The Greatest Sitcoms of All Time

MARTIN GITLIN

THE SCARECROW PRESS, INC.
Lanham • Toronto • Plymouth, UK
2014

Published by Scarecrow Press, Inc.
A wholly owned subsidary of The Rowman & Littlefield Publishing Group, Inc.
4501 Forbes Boulevard, Suite 200, Lanham, Maryland 20706
www.rowman.com

10 Thornbury Road, Plymouth PL6 7PP, United Kingdom

British Library Cataloguing in Publication Information Available

Library of Congress Cataloging-in-Publication Data

Gitlin, Marty.
  The greatest sitcoms of all time / Martin Gitlin.
      pages cm
  Includes bibliographical references and index.
  ISBN 978-0-8108-8724-4 (cloth : alk. paper) — ISBN 978-0-8108-8725-1 (ebook) 1.
Situation comedies (Television programs)—United States. I. Title.
  PN1992.8.C66G58 2014
  791.45'617—dc23   2013023335

∞™ The paper used in this publication meets the minimum requirements of American National
Standard for Information Sciences—Permanence of Paper for Printed Library Materials, ANSI/
NISO Z39.48-1992.

Printed in the United States of America.

Contents

Introduction

Rating sitcoms is not like comparing apples to oranges. It is far more complicated. It is like comparing apples to hamburgers to asparagus to mashed potatoes. That is how vast the differences can be between one television comedy and another. But I figured what the heck, let's give it a shot. Why? Because it was going to be tremendous fun, and a ranking of the best had yet to be attempted in book form. It was understood that television viewers feel passionate about their favorites and that heated discussions would result. But good-natured debate is one of the spices of life.

The task was indeed overwhelming because of the various factors that influenced the writing, production, performance, and success of sitcoms from 1950 to the present. The green light hoisted by *All in the Family* to social and political themes in the early 1970s launched a new era in the genre. Every sitcom that came before it had to be judged by the unspoken limitations placed upon them in regard to comedic fodder. For example, *Will & Grace* cannot be examined in the same light as *Leave It to Beaver*, yet both were breakthrough shows, the latter for its primary spotlight on youth and the former for its focus on gay characters. The ranking of each program listed in this book had the era in which it aired taken into strong consideration. Individual rankings were based on the following factors, all of which were taken with many grains of salt:

Impact: Shows that made an impression on the direction of television comedy or the society in which we live or merely explored new territory were rare. They took chances, which is certainly important. But I was particularly careful not to place too much emphasis on this category. After all, forays into uncharted waters were virtually impossible for shows in the 1950s and 1960s, which were hamstrung by the restraints of their times. It would be unfair to punish them for something they could not control. And those who created other shows had no intention of making a statement. It can certainly be argued that they, too, are not to blame for creating shows with the sole purpose of making viewers laugh. The number one choice is a prime example (you don't think I was going to give that away in the introduction, do you?).

Longevity: As the great Martin Luther King Jr. once famously said about a topic far more important (his own mortality), longevity has its place. It does in the world of television comedy. The ability of producers, directors, writers, and actors to maintain viability and viewership for long periods of time cannot be underrated. But it is foolish to give that too much credence. There are sitcoms that earned spots on this list that lasted two seasons or less, and others never considered to have longevity approached a decade on the air. Longevity does not always translate to greatness.

Ratings: Although this category ties in with longevity, they are not identical. Some shows (*The Adventures of Ozzie and Harriett* immediately comes to mind) remained on television for ten years or longer without garnering ratings worthy of sticking around that long. Other shows earned tremendous Nielsens but were panned by the critics and unworthy of selection. Most often this was a credible reflection on the worthiness of a sitcom, but popularity does not always translate to greatness in any form of entertainment.

Awards: Emmys and Golden Globes were strongly considered in the rankings, although one must be careful to prevent linking them with surefire greatness, particularly in the 1950s and 1960s, when there were fewer awards to go around and some of the most watched, beloved, and generally respected sitcoms were shut out. Those accepted as the premier shows in television history, however, were generously awarded, and that was reflected in the rankings, particularly at the upper levels.

Humor: This is certainly the most subjective of the considerations, but not wholly. Not everything in entertainment is subjective. The Beatles were a better band than The Bay City Rollers. Period. And *Seinfeld* was a better sitcom than *The Ropers*. Period. The talent in production, direction, writing, and comedic performance can be judged objectively. And some shows simply elicited more laughs than others. On the other hand, there is no doubt that subjective opinion enters strongly into the equation when ranking the seventy best sitcoms. It is a difficult task. And subjectivity was certainly a factor when I was separating (for instance) number forty-seven from number forty-eight. Debate away.

Legacy: How shows of the past are respected or disrespected by later generations through syndication and reputation was factored into the rankings. Many old sitcoms, like *The Honeymooners*, are far more respected and popular in the modern era than when they aired, but I was careful not to overrate the importance of this category. *Gilligan's Island* and *The Brady Bunch* (both Sherwood Schwartz creations) are two examples of sitcoms whose reputations beyond their runs on the airwaves far exceeded their greatness due to their iconic statuses through syndication.

An equally daunting task to ranking the top seventy sitcoms once they were established was deciding which ones to leave out. Some were award winners, many earned high ratings, and still others shine brightly in the spotlight of television history. That is where a healthier mix of subjectivity and objectivity entered into the equation. It was not difficult identifying most of the sitcoms in the book as worthy of inclusion. I flipped no coins in making decisions. I was careful to weigh the aforementioned criteria to determine which sitcoms belonged and which did not. It was the difficulty of that task that motivated me to add a Top 10 list of sitcoms from each decade that fell short. Each deserved the recognition.

I believe you will enjoy reading about the shows that have made us laugh, and sometimes cry. Our favorites have brought joy to our lives. It matters not if they are on this list. They say laughter is the best medicine. Any show that has made a viewer feel better after a miserable day has fulfilled its purpose. It's just that the following sitcoms fulfilled that purpose more successfully than the others. Enjoy!

✳ 1 ✳

Seinfeld

(1989–1998)

Cast: Jerry Seinfeld (Jerry Seinfeld), Jason Alexander (George Costanza), Julia Louis-Dreyfus (Elaine Benes), Michael Richards (Cosmo Kramer), Wayne Knight (Newman), Jerry Stiller (Frank Costanza), Estelle Harris (Estelle Costanza), Liz Sheridan (Helen Seinfeld), Barney Martin (Morty Seinfeld)

Created by: Executive producer and writer Larry David

Network: NBC

First Air Date: July 5, 1989 (pilot)

Last Air Date: May 14, 1998

Broadcast History:
    May 1990–July 1990: Thursday at 9:30–10:00 PM
    January 1991–February 1991: Wednesday at 9:30–10:00 PM
    April 1991–June 1991: Thursday at 9:30–10:00 PM
    June 1991–December 1991: Wednesday at 9:30–10:00 PM
    December 1991–January 1993: Wednesday at 9:00–9:30 PM
    February 1993–August 1993: Thursday at 9:30–10:00 PM
    August 1993–September 1998: Thursday at 9:00–9:30 PM
    January 1998–September 1998: Wednesday at 8:30–9:00 PM

Seasons: 9

Episodes: 180

Ratings History: 1990–1991 (not in Top 30), 1991–1992 (not in Top 30), 1992–1993 (25), 1993–1994 (3), 1994–1995 (1), 1995–1996 (2), 1996–1997 (2), 1997–1998 (1)

Jason Alexander, Julia Louis-Dreyfus, Jerry Seinfeld, Michael Richards. *NBC/Columbia TriStar Television/Photofest ©NBC/Columbia TriStar Television*

Overview

The notion that a viewer must like a character in a personal sense to like them in a comedic sense was blasted to all eternity by *Seinfeld*, which many believe is the flat-out funniest sitcom to ever grace the small screen. The four main characters were self-absorbed, misdirected meddlers who disregarded all tendencies toward generally accepted societal values and moral righteousness. They trampled upon the feelings of others to fulfill their own, often hedonistic, desires. Yet, viewers embraced them, perhaps because the quirky quartet spoke to their own selfish individual needs and certainly because they were downright hilarious.

Seinfeld promoted itself as being "a show about nothing," but rather it was a show about everything unimportant. It was about breaking up with a woman for eating her peas one at a time. It was about the second toe fighting to gain supremacy over the big toe—the coup de toe. It was about getting caught picking your nose and claiming it was a scratch. It was about sneaking unauthorized cucumbers into restaurants to slice into salads. It was about the inevitable shrinkage of a male sexual organ after a dip in cold water.

Creator Larry David and title character Jerry Seinfeld were the driving forces behind the humor, which was based on observations of everyday trivialities. The show was based in New York City and featured main characters drifting through life, eschewing compassion for selfish personal goals, rarely uttering a kind word about anybody, and discussing every meaningless occurrence in their emotionally barren existences and how it affected whatever challenges they faced during that particular half-hour program. The rest of the world and those unfortunate to stumble into it were no match for their simplistic and egotistical motivations, portrayed by arguably the funniest cast ever assembled.

The Jerry Seinfeld role was the most true to its basic form. The New York-based comedian played himself; he sometimes joked within the script of his inability to act, although his dialogue and acting grew in believability as the show progressed. The most humorous aspect of his character was his almost weekly dispatching of girlfriends or their dispatching of him for the most insignificant peculiarities. He broke up with one woman because she objected to him pretending her belly button was talking to him while she slept. He ended the relationship with another for eating her peas one at a time—which proved vexing because she scooped her corn niblets with a spoon. He sent another woman packing because she had "man hands." Yet another dumped him because he had sent friend Elaine (Julia Louis-Dreyfus) into a sauna to fall into her breasts and find out if they were real.

Elaine also lost one potential relationship after another through her own idiosyncratic judgments and self-centered decision making. She lost one boyfriend because she chastised him for failing to place an exclamation point on the end of a note informing her that her friend had given birth. Another promising relationship was snuffed out when her boyfriend discovered she had stopped off to buy a pack of Jujyfruits candy upon learning he had been taken to the hospital following a car accident. Misfortune also followed Elaine into the workplace, sometimes due to the interfering of the other main characters. One promotion was squelched when Jerry chased out of the building and into the street her competitor for the job, with whom he was angry for heckling him during his routine at a local comedy club. The frightened woman ran into the street and had her pinkie toe severed by a street sweeper. Her boss felt so sorry for her that he gave her the promotion instead of Elaine.

George Costanza (Jason Alexander), a despicable lout and the most self-centered of the group, best captured the strange dichotomy between negative characterization and humor. George was easily the biggest loser among the four, and he deserved every ounce of misfortune he received. He lied his way through life, yet lamented his inability to find professional or personal fulfillment. The depth of his inconsideration for others boggled the mind. He knocked over a frail old woman in a walker and pushed past children at a birthday party to escape what turned out to be a small grease fire in the kitchen. He attempted a switch to the Latvian Orthodox religion behind the backs of his parents to maintain a relationship with a woman who was devout, but cheated to pass the conversion test. He got fired from a proofreading job procured for him by Elaine after engaging in sex on his desk with the cleaning woman and then claimed his ignorance of wrongdoing, asking his soon-to-be former-boss, "Was that wrong?," and offering that he wished someone had informed him that such behavior was "frowned upon." He even accidentally killed his fiancé by buying cheap envelopes (for the wedding invitations) with toxic glue, with which she licked herself to death—and he hardly cared a lick. Many fans consider George the funniest character on *Seinfeld* and perhaps the most humorous in the history of the American sitcom.

Others, however, do not believe George is even the funniest character on the show. They feel it is the irrepressible Cosmo Kramer (Michael Richards), the only one of the four almost exclusively referred to by a last name, since the strange first name of this strangest of characters was not even revealed until the sixth season. The directionless Kramer temporarily embraced whatever persona or role had somehow attached itself to him in any point of his life or simply created a new one. In one episode, he was accidentally swept into a business office by a wave of people and began working there without being hired—suitcase, ulcer, and all. In another, he found furniture from the set of the 1970s *Merv Griffin Show* in a trash dumpster, reconfigured it into his apartment, and transformed himself into an old-school talk show host, inviting his puzzled friends in for impromptu interviews. In yet another, he "hired" an intern to help him run "Kramerica Industries," which seemed to serve no purpose whatsoever.

It seemed that each main character, save Jerry, evolved throughout the course of the show, but always in a more humorous way. George began the show as far less a loser than he became. He boasted a decent job as a real estate agent and prided himself as somewhat of an intellectual. He soon became unemployed, as it was apparently decided he would be a funnier, less sympathetic character living with his parents. His later years as a working man brought little growth as his pathetic work ethic rose to the fore. As the series neared its end, his traits became exaggerated and lost all sense of realism. His bitterness and frustration became more pronounced, which, in turn, drained at least some of the humor from his character.

The same could be claimed about Elaine and Kramer toward the end of the run. Elaine grew angry and tough as the limited softness of her character was removed. All sense of realism was extracted from the Kramer character in the late episodes. In one, for instance, he began using butter to shave himself, and the always-hungry Newman began eyeing him like a cannibal. What was silly about Kramer became ridiculous and over the top.

The distinctive, offbeat personalities of the side characters added to the show's allure. Among them was an angry, socially frustrated, roly-poly neighbor known simply as Newman (Wayne Knight), a name spoken with derision by the hated Jerry. The parents of both Jerry and George also added to the brilliant comedy. One might believe that a couple that argues with the ferocity of Frank Costanza (Jerry Stiller) and Estelle Costanza (Estelle Harris) would make viewers uncomfortable, but that was never the case. Their clashes simply added to the humor of their characters.

Common practice in the 1990s and beyond for the fan of the American sitcom has been to identify what is perceived as the funniest *Seinfeld* episode. Was it "The Contest," which began when George revealed that his mother caught him masturbating, leading the four to wager as to which one could hold off the longest without sexual gratification? Was it "The Junior Mint," which featured Kramer accidentally tossing the small candy into the chest cavity of Elaine's boyfriend during surgery? Was it "The Hamptons," which took a disturbing and hilarious turn when Jerry's girlfriend walked in on George naked, revealing a private part that, much to his dismay, had undergone "significant shrinkage" after a trip to the pool, filled with cold water?

No sitcom has slipped phrases into the American lexicon with greater frequency and success than *Seinfeld*. Throwaway lines from various episodes were tossed out whenever they were deemed appropriate or when memories from the show come flooding back. There was the line from the episode in which the "Soup Nazi" refused to serve customers whose ordering he deemed disrespectful: "No soup for you!" There was the farewell proclamation uttered by the woman about her breasts to Jerry, who had blown his chance to get intimate with her: "They're real and they're *spectacular*." There was the repeated claim from Jerry and George pronouncing their heterosexuality while defending the rights of homosexuals in a case of mistaken identity, as they had been labeled as gay: "Not that there's anything wrong with that." And there was the one line Kramer was rehearsing with conviction for his part in a Woody Allen movie being filmed in New York: "These pretzels are making me thirsty."

The last episode, a highly rated, highly publicized hour-long show, spotlighted those exaggerations in the characterizations. The four landed in jail for making jokes and filming while watching an obese man being robbed at gunpoint. The show was able to create positive viewership despite featuring unsympathetic characters, but their enjoyment of such an event on the street went beyond a lack of empathy to downright cruelty, which is one reason the final episode was considered by many to be a disappointment.

Yet, the negative perceptions of how the show ended could not begin to erase the brilliance of the writing, the simple humor of both the main and side characters, and how the characters were utilized to form on-screen relationships that remained as funny as any in the history of television until they arguably lost some of their freshness in the last season.

The Best Jerry Breakups

Jerry Seinfeld was fussy when it came to women. It was no wonder he remained single throughout the show and never maintained a long-term relationship. Here are some of the women he dated and why they did not stay together:

- Donna (Gretchen German): She liked the Dockers pants commercial he detested.
- Naomi (Jessica Lundy): She laughed like Elmer Fudd sitting on a juicer.
- Tia (Jennifer Campbell): She caught him picking his nose, although he claimed it to be a scratch.
- Sidra (Teri Hatcher): She learned that he sent Elaine into the sauna to find out if her breasts were real.
- Jody (Jennifer Coolidge): She was a masseuse who refused to give him a massage.
- Audrey (Suzanne Snyder): She refused to eat apple pie and wouldn't tell him why.
- Rachel (Melanie Smith): Her parents cut it off because they learned from Newman that they had made out during *Schindler's List*.
- Julie (Marita Geraghty): She had actually dated—and was dumped by—Newman.

- Melanie (Athena Massey): She ate her peas one at a time, but scooped her corn niblets.
- Christie (Lisa Deane): She always wore the same dress.
- Gillian (Kristin Bauer): She had "man hands."
- Claire (Sara Rose Peterson): She wouldn't allow Jerry to pretend her belly button was talking to him when she was asleep.
- Celia (Julia Pennington): She wouldn't let Jerry play with her vintage toy collection.

From Julia to Eileen to Elaine to Ellie to Old Christine to Selina

Julia Louis-Dreyfus was the only major *Seinfeld* character to land a successful sitcom after the show was cancelled. She played the role of single mother Christine Campbell in *The New Adventures of Old Christine* from 2006 to 2010. Louis-Dreyfus caught her first big break as a cast member of *Saturday Night Live* during its years of struggle in the early 1980s. She also played Eileen Swift in the short-lived sitcom *Day by Day* (1988–1989), Ellie Riggs in the shorter-lived sitcom *Watching Ellie* (2002–2003), and Selina Meyer in *Veep* before and after her time on *Seinfeld* and *The New Adventures of Old Christine*.

Did You Know?

There was at least one Superman reference in the vast majority of *Seinfeld* episodes. He was Jerry's hero.

They Said It

> **Mr. Lippman [George's boss]:** It's come to my attention that you and the cleaning woman have engaged in sexual intercourse on the desk in your office. Is that correct?
> **George:** Who said that?
> **Mr. Lippman:** She did.
> **George:** [after a hesitation] Was that wrong? Should I not have done that? I tell you, I gotta plead ignorance on this thing because if anyone had said anything to me at all when I first started here that that sort of thing is frowned upon . . . you know, cause I've worked in a lot of offices, and I tell you, people do that all the time.
> **Mr. Lippman:** You're fired.
> **George:** Well, you didn't have to say it like that.

> **Jerry:** [at a Confessional] I need to talk to you about my friend, Dr. Tim Whatley. I think he's converted to Judaism just for the jokes.
> **Priest:** And this offends you as a Jewish person?
> **Jerry:** No, it offends me as a comedian.

Kramer: It's a write-off for them.

Jerry: How is it a write-off?

Kramer: They just write it off.

Jerry: You don't even know what a write-off is.

Kramer: Do you?

Jerry: No, I don't.

Kramer: [slowly for effect] But they do . . . and they're the ones . . . writing it off.

Jerry: [answering the phone] This isn't a good time.

Telemarketer: When would be a good time to call back, sir?

Jerry: I have an idea—why don't you give me your home number and I'll call you back later?

Telemarketer: Umm, we're not allowed to do that.

Jerry: Oh, I guess because you don't want strangers calling you at home.

Telemarketer: Umm, no.

Jerry: Well, now you know how I feel. [hangs up]

George: [referring to his girlfriend skimming over facts in a story] You don't think she'd "yada, yada" sex?

Elaine: I've "yada yada'd" sex.

George: Really?

Elaine: Yeah, I met this lawyer, we went out to dinner, I had the lobster bisque, we went back to my place, yada, yada, yada, I never heard from him again.

Jerry: But you yada yada'd over the best part.

Elaine: No . . . I mentioned the bisque.

Frank: [at a fancy dinner with the wealthy parents of Susan Ross, George's fiancé] You have the rooster, the hen, and the chicken. The rooster goes with the chicken. . . . So who's having sex with the hen? Something's missing!

Mrs. Ross: [drinking wine and staring at Frank] Something's missing, all right.

Elaine: [announcing Kramer at a bachelor auction] OK, our next bachelor is Cosmo Kramer. He's a high school graduate.

Kramer: [whispering to Elaine] Equivalency.

Elaine: Equivalency. High school equivalency program graduate. He's, uh . . . I don't know, six foot three, one hundred ninety pounds. He likes . . . fruit, and he just got, um . . . a haircut. [Kramer slips off the runway and falls onto a table below.] Do I hear . . . five bucks?

Major Awards

EMMY AWARD WINS (10)

1992 (2): Outstanding Individual Achievement in Writing in a Comedy Series (Elaine Pope and Larry Charles for "The Fix-Up"); Outstanding Individual Achievement in Editing for a Series, Multi-Camera Production (Janet Ashikaga for "The Subway")

1993 (3): Outstanding Comedy Series; Outstanding Individual Achievement in Writing in a Comedy Series (Larry David for "The Contest"); Outstanding Supporting Actor in a Comedy Series (Michael Richards)

1994 (2): Outstanding Supporting Actor in a Comedy Series (Michael Richards); Outstanding Individual Achievement in Editing for a Series, Multi-Camera Production (Janet Ashikaga for "The Opposite")

1995 (1): Outstanding Individual Achievement in Editing for a Series, Multi-Camera Production (Janet Ashikaga for "The Diplomats Club")

1996 (1): Outstanding Supporting Actress in a Comedy Series (Julia Louis-Dreyfus)

1997 (1): Outstanding Supporting Actor in a Comedy Series (Michael Richards)

EMMY AWARD NOMINATIONS, IN ADDITION TO WINS (58)

1990 (1): Outstanding Editing for a Miniseries or a Special, Multi-Camera Production (Robert Souders for "The Stakeout")

1991 (3): Outstanding Writing in a Comedy Series (Larry David for "The Deal"); Outstanding Writing in a Comedy Series (Larry David and Jerry Seinfeld for "The Pony Remark"); Outstanding Directing in a Comedy Series (Tom Cherones for "The Pony Remark")

1992 (7): Outstanding Comedy Series; Outstanding Lead Actor in a Comedy Series (Jerry Seinfeld); Outstanding Supporting Actor in a Comedy Series (Jason Alexander); Outstanding Supporting Actress in a Comedy Series (Julia Louis-Dreyfus); Outstanding Individual Achievement in Writing in a Comedy Series (Larry David for "The Parking Garage"); Outstanding Individual Achievement in Writing in a Comedy Series (Larry David, Bob Shaw, and Don McEnery for "The Tape"); Outstanding Individual Achievement in Directing in a Comedy Series (David Steinberg for "The Tape"); Outstanding Individual Achievement in Editing for a Series, Multi-Camera Production (Janet Ashikaga for "The Subway")

1993 (8): Outstanding Lead Actor in a Comedy Series (Jerry Seinfeld); Outstanding Supporting Actor in a Comedy Series (Jason Alexander); Outstanding Supporting Actress in a Comedy Series (Julia Louis-Dreyfus); Outstanding Guest Actor in a Comedy Series (Bill Erwin); Outstanding Individual Achievement in Writing in a Comedy Series (Larry Charles for "The Outing"); Outstanding Individual Achievement in Directing in a Comedy Series (Tom Cherones for "The Contest"); Outstanding Individual Achievement in Editing for a Series, Multi-Camera Production (Janet Ashikaga for "The Pilot"); Outstanding Individual Achievement in Sound Mixing for a Comedy Series or a Special (Charlie McDaniel, Craig Porter, and Peter San Filipo for "The Airport")

1994 (10): Outstanding Comedy Series; Outstanding Lead Actor in a Comedy Series (Jerry Seinfeld); Outstanding Supporting Actor in a Comedy Series (Jason Alexander); Outstanding Supporting Actress in a Comedy Series (Julia Louis-Dreyfus); Outstanding Guest Actor in a Comedy Series (Judge Reinhold for "The Raincoats"); Outstanding Guest Actress in a Comedy Series (Marlee Matlin for

"The Lip Reader"); Outstanding Individual Achievement in Writing in a Comedy Series (Larry David for "The Puffy Shirt"); Outstanding Individual Achievement in Writing in a Comedy Series (Larry David and Lawrence Levy for "The Mango"); Outstanding Individual Achievement in Directing in a Comedy Series (Tom Cherones for "The Mango"); Outstanding Individual Achievement in Sound Mixing for a Comedy Series or a Special (Larry Ellena, Charlie McDaniel, Craig Porter, Peter San Filipo for "The Bris")

1995 (6): Outstanding Comedy Series; Outstanding Lead Actor in a Comedy Series (Jerry Seinfeld); Outstanding Supporting Actor in a Comedy Series (Jason Alexander); Outstanding Supporting Actor in a Comedy Series (Michael Richards); Outstanding Supporting Actress in a Comedy Series (Julia Louis-Dreyfus); Outstanding Individual Achievement in Directing for a Comedy Series (Andy Ackerman for "The Jimmy")

1996 (10): Outstanding Comedy Series; Outstanding Lead Actor in a Comedy Series (Jerry Seinfeld); Outstanding Supporting Actor in a Comedy Series (Jason Alexander); Outstanding Supporting Actor in a Comedy Series (Michael Richards); Outstanding Guest Actor in a Comedy Series (Larry Thomas for "The Soup Nazi"); Outstanding Individual Achievement in Writing for a Comedy Series (Spike Feresten for "The Soup Nazi"); Outstanding Individual Achievement in Directing for a Comedy Series (Andy Ackerman for "The Soup Nazi"); Outstanding Individual Achievement in Casting for a Series; Outstanding Individual Achievement in Editing for a Series, Multi-Camera Production (Janet Ashikaga for "The Rye"); Outstanding Individual Achievement in Sound Mixing for a Comedy Series or a Special (Charlie McDaniel, Craig Porter, Peter San Filipo for "The Cadillac")

1997 (8): Outstanding Comedy Series; Outstanding Supporting Actor in a Comedy Series (Jason Alexander); Outstanding Supporting Actress in a Comedy Series (Julia Louis-Dreyfus); Outstanding Guest Actor in a Comedy Series (Jerry Stiller); Outstanding Writing for a Comedy Series (Peter Mehlman and Jill Franklyn for "The Yada Yada"); Outstanding Directing for a Comedy Series (Andy Ackerman for "The Pothole"); Outstanding Casting for a Series; Outstanding Editing for a Series, Multi-Camera Production (Skip Collector for "The Pothole")

1998 (5): Outstanding Comedy Series; Outstanding Supporting Actor in a Comedy Series (Jason Alexander); Outstanding Supporting Actress in a Comedy Series (Julia Louis-Dreyfus); Outstanding Guest Actor in a Comedy Series (Lloyd Bridges for "The Blood"); Outstanding Multi-Camera Picture Editing for a Series (Skip Collector for "The Finale")

GOLDEN GLOBE WINS (3)

1994 (3): Best TV Series, Musical/Comedy; Best Performance by an Actor in a TV Series, Musical/Comedy (Jerry Seinfeld); Best Performance by an Actress in a Supporting Role in a Series, Mini-Series, or Motion Picture Made for TV (Julia Louis-Dreyfus)

GOLDEN GLOBE NOMINATIONS, IN ADDITION TO WINS (12)

1993 (1): Best Performance by an Actor in a Supporting Role in a Series, Mini-Series, or Motion Picture Made for TV (Jason Alexander)

1994 (1): Best Performance by an Actor in a Supporting Role in a Series, Mini-Series, or Motion Picture Made for TV (Jason Alexander)

1995 (4): Best TV Series, Musical/Comedy; Best Performance by an Actor in a TV Series, Musical/Comedy (Jerry Seinfeld); Best Performance by an Actor in a Supporting Role in a Series, Mini-Series, or Motion Picture Made for TV (Jason Alexander); Best Performance by an Actress in a Supporting Role in a Series, Mini-Series, or Motion Picture Made for TV (Julia Louis-Dreyfus)

1996 (2): Best TV Series, Musical/Comedy; Best Performance by an Actor in a TV Series, Musical/Comedy (Jerry Seinfeld)

1997 (1): Best TV Series, Musical/Comedy

1998 (3): Best TV Series, Musical/Comedy; Best Performance by an Actor in a TV Series, Musical/Comedy (Jerry Seinfeld); Best Performance by an Actor in a Supporting Role in a Series, Mini-Series, or Motion Picture Made for TV (Jason Alexander)

PEABODY AWARD

1993: NBC

Further Reading

Delaney, Tim. *Seinology: The Sociology of Seinfeld.* Amherst, N.Y.: Prometheus Books, 2006.

Irwin, William. *Seinfeld and Philosophy: A Book about Everything and Nothing.* Chicago, Open Court Publishing, 1999.

Wild, David. *Seinfeld: The Totally Unauthorized Tribute.* New York: Three Rivers Press, 1998.

✳ **2** ✳
All in the Family
(1971–1979)

Cast: Carroll O'Connor (Archie Bunker), Jean Stapleton (Edith Bunker), Rob Reiner (Mike Stivic), Sally Struthers (Gloria Bunker-Stivic)

Created by: Producer and writer Norman Lear and producer Bud Yorkin, based on the British program *Till Death Us Do Part* (created by Johnny Speight)

Network: CBS

First Air Date: January 12, 1971

Last Air Date: April 8, 1979

Broadcast History:
    January 12–April 6, 1971: Tuesday at 9:30–10:00 PM
    September 18, 1971–March 8, 1975: Saturday at 8:00–8:30 PM
    September 8, 1975–March 8, 1976: Monday at 9:00–9:30 PM
    September 22–October 27, 1976: Wednesday at 9:00–9:30 PM
    November 6, 1976–March 12, 1977: Saturday at 9:00–9:30 PM
    October 9, 1977–October 1, 1978: Sunday at 9:00–9:30 PM
    October 8, 1978–April 8, 1979: Sunday at 8:00–8:30 PM

Seasons: 8

Episodes: 208

Ratings History: 1971–1972 (1), 1972–1973 (1), 1973–1974 (1), 1974–1975 (1), 1975–1976 (1), 1976–1977 (12), 1977–1978 (4), 1978–1979 (9)

Clockwise from top left: Rob Reiner, Sally Struthers, Carroll O'Connor, and Jean Stapleton. *CBS/Photofest ©CBS*

Overview

Television and postwar America were born and raised together, but the reality of the times could be grasped only through watching the news. Sitcoms lagged farther behind than any entertainment genre in dealing with social and political issues. In fact, such topics were avoided quite intentionally.

During the 1950s and 1960s, network executives believed in winning the hearts and minds of the viewer through escapism and wholesome family portrayals. The latter was most prevalent in the 1950s and early 1960s through such sitcoms as *Make Room for Daddy, Ozzie and Harriett, Father Knows Best,* and *Leave It to Beaver.* Even more manic humor written into the scripts of such 1950s stalwarts as *I Love Lucy* and *The Honeymooners* did not dabble in anything perceived as controversial. Sex could not even be implied in such shows during a time when spouses slept in separate beds.

The mid- to late 1960s brought explosive new social and political issues, only to push the sitcom more distant from reality. The embraced philosophy was that the more problems faced by American society, the deeper its TV viewers wished to escape.

Americans witnessed enough bitter reality on the nightly news. They saw thousands of countrymen killed in the fields of Vietnam. They watched in horror the assassinations of President John F. Kennedy and brother Robert Kennedy, as well as civil rights leader Martin Luther King Jr. They squirmed in their seats at the dinner table at the sight of riots in the streets of inner cities and college campuses. It's no wonder that by prime time they could not wait to leave that world for that of a talking horse, or, for that matter, a Martian (*My Favorite Martian*), hillbilly Marine (*Gomer Pyle*), flying nun (*The Flying Nun*), witch (*Bewitched*), genie (*I Dream of Jeannie*), and two ghoulish families (*The Munsters* and *The Addams Family*). A laugh track deepened the foray into unreality.

A revolution began, albeit quietly and with no fanfare, on Wednesday night, January 12, 1971, when a midseason replacement called *All in the Family* first aired. CBS gave the program a mere thirteen-episode commitment. Everything about the show ran contrary to American sitcom trends since the birth of television. There was nothing controversial about the basic format, which featured a middle-aged couple (Archie and Edith Bunker), their daughter (Gloria Stivic), and her husband (Michael Stivic), but everything else about *All in the Family* was indeed shocking.

The show was the brainchild of producers Norman Lear and Bud Yorkin, who were inspired by a mid-1960s British comedy series featuring a racist dockworker entitled *Till Death Us Do Part*. Lear and Yorkin obtained the rights to *Till Death Us Do Part* with the intention of selling a sitcom starring famed movie actor Mickey Rooney called *Those Were the Days* to ABC. When that network turned it down, the project appeared doomed.

CBS president Robert D. Wood came to the rescue. He recognized that changes in American culture had spawned more sophisticated audiences that yearned for socially and politically relevant fare. He sought to replace rural sitcoms like *Green Acres*, *Gomer Pyle, U.S.M.C.*, *Petticoat Junction*, and *The Beverly Hillbillies* with programs that would attract a more affluent demographic. He understood that making any commitment to the show now known as *All in the Family* was a risk, which is why he gave it such a limited initial commitment.

The unique nature of the show, particularly filming in front of a live audience in more of a theater setting, called for a different approach to casting. Carroll O'Connor boasted extensive experience as a play actor before finding some success in TV character roles in the 1960s. Jean Stapleton was born into an acting family and was even more polished as a stage actress, having appeared in several Broadway plays in the 1950s and 1960s. Rob Reiner received inspiration from his Emmy-winning father, Carl Reiner, who created and acted in *The Dick Van Dyke Show*. Rob began his career in theater before landing roles in his late teens and early twenties in such hit sitcoms as *The Andy Griffith Show*, *Gomer Pyle, U.S.M.C.*, *That Girl*, and *Room 222*. Sally Struthers trained at the Pasadena Playhouse College of Theatre Arts before gaining experience as an actor and dancer on variety shows the likes of *The Smothers Brothers Comedy Hour* and *The Tim Conway Comedy Hour*.

The chemistry between the four principal cast members proved to be one of the primary reasons for the show's unprecedented success, but ratings for the early episodes were so abysmal that it seemed likely to be cancelled. *Life* magazine critic John Leonard complained in March 1971 that the show was "wretched." The few Americans who did tune in could scarcely believe what they heard. They listened to the hopelessly bigoted Archie, a dockworker like his fictional British predecessor, refer to blacks as "Spades," Chinese as "Chinks," Vietnamese as "Gooks," Hispanics as "Spics," and Jews as "Hebes." They heard him debate heatedly, ignorantly, and hilariously with Mike, the liberal college student, about such formerly taboo subjects as the plight of minorities, gun control, homosexuality, and the war in Vietnam. They heard Gloria complain about her period and embrace the fledgling women's liberation movement. They even heard the first belch (from Archie, of course) and toilet flush in the history of the American sitcom.

All in the Family did not merely break through barriers. It shattered them. The groundswell of interest took hold. Soon, millions of curious Americans were tuning in. They were not only taken aback by the fact that virtually no subject was sacred, at least for that television era, but they were also thoroughly entertained. They laughed when Archie referred to the simple-minded, nonconfrontational Edith as "dingbat" or Mike as "meathead." The nicknames quickly became part of the American lexicon. They laughed when Archie, appearing on television to express a rebuttal to an editorial, claimed in dead seriousness that the way to end skyjackings was to provide every passenger with a gun. They laughed when he complained that Mike and Gloria would not be so thrilled that a black family moved next door when the watermelon rinds began flying out the window. The notion of and sensitivity regarding political correctness would preclude such views from being expressed by fictional characters today, but they were accepted merely as the ranting of an ignorant buffoon in the early 1970s.

The impact of *All in the Family* was all-pervasive throughout the television industry. Such issues as sex, drugs, war, women's rights, and race relations became fair game, even on family shows like *Eight Is Enough*. As the forerunner to social progressiveness on television and with *All in the Family* leading the way, CBS began dominating the ratings, particularly with a Saturday night lineup that many still consider the best in television history. Sitcoms the likes of *M*A*S*H* and *The Mary Tyler Moore Show* blazed new territory, and the viewing public was happy to come along for the ride.

While the four members of the Bunker household quickly emerged as some of the most memorable characters in American television history, their neighbors and extended family members on the show proved intriguing as well. One appearance as Edith's cousin Maude landed Bea Arthur her own sitcom. Another spinoff was *The Jeffersons*, who gained fame by playing the black family that lived next door to the Bunkers.

By the end of its first half-season, *All in the Family* was a megahit. It not only soared to the top of the Nielsen ratings, it earned the admiration of critics and garnered numerous Emmy and Golden Globe awards. For the next few years, scriptwriters embraced the formula that made it perhaps the most successful, and certainly the most impactful, sitcom in television history.

Times, however, were changing. American involvement in Vietnam had all but ended by the early 1970s, as had the era of race riots and college protests. The issues debated by Archie and Mike were no longer in the spotlight. *All in the Family* slowly moved in a different direction. Mike completed graduate school and moved next door, along with Gloria. Archie mellowed. His arguments with Mike became tamer. He traded his job on the loading dock with what he deemed more prideful work as a saloon owner. His anger and bigotry softened, as did Mike in his staunchly liberal stances. The show remained a huge success both critically and in the ratings, but many believe it lost its edge when Archie's anger was replaced by frustration and a greater understanding of others.

The softer side of Archie was cultivated after Reiner and Struthers left the show and a young girl named Stephanie moved into the Bunker home. The focus had shifted almost exclusively to his saloon when Edith was killed off in 1980 and the program morphed into *Archie Bunker's Place*. By that time, the program bore little resemblance to the sitcom that had altered the face of television nine years earlier, but it will always be remembered for changing television and, to a great extent, American society through plotlines dealing with issues of social and political significance. It promoted the freedom to discuss and debate controversial social and political issues and confront ignorance. It is also arguably the best-written and downright funniest sitcom in television history.

Sammy!

Perhaps the most notable episode of *All in the Family* features a real-life Sammy Davis Jr., who visited the Bunker home on 704 Houser Street to retrieve a briefcase he left in Archie's cab. His stopover naturally caused chaos in the neighborhood, but also an opportunity for Archie to present his skewed views on race relations to one of the biggest stars in entertainment. The highlight of their conversation was when Archie attempted to defend himself by stressing that he was "always dead set against slavery." Sammy sickened Archie at the end of the episode when he kissed him on the cheek as they posed for a picture together.

Not so Glorious *Gloria*

The least successful spin-off of *All in the Family* featured Sally Struthers as a now-divorced woman. *Gloria* ran for one season before CBS yanked it off the air in September 1983. It was explained that Gloria's husband Mike left her to live on a commune with a flower child, although in one episode of *All in the Family*, controversy reigned after the couple moved to California as it was revealed that Gloria had an affair with one of Mike's friends. In *Gloria*, she had taken herself and son Joey to upstate New York, where she had found work as an assistant to veterinarian Willard Adams (Burgess Meredith). Carroll O'Connor, who played her father in *All in the Family* and was involved in the creation of *Gloria*, later complained that its writers and producer were replaced behind his back.

They Said It

Mike: [on what Buddhists say after sneezing instead of "God bless you."] Why couldn't they say 'Buddha bless you' in Chinese?
Archie: Because they don't say that, that's why. If they say . . . well, if they say anything at all, it's 'Sayonara.'
Mike: [incredulous] That's Japanese.
Archie: What are you talking about? You put a Jap and a Chink together, you gonna tell me which is which?
Mike: That's right, because I find out about them. I talk to them as individuals.
Archie: Sure you talk to them. You say, 'Which one of you guys is the Chink?'

Gloria: [angrily explaining that Archie should strive to make life easier for her] You've got the satisfaction of knowing that you're helping your child be better off than you. Every father wants his kid to be better than him.
Archie: That don't always work that way, little girl. You look at the world around you there. Take a look at your animal kingdom for example there. I mean, take your gorilla. Your gorilla wants his kid to grow up better than him too. But the kid grows up and there he is, still a gorilla!

Archie: [reacting to a TV editorial] I *hate* that jerk on TV!
Mike: Oh, I get it, I get it. When you thought he was talking about V.D. and a permissive society, he was smart. You find out he was talking about gun control, he's a jerk?
Archie: That's right and I'm gonna prove it to you. How many people in this U.S. of A. would like to have guns?
Mike: Too many. Thousands.
Archie: [making his final point] BUT . . . how many people would like to have V.D.?

Archie: What the hell am I eatin' here?
Edith: Yankee stew.
Archie: Well, the Yankees struck out. Pass me the ketchup.

Major Awards

EMMY AWARD WINS (22)

1971 (3): Outstanding Series: Comedy; Outstanding New Series; Outstanding Continued Performance by an Actress in a Leading Role in a Comedy Series (Jean Stapleton)
1972 (7): Outstanding Series, Comedy; Outstanding Continued Performance by an Actor in a Leading Role in a Comedy Series (Carroll O'Connor); Outstanding Continued Performance by an Actress in a Leading Role in a Comedy Series (Jean Stapleton); Outstanding Performance by an Actress in a Supporting Role

in Comedy (Sally Struthers); Outstanding Directorial Achievement in Comedy (John Rich for "Sammy's Visit"); Outstanding Writing Achievement in Comedy (Burt Styler for "Edith's Problem"); Outstanding Achievement in Live or Tape Sound Mixing (Norman Dewes for "The Elevator Story")

1973 (2): Outstanding Comedy Series; Outstanding Writing Achievement in Comedy (Michael Ross, Bernard West, and Lee Kalcheim for "The Bunkers and the Swingers")

1974 (1): Best Supporting Actor in Comedy (Rob Reiner)

1977 (1): Outstanding Lead Actor in a Comedy Series (Carroll O'Connor)

1978 (6): Outstanding Comedy Series; Outstanding Lead Actor in a Comedy Series (Carroll O'Connor); Outstanding Lead Actress in a Comedy Series (Jean Stapleton); Outstanding Continued Performance by a Supporting Actor in a Comedy Series (Rob Reiner); Outstanding Directing in a Comedy Series (Paul Bogart for "Edith's 50th Birthday"); Outstanding Writing Achievement in Comedy (Bob Weiskopf, Bob Schiller, Barry Harman, and Harve Brosten for "Cousin Liz")

1979 (2): Outstanding Lead Actor in a Comedy Series (Carroll O'Connor); Outstanding Supporting Actress in Comedy or Comedy, Variety or Music Series (Sally Struthers)

EMMY AWARD NOMINATIONS, IN ADDITION TO WINS (34)

1971 (4): Outstanding Continued Performance by an Actor in a Leading Role in a Comedy Series (Carroll O'Connor); Outstanding Writing Achievement in Comedy (Stanley Ralph Ross for "Oh, My Aching Back"); Outstanding Writing Achievement in Comedy (Norman Lear for "Meet the Bunkers"); Outstanding Directorial Achievement in Comedy (John Rich for "Gloria's Pregnancy")

1972 (4): Outstanding Single Program, Drama or Comedy (for "Sammy's Visit"); Outstanding Performance by an Actor in a Supporting Role in Comedy (Rob Reiner); Outstanding Writing Achievement in Comedy (Burt Styler and Norman Lear for "The Saga of Cousin Oscar"); Outstanding Writing Achievement in Comedy (Phil Mishkin and Alan J. Levitt for "Mike's Problem")

1973 (5): Outstanding Continued Performance by an Actor in a Leading Role in a Comedy Series (Carroll O'Connor); Outstanding Continued Performance by an Actress in a Leading Role in a Comedy Series (Jean Stapleton); Outstanding Performance by an Actor in a Supporting Role in Comedy (Rob Reiner); Outstanding Performance by an Actress in a Supporting Role in Comedy (Sally Struthers); Outstanding Directorial Achievement in Comedy (John Rich and Bob LaHendro for "The Bunkers and the Swingers")

1974 (4): Outstanding Comedy Series; Best Lead Actor in a Comedy Series (Carroll O'Connor); Best Lead Actress in a Comedy Series (Jean Stapleton); Best Supporting Actress in a Comedy Series (Sally Struthers)

1975 (4): Outstanding Comedy Series; Best Lead Actor in a Comedy Series (Carroll O'Connor); Best Lead Actress in a Comedy Series (Jean Stapleton); Outstanding Continuing Performance by a Supporting Actor in a Comedy Series (Rob Reiner)

1976 (1): Outstanding Comedy Series

1977 (4): Outstanding Comedy Series; Best Lead Actress in a Comedy Series (Jean Stapleton); Outstanding Directing in a Comedy Series (Paul Bogart for "The Draft Dodger"); Outstanding Art Direction or Scenic Design for a Comedy Series (Don Roberts for "The Unemployment Story: Part II")

1978 (3): Outstanding Continuing Performance by a Supporting Actress in a Comedy Series (Sally Struthers); Outstanding Writing in a Comedy Series (Mel Tolkin, Larry Rhine, and Erik Tarloff for "Edith's Crisis of Faith: Part II); Outstanding Writing in a Comedy Series (Bob Weiskopf and Bob Schiller for "Edith's 50th Birthday")

1979 (5): Outstanding Comedy Series; Outstanding Lead Actress in a Comedy Series (Jean Stapleton); Outstanding Writing in a Comedy or Comedy Variety or Music Series (Milt Josefsberg, Phil Sharp, Bob Schiller, and Bob Weiskopf for "California, Here We Are: Part II"); Outstanding Directing in a Comedy or Comedy Variety or Music Series (Paul Bogart); Outstanding Video Tape Editing for a Series (Harvey Berger and Hal Collins for "The 200th Episode Celebration of 'All in the Family'")

GOLDEN GLOBE WINS (8)

1972 (2): Best TV Show, Musical/Comedy; Best TV Actor, Musical/Comedy (Carroll O'Connor)

1973 (2): Best TV Show, Musical/Comedy; Best TV Actress, Musical/Comedy (Jean Stapleton)

1974 (2): Best TV Show, Musical/Comedy; Best TV Actress, Musical/Comedy (Jean Stapleton)

1975 (1): Best Supporting Actress, Television (Betty Garrett)

1978 (1): Best TV Series, Musical/Comedy

GOLDEN GLOBE NOMINATIONS, IN ADDITION TO WINS (20)

1972 (3): Best TV Actress, Musical/Comedy (Jean Stapleton); Best Supporting Actor, Television (Rob Reiner); Best Supporting Actress, Television (Sally Struthers)

1973 (3): Best TV Actor, Musical/Comedy (Carroll O'Connor); Best Supporting Actor, Television (Rob Reiner); Best Supporting Actress, Television (Sally Struthers)

1974 (3): Best TV Actor, Musical/Comedy (Carroll O'Connor); Best Supporting Actor, Television (Rob Reiner); Best Supporting Actress, Television (Sally Struthers)

1975 (3): Best TV Show, Musical/Comedy; Best TV Actor, Musical/Comedy (Carroll O'Connor); Best TV Actress, Musical/Comedy (Jean Stapleton)

1976 (2): Best TV Actor, Musical/Comedy (Carroll O'Connor); Best Supporting Actor, Television (Rob Reiner)

1977 (2): Best Supporting Actor, Television (Rob Reiner); Best Supporting Actress, Television (Sally Struthers)

1978 (2): Best TV Actor, Musical/Comedy (Carroll O'Connor); Best TV Actress, Musical/Comedy (Jean Stapleton)
1979 (2): Best TV Series, Musical/Comedy; Best TV Actress, Musical/Comedy (Jean Stapleton)

HUMANITAS PRIZE

1978: 30-Minute Category (Larry Rhine and Mel Tolkin)

HUMANITAS PRIZE NOMINATIONS

1977: 30-Minute Network or Syndicated Television (Larry Rhine and Mel Tolkin)
1979: 30-Minute Network or Syndicated Television (Larry Rhine and Mel Tolkin)

PEABODY AWARD

1978: Norman Lear

Further Reading

McCrohan, Donna. *Archie & Edith, Mike & Gloria: The Tumultuous History of* All in the Family. New York: Workman, 1988.
Museum of Broadcast Communications. "All in the Family." Available online at www.museum .tv/eotvsection.php?entrycode=allinthefa.

✳ 3 ✳

*M*A*S*H*

(1972–1983)

Cast: Alan Alda (Captain Benjamin Franklin "Hawkeye" Pierce), Wayne Rogers (Captain John Francis "Trapper" McIntyre), McLean Stevenson (Colonel Henry Blake), Loretta Swit (Major Margaret "Hot Lips" Houlihan), Larry Linville (Major Frank Burns), Gary Burghoff (Corporal Walter "Radar" O'Reilly), Jamie Farr (Corporal Maxwell "Max" Klinger), William Christopher (Captain Father John Francis Patrick Mulcahy), Mike Farrell (Captain B. J. Hunnicutt), Harry Morgan (Colonel Sherman T. Potter), David Ogden Stiers (Major Charles Emerson Winchester III)

Created by: Producer, director, and writer Larry Gelbart, based on the 1970 film of the same title

Network: CBS

First Air Date: September 17, 1972

Last Air Date: February 8, 1983

Broadcast History:
September 17, 1972–September 1973: Sunday at 8:00–8:30 PM
September 1973–September 1974: Saturday at 8:30–9:00 PM
September 1974–September 1975: Tuesday at 8:30–9:00 PM
September 1975–November 1975: Friday at 8:30–9:00 PM
December 1975–January 1978: Tuesday at 9:00–9:30 PM
January 1978–September 1983: Monday at 9:00–9:30 PM

Seasons: 11

Episodes: 251

Ratings History: 1972–1973 (46), 1973–1974 (4), 1974–1975 (5), 1975–1976 (15), 1976–1977 (4), 1977–1978 (9), 1978–1979 (7), 1979–1980 (5), 1980–1981 (4), 1981–1982 (9), 1982–1983 (3)

Alan Alda, Loretta Swit, McLean Stevenson, Wayne Rogers, and Larry Linville. *CBS/ Photofest ©CBS*

Overview

The television "dramedy" was born when perhaps the most critically acclaimed program in television history debuted on September 17, 1972. One could hardly detect the drama through the laugh track and silliness in the early episodes of the adaptation of a namesake 1970 hit film, but when *M*A*S*H* hit its stride as the mid-1970s approached, it succeeded in drawing out a range of emotions from its viewers through humor and taut personal conflicts and challenges.

Although it never rose above number three in the annual Nielsen ratings, the show was among the most respected and beloved to ever appear on the small screen. The complexities of such featured characters as Benjamin "Hawkeye" Pierce (Alan Alda) and Margaret "Hot Lips" Houlihan (Loretta Swit) resulted in multidimensional portrayals and a strong sense of realism. Their personalities and motivations evolved, taking the loyal audience with them on their emotional journeys.

M*A*S*H was set at a mobile army surgical hospital (hence, the title) during the Korean War in the early 1950s, although there was no attempt to escape the obvious parallel between its antiwar theme and the unpopularity of the Vietnam War, which was drawing down at the time of the show's launch. The rare fruitful and effective sitcom remake of a movie came courtesy of creator Larry Gelbart, who had honed his talents writing for such comedic giants as Bob Hope and Sid Caesar and for such hit Broadway plays as *A Funny Thing Happened on the Way to the Forum*. Gelbart and Alda immediately placed their imprints on *M*A*S*H* through purposefully sophomoric humor and rebelliousness against the backdrop of the tragedies of war. The effective contrasting of the humor and drama was most evident in the operating room, where Hawkeye—one of several surgeons up to his elbows in blood and both horrified and angered by the perceived senselessness of the death and destruction—cracked jokes to maintain his sanity.

Alda established his Hawkeye persona as the central character from the start. The son of actor Robert Alda (who made several appearances on the show as a fellow surgeon) received his training in the New York theaters before finding small parts on various television programs in the 1960s. His casting in *M*A*S*H* proved to be his breakthrough and would remain his signature role, although he did gain success as both an actor and director well beyond.

The protagonists and antagonists were unmistakable in the early years. Ground zero was "The Swamp," a shambles of a hut that housed Pierce, best friend John "Trapper" McIntyre (Wayne Rogers), and foil Frank Burns (Larry Linville), whose lack of intelligence and surgical skills prompted constant derision from his roommates. Adding to the early humor was the not-so-secret love affair between the married Burns and head nurse "Hot Lips" Houlihan, who otherwise sought to promote "army discipline" in a unit devoid of it thanks greatly to the "leadership" of Colonel Henry Blake (McLean Stevenson), a confirmed civilian and inept officer. The occasional spotlight on cross-dressing Corporal Max Klinger (Jamie Farr), who wore women's clothes in bucking for a discharge, supplemented the wackiness of the early years of the show.

The comic tone of *M*A*S*H* took a dramatic turn in the mid- to late 1970s. The seeds were planted by the dissatisfaction of both Stevenson and Rogers, who had grown tired of taking a back seat to Alda in the comic hierarchy and decided to leave the series. The change was signaled in the 1975 season finale, perhaps the most shocking episode in the history of the American sitcom. The words uttered by Corporal Walter "Radar" O'Reilly (Gary Burghoff) to the other cast members toiling in the operating room in the final scene remained a secret to them until the final moment and revealed the fate of the Stevenson character. A somber O'Reilly informed the others that Blake's plane home had been shot down over the Sea of Japan. "There were no survivors," he concluded as the room fell silent.

Cast changes and greater artistic control by Alda brought with them a more even mix of humor and drama. Alda yearned not only to make audiences laugh, but to make a statement with each episode and through the overall message of the show, which became increasingly moralistic, antiwar, and, much of the dismay of some loyal viewers, outwardly preachy. Cast replacements, including Colonel Sherman T. Potter (Harry Morgan) and Captain B. J. Hunnicutt (Mike Farrell), displayed a greater depth, seriousness, and sense of morality than their predecessors. The pure comic relief of the bumbling Burns was eventually replaced by the Harvard educated Major Charles Emerson Winchester III (David Ogden Stiers), whose wealth, breeding, and intelligence made him a far more challenging antagonist to Pierce and Hunnicutt. Linville had left the show because he had reached the conclusion that he could take his incompetent, morally bankrupt, one-dimensional character no further.

There would be no other major additions to the cast throughout the show's run. The last several years of the show spotlighted the emotional growth of several characters, particularly Houlihan, Winchester, and Pierce. That of Houlihan proved to be the most dramatic, as the shallow, needy, immature nurse of the early years blossomed into a strong, self-actualized, independent woman. Winchester became far less self-absorbed as he was touched by the horrors of war and how they affected the native Korean population. And the confirmed bachelor Pierce, a thoughtless, disrespectful womanizer early in the show, grew finely in tune with the feelings and emotions of the opposite sex as the women's movement in the United States took hold and grew in the 1970s.

The antiwar theme of *M*A*S*H* remained a constant through a dramatic shift in the American political landscape. The show was launched during a period of rampant antiwar sentiment nurtured by the growing unpopularity of the Vietnam War, which had peaked in the early 1970s. By the late 1970s and early 1980s, when the sitcom was in its final years, the nation had been swept by a wave of conservatism and patriotism personified by popular president Ronald Reagan, but the seeming disconnect between the moral message pumped out by Alda and the show and the political leanings of the country did not affect ratings. *M*A*S*H* remained one of the most-watched programs in the United States throughout that time period.

That certainly remained true on February 8, 1983, when the final two-and-a-half-hour program aired in front of what remains the top-rated series episode in television history. A mind-boggling 106 million viewers—almost 77 percent of American TV-watching households—tuned in to say good-bye to the characters that had been part of their lives for more than a decade. The farewell show, entitled "Goodbye, Farewell, and Amen," features a twist in the plot, in which Hawkeye experiences an emotional breakdown after having forced a Korean woman to smother her crying baby on a bus with enemy soldiers nearby. The series finale takes viewers through his emotional hell and back, while also focusing on the relationships between the other characters as they experience the joy of learning they are about to return home and the sadness of departing from their friends of many years.

Not So Hot Spin-Off

The departure of the *M*A*S*H* characters from Korea didn't translate into their departure from the small screen. The show spawned a spin-off in *After M*A*S*H*, which spotlights the postwar work of Potter, Klinger, and Father Mulcahy (William Christopher) at a stateside hospital. It lasted just two seasons.

Did You Know?

Gary Burghoff, who played Radar O'Reilly, has just three fingers on his left hand, which he hid during filming. He was also an accomplished drummer, which he displayed on occasion on the show.

They Said It

Frank: Funny thing, war: never have so many suffered so much so so few could be so happy.
Margaret: We're lucky to be two of the few and not the many.
Frank: I know, darling, and I love being both of us.

Frank: I'm sick of hearing about the wounded. What about all the thousands of wonderful guys who are fighting this war without any of the credit or the glory that always goes to those lucky few who just happen to get shot?

Hawkeye: Nurse! Nurse!
Nurse: Did you call me, doctor?
Hawkeye: Why should I call you 'doctor?' I'm the surgeon.

Frank: I know I'm a real asset.
Hawkeye: You're only off by two letters.

Sherman: [as the surgeons operate on a little Korean girl] Someone dropped a bomb on her village from an airplane.
Captain Hathaway [a bomber]: Who did it?
Hawkeye: He just dropped it. He didn't autograph it.
Captain Hathaway: No, I mean was it one of theirs or one of ours?
Sherman: What difference does that make?
Captain Hathaway: A lot. It makes a lot of difference.
Sherman: Not to her.

Major Awards

EMMY AWARD WINS (14)

1974 (4): Outstanding Comedy Series; Best Lead Actor in a Comedy Series (Alan Alda); Actor of the Year, Series (Alan Alda); Best Directing in a Comedy (Jackie Cooper for "Carry On, Hawkeye")

1975 (1): Outstanding Director in a Comedy Series (Gene Reynolds for "O.R.")

1976 (2): Outstanding Director in a Comedy Series (Gene Reynolds for "Welcome to Korea"); Outstanding Achievement in Film Editing for Entertainment Programming for a Series, for a Single Episode of a Comedy Series (Stanford Tischler and Fred W. Berger for "Welcome to Korea")

1977 (2): Outstanding Continuing Performance by a Supporting Actor in a Comedy Series (Gary Burghoff); Outstanding Directing in a Comedy Series (Alan Alda for "Dear Sigmund")

1979 (1): Outstanding Writing in a Comedy or Comedy-Variety or Music Series (Alan Alda for "Inga")

1980 (2): Outstanding Supporting Actress in a Comedy or Comedy-Variety or Music Series (Loretta Swit); Outstanding Supporting Actor in a Comedy or Comedy-Variety or Music Series (Harry Morgan)

1982 (2): Outstanding Lead Actor in a Comedy Series (Alan Alda); Outstanding Supporting Actress in a Comedy or Comedy-Variety or Music Series (Loretta Swit)

EMMY AWARD NOMINATIONS, IN ADDITION TO WINS (95)

1973 (8): Outstanding Comedy Series; Outstanding New Series; Outstanding Continued Performance by an Actor in a Leading Role in a Comedy Series (Alan Alda); Outstanding Performance by an Actor in a Supporting Role in Comedy (Gary Burghoff); Outstanding Performance by an Actor in a Supporting Role in Comedy (McLean Stevenson); Outstanding Writing Achievement in Comedy (Larry Gelbart for the pilot); Outstanding Directorial Achievement in Comedy (Gene Reynolds); Outstanding Achievement in Film Editing for Entertainment Programming, for a Series or a Single Program of a Series

1974 (7): Best Supporting Actor in Comedy (Gary Burghoff); Best Supporting Actor in Comedy (McLean Stevenson); Best Supporting Actress in Comedy (Loretta Swit); Best Writing in Comedy (Linda Bloodworth-Thomason and Mary Kay Place for "Hot Lips and Empty Arms"); Best Writing in Comedy (McLean Stevenson for "The Trial of Henry Blake"); Best Directing in Comedy (Gene Reynolds); Best Film Editing for Entertainment Programming, for a Series or a Single Program of a Series

1975 (10): Outstanding Comedy Series; Outstanding Lead Actor in a Comedy Series (Alan Alda); Outstanding Continuing Performance by a Supporting Actor in a Comedy Series (Gary Burghoff); Outstanding Continuing Performance by a Supporting Actor in a Comedy Series (McLean Stevenson); Outstanding Continuing Performance by a Supporting Actress in a Comedy Series (Loretta Swit); Outstanding Single Performance by a Supporting Actor in a Comedy or Drama Series (Harry Morgan); Outstanding Directing in a Comedy Series (Alan Alda); Outstanding Directing in a Comedy Series (Hy Averback); Outstanding Film Editing for Entertainment Programming for a Series, for a Single Episode of a Comedy Series; Outstanding Achievement in Cinematography for Entertainment Programming for a Series

1976 (9): Outstanding Comedy Series; Outstanding Lead Actor in a Comedy Series (Alan Alda); Outstanding Continuing Performance by a Supporting Actor in a Comedy Series (Gary Burghoff); Outstanding Continuing Performance by a Supporting Actor in a Comedy Series (Harry Morgan); Outstanding Continuing Performance by a Supporting Actress in a Comedy Series (Loretta Swit); Outstanding Writing in a Comedy Series (Larry Gelbart and Gene Reynolds for "The More I See You"); Outstanding Writing in a Comedy Series (Larry Gelbart and Simon Muntner for "Hawkeye"); Outstanding Directing in a Comedy Series (Alan Alda); Outstanding Achievement in Cinematography for Entertainment Programming for a Series

1977 (9): Outstanding Comedy Series; Outstanding Lead Actor in a Comedy Series (Alan Alda); Outstanding Continuing Performance by a Supporting Actor in a Comedy Series (Harry Morgan); Outstanding Continuing Performance by a Supporting Actress in a Comedy Series (Loretta Swit); Outstanding Writing in a Comedy Series (Alan Alda for "Dear Sigmund"); Outstanding Directing in a Comedy Series (Joan Darling for "The Nurses"); Outstanding Directing in a Comedy Series (Alan Rafkin for "Lt. Radar O'Reilly"); Outstanding Film Editing in a Comedy Series (Samuel E. Beetley and Stanford Tischler for "Dear Sigmund"); Outstanding Cinematography in Entertainment Programming for a Series (William K. Jurgensen for "Dear Sigmund")

1978 (8): Outstanding Comedy Series; Outstanding Lead Actor in a Comedy Series (Alan Alda); Outstanding Continuing Performance by a Supporting Actor in a Comedy Series (Gary Burghoff); Outstanding Continuing Performance by a Supporting Actor in a Comedy Series (Harry Morgan); Outstanding Continuing Performance by a Supporting Actress in a Comedy Series (Loretta Swit); Outstanding Writing in a Comedy Series (Alan Alda for "Fallen Idol"); Outstanding Directing in a Comedy Series (Alan Alda and Burt Metcalfe for "Comrade in Arms: Part I"); Outstanding Film Editing in a Comedy Series (Stanford Tischler and Larry L. Mills for "Fade Out, Fade In")

1979 (9): Outstanding Comedy Series; Outstanding Lead Actor in a Comedy Series (Alan Alda); Outstanding Supporting Actor in a Comedy or Comedy-Variety or Music Series (Gary Burghoff); Outstanding Supporting Actor in a Comedy or Comedy-Variety or Music Series (Harry Morgan); Outstanding Supporting Actress in a Comedy or Comedy-Variety or Music Series (Loretta Swit); Outstanding Writing in a Comedy or Comedy-Variety or Music Series (Ken Levine and David Isaacs for "Point of View"); Outstanding Directing in a Comedy or Comedy-Variety or Music Series (Alan Alda for "Dear Sis"); Outstanding Directing in a Comedy or Comedy-Variety or Music Series (Charles S. Dubin for "Point of View"); Outstanding Film Editing in a Comedy Series (Larry L. Mills and Stanford Tischler for "The Billfold Syndrome")

1980 (9): Outstanding Comedy Series; Outstanding Lead Actor in a Comedy Series (Alan Alda); Outstanding Supporting Actor in a Comedy or Comedy-Variety or Music Series (Mike Farrell); Outstanding Writing in a Comedy Series (Ken Levine and David Isaacs for "Goodbye Radar: Part II"); Outstanding Directing in a Comedy Series (Charles S. Dubin for "Period of Adjustment"); Outstanding

Directing in a Comedy Series (Burt Metcalfe for "Bottle Fatigue"); Outstanding Directing in a Comedy Series (Alan Alda for "Dreams"); Outstanding Directing in a Comedy Series (Harry Morgan for "Stars and Stripes"); Outstanding Achievement in Film Editing for a Series (Larry L. Mills and Stanford Tischler for "The Yalu Brick Road")

1981 (9): Outstanding Comedy Series; Outstanding Lead Actor in a Comedy Series (Alan Alda); Outstanding Supporting Actor in a Comedy or Comedy-Variety or Music Series (Harry Morgan); Outstanding Supporting Actor in a Comedy or Comedy-Variety or Music Series (David Ogden Stiers); Outstanding Supporting Actress in a Comedy or Comedy-Variety or Music Series (Loretta Swit); Outstanding Writing in a Comedy Series (Mike Farrell, John Rappaport, Dennis Koenig, Thad Mumford, Dan Wilcox, and Burt Metcalfe for "Death Takes a Holiday"); Outstanding Directing in a Comedy Series (Alan Alda for "The Life You Save"); Outstanding Directing in a Comedy Series (Burt Metcalfe for "No Laughing Matters"); Outstanding Achievement in Film Editing for a Series (Larry L. Mills and Stanford Tischler for "Death Takes a Holiday")

1982 (8): Outstanding Comedy Series; Outstanding Supporting Actor in a Comedy or Comedy-Variety or Music Series (Harry Morgan); Outstanding Supporting Actor in a Comedy or Comedy-Variety or Music Series (David Ogden Stiers); Outstanding Writing in a Comedy Series (Alan Alda for "Follies of the Living—Concerns of the Dead"); Outstanding Directing in a Comedy Series (Alan Alda for "Where There's a Will, There's a War"); Outstanding Directing in a Comedy Series (Hy Averback for "Sons and Bowlers"); Outstanding Directing in a Comedy Series (Charles S. Dubin for "Pressure Points"); Outstanding Directing in a Comedy Series (Burt Metcalfe for "Picture This")

1983 (9): Outstanding Comedy Series; Outstanding Lead Actor in a Comedy Series (Alan Alda); Outstanding Supporting Actor in a Comedy or Comedy-Variety or Music Series (Harry Morgan); Outstanding Supporting Actress in a Comedy or Comedy-Variety or Music Series (Loretta Swit); Outstanding Directing in a Comedy Series (Alan Alda for "Goodbye, Farewell, and Amen"); Outstanding Directing in a Comedy Series (Burt Metcalfe for "The Joker Is Wild"); Outstanding Film Editing for a Series (Larry L. Mills and Stanford Tischler for "Goodbye, Farewell, and Amen"); Outstanding Sound Editing for a Series (Richard Sperber, David M. Ice, Edward Rossi, William Hartman, Godfrey Marks, and Don Issacs for "Goodbye, Farewell, and Amen"); Outstanding Individual Achievement, Costumers (Albert H. Frankel and Rita Bennett for "Goodbye, Farewell, and Amen")

GOLDEN GLOBE WINS (7)

1974 (1): Best Supporting Actor, Television (McLean Stevenson)
1975 (1): Best TV Actor, Musical/Comedy (Alan Alda)
1976 (1): Best TV Actor, Musical/Comedy (Alan Alda)
1980 (1): Best TV Actor, Musical/Comedy (Alan Alda)
1981 (1): Best Performance by an Actor in a TV Series, Musical/Comedy (Alan Alda)
1982 (1): Best Performance by an Actor in a TV Series, Musical/Comedy (Alan Alda)
1983 (1): Best Performance by an Actor in a TV Series, Musical/Comedy (Alan Alda)

GOLDEN GLOBE NOMINATIONS, IN ADDITION TO WINS (13)

1973 (2): Best TV Show, Musical/Comedy; Best TV Actor, Musical/Comedy (Alan Alda)
1974 (2): Best TV Actor, Musical/Comedy (Alan Alda); Best Supporting Actress, Television (Loretta Swit)
1977 (2): Best TV Series, Musical/Comedy; Best TV Actor, Musical/Comedy (Alan Alda)
1978 (1): Best TV Actor, Musical/Comedy (Alan Alda)
1979 (1): Best TV Actor, Musical/Comedy (Alan Alda)
1980 (1): Best TV Series, Musical/Comedy; Best TV Actress (Loretta Swit)
1981 (1): Best TV Series, Musical/Comedy
1982 (1): Best Performance by an Actress in a TV Series, Musical/Comedy (Loretta Swit)
1983 (2): Best TV Series, Musical/Comedy; Best Performance by an Actress in a Supporting Role in a Series, Mini-Series, or Motion Picture Made for TV (Loretta Swit)

HUMANITAS PRIZE

1976: 30-Minute Category (Larry Gelbart)
1980: 60-Minute Category (Alan Alda and James Jay Rubinfier)
1982: 30-Minute Category (David Pollock and Elias Davis)
1983: 30-Minute Category (David Pollock and Elias Davis)

HUMANITAS PRIZE NOMINATIONS

1976: 30-Minute Category (Burt Prelutsky)
1977: 30-Minute Category (Alan Alda)
1979: 30-Minute Category (Ken Levine and David Isaacs)
1981: 30-Minute Category (David Pollock and Elias Davis)

PEABODY AWARD

1976: CBS

Further Reading

Kalter, Suzy. *The Complete Book of M*A*S*H*. New York: Harry Abrams, 1988.
Reiss, David S. *M*A*S*H: The Exclusive Inside Story of TVs Most Popular Show*. London: MacMillan, 1983.

4

I Love Lucy

(1951–1957)

Cast: Lucille Ball (Lucy Ricardo), Desi Arnaz (Ricky Ricardo), Vivian Vance (Ethel Mertz), William Frawley (Fred Mertz), Richard Keith (Little Ricky)

Created by: Producer and writer Jess Oppenheimer

Network: CBS

First Air Date: October 15, 1951

Last Air Date: May 6, 1957

Broadcast History:
October 15, 1951–May 6, 1957: Monday at 9:00–9:30 PM

Seasons: 6

Episodes: 179

Ratings History: 1951–1952 (3), 1952–1953 (1), 1953–1954 (1), 1954–1955 (1), 1955–1956 (2), 1956–1957 (1)

Overview

The visions are ingrained in the memories of millions, perhaps billions, of people around the world. They picture Lucy stuffing gobs of chocolate into her mouth in fear of losing her job as a candy wrapper while the conveyer belt spitting out the goodies churns faster. They picture her standing in a giant vat in Italy, where a case of mistaken identity has forced her to stomp grapes with her feet for a wine

Top: Vivian Vance and Lucille Ball; bottom: William Frawley and Desi Arnaz. *CBS/ Photofest ©CBS*

manufacturer. They picture the beloved redhead, mouth open wide, crying at the top of her lungs over one of the many disappointments in her life. And somehow they can empathize with her.

Many consider *I Love Lucy* to be the greatest sitcom ever produced. Although the talents of the other cast members should not be dismissed, Lucille Ball stole the show. She is generally accepted to be the funniest female comedian in the history of American entertainment. The wacky behavior of her front-of-the-camera persona remained in direct contrast to that of her real-life personality and drive. Ball was a thoughtful and savvy businesswoman who took comedy seriously. Lucy Ricardo was as madcap as any character that has ever graced a television screen.

The sitcom was one of just a few to dominate an era. Only *All in the Family*, which earned the number one spot in the Nielsen ratings six straight years, proved a bigger hit among viewers. *I Love Lucy* ranked among the top three in all six of its seasons and earned the top spot in four of them. It left the air in 1957, as the top-rated show on television. A severe case of cast-member burnout, rather than shrinking viewership, caused its cancellation that year.

The show revolved around the zany antics of Lucy Ricardo, who was married to real-life husband Ricky Ricardo (Desi Arnaz), a Cuban bandleader at the Tropicana Club in New York. Lucy worked feverishly, and mostly in vain, to convince Ricky to put her in his show despite her distinct lack of talent as a singer or dancer. The scatterbrained, but determined, Lucy went to great lengths to accomplish goals of acquiring personal satisfaction or fame and fortune for herself and Ricky, leading to hilariously disastrous consequences. His exasperation with her often caused him to lose his ability to speak fluid English and instead toss a string of insults at her in Spanish.

Lucy's sidekick and often-unwitting accomplice to her shenanigans was neighbor and best friend Ethel Mertz (Vivian Vance), who was married to notorious tightwad Fred Mertz (William Frawley). The plots created by show creator Jess Oppenheimer and fellow writers Madelyn Pugh and Bob Carroll Jr. sometimes pitted Lucy and Ethel against Desi and Fred in some form of battle of the sexes. Some placed the Ricardos against the Mertzes in a family feud. Others simply featured Lucy in a personal struggle to reach a goal. But all of them were highlighted by her zany, creative schemes resulting in calamity for herself and all her hapless victims.

Global syndication that has aired the show to billions of people too young to remember its initial run have turned on generation after generation to its brilliance. Both passionate and casual viewers of *I Love Lucy* embrace their favorite episodes. The most critically acclaimed was "Lucy Does a TV Commercial," which ranked third on the list of all-time sitcom episodes (behind *Seinfeld's* "The Contest" and *The Mary Tyler Moore Show's* "Chuckles Bites the Dust"), as ranked by *TV Guide* in 2009. In that episode, Lucy is hired to hawk a new tonic called Vitameatavegamin, which, unbeknownst to her, contains 23 percent alcohol. She becomes drunker with each gulp and fails to spit out her lines in the rehearsal. She is nowhere to be seen for the live taping, which was slated for the same time and location as Ricky's show. A still-smashed Lucy is seen stumbling around before finally joining him in the middle of a song. She sings jibberish in front of the camera, stopping only to say hello to Fred and Ethel in TV land. After she slurs a few words about Vitameatavegamin, her horrified husband finally carries her off the stage. The scene exemplifies the talent of Ball as a physical comedian.

The incredible long-term success of the program in syndication can be partly attributed to the decision to film episodes before a live audience, thereby ensuring the ability to make quality prints of *I Love Lucy* for reruns the producers or actors likely had no idea at the time would be shown well into the next century. The show has been translated into dozens of languages and seen around the world, but it wasn't until the launch of *All in the Family* nearly two decades later that another situation comedy was filmed before a live audience. The use of a laugh track in the 1950s and 1960s gave sitcoms a sense of unreality. The live audience reaction to Lucy and her cohorts brought a feeling of authenticity to the program.

Despite the wackiness of the Lucy character, the writers sought to bring realism to the show. They turned the real-life birth of her son into an episode in which Ricky Jr. was born. Two different babies were shown to be their son until a child actor named Richard Keith, who was discovered by the two stars, assumed the speaking role in the final season. By that time, the twenty-year marriage of Lucy and Desi had become strained.

"[Ball] told me that by 1956 it wasn't even a marriage anymore," said Ball biographer Bart Andrews. They were just going through a routine for the children. She told me that for the last five years of their marriage, it was 'just booze and broads.' That was in the divorce papers, as a matter of fact."

I Love Lucy ended on top of the ratings world. It remains arguably the most beloved sitcom in television history. And while the talents of the other cast members and personalities of their characters contributed greatly to the success of the show, it's undeniable that it would hardly have made a dent on the television scene without the comedic brilliance of Lucille Ball.

Critics Had Some "Splainin' to Do"

The continued popularity of the cancelled *I Love Lucy* program in 1958 motivated CBS to ask approximately 155 television critics and columnists to choose their favorite episodes. The top thirteen were aired that summer as a replacement series for *The Danny Thomas Show*, which was on hiatus. The network decided that *The Top Ten Lucy Shows* would be a snappy title for the series, despite the fact that they aired three more than that.

The top three on the list are not considered among the favorites of current *I Love Lucy* fans. They featured luminaries of the day, including country singer Tennessee Ernie Ford, comedian Bob Hope, and famed journalist Edward R. Murrow, none of whom resonates with more recent generations. Such critically acclaimed episodes as "Lucy Does a TV Commercial" (in which she gets drunk on Vitameatavegamin) and "Lucy's Italian Movie" (in which she stomps grapes in Italy) did make the cut. Mysteriously absent is "Job Switching," which features Lucy and Ethel failing to keep up with their task of wrapping chocolates sliding by on a conveyer belt. That episode is the all-time favorite of many fans of the show.

Definitely Not One and Done

Many sitcom stars fade from popularity after their shows are cancelled or are remembered only through syndication. This was not the case with Lucille Ball. The wacky redhead remained hot well into the 1970s. She followed *I Love Lucy* with *The Lucy Show* (1962–1968) and *Here's Lucy* (1968–1972). Both shows remained in the Top 10 of the Nielsen ratings from 1962 to 1971. *The Lucy Show* peaked at number two in the 1966–1967 season.

The former featured her as Lucy Carmichael, a widow with two children living in Danbury, Connecticut, and sharing her home with divorced friend Vivian Bagley (Vivian Vance). That character left the show in 1965, when Carmichael hightailed it to San Francisco. The star's name was changed to Lucy Carter and the show renamed *Here's Lucy* in 1968. The character still had two kids, but they were played by her real-life son (Desi Arnaz Jr.) and daughter (Lucie Arnaz).

The only constant was Gale Gordon, who played Lucy's long-suffering boss from 1963 to 1974, when the show finally left the air. Gordon had gained fame through his role as blustery school principal Osgood Conklin in *Our Miss Brooks* and the always-exasperated Mr. Wilson on *Dennis the Menace*.

They Said It

Fred: She said my mother looks like a weasel.
Lucy: Ethel, apologize.
Ethel: I'm sorry your mother looks like a weasel.

Lucy: If some other woman were to take Fred away from you, you'd be singing a different tune, too.
Ethel: Yeah, 'Happy Days Are Here Again.'

Ethel: Imagine me meeting a queen face to face. I'm scared.
Fred: You're scared? Think of the queen.

Major Awards

EMMY AWARD WINS (4)

1953 (1): Best Situation Comedy
1954 (2): Best Situation Comedy; Best Series Supporting Actress (Vivian Vance)
1956 (1): Best Actress, Continuing Performance (Lucille Ball)

EMMY AWARD NOMINATIONS, IN ADDITION TO WINS (16)

1952 (1): Best Comedy Show
1954 (2): Best Female Star of a Regular Series (Lucille Ball); Best Series Supporting Actor (William Frawley)
1955 (5): Best Situation Comedy Series; Best Actress Starring in a Regular Series (Lucille Ball); Best Supporting Actor in a Regular Series (William Frawley); Best Supporting Actress in a Regular Series (Vivian Vance); Best Written Comedy Material (Jess Oppenheimer, Bob Carroll Jr., and Madelyn Davis)

1956 (2): Best Actor in a Supporting Role (William Frawley); Best Comedy Writing (Jess Oppenheimer, Bob Carroll Jr., Madelyn Davis, Bob Schiller, and Bob Weiskopf for "L.A. at Last")

1957 (3): Best Continuing Performance by a Comedienne in a Series (Lucille Ball); Best Supporting Performance by an Actor (William Frawley); Best Supporting Performance by an Actress (Vivian Vance)

1958 (3): Best Continuing Performance (Female) in a Series by a Comedienne, Singer, Hostess, Dancer, M.C., Announcer, Narrator, Panelist, or Any Person Who Essentially Plays Herself (Lucille Ball); Best Continuing Supporting Performance by an Actor in a Dramatic or Comedy Series (William Frawley); Best Continuing Supporting Performance by an Actress in a Dramatic or Comedy Series (Vivian Vance)

Further Reading

Edwards, Elizabeth. *I Love Lucy: Celebrating 50 Years of Love and Laughter.* Philadelphia, PA: Running Press, 2010.

Jones, Chris. "'I Love Lucy Live on Stage' Only a Warm Facsimile." *Chicago Tribune,* September 20, 2012. Available online at http://articles.chicagotribune.com/2012-09-20/entertainment/ct-ott-0921-lucy-review-20120920_1_love-lucy-live-lucille-ball-lucy-ricardo.

Sanders, Coyne S., and Tom Gilbert. *Desilu: The Story of Lucille Ball and Desi Arnaz.* New York: It Books, 2011.

✯ **5** ✯

The Mary Tyler Moore Show

(1970–1977)

Cast: Mary Tyler Moore (Mary Richards), Ed Asner (Lou Grant), Valerie Harper (Rhoda Morgenstern), Ted Knight (Ted Baxter), Gavin MacLeod (Murray Slaughter), Cloris Leachman (Phyllis Lindstrom), Betty White (Sue Ann Nivens), Georgia Engel (Georgette Franklin Baxter)

Created by: Executive producers James L. Brooks and Allan Burns

Network: CBS

First Air Date: September 19, 1970

Last Air Date: September 3, 1977

Broadcast History:
September 19, 1970–December 1971: Saturday at 9:30–10:00 PM
December 1971–September 1972: Saturday at 8:30–9:00 PM
September 1972–March 8, 1976: Saturday at 9:00–9:30 PM
November 1976–September 3, 1977: Saturday at 8:00–8:30 PM

Seasons: 7

Episodes: 168

Ratings History: 1970–1971 (22), 1971–1972 (10), 1972–1973 (7), 1973–1974 (9), 1974–1975 (11), 1975–1976 (19), 1976–1977 (not in Top 30)

Mary Tyler Moore. *CBS/Photofest ©CBS*

Overview

The greatness of *The Mary Tyler Moore Show* extended far beyond its social impact as the first American sitcom to spotlight a proud, successful, independent, romantically unattached working woman. Its brilliance as perhaps the finest television comedy ever produced can be attributed to character-based humor achieved through a depth of talent arguably unmatched in the history of the medium.

Supremely funny and multidimensional characters peppered the cast in both the professional and personal lives of Mary Richards (Mary Tyler Moore). The proof was in the Emmys. Every significant performer portraying a colleague at the pitiful WJM newsroom or friend living in her Minneapolis apartment earned one except Gavin MacLeod, who played copywriter Murray Slaughter.

There was Ed Asner playing a combination of tough, cantankerous, but fair producer and sensitive, cuddly, teddy bear Lou Grant. There was Ted Knight as the preposterously inept, dimwitted egomaniac and anchorman Ted Baxter. There was legendary Betty White playing happy homemaker Sue Ann Nivens, who, in a rare moment of self-reflection, described herself quite accurately as a "vain, selfish, egotistical middle-aged shrew." There was Valerie Harper as witty and self-deprecating neighbor and best friend Rhoda Morgenstern. There was Cloris Leachman as the hip feminist and meddler Phyllis Lindstrom. And, of course, there was Moore as Richards, proud, ambitious, yet vulnerable, fearful of spending her life alone, but unwilling to compromise her career for any man.

The theme song explains the story of Mary Richards, who has arrived in Minneapolis after ending a long-term relationship. She is hired by Grant as an associate producer, despite a profound lack of experience, because, as the boss later explains, she bumped into a desk and apologized to it. She expresses her love and affection for her coworkers and neighbors far more easily than she develops an emotional bond with the many suitors that cross her path. But she was no prude; one episode in which she arrives home early in the morning after a date and is scolded by her phoning father proves that she was not waiting for marriage to consummate strong relationships. She was, after all, in her thirties.

Lou has his own personal and professional soap operas. Longtime wife Edie (Priscilla Morrill) left him for reasons never satisfactorily explained and later married another man. He is tortured daily by the inane Ted. Yet, he keeps his sanity and concludes most episodes with a satisfying smile.

Murray is in love with Mary—and finally admits it in one notable episode. He is the perpetrator and victim of the only put-down humor in the show. Murray regularly jokes to Ted about his incompetence and Sue Ann about her promiscuity. Only the latter returns the favor, matching such insults with ones of her own about Murray's baldness. But Murray is, most of all, kindhearted and selfless, despite his inner resentment, rarely expressed, about his lack of appreciation or financial reward at WJM.

Ted arguably evolves more than any other character on the program, although that just makes him less of a buffoon. Knight yearned for his character to grow, a wish that was granted through his relationship with his girlfriend, then wife Georgette (Georgia Engel). But he remains a fool, even in the later episodes, for example, when he tries to convince Lou that he is an intellectual by taking out books from the library, including "Victor Hugo's latest."

Sue Ann, who arrives on the scene in the fourth season, shamelessly pursues Lou and masks her fears with a painted-on smile that, as she is proud to point out, accentuates her dimples. She bosses around her lackeys on the set of *The Happy Homemaker*, yet shows her vulnerability and sensitivity when rebuffed, for instance, when two plumbers at a convention ignore her advances and gravitate toward Mary.

The sarcastic, droll Rhoda gained self-assuredness as the show progressed. The window dresser seeks love with a desperation never seen from Mary, but her lack of confidence grows in the early episodes with every rejection. She never attempts to garner respect from Phyllis, who believes her to be unworthy of Mary's friendship. The performance of Harper resulted in a successful spin-off entitled *Rhoda* that forced her to leave *The Mary Tyler Moore Show* after four seasons.

A sitcom of her own also lured Leachman away after five years. She landed the title role in the spin-off *Phyllis* after playing Mary's landlord with aplomb and passion. Her facial expressions (for example, the time she tastes her own apple pie and realizes just how horrible a baker she is) communicate masked feelings. The humor involving Phyllis often revolves around the blandness of husband Lars, who is never shown.

The plotlines proved as intriguing and humorous as the characters themselves. The episode "Chuckles Bites the Dust" has been ranked as the funniest single episode in the history of television. It revolves around the death of Chuckles the Clown, who was dressed up as a peanut in a parade and shelled into oblivion by a rogue elephant.

The Mary Tyler Moore Show gained greater critical acclaim as one of the most highly awarded sitcoms in television history than it did viewership. Although it remained in the Top 22 in the Nielsen ratings in each of its first six seasons, it never vaulted into the Top 5. But it remained a staple in the powerful CBS Saturday night lineup of the 1970s—perhaps the finest ever—throughout its run.

The show was cancelled in 1977, despite strong ratings. In a final, fitting bit of irony, everyone in the WJM newsroom is fired but Ted, which is just one more reason to remember *The Mary Tyler Moore Show* with the fondness and respect befitting one of the funniest and important sitcoms ever to grace the airwaves.

Ordinary People, Extraordinary Performance

Mary Tyler Moore proved her versatility as an actress with her performance as a calculating, bitter wife and mother in the 1980 Academy Award-winning movie *Ordinary People*, for which she was nominated for an Oscar. Noted *Boston Phoenix* critic Stephen Schiff summarizes her brilliance in the film in the following piece:

> Most remarkable of all, however, is Mary Tyler Moore, whose portrayal of a Lake Forest ice princess is so cool, brittle, and nasty that it borders on the perverse. By all rights, Beth should not seem a villain. Her inability to express emotion is a reflection of her son's, and because she's a hopeless case, the filmmakers would like us to pity her. But the ear-to-ear smile of Mary Tyler Moore is too familiar, too comfortable, and practiced to seem the panoply of an Illinois housewife. It's a star's smile, intense and ferocious, and when we detect hatred or duplicity beneath it, it's so powerful that it comes to seem evil: the deceptive grin of a monster.

Good Knight, Early Good-bye

Ted Knight bounced from one minor guest appearance to the next in sitcoms and dramas before landing his signature role of Ted Baxter on *The Mary Tyler Moore Show*. He parlayed that into his own series entitled *Too Close for Comfort*, which was rolling into its seventh season when he died of cancer at the comparatively tender age of sixty-two. But aside from his Baxter role, he might be remembered most as the outrageous Judge Elihu Smails in the goofy 1980 comedy film *Caddyshack*.

They Said It

> **Ted:** I did a report on unemployment. It's at an all-time high. Or was it low?
> **Murray:** [exasperated] High, Ted.
> **Ted:** Hi, Murr.

Mary: [drunk and depressed that a WJM documentary on an honest politician bombed] If it weren't for all the rotten things that happen in this world we couldn't put on a news show. We should be grateful to all the people who do those rotten things. We should stop them in the streets and say, 'Thank you Mr. Mugger, thank you Mr. Thief, thank you Mr. Maniac.'

Phyllis: [to a beau of Mary's she wants to impress] My name is Phyllis, but my friends call me 'Phyl.'
Rhoda: Her really good friends call her 'Ph.'

Ted: [introducing wife Georgette to former WJM weatherman Gordy, of whom he's insanely jealous for hitting it big in New York] I'd like you to meet my wife Georgette, a woman I'd much rather have than two hundred and fifty thousand dollars a year. Wouldn't you?
Gordy: [embarrassed] Yeah, Ted, yeah.
Ted: Want to trade?

Ted: [upon learning that Sue Ann earns a higher salary than him] Mary, do you know what Sue Ann takes home every week?
Mary: Three sailors, a tree surgeon, and a boy in the mail room.

Murray: [after everyone but Ted was fired] Being fired is like being violated.
Sue Ann: Leave it to Murray to find a bright spot.

Major Awards

EMMY AWARD WINS (29)

1971 (4): Outstanding Performance by an Actor in a Supporting Role in Comedy (Ed Asner); Outstanding Performance by an Actress in a Supporting Role in Comedy (Valerie Harper); Outstanding Writing Achievement in Comedy (James L. Brooks and Allan Burns for "Support Your Local Mother"); Outstanding Directorial Achievement in Comedy (Jay Sandrich)
1972 (2): Outstanding Performance by an Actor in a Supporting Role in Comedy (Ed Asner); Outstanding Performance by an Actress in a Supporting Role in Comedy (Valerie Harper)
1973 (4): Outstanding Continued Performance by an Actress in a Leading Role in a Comedy Series (Mary Tyler Moore); Outstanding Performance by an Actor in a Supporting Role in Comedy (Ted Knight); Outstanding Performance by an Actress in a Supporting Role in Comedy (Valerie Harper); Outstanding Directorial Achievement in Comedy (Jay Sandrich)
1974 (5): Actress of the Year, Series (Mary Tyler Moore); Best Lead Actress in a Series (Mary Tyler Moore); Best Supporting Actress in Comedy (Cloris Leachman); Best Writing in Comedy (Treva Silverman for "The Lou and Edie Story"); Writer of the Year, Series (Treva Silverman for "The Lou and Edie Story")

1975 (6): Outstanding Comedy Series; Outstanding Performance by a Supporting Actor in a Comedy Series (Ed Asner); Outstanding Performance by a Supporting Actress in a Comedy Series (Betty White); Outstanding Single Performance by a Supporting Actress in a Comedy or Drama Series (Cloris Leachman for "Phyllis Whips Inflation"); Outstanding Writing in a Comedy Series (Ed. Weinberger and Stan Daniels for "Mary Richards Goes to Jail"); Outstanding Film Editing for Entertainment Programming for a Series, for a Single Episode of a Comedy Series (Douglas Hines for "An Affair to Forget")

1976 (5): Outstanding Comedy Series; Outstanding Lead Actress in a Comedy Series (Mary Tyler Moore); Outstanding Continuing Performance by a Supporting Actor in a Comedy Series (Ted Knight); Outstanding Continuing Performance by a Supporting Actor in a Comedy Series (Betty White); Outstanding Writing in a Comedy Series (David Lloyd for "Chuckles Bites the Dust")

1977 (3): Outstanding Comedy Series; Outstanding Writing in a Comedy Series (James L. Brooks, Allan Burns, Ed. Weinberger, Stan Daniels, David Lloyd, and Bob Ellison for "The Last Show"); Outstanding Film Editing in a Comedy Series (Douglas Hines for "Murray Can't Lose")

EMMY AWARD NOMINATIONS, IN ADDITION TO WINS (38)

1971 (4): Outstanding Series, Comedy; Outstanding New Series; Outstanding Continued Performance by an Actress in a Leading Role in a Comedy Series (Mary Tyler Moore); Outstanding Directorial Achievement in Comedy (Alan Rafkin for "Support Your Local Mother")

1972 (6): Outstanding Series, Comedy; Outstanding Continued Performance by an Actress in a Leading Role in a Comedy Series (Mary Tyler Moore); Outstanding Performance by an Actor in a Supporting Role in Comedy (Ted Knight); Outstanding Performance by an Actress in a Supporting Role in Comedy (Cloris Leachman); Outstanding Directorial Achievement in Comedy (Jay Sandrich for "Thoroughly Unmilitant Mary"); Outstanding Directorial Achievement in Comedy (Peter Baldwin for "Where There's Smoke, There's Rhoda")

1973 (5): Outstanding Comedy Series; Outstanding Performance by an Actor in a Supporting Role in Comedy (Ed Asner); Outstanding Performance by an Actress in a Supporting Role in Comedy (Cloris Leachman); Outstanding Writing Achievement in Comedy (James L. Brooks and Allan Burns for "The Good-Time News"); Outstanding Achievement in Film Editing for Entertainment Programming, for a Series or a Single Program of a Series (Douglas Hines)

1974 (6): Outstanding Comedy Series; Best Supporting Actor in Comedy (Ed Asner); Best Supporting Actor in Comedy (Ted Knight); Best Supporting Actress in Comedy (Valerie Harper); Best Directing in Comedy (Jay Sandrich for "Lou's First Date"); Best Film Editing for Entertainment Program, for a Series or a Single Program of a Series (Douglas Hines and Bud S. Isaacs)

1975 (3): Outstanding Lead Actress in a Comedy Series (Mary Tyler Moore); Outstanding Continuing Performance by a Supporting Actor in a Comedy Series

(Ted Knight); Outstanding Writing in a Comedy Series (David Lloyd for "Lou and That Woman")

1976 (5): Outstanding Continuing Performance by a Supporting Actor in a Comedy Series (Ed Asner); Outstanding Continuing Performance by a Supporting Actress in a Comedy Series (Georgia Engel); Outstanding Single Performance by a Supporting Actress in a Drama or Comedy Series (Eileen Heckart for "Mary's Aunt"); Outstanding Directing in a Comedy (Joan Darling for "Chuckles Bites the Dust"); Outstanding Achievement in Film Editing for Entertainment Programming for a Series, for a Single Episode of a Comedy Series (Douglas Hines for "Chuckles Bites the Dust")

1977 (9): Outstanding Lead Actress in a Comedy Series (Mary Tyler Moore); Outstanding Continuing Performance by a Supporting Actor in a Comedy Series (Ed Asner); Outstanding Continuing Performance by a Supporting Actor in a Comedy Series (Ted Knight); Outstanding Continuing Performance by a Supporting Actress in a Comedy Series (Georgia Engel); Outstanding Continuing Performance by a Supporting Actress in a Comedy Series (Betty White); Outstanding Single Performance by a Supporting Actress in a Drama or Comedy Series (Eileen Heckart for "Lou Proposes"); Outstanding Writing in a Comedy Series (David Lloyd for "Mary Midwife"); Outstanding Writing in a Comedy Series (Earl Pomerantz for "Ted's Change of Heart"); Outstanding Directing in a Comedy Series (Jay Sandrich for "The Last Show")

GOLDEN GLOBE WINS (3)

1971 (1): Best TV Actress, Musical/Comedy (Mary Tyler Moore)
1972 (1): Best Supporting Actor, Television (Ed Asner)
1976 (1): Best Supporting Actor, Television (Ed Asner)

GOLDEN GLOBE NOMINATIONS, IN ADDITION TO WINS (18)

1972 (2): Best TV Show, Musical/Comedy; Best TV Actress, Musical/Comedy (Mary Tyler Moore)

1973 (5): Best TV Show, Musical/Comedy; Best TV Actress, Musical/Comedy (Mary Tyler Moore); Best Supporting Actor, Television (Ed Asner); Best Supporting Actor, Television (Ted Knight); Best Supporting Actress, Television (Valerie Harper)

1974 (4): Best TV Show, Musical/Comedy; Best TV Actress, Musical/Comedy (Mary Tyler Moore); Best Supporting Actor, Television (Ed Asner); Best Supporting Actress, Television (Valerie Harper)

1975 (3): Best TV Actor, Musical/Comedy (Ed Asner); Best TV Actress, Musical/Comedy (Mary Tyler Moore); Best Supporting Actor, Television (Gavin MacLeod)

1976 (2): Best TV Actress, Musical/Comedy (Mary Tyler Moore); Best Supporting Actor, Television (Ted Knight)

1977 (2): Best TV Actress, Musical/Comedy (Mary Tyler Moore); Best Supporting Actor, Television (Gavin MacLeod)

HUMANITAS PRIZE

1977: 30-Minute Category (Earl Pomerantz)

PEABODY AWARD

1978: MTM Enterprises

Further Reading

Alley, Robert S., and Irby B. Brown. *Love Is All Around: The Making of the Mary Tyler Moore Show*. New York: Delta, 1989.
Armstrong, Jennifer Keishin. *Mary and Lou and Rhoda and Ted: And All the Brilliant Minds Who Made* The Mary Tyler Moore Show *a Classic*. New York: Simon & Schuster, 2013.
Dow, Bonnie. "Hegemony, Feminist Criticism, and *The Mary Tyler Moore Show*." *Critical Studies in Mass Communication* 7 (September 1990): 261–74.
"Rhoda and Mary: Love Laughs." *Time Magazine*, October 28, 1974, p. 10.

6

Cheers

(1982–1993)

Cast: Ted Danson (Sam Malone), Shelley Long (Diane Chambers), Rhea Perlman (Carla Tortelli LeBec), Nicholas Colasanto (Ernie "Coach" Pantusso), George Wendt (Norm Peterson), John Ratzenberger (Cliff Clavin), Kelsey Grammer (Dr. Frasier Crane), Woody Harrelson (Woody Boyd), Kirstie Alley (Rebecca Howe), Bebe Neuwirth (Dr. Lilith Sternin), Tom Skerritt (Evan Drake), Jay Thomas (Eddie LeBec), Roger Rees (Robin Colcord), Jackie Swanson (Kelly Gaines)

Created by: Producer, director, and writer James Burrows; producers and writers Glen Charles and Les Charles

Network: NBC

First Air Date: September 30, 1982

Last Air Date: May 20, 1993

Broadcast History:
September 30, 1982–December 1982: Thursday at 9:00–9:30 PM
January 1983–December 1983: Thursday at 9:30–10:00 PM
December 1983–August 1993: Thursday at 9:00–9:30 PM
February 1993–May 20, 1993: Thursday at 8:00–8:30 PM

Seasons: 11

Episodes: 275

Ratings History: 1982–1983 (not in Top 30), 1983–1984 (not in Top 30), 1984–1985 (12), 1985–1986 (5), 1986–1987 (3), 1987–1988 (3), 1988–1989 (4), 1989–1990 (3), 1990–1991 (1), 1991–1992 (4), 1992–1993 (8)

Front row, from left: Ted Danson and Shelley Long; back row, from left: John Ratzenberger, Nicholas Colasanto, Rhea Perlman, and George Wendt. *NBC/Photofest* *©NBC*

Overview

Few sitcoms have ever established the level of identity and unique characterization as the one about a Boston bar. When its patrons screamed "Norm!" in unison upon the inevitable daily entrance of Norm Peterson (George Wendt), television viewers felt like chiming in as well. Cheers was indeed the place where everybody knew your name.

The namesake show boasted arguably the deepest and most talented cast in the history of the American sitcom. And it's strange, too. None were major stars when this brilliant program first hit the airwaves on September 30, 1982. Soon they were household names who had introduced some of the most distinctive, complex, and downright funny characters ever seen on the small screen. It's no wonder that the show's record of eleven Emmy nominations for Outstanding Comedy Series ties the sitcom for first all-time with *M*A*S*H*, and its record of four wins ties it for second with *All in the Family* and places it behind only *Frasier*.

Viewer identification resulted from eleven seasons on the air, several stalwart players who stayed for the duration, and showing only occasional scenes outside the bar setting. Home lives were discussed often, but usually within the confines of the establishment. Frequent cast shifts, which destroyed other sitcoms throughout the years, could not make a dent in the quality of *Cheers*. Equally intriguing and funny characters replaced those who left.

The popularity of the show certainly would have taken a hit, however, had Ted Danson or Rhea Perlman walked. The former plays slow-witted, ruggedly handsome recovering alcoholic and former Boston Red Sox relief pitcher Sam Malone, who struggles between his desire to maintain the freedom of bachelorhood and finding emotional contentment with a woman he loves. The female character with whom he develops a love-hate relationship is flighty blonde intellectual Diane Chambers (Shelley Long), who is wildly attracted to his Cro-Magnon good looks and recoils at his Cro-Magnon intellect. The woman he desires is statuesque gold digger Rebecca Howe (Kirstie Alley, who replaced Long in 1987). The bond between Sam and Rebecca, who seek wealthy suitors, degenerates into a power struggle as both take turns assuming control of the bar. Perlman plays sarcastic, mean-spirited waitress Carla Tortelli, a baby-making machine whose derision can be directed at anyone, even her own children. Carla, too, seeks love and affection but spends the run of the show on an emotional rollercoaster.

The other two characters who stuck it out from the beginning to the end of the series were self-deprecating Norm and lonely, annoying Cliff Clavin (John Ratzenberger), who spend much of their time trading barbs as they drink beer with their butts firmly planted on barstools resting next to one another. Norm not only enjoys the company of his fellow patrons, he uses Cheers as an escape from nagging wife Vera, perhaps the most well-known never-seen character in television history. Ratzenberger was initially rejected before suggesting he assume the part of a bar know-it-all, which he performed to a tee.

The characters that came and went proved equally memorable. Perpetually muddled bartender Ernie "Coach" Pantusso brought a sweetness and innocence to the show that was lost when actor Nicholas Colasanto died. He was replaced by ignorant country bumpkin Woody Boyd (Woody Harrelson). One of the two most memorable additions to *Cheers* was Rebecca, whose desire for wealth motivates pursuits that border on stalking of such powerful men in her life as British tycoon Robin Colcord (Roger Rees) and rich and handsome boss Evan Drake (Tom Skerritt). The other was pompous intellectual Dr. Frasier Crane (Kelsey Grammer), whose sophistication so attracts Diane that they nearly wed. Frasier finally marries Dr. Lilith Sternin (Bebe Neuwirth), whose icy exterior masks her social inadequacies, yet she dominates her husband emotionally.

One marvels at the fact that *Cheers* was a ratings disaster in its first season, despite the growing sexual tension between Sam and Diane and the humor brought forth by such characters as Carla, Coach, Norm, and Cliff. That none were heavyweights in American entertainment undoubtedly played a role in the fact that the sitcom lacked identity with viewers and was nearly yanked off the air when it hit rock bottom in the Nielsens. The show slowly built viewership through its character-driven humor before catapulting to number twelve in the ratings in its third season and remaining in the Top 10 in each of its last seven years, peaking at the top spot in 1990–1991.

The ninety-eight-minute final episode, aired on May 20, 1993, attracted an estimated 42 million viewers, garnering one of the top ratings of any sitcom in history. It features the return of Diane as a successful TV writer after six seasons away from the show and several strange twists, including Woody being elected to city council and an impulsive Rebecca marrying a plumber. It also set the hearts of *Cheers* fans racing as Sam and Diane run off to get married but call it off at the last minute. The on-again, off-again romance that had captivated audiences to a greater extent than arguably any in sitcom history ends with the show. The final scenes feature the cast members philosophizing about the meaning of life—Cliff appropriately offers that it was "shoes"—and the lights go off on the bar and one of the best television shows ever for the final time.

"Sudden Sam" and Sam Malone

The inspiration for the Sam Malone character was immensely talented Cleveland Indians left-handed pitcher "Sudden Sam" McDowell, who starred in the 1960s. He was given that nickname because it was said that his blazing fastball arrived at the plate "all of a sudden." Alcoholism prevented McDowell from reaching his full potential, despite the fact that he made six American League All-Star teams. His career faded in the early 1970s, after he was traded from Cleveland, as his disease worsened. McDowell sobered up after his playing career, just as Malone did, and he later worked with Major League Baseball as a consultant helping a new generation of players avoid the same pitfalls that plagued him throughout his career.

Gobble, Gobble, Food in the Face

Perhaps the most memorable moment in *Cheers* history is a Thanksgiving episode written by Cherie and Bill Steinkellner. In a rare scene outside the bar, the regulars gather at Carla's house for a turkey dinner. Tension mounts as they become irritated waiting for the bird to be ready. The first bit of anger is expressed by Frasier, who yells at Norm for calling the turkey thermometer "that little pop thing." Carla begins tossing a few carrots in Norm's face. Woody throws gravy at Cliff, and the others are about to pick up food to toss when Diane, wearing a Pilgrim outfit, screams out, "Stop this immediately!" She is struck by cranberries tossed by Sam, whereupon all hell breaks loose. Cliff gets Woody in a headlock and shoves mashed potatoes in his face. The cast members continue the food fight for half an hour, slipping and sliding as they pick up more to throw. They then eat their dinner with food all over them. Rhea Perlman later stated that it was by far her favorite episode.

They Said It

Diane: He's trying to make a mountain out of a molehill.
Carla: He wants you to wear a padded bra?

Norm: It's a dog-eat-dog world, and I'm wearing Milkbone underwear.

Sam: I've never met an intelligent woman I'd want to date.
Diane: On behalf of all the intelligent women in America, may I just say: 'Whew.'

Woody: What's shakin', Mr. Peterson?
Norm: All four cheeks and a couple of chins.

Cliff: What a pathetic display. I'm ashamed God made me a man.
Carla: I don't think God's doing a lot of bragging either.

Major Awards

EMMY AWARD WINS (28)

1983 (5): Outstanding Comedy Series; Outstanding Lead Actress in a Comedy Series (Shelley Long); Outstanding Writing in a Comedy Series (Glen Charles and Les Charles for "Give Me a Ring Sometime"); Outstanding Directing in a Comedy Series (James Burrows for "Showdown: Part II"); Outstanding Individual Achievement, Graphic Design and Title Sequences (James Castle and Bruce Bryant for "Showdown: Part I")
1984 (4): Outstanding Comedy Series; Outstanding Supporting Actress in a Comedy Series (Rhea Perlman); Outstanding Writing in a Comedy Series (David Angell for "Old Flames"); Outstanding Film Editing for a Series (Andrew Chulack for "Old Flames")
1985 (2): Outstanding Supporting Actress in a Comedy Series (Rhea Perlman); Outstanding Live and Tape Sound Mixing and Sound Effects for a Series (Michael Ballin, Sam Black, Doug Gray, and Thomas J. Huth for "The Executive's Executioner")
1986 (2): Outstanding Supporting Actress in a Comedy Series (Rhea Perlman); Outstanding Sound Mixing for a Comedy Series or a Special (Michael Ballin, Robert Douglass, Doug Gray, and Thomas J. Huth for "Fear Is My Co-Pilot")
1987 (2): Outstanding Guest Performer in a Comedy Series (John Cleese for "Simon Says"); Outstanding Sound Mixing for a Comedy Series or a Special (Michael Ballin, Robert Douglass, Doug Gray, and Thomas J. Huth for "The Proposal")
1988 (1): Outstanding Editing for a Series, Multi-Camera Production (Andy Ackerman for "The Big Kiss-Off")

1989 (3): Outstanding Comedy Series; Outstanding Supporting Actor in a Comedy Series (Woody Harrelson); Outstanding Supporting Actress in a Comedy Series (Rhea Perlman)

1990 (3): Outstanding Lead Actor in a Comedy Series (Ted Danson); Outstanding Supporting Actress in a Comedy Series (Bebe Neuwirth); Outstanding Sound Mixing for a Comedy Series or a Special (Sam Black, Robert Crosby, Robert Douglass, and Thomas J. Huth for "The Stork Brings a Crane")

1991 (4): Outstanding Comedy Series; Outstanding Lead Actress in a Comedy Series (Kirstie Alley); Outstanding Supporting Actress in a Comedy Series (Bebe Neuwirth); Outstanding Directing in a Comedy Series (James Burrows for "Woody Interruptus")

1993 (2): Outstanding Lead Actor in a Comedy Series (Ted Danson); Outstanding Individual Achievement in Editing for a Series, Multi-Camera Production (Robert Bramwell for "One for the Road")

EMMY AWARD NOMINATIONS, IN ADDITION TO WINS (91)

1983 (8): Outstanding Lead Actor in a Comedy Series (Ted Danson); Outstanding Supporting Actor in a Comedy, Variety, or Music Series (Nicholas Colasanto); Outstanding Supporting Actress in a Comedy, Variety, or Music Series (Rhea Perlman); Outstanding Writing in a Comedy Series (David Lloyd for "Diane's Perfect Date"); Outstanding Writing in a Comedy Series (Ken Levine and David Isaacs for "The Boys in the Bar"); Outstanding Film Editing for a Series (Andrew Chulack for "Endless Slumper"); Outstanding Art Direction for a Series (Richard Sylbert and George Gaines for "Give Me a Ring Sometime"); Outstanding Achievement in Music and Lyrics (Gary Portnoy and Judy Hart-Angelo for pilot, "Where Everybody Knows Your Name")

1984 (8): Outstanding Lead Actor in a Comedy Series (Ted Danson); Outstanding Lead Actress in a Comedy Series (Shelley Long); Outstanding Supporting Actor in a Comedy Series (Nicholas Colasanto); Outstanding Supporting Actor in a Comedy Series (George Wendt); Outstanding Writing in a Comedy Series (Glen Charles and Les Charles for "Power Play"); Outstanding Writing in a Comedy Series (David Lloyd for "Homicidal Ham"); Outstanding Directing in a Comedy Series (James Burrows for "Old Flames"); Outstanding Live and Tape Sound Mixing and Sound Effects for a Series (Sam Black, Doug Gray, Thomas J. Huth, and Gordon Klimuck for "No Help Wanted")

1985 (10): Outstanding Comedy Series; Outstanding Lead Actor in a Comedy Series (Ted Danson); Outstanding Lead Actress in a Comedy Series (Shelley Long); Outstanding Supporting Actor in a Comedy Series (Nicholas Colasanto); Outstanding Supporting Actor in a Comedy Series (George Wendt); Outstanding Supporting Actor in a Comedy Series (John Ratzenberger); Outstanding Writing in a Comedy Series (Glen Charles and Les Charles for "Rebound: Part II"); Outstanding Writing in a Comedy Series (Peter Casey and David Lee for "I Call Your

Name"); Outstanding Writing in a Comedy Series (David Lloyd for "Sam Turns the Other Cheek"); Outstanding Directing in a Comedy Series (James Burrows for "Cheerio")

1986 (9): Outstanding Comedy Series; Outstanding Lead Actor in a Comedy Series (Ted Danson); Outstanding Lead Actress in a Comedy Series (Shelley Long); Outstanding Supporting Actor in a Comedy Series (John Ratzenberger); Outstanding Supporting Actor in a Comedy Series (George Wendt); Outstanding Writing in a Comedy Series (Peter Casey and David Lee for "2 Be 2 Good 4 Real"); Outstanding Directing in a Comedy Series (James Burrows for "The Triangle"); Outstanding Editing for a Series, Multi-Camera Production (Andy Ackerman for "Birth, Death, Love, and Rice"); Outstanding Editing for a Series, Multi-Camera Production (Douglas Hines for "The Triangle")

1987 (8): Outstanding Comedy Series; Outstanding Lead Actor in a Comedy Series (Ted Danson); Outstanding Supporting Actor in a Comedy Series (Woody Harrelson); Outstanding Supporting Actor in a Comedy Series (George Wendt); Outstanding Supporting Actress in a Comedy Series (Rhea Perlman); Outstanding Writing in a Comedy Series (Janet Leahy for "Abnormal Psychology"); Outstanding Directing in a Comedy Series (James Burrows for "Chambers vs. Malone"); Outstanding Editing for a Series, Multi-Camera Production (Andy Ackerman for "Cheers: The Motion Picture")

1988 (10): Outstanding Comedy Series; Outstanding Lead Actor in a Comedy Series (Ted Danson); Outstanding Lead Actress in a Comedy Series (Kirstie Alley); Outstanding Supporting Actor in a Comedy Series (Woody Harrelson); Outstanding Supporting Actor in a Comedy Series (Kelsey Grammer); Outstanding Supporting Actor in a Comedy Series (George Wendt); Outstanding Supporting Actress in a Comedy Series (Rhea Perlman); Outstanding Writing in a Comedy Series (Glen Charles and Les Charles for "Home Is the Sailor"); Outstanding Directing in a Comedy Series (James Burrows for "Backseat Becky, Up Front"); Outstanding Sound Mixing for a Comedy Series or a Special (Doug Gray, Robert Douglass, Thomas J. Huth, and Pete San Filipo Sr. for "The Last Angry Mailman")

1989 (4): Outstanding Lead Actor in a Comedy Series (Ted Danson); Outstanding Supporting Actor in a Comedy Series (George Wendt); Outstanding Directing in a Comedy Series (James Burrows for "The Visiting Lecher"); Outstanding Sound Mixing for a Comedy Series or a Special (Sam Black, Robert Crosby, Robert Douglass, and Thomas J. Huth for "Jumping Jerks")

1990 (9): Outstanding Comedy Series; Outstanding Lead Actress in a Comedy Series (Kirstie Alley); Outstanding Supporting Actor in a Comedy Series (Kelsey Grammer); Outstanding Supporting Actor in a Comedy Series (Woody Harrelson); Outstanding Supporting Actress in a Comedy Series (Rhea Perlman); Outstanding Guest Actress in a Comedy Series (Georgia Brown for "The Ghost and Mrs. LeBec"); Outstanding Guest Actress in a Comedy Series (Alexis Smith for "Sammy and the Professor"); Outstanding Directing in a Comedy Series (James Burrows for "Woody Interruptus"); Outstanding

Writing in a Comedy Series (Ken Levine and David Isaacs for "Death Takes a Holiday on Ice")

1991 (11): Outstanding Lead Actor in a Comedy Series (Ted Danson); Outstanding Supporting Actor in a Comedy Series (Woody Harrelson); Outstanding Supporting Actress in a Comedy Series (Rhea Perlman); Outstanding Guest Actor in a Comedy Series (Sheldon Leonard for "Grease"); Outstanding Guest Actress in a Comedy Series (Frances Sternhagen for "Ma Always Liked You Best"); Outstanding Guest Actress in a Comedy Series (Sada Thompson for "Honor Thy Mother"); Outstanding Editing for a Miniseries or a Special, Multi-Camera Production (Andy Ackerman for "200th Anniversary Special"); Outstanding Editing for a Series, Multi-Camera Production (Andy Ackerman for "The Days of Wine and Neuroses"); Outstanding Editing for a Miniseries or a Special, Multi-Camera Production (Shelia Amos for "Rat Girl"); Outstanding Informational Special (for "200th Anniversary Special"); Outstanding Sound Mixing for a Comedy Series or a Special (Sam Black, Robert Crosby, Robert Douglass, and Thomas J. Huth for "The Days of Wine and Neuroses")

1992 (8): Outstanding Comedy Series; Outstanding Lead Actor in a Comedy Series (Ted Danson); Outstanding Lead Actress in a Comedy Series (Kirstie Alley); Outstanding Supporting Actor in a Comedy Series (Harvey Fierstein); Outstanding Supporting Actress in a Comedy Series (Frances Sternhagen); Outstanding Individual Achievement in Directing in a Comedy Series (James Burrows for "An Old Fashioned Wedding"); Outstanding Individual Achievement in Editing for a Series, Multi-Camera Production (Robert Bramwell and Peter Chakos for "An Old Fashioned Wedding"); Outstanding Individual Achievement in Sound Mixing for a Comedy Series or a Special (Sam Black, Robert Crosby, Robert Douglass, and Thomas J. Huth for "Bar Wars IV: This Time It's for Real")

1993 (6): Outstanding Comedy Series; Outstanding Lead Actress in a Comedy Series (Kirstie Alley); Outstanding Supporting Actress in a Comedy Series (Rhea Perlman); Outstanding Guest Actor in a Comedy Series (Tom Berenger for "One for the Road"); Outstanding Guest Actress in a Comedy Series (Shelley Long for "One for the Road"); Outstanding Individual Achievement in Directing in a Comedy Series (James Burrows for "One for the Road")

GOLDEN GLOBE WINS (6)

1983 (1): Best Performance by an Actress in a Supporting Role in a Series, Mini-Series, or Motion Picture Made for TV (Shelley Long)

1985 (1): Best Performance by an Actress in a TV Series, Musical/Comedy (Shelley Long)

1990 (1): Best Performance by an Actor in a TV Series, Musical/Comedy (Ted Danson)

1991 (3): Best TV Series, Musical/Comedy; Best Performance by an Actor in a TV Series, Musical/Comedy (Ted Danson); Best Performance by an Actress in a TV Series, Musical/Comedy (Kirstie Alley)

GOLDEN GLOBE NOMINATIONS, IN ADDITION TO WINS (25)

1983 (1): Best TV Series, Musical/Comedy
1984 (3): Best TV Series, Musical/Comedy; Best Performance by an Actor in a TV Series, Musical/Comedy (Ted Danson); Best Performance by an Actress in a TV Series, Musical/Comedy (Shelley Long)
1985 (3): Best TV Series, Musical/Comedy; Best Performance by an Actor in a TV Series, Musical/Comedy (Ted Danson); Best Performance by an Actress in a Supporting Role in a Series, Mini-Series, or Motion Picture Made for TV (Rhea Perlman)
1987 (3): Best TV Series, Musical/Comedy; Best Performance by an Actor in a TV Series, Musical/Comedy (Ted Danson); Best Performance by an Actress in a Supporting Role in a Series, Mini-Series, or Motion Picture Made for TV (Rhea Perlman)
1988 (2): Best TV Series, Musical/Comedy; Best Performance by an Actress in a Supporting Role in a Series, Mini-Series, or Motion Picture Made for TV (Rhea Perlman)
1989 (3): Best TV Series, Musical/Comedy; Best Performance by an Actor in a TV Series, Musical/Comedy (Ted Danson); Best Performance by an Actress in a Supporting Role in a Series, Mini-Series, or Motion Picture Made for TV (Rhea Perlman)
1990 (3): Best TV Series, Musical/Comedy; Best Performance by an Actress in a TV Series, Musical/Comedy (Kirstie Alley); Best Performance by an Actress in a Supporting Role in a Series, Mini-Series, or Motion Picture Made for TV (Rhea Perlman)
1992 (4): Best TV Series, Musical/Comedy; Best Performance by an Actor in a TV Series, Musical/Comedy (Ted Danson); Best Performance by an Actress in a TV Series, Musical/Comedy (Kirstie Alley); Best Performance by an Actress in a Supporting Role in a Series, Mini-Series, or Motion Picture Made for TV (Rhea Perlman)
1993 (3): Best TV Series, Musical/Comedy; Best Performance by an Actor in a TV Series, Musical/Comedy (Ted Danson); Best Performance by an Actress in a TV Series, Musical/Comedy (Kirstie Alley)

Further Reading

Harris, Mark. "Cheers!" *Entertainment Weekly*, October 26, 1990, cover story.
Wenger, Mark. *The Cheers Trivia Book*. New York: Citadel Press, 1994.

✴ 7 ✴
The Andy Griffith Show
(1960–1968)

Cast: Andy Griffith (Andy Taylor), Don Knotts (Barney Fife), Ron Howard (Opie Taylor), Frances Bavier (Aunt Bee), Howard McNear (Floyd Lawson), Jim Nabors (Gomer Pyle), George Lindsey (Goober Pyle), Aneta Corsaut (Helen Crump), Betty Lynn (Thelma Lou), Hal Smith (Otis Campbell), Jack Dodson (Howard Sprague), Paul Hartman (Emmett Clark)

Created by: Executive producers Sheldon Leonard and Danny Thomas; producer Aaron Ruben

Network: CBS

First Air Date: October 3, 1960

Last Air Date: April 1, 1968

Broadcast History:
October 3, 1960–September 1964: Monday at 9:30–10:00 PM
September 1964–June 1965: Monday at 8:30–9:00 PM
September 1965–September 1968: Monday at 9:00–9:30 PM

Seasons: 8

Episodes: 249

Ratings History: 1960–1961 (4), 1961–1962 (7), 1962–1963 (6), 1963–1964 (5), 1964–1965 (4), 1965–1966 (6), 1966–1967 (3), 1967–1968 (1)

Andy Griffith and Don Knotts. *CBS/Photofest ©CBS*

Overview

The town of Mayberry is fictional, but it is wonderfully real in the hearts and minds of millions of Americans who grew up embracing the homespun characters that made up its citizenry. The sleepy village in rural North Carolina became a home away from home, at least for a half-hour every week, for many television viewers in the 1960s. And thanks to its tremendous popularity in syndication, it has earned a reputation as one of the most-watched and beloved television programs ever. New generations have adopted Mayberry as their imaginary town of choice.

The Andy Griffith Show proved to be escapism at its most comforting during a decade in which news accounts of riots, assassinations, and war seemed like nightly events. The laid-back, quiet confidence of main character Sheriff Andy Taylor (Andy Griffith) provided viewers with a sense of assurance that everything was going to be all right. His family, which included son Opie and Aunt Bee, became our family through the writing and characterizations of one of the most successful sitcoms in history. It seemed that they had invited and welcomed American viewers into their home. Their friends were our friends.

The creation of the program was part of a strong push toward rural comedy that began in the late 1950s, with such sitcoms as *The Real McCoys*, and picked up steam in the early 1960s. The trend featured a spotlight on unpretentious country characters that made up for a lack of education, with strong morals and values. The success of

The Andy Griffith Show paved the way for other rural sitcoms, including *The Beverly Hillbillies*, *Green Acres*, and *Petticoat Junction*. It also directly resulted in the popular spinoff *Gomer Pyle, U.S.M.C.* The title character, played by Jim Nabors, was presented to the television world as a painfully naïve gas station attendant in Mayberry before deciding to test his manhood by joining the U.S. Marines.

The pilot episode of *The Andy Griffith Show* was a spin-off of *Make Room for Daddy*, which features established sitcom star Danny Thomas. Andy Taylor is introduced to America when he arrests the Thomas character (Danny Williams) for running a stop sign in Mayberry and places him behind bars.

The show became an immediate hit, debuting in its first year at number four in the Nielsen ratings. The reason for the success was viewer identification with the main and side characters, as well as the writing, which gave the show a greater sensitivity than other sitcoms of its generation. *The Andy Griffith Show* was more than a comedy. The relationship between widower Andy Taylor and Opie, played by future *Happy Days* star and movie director Ron Howard, was more thoughtful and serious than most, as the father sought to impart wisdom and a moral foundation to his young son. Viewers also identified with Aunt Bee (Frances Bavier) more as a loving surrogate mother for Opie and caring older relative to Andy than a comic character. She was known for making the best fried chicken and apple pie in Mayberry and adding to the reputation of the small town as a center of gossip, while bringing a sense of values to her home and community.

The humor emanating from the Taylor household was rather subtle. That is, until Deputy Barney Fife (Don Knotts) paid a visit. The bumbling Fife provided the brazen comedy for the show with a manic personality, false machismo, and tendency to make the worst of any situation. He claimed himself to be an expert on any subject until the mildest of tests proved his ignorance. One hilarious example is when he brags to Opie about his knowledge of the Emancipation Proclamation. When pressed by Andy, he gets flustered as it becomes apparent he knows nothing about it. He finally blurts out that it was a proclamation for emancipation and storms out of the house. Barney also overreacted to every minor offense committed on the streets of Mayberry, lambasting Aunt Bee on one occasion for jaywalking, but when confronted with real criminals, he was easily duped and sometimes unwittingly helped them commit their crimes, only to be saved by the sheriff. In one episode, the overzealous Fife, trying to prove that he is as tough as those who ran the most notorious jails in the land, allows his prisoners to repeatedly escape, only to be recaptured by Sheriff Taylor. But Andy always looked out for the best interest and emotional well-being of the inept Barney, who had been his friend since childhood. All was well when it turned out well—and Andy would give Barney credit for saving the day, even when he rarely did.

The side characters provided challenges and friendship for Andy and Barney in both their personal and professional lives. The most humorous—and the one who would be considered the most socially incorrect in the modern era—was Otis Campbell (Hal Smith). The town drunk would stumble in every weekend night with a "snootfull" (on one occasion after riding a cow that he thought was a horse into town) and let himself into his favorite jail cell with the key hung right next to the door. He would sleep it off and enjoy a cup of hot coffee from Andy or Barney or a fine breakfast brought in from Aunt Bee the next morning. No one was really punished in Mayberry.

The two jail cells were more a home away from home for those who Andy believed had fallen into some sort of misfortune in their lives, and he did not want to make them feel any worse than they already did. Andy was never judgmental about his fellow townspeople. He treated them all as friends.

The show focused equally on the personal and professional lives of Andy and Barney. The writers worked diligently to find romantic interests for Andy from the start. His first girlfriend was "lady druggist" Ellie Walker, played by Elinor Donahue, who had made her mark as the teenage daughter in the family sitcom *Father Knows Best* in the 1950s. Donahue even earned mention in the opening credits during the first year of *The Andy Griffith Show* and was firmly established as his girlfriend, but she opted out of her contract after one season.

Barney began working feverishly as a Mayberry Cupid in seeking potential wives for his friend. In one episode, he lures every unmarried woman to Andy's house on a ruse in an effort to provide him an opportunity to select the ones he wants to date and discards the others. That effort fails, but later, in the same episode, he is matched up with Opie's teacher, Helen Crump (Aneta Corsaut). Although Barney decides that Helen is no match for his buddy after sizing her up (she has no idea how to cook leg of lamb, Andy's favorite dish), Andy feels an immediate attraction. They become a couple and eventually wed. Many episodes feature the interrelationships between Andy, Helen, Barney, and Thelma Lou (Betty Lynn). Thelma Lou eventually becomes the love interest for Barney, who requires great patience and understanding on her part.

The only personality to drastically change during the eight-year run of the show was that of Andy. He portrayed a hick country bumpkin with a thick Southern drawl early in the show, but lost the heavy accent by the second year and was portrayed as a much calmer and wiser character through the fifth season. *The Andy Griffith Show*, however, then took a dramatic turn. Knotts left after five years to pursue other professional interests. The loss of an actor who had won three Emmys for Best Supporting Actor proved to be a crucial one from an artistic standpoint. The Fife character was replaced by Warren Ferguson (Jack Burns), who failed to match his predecessor's attractive personality or sense of comic timing as the new deputy.

The loss of Nabors and Knotts, as well as the transformation of the show from black-and-white to color in 1965, marked the end of its attraction of millions of fans, although the show remained, at the time, a ratings smash. Such new characters as county clerk Howard Sprague (Jack Dodson) and fix-it man Emmett Clark (Paul Hartman) are considered by most passionate fans of the show to be more thoughtful than funny. The attempt to turn the sitcom into one in which the moral messages superseded the humor dramatically changed the personality of Andy. He traded in his good-natured patience for a quick temper and tendency to whine and complain.

The Andy Griffith Show is a reminder of a simpler time in a bygone era, one of innocence and community. The portrayal of characters content to while away their time whittling or singing to a guitar being strummed on the front porch will most likely never return to the small screen. One of the most embraced episodes, entitled "Man in a Hurry," spotlights the contrast between life in Mayberry and that of the big-city world personified by a rushed businessman named Malcolm Tucker, whose car broke down on the outskirts of town. He is eager to get to Charlotte, where he has important business, but he is stuck in Mayberry, where nothing is open on Sunday, including the garage in which his car could be fixed. He paces about anxiously, but is eventually seduced and soothed by the friendliness of the people and slow pace of life in the sleepy town. He is eventually calmed to the point where, even after his car has been repaired, he decides to stay in Mayberry overnight. The episode closes with a shot of Malcolm napping contentedly on the Taylor front porch.

Andy expresses his philosophy in an episode about his high school reunion. He states that his goal in life was simply to be happy. His show indeed made its viewers happy.

You *Can* Go Home Again

Betty Lynn, who played Barney's love interest Thelma Lou, fulfilled the dream of many who saw Mayberry as a utopia. She moved there in 2007. Okay, she didn't exactly move to Mayberry, which, of course, is fictional. She did leave her home of fifty-seven years in West Hollywood, to live in Mount Airy, North Carolina, on which Mayberry was based. Lynn sought tranquility after her California home had been broken into twice and couldn't think of a more peaceful town than Mount Airy. She told the Associated Press in a 2007 interview that there was no place like it, unless it was heaven.

The Nervous Barber

Among the many memorable characters that made *The Andy Griffith Show* special was Floyd the Barber (Howard McNear). Floyd was so nervous he could hardly put a complete sentence together, but that didn't stop him from yakking up a storm to whoever would listen. It was in his barbershop that games of checkers were played and the albeit not exactly earth-shattering news of the day in Mayberry was discussed. McNear suffered a stroke during the third season, resulting in the loss of mobility and forcing him to be seen sitting most of the time. He died of another stroke in 1969.

They Said It

> **Barney:** [reacting to Andy telling singing competitor and townie Rafe Hollister, who boasted a surprisingly gifted voice, to try out for a local musical] I'm surprised at you, Andy. They want people who have had musical training. Why, suppose they ask Rafe to do something he don't know. Rafe, if they asked you to sing a cappella, could you do it?
> **Rafe:** No.
> **Andy:** Hey, Barn, what if they was to ask you if you could sing a cappella, what would you do?

Barney: Why I'd do it. [Snapping his fingers in rhythm and singing to the tune of *La Cucaracha*] A cappella, a cappella. . . . Well, I don't remember all the words.

Barney: [explaining to Opie why he didn't need to worry about a pack of dogs in an open field during a thunderstorm, but losing his conviction] If they was giraffes they'd been hit by now. But dogs are short and they take care of their own. Giraffes don't. Giraffes don't at all. . . . Boy, giraffes are selfish.

Barney: [to a detective in town to investigate a spate of cow thievery and who was informed by Andy they have decided not to make a mélange, a plaster cast of the footprints outside a barn from which a cow was stolen] Yeah, that's right, we decided not to make a mélange. Oh, we told a few people, but we decided it didn't make sense upsetting folks, running around, blabbing, making a big mélange out of it.

Major Awards

EMMY AWARD WINS (6)

1961 (1): Outstanding Performance in a Supporting Role by an Actor or Actress in a Series (Don Knotts)
1962 (1): Outstanding Performance in a Supporting Role by an Actor or Actress in a Series (Don Knotts)
1963 (1): Outstanding Performance in a Supporting Role by an Actor or Actress in a Series (Don Knotts)
1966 (1): Outstanding Performance by an Actor in a Supporting Role in a Comedy (Don Knotts)
1967 (2): Outstanding Performance by an Actor in a Supporting Role in a Comedy (Don Knotts); Outstanding Performance by an Actress in a Supporting Role in a Comedy (Frances Bavier)

EMMY AWARD NOMINATIONS, IN ADDITION TO WINS (3)

1961 (1): Outstanding Program Achievement in the Field of Humor
1962 (1): Outstanding Program Achievement in the Field of Humor
1967 (1): Outstanding Comedy Series

Further Reading

Beck, Ken, and Jim Clark. *The Andy Griffith Show Book.* New York: St. Martin's Griffin, 2010.
Fann, Joey. *The Way Back to Mayberry: Lessons from a Simpler Time.* Nashville, TN: B&H Books, 2010.
Gray, Beverly. *Ron Howard: From Mayberry to the Moon . . . and Beyond.* Nashville, TN: Thomas Nelson, 2003.

Frasier

(1993–2004)

Cast: Kelsey Grammer (Dr. Frasier Crane), David Hyde Pierce (Dr. Niles Crane), John Mahoney (Martin Crane), Jane Leeves (Daphne Moon Crane), Peri Gilpin (Roz Doyle), Dan Butler (Bob "Bulldog" Briscoe)

Created by: Executive producer, director, and writer David Lee; executive producers and writers David Angell and Peter Casey

Network: NBC

First Air Date: September 16, 1993

Last Air Date: May 13, 2004

Broadcast History:
  September 16, 1993–September 1994: Thursday at 9:30–10:00 PM
  September 1994–September 1998: Tuesday at 9:00–9:30 PM
  June 1998–July 1998: Sunday at 9:00–9:30 PM
  September 1998–July 2000: Thursday at 9:00–9:30 PM
  July 1999–September 1999: Thursday at 9:30–10:00 PM
  April 2000–May 2000: Thursday at 9:30–10:00 PM
  July 2000–July 2003: Tuesday at 9:00–9:30 PM
  May 2001–June 2001: Tuesday at 9:30–10:00 PM
  January 2002–May 2002: Tuesday at 8:00–8:30 PM
  May 2003–July 2003: Thursday at 9:30–10:00 PM
  August 2003–May 2004: Tuesday at 9:00–9:30 PM
  February 2004–March 2004: Saturday at 9:00–9:30 PM
  April 2004–May 2004: Monday at 8:30–9:30 PM
  May 13, 2004: Thursday at 8:00–10:00 PM

Seasons: 11

Episodes: 263

Ratings History: 1993–1994 (7), 1994–1995 (15), 1995–1996 (11), 1996–1997 (16), 1997–1998 (10), 1998–1999 (3), 1999–2000 (6), 2000–2001 (17), 2001–2002 (16), 2002–2003 (26), 2003–2004 (not in Top 30)

Clockwise from top left: David Hyde Pierce, Jane Leeves, Peri Gilpin, Moose, Kelsey Grammer, and John Mahoney. *NBC/Photofest ©NBC; Photographer: Chris Haston*

Overview

The history of television has been peppered with examples of fine spin-offs (*Maude* and *Laverne and Shirley* come to mind), but there have been far more bombs when attempts have been made to give characters from one show a sitcom of their own. Only one stands out for brilliance that rivals that of a critically acclaimed program, and that is *Frasier*.

Intellectual blowhard Frasier Crane (Kelsey Grammer) took *Cheers* by storm upon his arrival in 1984. His neurotic tendencies, false sense of pride, and desire to be one of the boys despite his contrasting personality and interests made him an immediately intriguing and attractive character. Several cast members from *Cheers* could have proven to be excellent subject material for a spin-off, but fate would only have that in store for Grammer.

The success of *Frasier* might have come as little surprise considering it was created by David Angell and Peter Casey, both of whom had written extensively for *Cheers*, as well as the well-received 1990s sitcom *Wings*. The pair had a good read on Grammer and his character and translated it well into the new project. Frasier was the same emotionally frustrated, pompous highbrow on his new sitcom, but he had divorced irritating wife Lilith and hightailed it across country from Boston to Seattle, where he landed a job as a host on radio station KACL giving advice based on his experience in his field of psychology. He traded in spending countless hours of banter with his bar buddies for bonding with haughty brother Niles (David Hyde Pierce) and his father, Martin (John Mahoney), a former cop and a down-to-earth guy who spent the entire run of the program wondering how he spawned two such self-important snobs. The differences in the Crane dad and his sons were represented by his old-school easy chair that stuck out like a sore thumb in the middle of Frasier's ultramodern high-rise apartment, providing a breathtaking view of the Seattle skyline. Niles was a frequent visitor, greatly because he fell madly in love with the third British accent named Daphne Moon (Jane Leeves), whom he somehow eventually convinced to be his wife. Many fans of the show believe his desperate pursuit of Daphne, which turned him into a babbling schoolboy when he was around her, was far more intriguing and humorous than his relationship with her once they were wed.

One reason for the ratings success of *Frasier*, which not only remained in the Top 20 in the Nielsens in each of its first nine seasons, but also earned more Emmy wins (thirty-seven) than any other sitcom, was that those involved with the title character professionally were equally humorous. The wackiest was brash, self-absorbed sports talk show host Bob "Bulldog" Briscoe (Dan Butler), who neither had nor desired a filter for the acerbic, insulting words that left his mouth. Equally interesting was Roz Doyle (Peri Gilpin), producer and call screener for Frasier's show, who seemingly boasted another boyfriend in every episode and certainly had a more active sex life than any other main character on the show.

Even the unseen character on the show was funny. Niles often referred hilariously to Maris, his intolerable social-climbing wife who became his former wife. Although she was never shown, viewers understood that Niles' usually dour, depressed moods (at least until he snagged Daphne) were the result of the latest run-in with his dominating ex. They separated in 1997, leading to a divorce and a financial battle in which Maris sought to suck every penny from his bank account. Niles spoke with contempt about Maris and described with relish her shockingly rapid transformation from skinny rail to tub of lard.

Some of the humor revolved around the sibling rivalry between Frasier and Niles that can best be described as a snobbery competition as they sought to raise their social statuses with often-disastrous results. One wonders why they didn't follow in the footsteps of their father, who was comfortable enough in his own skin to care nary a wit about his standing among the wealthy and cultured in Seattle.

Cast changes and occasional appearances by such *Cheers* alumni as Ted Danson, Bebe Neuwirth, Shelley Long, and Woody Harrelson kept *Frasier* fresh. So did the engagement between Daphne and Miles, who had grown so frustrated in his desire for her that he eloped with Dr. Melinda Karnofsky (Jane Adams), who had been Frasier's girlfriend. His love for Daphne motivated him to divorce "Mel" and step up his pursuit of her. She was taken in once he expressed his love for her, and by the 2000–2001 season they were engaged. Their relations, as well as many viewers, were disappointed when they ran off to Nevada to wed in September 2002, which was considered a wasted opportunity for a wedding episode in the imaginations of the creative writers.

The final episode is highlighted by Daphne giving birth to baby boy David and the nuptials of Martin and outgoing, flirty Ronee Lawrence (Wendie Malick), who had babysat Martin's sons when they were kids. Frasier, meanwhile, quits his job at KACL. He announces that he is moving to San Francisco for another professional opportunity, but instead decides to chase after Charlotte, the latest of his string of girlfriends, who had moved to Chicago. The final scene shows Frasier's plane touching down in the Windy City. And so ended one of the most well-rounded programs in American television history, one that provided humor and a depth of characterization that matched the sitcom from which it was spawned.

Addition by Addition

The writers originally intended for Frasier to be an only child in his namesake sitcom. In fact, a reference to Frasier as having no siblings had been made during his time on *Cheers*, but when a producer stumbled upon a headshot of David Hyde Pierce, he decided he looked like Kelsey Grammer did in early episodes of *Cheers*, and soon they were cast as brothers. *Cheers* star character Sam Malone (Ted Danson) marveled at the facial similarity in a second-season episode of *Frasier*.

The Staring Terrier

Even the main mutt on *Frasier* was entertaining. The Jack Russell Terrier owned by Martin Crane was named Eddie. The dog delighted viewers by his ability to fix a glare on Frasier for long periods of time. Eddie was played by a dog named Moose. Moose obviously ate well. When his part called for him to lick characters on the show, liver pate was dabbed behind their ears. He was also quite popular; he received more fan mail than any of the human stars on *Frasier*. Moose died at age sixteen in Los Angeles in 2006.

Did You Know?

Peri Gilpin beat out future *Friends* star Lisa Kudrow for the role of Roz Doyle. The latter nearly got the part because her line readings received a better response, but the show creators believed she lacked the forcefulness required to play Roz.

They Said It

Frasier: Niles, is there a light bulb over my head?
Niles: You have an idea?
Frasier: No. I'm asking if there's actually a light bulb over my head.

Bulldog: [slamming his hand on the table angrily] Where's my pen? . . . THIS STINKS! THIS IS TOTAL BS! THIS IS . . . oh, here it is.

Frasier: [responding to a caller] Roger, at Cornell University they have an incredible piece of scientific equipment known as the Tunneling Electron Microscope. Now, this microscope is so powerful that by firing electrons you can actually see images of the atom, the infinitesimally minute building blocks of our universe. Roger, if I were using that microscope right now, I still wouldn't be able to locate my interest in your problem.

Frasier: You know the expression, 'Living well is the best revenge'?
Niles: It's a wonderful expression. I just don't know how true it is. You don't see it turning up in a lot of opera plots. 'Ludwig, maddened by the poisoning of his entire family, wreaks vengeance on Gunther in the third act by living well.'
Frasier: All right, Niles.
Niles: 'Whereupon Woton, upon discovering his deception, wreaks vengeance on Gunther in the third act again by living even better than the Duke.'
Frasier: Oh, all right!

Major Awards

EMMY AWARD WINS (37)

1994 (5): Outstanding Comedy Series; Outstanding Lead Actor in a Comedy Series (Kelsey Grammer); Outstanding Individual Achievement in Writing in a Comedy Series (David Angell, Peter Casey, and David Lee for "The Good Son"); Outstanding Individual Achievement in Directing in a Comedy Series (James Burrows for "The Good Son"): Outstanding Individual Achievement in Editing for a Series, Multi-Camera Production (Ron Volk for "The Show Where Lilith Comes Back")

1995 (5): Outstanding Comedy Series; Outstanding Lead Actor in a Comedy Series (Kelsey Grammer); Outstanding Supporting Actor in a Comedy Series (David Hyde Pierce); Outstanding Individual Achievement in Writing for a Comedy Series (Chuck Ranberg and Anne Flett-Giordano for "An Affair to Forget"); Outstanding Individual Achievement in Directing for a Comedy Series (David Lee for "The Matchmaker")

1996 (4): Outstanding Comedy Series; Outstanding Individual Achievement in Writing for a Comedy Series (Joe Keenan, Christopher Lloyd, Rob Greenberg, Jack

Burditt, Chuck Ranberg, Anne Flett-Giordano, Linda Morris, and Vic Rauseo for "Moondance"); Outstanding Individual Achievement in Editing for a Series, Multi-Camera Production (Ron Volk for "The Show Where Diane Comes Back"); Outstanding Individual Achievement in Sound Mixing for a Comedy Series or a Special (Robert Douglass, Thomas J. Huth, Dana Mark McClure, and David M. Weishaar for "Kisses Sweeter Than Wine")

1997 (2): Outstanding Comedy Series; Outstanding Directing for a Comedy Series (David Lee for "To Kill a Talking Bird")

1998 (4): Outstanding Comedy Series; Outstanding Lead Actor in a Comedy Series (Kelsey Grammer); Outstanding Supporting Actor in a Comedy Series (David Hyde Pierce); Outstanding Multi-Camera Picture Editing for a Series (Ron Volk for "Room Service")

1999 (2): Outstanding Supporting Actor in a Comedy Series (David Hyde Pierce); Outstanding Writing for a Comedy Series (Jay Kogen for "Merry Christmas, Mrs. Moskowitz")

2000 (2): Outstanding Guest Actress in a Comedy Series (Jean Smart); Outstanding Multi-Camera Picture Editing for a Series (Ron Volk and Scott Maisano for "Something Borrowed, Someone Blue")

2001 (3): Outstanding Guest Actor in a Comedy Series (Derek Jacobi for "The Show Must Go Off"); Outstanding Guest Actress in a Comedy Series (Jean Smart); Outstanding Multi-Camera Picture Editing for a Series (Ron Volk for "Daphne Returns")

2002 (3): Outstanding Guest Actor in a Comedy Series (Anthony LaPaglia for "The Mother Lode"); Outstanding Multi-Camera Picture Editing for a Series (Ron Volk for "The Proposal"); Outstanding Multi-Camera Sound Mixing for a Series or a Special (Andre Caporaso, Robert Douglass, Thomas J. Huth, and Dana Mark McClure for "Bla-Z-Boy")

2003 (1): Outstanding Multi-Camera Picture Editing for a Series (Ron Volk for "Rooms with a View")

2004 (6): Outstanding Lead Actor in a Comedy Series (Kelsey Grammer); Outstanding Supporting Actor in a Comedy Series (David Hyde Pierce); Outstanding Guest Actress in a Comedy Series (Laura Linney); Outstanding Art Direction for a Multi-Camera Series (Roy Christopher, Amy Skjonsby-Winslow, and Ron Olsen for "Freudian Sleep/Caught in the Act"); Outstanding Multi-Camera Picture Editing for a Series (Ron Volk for "Goodnight, Seattle"); Outstanding Multi-Camera Sound Mixing for a Series or a Special (Andre Caporaso, Robert Douglass, Thomas J. Huth, and Dana Mark McClure for "The Doctor Is Out")

EMMY AWARD NOMINATIONS, IN ADDITION TO WINS (73)

1994 (6): Outstanding Supporting Actor in a Comedy Series (David Hyde Pierce); Outstanding Guest Actor in a Comedy Series (John Glover for "Oops"); Outstanding Individual Achievement in Writing in a Comedy Series (Ken Levine and David Isaacs for "The Show Where Lilith Comes Back"); Outstanding Individual

Achievement in Art Direction for a Series (Roy Christopher, Sharon Vijoen, and Ron Olsen for "A Midwinter's Night Dream"); Outstanding Individual Achievement in Main Title Theme Music (Bruce Miller and Darryl Phinnessee); Outstanding Individual Achievement in Sound Mixing for a Comedy Series or a Special (Sam Black, Robert Crosby, Robert Douglass, and Thomas J. Huth for "A Midwinter's Night Dream")

1995 (7): Outstanding Guest Actor in a Comedy Series (Nathan Lane for "Fool Me Once, Shame on You, Fool Me Twice . . ."); Outstanding Guest Actress in a Comedy Series (Bebe Neuwirth for "Adventures in Paradise: Part II"); Outstanding Guest Actress in a Comedy Series (JoBeth Williams for "Adventures in Paradise: Part II"); Outstanding Individual Achievement in Writing for a Comedy Series (Joe Keenan for "The Matchmaker"); Outstanding Individual Achievement in Art Direction for a Series (Roy Christopher and Ron Olsen for "The Innkeepers"); Outstanding Individual Achievement in Editing for a Series, Multi-Camera Production (Ron Volk for "The Matchmaker"); Outstanding Individual Achievement in Sound Mixing for a Comedy Series or a Special (Robert Douglass, Thomas J. Huth, Dana Mark McClure, and David M. Weishaar for "Adventures in Paradise, Part II")

1996 (7): Outstanding Lead Actor in a Comedy Series (Kelsey Grammer); Outstanding Supporting Actor in a Comedy Series (David Hyde Pierce); Outstanding Guest Actor in a Comedy Series (Griffin Dunne for "The Friend"); Outstanding Guest Actor in a Comedy Series (Harris Yulin for "A Word to the Wiseguy"); Outstanding Guest Actress in a Comedy Series (Shelley Long for "The Show Where Diane Comes Back"); Outstanding Individual Achievement in Casting for a Series (Jeff Greenberg); Outstanding Individual Achievement in Editing for a Series, Multi-Camera Production (Timothy Mozer for "The Adventures of Bad Boy and Dirty Girl")

1997 (7): Outstanding Lead Actor in a Comedy Series (Kelsey Grammer); Outstanding Supporting Actor in a Comedy Series (David Hyde Pierce); Outstanding Guest Actor in a Comedy Series (James Earl Jones for "Roz's Krantz and Gouldenstein Are Dead"); Outstanding Guest Actress in a Comedy Series (Marsha Mason for "Dad Loves Sherry, the Boys Just Whine"); Outstanding Casting for a Series (Jeff Greenberg); Outstanding Editing for a Series, Multi-Camera Production (Ron Volk for "To Kill a Talking Bird"); Outstanding Sound Mixing for a Comedy Series or a Special (Andre Caporaso, Robert Douglass, Dana Mark McClure, and John Reiner for "Liar, Liar")

1998 (7): Outstanding Supporting Actress in a Comedy Series (Jane Leeves); Outstanding Guest Actress in a Comedy Series (Patti LuPone for "Beware of Greeks"); Outstanding Writing for a Comedy Series (Joe Keenan for "The Ski Lodge"); Outstanding Casting for a Series (Jeff Greenberg); Outstanding Costume Design for a Series (Audrey M. Bansmer for "Halloween"); Outstanding Multi-Camera Picture Editing for a Series (Janet Ashikaga for "Roz and the Schnoz"); Outstanding Sound Mixing for a Comedy Series or a Special (Andre Caporaso, Robert Douglass, Dana Mark McClure, and John Reiner for "Beware of Greeks")

1999 (8): Outstanding Comedy Series; Outstanding Lead Actor in a Comedy Series (Kelsey Grammer); Outstanding Supporting Actor in a Comedy Series (John Mahoney); Outstanding Guest Actor in a Comedy Series (Woody Harrelson for

"The Show Where Woody Shows Up"); Outstanding Guest Actress in a Comedy Series (Christine Baranski for "Dr. Nora"); Outstanding Guest Actress in a Comedy Series (Piper Laurie for "Dr. Nora"); Outstanding Multi-Camera Picture Editing for a Series (Ron Volk for "Shutout in Seattle"); Outstanding Sound Mixing for a Comedy Series or a Special (Andre Caporaso, Robert Douglass, Thomas J. Huth, and Dana Mark McClure for "Three Valentines")

2000 (7): Outstanding Comedy Series; Outstanding Lead Actor in a Comedy Series (Kelsey Grammer); Outstanding Supporting Actor in a Comedy Series (David Hyde Pierce); Outstanding Guest Actor in a Comedy Series (Anthony LaPaglia); Outstanding Writing for a Comedy Series (Christopher Lloyd and Joe Keenan for "Something Borrowed, Someone Blue"); Outstanding Multi-Camera Picture Editing for a Series (Ron Volk for "Dark Side of the Moon"); Outstanding Sound Mixing for a Comedy Series or a Special (Andre Caporaso, Robert Douglass, Thomas J. Huth, and Dana Mark McClure for "Something Borrowed, Someone Blue")

2001 (8): Outstanding Comedy Series; Outstanding Lead Actor in a Comedy Series (Kelsey Grammer); Outstanding Supporting Actor in a Comedy Series (David Hyde Pierce); Outstanding Guest Actor in a Comedy Series (Victor Garber for "Taking Liberties"); Outstanding Art Direction for a Multi-Camera Series (Roy Christopher and Ron Olsen for "Cranes Go Caribbean"); Outstanding Casting for a Comedy Series (Jeff Greenberg); Outstanding Cinematography for a Multi-Camera Series (Ken Lamkin for "And the Dish Ran Away with the Spoon"); Outstanding Multi-Camera Sound Mixing for a Series or a Special (Andre Caporaso, Robert Douglass, Thomas J. Huth, and Dana Mark McClure for "Hooping Cranes")

2002 (6): Outstanding Lead Actor in a Comedy Series (Kelsey Grammer); Outstanding Supporting Actor in a Comedy Series (David Hyde Pierce); Outstanding Guest Actor in a Comedy Series (Adam Arkin for "The Two Hundredth"); Outstanding Guest Actor in a Comedy Series (Brian Cox for "The Moons over Seattle"); Outstanding Casting for a Comedy Series (Jeff Greenberg); Outstanding Cinematography for a Multi-Camera Series (Ken Lamkin for "Deathtrap")

2003 (4): Outstanding Supporting Actor in a Comedy Series (David Hyde Pierce); Outstanding Supporting Actor in a Comedy Series (John Mahoney); Outstanding Cinematography for a Multi-Camera Series (Ken Lamkin for "Rooms with a View"); Outstanding Multi-Camera Sound Mixing for a Series or a Special (Andre Caporaso, Robert Douglass, Thomas J. Huth, and Dana Mark McClure for "Daphne Does Dinner")

2004 (3): Outstanding Guest Actor in a Comedy Series (Anthony LaPaglia); Outstanding Writing for a Comedy Series (Christopher Lloyd and Joe Keenan for "Goodnight, Seattle"); Outstanding Casting for a Comedy Series (Jeff Greenberg)

GOLDEN GLOBE WINS (3)

1995 (1): Best TV Series, Musical/Comedy

1996 (1): Best Performance by an Actor in a TV Series, Musical/Comedy (Kelsey Grammer)

2001 (1): Best Performance by an Actor in a TV Series, Musical/Comedy (Kelsey Grammer)

GOLDEN GLOBE NOMINATIONS, IN ADDITION TO WINS (20)

1994 (3): Best TV Series, Musical/Comedy; Best Performance by an Actor in a TV Series, Musical/Comedy (Kelsey Grammer); Best Performance by an Actor in a Supporting Role in a Series, Mini-Series, or Motion Picture Made for TV (John Mahoney)

1995 (3): Best Performance by an Actor in a TV Series, Musical/Comedy (Kelsey Grammer); Best Performance by an Actor in a Supporting Role in a Series, Mini-Series, or Motion Picture Made for TV (David Hyde Pierce); Best Performance by an Actress in a Supporting Role in a Series, Mini-Series, or Motion Picture Made for TV (Jane Leeves)

1996 (2): Best TV Series, Musical/Comedy; Best Performance by an Actor in a Supporting Role in a Series, Mini-Series, or Motion Picture Made for TV (David Hyde Pierce)

1997 (3): Best TV Series, Musical/Comedy; Best Performance by an Actor in a TV Series, Musical/Comedy (Kelsey Grammer); Best Performance by an Actor in a Supporting Role in a Series, Mini-Series, or Motion Picture Made for TV (David Hyde Pierce)

1998 (3): Best TV Series, Musical/Comedy; Best Performance by an Actor in a TV Series, Musical/Comedy (Kelsey Grammer); Best Performance by an Actor in a Supporting Role in a Series, Mini-Series, or Motion Picture Made for TV (David Hyde Pierce)

1999 (2): Best TV Series, Musical/Comedy; Best Performance by an Actor in a TV Series, Musical/Comedy (Kelsey Grammer)

2001 (3): Best TV Series, Musical/Comedy; Best Performance by an Actor in a Supporting Role in a Series, Mini-Series, or Motion Picture Made for TV (David Hyde Pierce); Best Performance by an Actor in a Supporting Role in a Series, Mini-Series, or Motion Picture Made for TV (John Mahoney)

2002 (1): Best TV Series, Musical/Comedy

HUMANITAS PRIZE

1996: 30-Minute Category (Steve Levitan)
2000: 30-Minute Category (Jay Kogen)

HUMANITAS PRIZE NOMINATIONS

1994: 30-Minute Category (David Angell, Peter Casey, and David Lee)
1998: 30-Minute Category (Jeffrey Richman and Suzanne Martin)
2001: 30-Minute Category (Jon Sherman and Dan O'Shannon)
2003: 30-Minute Category (Dan O'Shannon, Lori Kirkland Baker, and Bob Daily)

PEABODY AWARD

1995: NBC, Grub Street Productions, and Paramount Television

Further Reading

Graham, Jefferson. *Frasier: The Official Companion Book to the Award-Winning Paramount Television Comedy.* New York: Pocket Books, 1996.

Grammer, Kelsey. *So Far . . .* New York: Dutton, 1995.

Tucker, Ken. "TV Show Review: 'Frasier.'" *Entertainment Weekly*, October 22, 1993. Available online at www.ew.com/ew/article/0,,308507,00.html

✳ 9 ✳

The Dick Van Dyke Show

(1961–1966)

Cast: Dick Van Dyke (Robert Petrie), Mary Tyler Moore (Laura Petrie), Morey Amsterdam (Buddy Sorrell), Rose Marie (Sally Rogers), Larry Mathews (Ritchie Petrie), Rich Deacon (Mel Cooley), Ann Morgan Guilbert (Millie Helper), Jerry Paris (Jerry Helper), Carl Reiner (Alan Brady)

Created by: Carl Reiner

Network: CBS

First Air Date: October 3, 1961

Last Air Date: June 1, 1966

Broadcast History:
October 3, 1961–December 1961: Tuesday at 8:00–8:30 PM
January 1962–May 1964: Wednesday at 9:30–10:00 PM
September 1964–September 1965: Wednesday at 9:00–9:30 PM
September 1965–June 1, 1966: Wednesday at 9:30–10:00 PM

Seasons: 5

Episodes: 158

Ratings History: 1961–1962 (not in Top 30), 1962–1963 (9), 1963–1964 (3), 1964–1965 (7), 1965–1966 (16)

Overview

In one episode of *The Dick Van Dyke Show*, TV writer Rob Petrie creates a skit in which he speaks about his pride in the "level of sophistication" reached in the entertainment business, all the while executing pratfalls and the brilliant physical humor in which Dick Van Dyke excelled. But Petrie was right all along, despite the display

68

Clockwise from top left: Richard Deacon, Rose Marie, Morey Amsterdam, Dick Van Dyke, and Mary Tyler Moore. *CBS/Photofest ©CBS*

of slapstick in that scene. *The Dick Van Dyke Show* had indeed raised the American sitcom to a new level of sophistication.

The characters represented the new erudite, college-educated generation of young suburban adults as personified by President John F. Kennedy and his New Frontier of the early 1960s. Petrie's wife, Laura Petrie (Mary Tyler Moore), embodied a new wave of more self-actualized, cultured women whose primary concerns in life extended far beyond the shininess of her kitchen floor and cooking the perfect meal for her husband upon his return home from work. The decision to allow the character to don what became her trademark capri pants rather than a dress, as every TV housewife before her was quite unrealistically forced to wear, is considered one of the birth moments of the women's liberation movement.

The show and the Rob Petrie character were based greatly on the professional life of Reiner, who had worked in the mid- to late 1950s with an incredible stable of writers creating sketches for the legendary Sid Caesar in *Your Show of Shows* and *The Sid Caesar Show*. Among Reiner's colleagues were future award-winning playwright and screenwriter Neil Simon; *M*A*S*H* creator Larry Gelbart; Oscar-winning actor, writer, and director Woody Allen; and iconic comedy film writer and director Mel Brooks.

The Dick Van Dyke Show scenes rarely strayed beyond two locations. One was the office in which Petrie and fellow comedy writers Buddy Sorrell (Morey Amsterdam) and Sally Rogers (Rose Marie) created scripts for a variety program entitled *The Alan Brady Show* (which starred Reiner, who made occasional appearances). The other was the Petrie home, which housed Laura and young son Ritchie (Larry Mathews), who rarely played a significant role. Perhaps the most humorous conflicts were waged between the quick-witted Buddy and Reiner lackey producer Mel Cooley (Rich Deacon). The verbal sparring was quite one-sided, as Sorrell delivered one stinging and hilarious insult after another at Mel, who often replied by simply staring at Sorrell and exclaiming, "Yech!"

The problems of delivering funny scripts on time experienced by the three writers smacked of realism. So did the banter between the three as they dealt with severe cases of writer's block and periods of simply goofing off or discussing personal issues. The character that tugged the hardest at the heartstrings of the viewer was Rogers, an aging woman whose jokes about her inability to find love could not mask her loneliness and misery.

The sitcom also featured significant interaction between Rob's work and home life. Buddy and Sally often visited the Petries, sometimes for parties in which either impromptu or planned singing, dancing, or comedy routines showed off the talents of the cast members. The relationship between Rob and Laura was rarely combative. Their love and respect for one another remained evident throughout the course of the show, which quickly grew in popularity after hitting the air in October 1961. It catapulted into the Top 10 in the Nielsen ratings in its second season and remained in the Top 20 for the rest of its run.

Van Dyke never again reached the same level of professional success after his namesake sitcom left the air. He remained an icon in the entertainment world for decades thereafter, but not to the extent of Moore, who continued to blaze new trails for women in television as Mary Richards in *The Mary Tyler Moore Show*. But those both old enough to have watched her as Laura Petrie in the early 1960s, or fortunate enough to have seen the character in reruns, will always remember her trademark sobbing plea for help from her husband: "Oh, Rob!" American television viewers of that era wished they could have continued to hear those two words from Laura as she attempted in vain to control her emotions, but the show was cancelled despite continued high ratings to allow Van Dyke and other cast members to pursue other projects.

At Least He Didn't Snore

Jerry Van Dyke made four guest appearances on *The Dick Van Dyke Show*. The most notable is a two-part episode in which Jerry plays the familiar role of Dick's brother and the unfamiliar role of a somnambulist named Stacey Petrie, a painfully shy and unconfident banjo player who becomes outgoing and a brilliant musician only when asleep. His performance in that show launched the television career of the younger Petrie, who later starred in *My Mother the Car* and *Coach* (for which he earned four Emmy nominations for Best Supporting Actor) and has remained active as an actor past the age of eighty.

Did You Know?

The landscape of late-night television might have changed drastically if Johnny Carson had landed the role of Rob Petrie instead of Dick Van Dyke. The legendary talk show host was a leading contender for the part.

They Said It

Alan Brady: [to his staff members about a note regarding firing them] Didn't you see I crumpled it up?
Buddy: [after examining the paper] Yeah, that's his crumple.

Mel Cooley: Believe me, Rob, as the producer, I'm sorry.
Buddy: We believe you, Curly. You're a sorry producer.

Major Awards

EMMY AWARD WINS (15)

1962 (1): Outstanding Writing Achievement in Comedy (Carl Reiner)
1963 (3): Outstanding Program Achievement in the Field of Humor; Outstanding Writing Achievement in Comedy (Carl Reiner); Outstanding Directorial Achievement in Comedy (John Rich)
1964 (5): Outstanding Program Achievement in the Field of Comedy; Outstanding Continued Performance by a Lead Actor in a Series (Dick Van Dyke); Outstanding Continued Performance by a Lead Actress in a Series (Mary Tyler Moore); Outstanding Writing Achievement in Comedy or Variety (Carl Reiner, Sam Denoff, and Bill Persky for various episodes); Outstanding Directorial Achievement in Comedy (Jerry Paris)
1965 (2): Outstanding Program Achievements in Entertainment (Carl Reiner); Outstanding Individual Achievement in Entertainment, Actors and Performers (Dick Van Dyke)

1966 (4): Outstanding Comedy Series; Outstanding Continued Performance by an Actor in a Leading Role in a Comedy Series (Dick Van Dyke); Outstanding Continued Performance by an Actress in a Leading Role in a Comedy Series (Mary Tyler Moore); Outstanding Writing Achievement in Comedy (Sam Denoff and Bill Persky for "Coast to Coast Big Mouth")

EMMY AWARD NOMINATIONS, IN ADDITION TO WINS (10)

1962 (1): Outstanding Directorial Achievement in Comedy (John Rich)

1963 (3): Outstanding Continued Performance by a Lead Actor in a Series (Dick Van Dyke); Outstanding Continued Performance by a Lead Actress in a Series (Mary Tyler Moore); Outstanding Performance in a Supporting Role by an Actress (Rose Marie)

1964 (1): Outstanding Performance in a Supporting Role by an Actress (Rose Marie)

1965 (1): Outstanding Continued Achievement in Entertainment, Writers (Carl Reiner for "Never Bathe on Sunday")

1966 (4): Outstanding Performance by an Actor in a Supporting Role in a Comedy (Morey Amsterdam); Outstanding Performance by an Actress in a Supporting Role in a Comedy (Rose Marie); Outstanding Writing Achievement in Comedy (Sam Denoff and Bill Persky for "The Ugliest Dog in the World"); Outstanding Directorial Achievement in Comedy (Jerry Paris)

GOLDEN GLOBE WINS (2)

1964 (1): Best TV Show
1965 (1): Best TV Star, Female (Mary Tyler Moore)

Further Reading

Moore, Mary Tyler. *After All*. New York: Dell, 1996.

Van Dyke, Dick. *My Lucky Life In and Out of Show Business: A Memoir*. New York: Crown, 2011.

Weissman, Ginny, and Coyne Sanders. *The Dick Van Dyke Show: Anatomy of a Classic*. New York: St. Martin's, 1983.

Taxi

(1978–1983)

Cast: Judd Hirsch (Alex Rieger), Danny DeVito (Louie DePalma), Marilu Henner (Elaine O'Connor-Nardo), Tony Danza (Tony Banta), Jeff Conaway (Bobby Wheeler), Andy Kaufman (Latka Gravas), Christopher Lloyd (Reverend Jim Ignatowski), Carol Kane (Simka Dahblitz-Gravas), Randall Carver (John Burns)

Created by: Producers and writers Stan Daniels, James L. Brooks, Ed. Weinberger, and David Davis

Networks: ABC (1978–1982), NBC (1982–1983)

First Air Date: September 12, 1978

Last Air Date: July 27, 1983

Broadcast History:
September 12, 1978–October 1980: Tuesday at 9:30–10:00 PM
November 1980–January 1981: Wednesday at 9:00–9:30 PM
February 1981–December 1982: Thursday at 9:30–10:00 PM
January 1983–February 1983: Saturday at 9:30–10:00 PM
March 1983–May 1983: Wednesday at 9:30–10:00 PM
June 1983–July 27, 1983: Wednesday at 10:30–11:00 PM

Seasons: 5

Episodes: 114

Ratings History: 1978–1979 (9), 1979–1980 (13), 1980–1981 (not in Top 30), 1981–1982 (not in Top 30), 1982–1983 (not in Top 30)

Marilu Henner, Andy Kaufman, Judd Hirsch, and Tony Danza. *NBC/Photofest ©NBC*

Overview

If an all-star team of television comedy writers and producers needed to be organized in the late 1970s and 1980s, the task would have been simple. The lone requirement would have been contacting the folks that created *Taxi*. The group that served in those roles on this critically acclaimed sitcom (along with their previous and future credits) included Ed. Weinberger (*The Mary Tyler Moore Show* and *The Tonight Show Starring Johnny Carson*), James L. Brooks (*MTM*, *Room 222*, and *The Simpsons*), and David Davis (*MTM*, *The Bob Newhart Show*, and *Get Smart*). Add director James Burrows (*Will & Grace* and *Frasier*), who created *Cheers* alongside fellow *Taxi* contributors Glen Charles and Les Charles, and you have one of the finest crews ever assembled. The result was one of the finest comedies ever produced.

Taxi took the baton from *Barney Miller* as a sophisticated workplace-driven comedy and ran with it before handing it off to *Cheers*, but its viewership failed to match its brilliance. It debuted in the Top 10 in the Nielsen ratings and remained hot for two years before falling out of sight and going off the air. Such fate was unworthy of a sitcom that earned an Emmy for Outstanding Comedy Series in each of its first three seasons.

The main difference between *Taxi* and such intellectual workplace shows as *Barney Miller* and *Cheers* was the diminutive, mean-spirited, despicable, petty, outrageous Louie DePalma (Danny DeVito), who has been rated as the funniest sitcom character ever. The tyrannical DePalma served as the dispatcher for the Sunshine Cab Company in New York, which featured more sullen characters and darker storylines than the other two shows to which *Taxi* has been compared. Most of the main characters felt angst and expressed dissatisfaction with their lots in life and lack of success in other professions that landed them behind the wheel. Among them were Alex Rieger (Judd Hirsch), who seemed a better fit as a college psychology professor than a cabbie; failed boxer Tony Banta (Tony Danza); frustrated actor Bobby Wheeler (Jeff Conaway); and divorcee Elaine O'Connor-Nardo (Marilu Henner), whose artistic endeavors had taken her nowhere except into the gazes of lecherous Louie.

The wackier side of the cab company was personified by mechanic Latka Gravas (Andy Kaufman) and ultimate 1960s burnout "Reverend Jim" Ignatowski (Christopher Lloyd), who joined the cast in the second season. The former spoke pidgin English around an unrecognizable first language that left viewers blind to his ethnicity. The childlike Latka, who was bullied by Louie, later took on multiple personalities, including slick-talking womanizer Vic Ferrari. He forged a relationship with Simka Dahblitz-Gravas (Carol Kane), a woman from his homeland. The two spoke the same concocted language, fell in love, and finally wed at the end of the fourth season. Jim remained the same guy, who could have been the inspiration for the commercial that shows an egg frying and voiceover stating "this is your brain on drugs."

Taxi was respected enough to motivate a bidding war between HBO and NBC upon its cancellation from ABC in 1982. Promotional ads featuring DeVito claiming that the show was moving to a better network did not have their desired effect. By that time, the die was cast. The show had dropped out of the Top 30 in the Nielsen ratings, despite the three consecutive Outstanding Comedy Series Emmys, and was soon off the air, but history has been kind to *Taxi*, which is still considered one of the finest sitcoms ever produced.

Onward Taxi Drivers

The memorable cast members of *Taxi* forged successful careers. Tony Danza landed a lead role in the highly rated sitcom *Who's the Boss* soon after *Taxi* left the air and went on to earn recurring roles in such shows as *Hudson Street* and *Family Law*. Judd Hirsch starred in the underrated sitcom *Dear John* and hit action film *Independence Day* before snagging a role in the TV drama *Numb3rs*. Marilu Henner played the female lead alongside Burt Reynolds in the critically acclaimed sitcom *Evening Shade*.

The Strange World of Andy Kaufman

Andy Kaufman embarked on the weirdest foray into the theater of the absurd in the early 1980s by proclaiming himself the "Inter-Gender Wrestling Champion of the World" and offering $1,000 to any woman who could pin him in a match. Kaufman eventually launched a fake feud with professional wrestling champion Jerry "The King" Lawler, but their battles inside the ring were secondary to the prefight and postfight shenanigans. During an appearance on *Late Night with David Letterman*,

Kaufman showed up wearing a neck brace supposedly necessitated by an injury suffered at the hands of Lawler, who added insult and pain to injury by slapping the comic silly with the cameras rolling. Kaufman left the stage, only to return and hurl a string of profanity at Lawler and threaten a lawsuit. A story in the *Memphis Flyer* that ran in 1997—twelve years after Kaufman's death—quoted Lawler as confirming that the incident in which he supposedly caused the neck injury to Kaufman and the one on the Lettermen set were both improvised.

They Said It

Jim: [taking a written driving test] Pssssttt . . . what does the yellow light mean?
Bobby: Slow down.
Jim: What . . . does . . . the . . . yellow . . . light . . . mean?
Bobby: Slow down!
Jim: Whaaaat . . . dooooeeees . . . theeeee . . . yelllloowwww . . . liiiiight . . . meeeeean?

Louie: What's this?
Latka: It's a kebble.
Louie: What's a kebble?
Latka: 100 kebble make a lithnitch.
Louie: What's a lithnitch?
Latka: 270 lithnitch make a matta.
Louie: What's a matta?
Latka: I don't know, what's the matter with you?

Alex: Jim, when are you finally going to have some pride and stand up for yourself?
Jim: August!

Major Awards

EMMY AWARD WINS (18)

1979 (3): Outstanding Comedy Series; Outstanding Lead Actress in a Comedy Series (Ruth Gordon for "Sugar Mama"); Outstanding Film Editing for a Series (M. Pam Blumenthal for "Paper Marriage")
1980 (3): Outstanding Comedy Series; Outstanding Directing in a Comedy Series (James Burrows for "Louie and the Nice Girl"); Outstanding Achievement in Film Editing for a Series (M. Pam Blumenthal for "Louie and the Nice Girl")
1981 (6): Outstanding Comedy Series; Outstanding Lead Actor in a Comedy Series (Judd Hirsch); Outstanding Supporting Actor in a Comedy or Comedy-Variety or Music Series (Danny DeVito); Outstanding Writing in a Comedy Series (Michael Leeson for "Tony's Sister and Jim"); Outstanding Directing in a Comedy Series (James Burrows for "Elaine's Strange Triangle"); Outstanding Achievement

for Film Editing for a Series (M. Pam Blumenthal and Jack Michon for "Elaine's Strange Triangle")

1982 (3): Outstanding Lead Actress in a Comedy Series (Carol Kane); Outstanding Supporting Actor in a Comedy or Comedy-Variety or Music Series (Christopher Lloyd); Outstanding Writing in a Comedy Series (Ken Estin for "Elegant Iggy")

1983 (3): Outstanding Lead Actor in a Comedy Series (Judd Hirsch); Outstanding Supporting Actor in a Comedy or Comedy-Variety or Music Series (Christopher Lloyd); Outstanding Supporting Actress in a Comedy or Comedy-Variety or Music Series (Carol Kane)

EMMY AWARD NOMINATIONS, IN ADDITION TO WINS (16)

1979 (3): Outstanding Lead Actor in a Comedy Series (Judd Hirsch); Outstanding Supporting Actor in a Comedy or Comedy-Variety or Music Series (Danny DeVito); Outstanding Writing in a Comedy or Comedy-Variety or Music Series (Michael Leeson for "Blind Date")

1980 (2): Outstanding Lead Actor in a Comedy Series (Judd Hirsch); Outstanding Writing in a Comedy Series (Glen Charles and Les Charles for "Honor Thy Father")

1981 (3): Outstanding Lead Actress in a Comedy Series (Eileen Brennan for "The Boss's Wife"); Outstanding Writing in a Comedy Series (Glen Charles and Les Charles for "Going Home"); Outstanding Writing in a Comedy Series (David Lloyd for "Elaine's Strange Triangle")

1982 (5): Outstanding Comedy Series; Outstanding Lead Actor in a Comedy Series (Judd Hirsch); Outstanding Supporting Actor in a Comedy or Comedy-Variety or Music Series (Danny DeVito); Outstanding Writing in a Comedy Series (Barry Kemp and Holly Holmberg Brooks for "Jim the Psychic"); Outstanding Directing in a Comedy Series (James Burrows for "Jim the Psychic")

1983 (3): Outstanding Comedy Series; Outstanding Supporting Actor in a Comedy or Comedy-Variety or Music Series (Danny DeVito); Outstanding Writing in a Comedy Series (Ken Estin for "Jim's Inheritance")

GOLDEN GLOBE WINS (4)

1979 (1): Best TV Series, Musical/Comedy
1980 (2): Best TV Series, Musical/Comedy; Best TV Actor in a Supporting Role (Danny DeVito)
1981 (1): Best TV Series, Musical/Comedy

GOLDEN GLOBE NOMINATIONS, IN ADDITION TO WINS (22)

1979 (5): Best TV Actor, Musical/Comedy (Judd Hirsch); Best TV Actor in a Supporting Role (Jeff Conaway); Best TV Actor in a Supporting Role (Andy

Kaufman); Best TV Actor in a Supporting Role (Danny DeVito); Best TV Actress in a Supporting Role (Marilu Henner)

1980 (4): Best TV Actor, Musical/Comedy (Judd Hirsch); Best TV Actor in a Supporting Role (Jeff Conaway); Best TV Actor in a Supporting Role (Tony Danza); Best TV Actress in a Supporting Role (Marilu Henner)

1981 (4): Best Performance by an Actor in a TV Series, Musical/Comedy (Judd Hirsch); Best Supporting Actor in a Series, Mini-Series, or Motion Picture Made for TV (Andy Kaufman); Best Supporting Actor in a Series, Mini-Series, or Motion Picture Made for TV (Danny DeVito); Best Supporting Actress in a Series, Mini-Series, or Motion Picture Made for TV (Marilu Henner)

1982 (4): Best TV Series, Musical/Comedy; Best Performance by an Actor in a TV Series, Musical/Comedy (Judd Hirsch); Best Supporting Actor in a Series, Mini-Series, or Motion Picture Made for TV (Danny DeVito); Best Supporting Actress in a Series, Mini-Series, or Motion Picture Made for TV (Marilu Henner)

1983 (4): Best TV Series, Musical/Comedy; Best Performance by an Actor in a TV Series, Musical/Comedy (Judd Hirsch); Best Supporting Actress in a Series, Mini-Series, or Motion Picture Made for TV (Carol Kane); Best Supporting Actress in a Series, Mini-Series, or Motion Picture Made for TV (Marilu Henner)

1984 (1): Best TV Series, Musical/Comedy

HUMANITAS PRIZE

1979: 30-Minute Category (Michael Leeson)

Further Reading

Sorensen, Jeff. *The Taxi Book: The Complete Guide to Television's Most Lovable Cabbies.* New York: St. Martin's, 1987.

✳ 11 ✳

The Honeymooners

(1955–1956)

Cast: Jackie Gleason (Ralph Kramden), Audrey Meadows (Alice Kramden), Art Carney (Ed Norton), Joyce Randolph (Trixie Norton)

Created by: Jackie Gleason

Network: CBS

First Air Date: October 1, 1955

Last Air Date: September 22, 1956

Broadcast History:
October 1, 1955–February 1956: Saturday at 8:30–9:00 PM
February 1956–September 22, 1956: Saturday at 8:00–8:30 PM

Seasons: 1

Episodes: 39

Ratings History: 1955–1956 (20)

Overview

If Ralph Kramden proved to be as successful as the sitcom in which he was characterized, he would have been a billionaire. Kramden, a bus driver for the city of New York portrayed passionately and brilliantly by Jackie Gleason, had dreams matched only by his prodigious size. His harebrained, get-rich-quick schemes always failed, causing embarrassment, anger, and frustration, but not for a lack of trying. Ralph desired nothing more than to improve his lot in life and that of his wife, whom he understood deep in his heart was too good for him.

Art Carney and Jackie Gleason. *CBS/Photofest ©CBS*

It was Ralph's weekly battles with reality and the limitations of his intelligence, reason, and talent that made him one of the most memorable characters in television history, and *The Honeymooners* easily the best one-hit wonder of all American sitcoms. The show indeed lasted a mere thirty-nine episodes and one season, but the greatness of its legacy far exceeds that of many shows that have lasted ten times longer. It is considered by some the funniest sitcom ever produced, despite the short shelf life that leaves fans of classic television yearning for more.

Perhaps its success was the result of years of honing. *The Honeymooners* was born and raised as a recurring short sketch show filmed before live audiences on the Du-Mont network's *Cavalcade of Stars* and on *The Jackie Gleason Show* (CBS) from 1951 to 1955, before debuting as its own sitcom entity. It faced some heady competition when it debuted in that format, having been placed head-to-head in October 1955 against the highly popular *Perry Como Show*.

Gleason was considered a comedic genius by many in Hollywood, including iconic actor and director Orson Welles, who dubbed him simply "The Great One." He first gained success serving as a master of ceremonies in amateur shows in his native Brooklyn before trying his hand in a wide variety of tasks in the sports and entertainment worlds, including carnival barker, boxer, and even daredevil driver in carnivals. His rotund frame brought distinction and helped him land roles as a bit actor in such films as *Orchestra Wives* and *Springtime in the Rockies* before his career took off with the advent of television. Gleason was featured in the series *The Life of Riley* (1949–1950) before he gained stardom as host of DuMont's *Cavalcade of Stars*, during which he created such legendary characters as Ralph Kramden and Joe the Bartender. He starred in various variety programs, including *The Jackie Gleason Show* (1952–1957 and 1966–1970) and *Jackie Gleason: American Scene Magazine* (1962–1966). His most notable movie role came opposite Paul Newman in *The Hustler*, in which he plays a pool hustler named Minnesota Fats being challenged by a young upstart. Gleason earned an Academy Award nomination for his performance and showed he could thrive as both a serious and comedic actor.

The theme of *The Honeymooners* was a departure from other family sitcoms of the era, which most often featured larger families, with children, enjoying the economic fruits of the American dream. It was among the first to portray blue-collar couples struggling to make ends meet. The writing and characterizations embraced the depiction of people in a working-class environment. The setting was a tiny Brooklyn apartment with no frills—not even a telephone.

Although Ralph was the lead character in *The Honeymooners*, he shared plenty of camera time with effervescent best friend Ed Norton (Art Carney), whose madcap personality and penchant for taking life far less seriously than Ralph made him an ideal sidekick. Ralph bounced his ideas off Norton, a stupid sewer worker whom he often dragged down with him when the scheme flopped. But Norton was a supportive friend who did not seem to mind being used as a guinea pig for a failed experiment, despite knowing he had been manipulated. Indeed, he came to expect it and seemed to appreciate his friend Ralph thinking enough of him to use him for whatever half-baked plan he had concocted.

Perhaps the most famous scene in the history of the show was the result of Ralph having what he often described as a "BIIIIG MOUTH!" He bragged at his workplace about his talents as a golfer, despite the fact that he had never played the sport. He was corralled into a game with his boss and had to become proficient in a hurry. While it was wholly unrealistic for him to become as strong a golfer as he claimed to be in such a short period of time, he went full speed ahead rather than recant his claim. Ed joined him for an impromptu teaching session in Ralph's apartment. The result was hilarity as Ralph continued to flail away at air with his borrowed club as he aimed for a pincushion that served as the ball. Finally, Ed read a passage in a how-to book that informed Ralph that he needed to "address the ball." When asked by his friend its meaning, Ed took the club, looked down at the pincushion, gave it a salute, and said with conviction, "Hello, ball!," prompting roars of laughter from the audience.

If Ralph was the schlemiel, his wife Alice (Audrey Meadows) was the *schlimazel*. She was the victim of the mayhem he created. Viewers might have grown frustrated in the knowledge that an attractive, intelligent woman like Alice could instead have chosen a man who raised her station, especially considering that the period in question was twenty years before the time in which women generally sought to advance themselves professionally and financially, but Alice loved Ralph. She accepted her lot in life in tying her fortunes with that of her husband. She took her wedding vows literally and unquestioningly. So did Ed's wife, Trixie (Joyce Randolph), whose comparatively drab personality placed her in direct contrast to the more lively and thought-provoking Ralph, Ed, and Alice.

The small cast and small setting added up to big laughs. The tininess of the cramped apartment juxtaposed against Ralph's ample girth, about which Alice never missed an opportunity to joke at his expense, resulted in a visual that proved humorous without dialogue. The constant reminder of the dreary living quarters—radiator, window to the fire escape, and woefully archaic stove, sink, and icebox—could be sad to viewers but always seemed to bring laughs when Alice pointed out to her husband that she was not exactly living in the lap of luxury, thereby knocking him down a few pegs.

The Honeymooners has always been cherished for the loving, yet humorously confrontational, relationship between Ralph and Alice. He remained mindful of her importance in his life and the boundless love he felt for her, which motivated him to pursue avenues he believed would result in better professional or financial opportunities. He became angry or frustrated with her when she expressed doubt about the prospects of whatever wacky scheme in which he had become involved. His typical retort even promised violence—Ralph would clench his fist, show it to his wife, and yell, "To the moon, Alice!" or "Bang. . . . Zoom!" Such lines would never be allowed in today's politically correct television world, but they elicited howls of laughter from the live audiences fortunate enough to have soaked in a rare staging of *The Honeymooners*.

Just as threatening as Ralph was to his wife (although he would never have dreamed of delivering on such physical threats), he was sincerely apologetic when Alice was inevitably proven right and his plan had failed in some disastrous manner. He would hem and haw and words would fail him at first as he tried to explain away his motivation. And after Alice forgave him, he would often end the show with the throwaway line that made everything all right again: "Alice, you're the greatest."

The Honeymooners began to lose viewers to the hugely successful *Perry Como Show* in 1956. Gleason believed his program was running out of original ideas and its future excellence could not be maintained. He was too proud of the show to allow what he perceived as potential slippage, so he had it cancelled after one season, with $7 million remaining on his contract. Little could anyone have imagined that despite its brief run, it would be considered more than a half-century later as arguably the greatest sitcom ever produced.

Art Work

The greatness of Art Carney in the role of Ed Norton has never been disputed. The praise, which included a Best Actor Emmy in 1956 (the only Emmy win for the show), gained greater justification through his success in both movies and television into the 1990s. Carney had already earned two Emmys for his work in *The Jackie Gleason Show* and captured two more in the namesake variety program of the 1960s. Carney peaked as a movie actor with his portrayal of a retired New Yorker who embarked on a cross-country journey with his cat in *Harry and Tonto* (1975). He won both a Best Actor Oscar and Golden Globe for that performance.

Yabba Dabba Doo!

The popularity of *The Honeymooners* was indicative in a copycat cartoon of the 1960s. The main characters in the *The Flintstones* were patterned after those in the show, although the setting had been switched to prehistoric times. Fat Fred Flintstone was a mirror image of Ralph Kramden, while buddy Barney Rubble featured the same personality and temperament as Ed Norton.

They Said It

Ralph: Me and my silly pride. Well, I promise you this, Norton: I'm gonna learn. I'm gonna learn from here on out how to swallow my pride.
Norton: Well, that ought not to be too hard; you've learned how to swallow everything else.
Ralph: GET OUT!

Ralph: You're the type of person that would bend waaaaay over to pick up a purse on April Fools' Day. I wouldn't.
Alice: You couldn't.

Norton: Mind if I smoke?
Ralph: I don't care if you burn.

Major Awards

EMMY AWARD WINS (1)

1956 (1): Best Actor in a Supporting Role (Art Carney)

EMMY AWARD NOMINATIONS, IN ADDITION TO WINS (2)

1956 (2): Best Actor, Continuing Performance (Jackie Gleason); Best Actress in a Supporting Role (Audrey Meadows)

Further Reading

Crescenti, Peter, and Bob Columbe. *The Official Honeymooners Treasury*. New York: Perigee, 1990.
McCrohan, Donna. *The Honeymooners Companion*. New York: Workman, 1978.
Meadows, Audrey. *Love, Alice: My Life as a Honeymooner*. New York: Crown, 1994.

✴ 12 ✴

Murphy Brown

(1988–1998)

Cast: Candice Bergen (Murphy Brown), Faith Ford (Corky Sherwood), Charles Kimbrough (Jim Dial), Joe Regalbuto (Frank Fontana), Grant Shaud (Miles Silverberg), John Hostetter (John), Lily Tomlin (Kay Carter-Shepley)

Created by: Executive producer and writer Diane English

Network: CBS

First Air Date: November 14, 1988

Last Air Date: August 10, 1998

Broadcast History:
November 14, 1988–February 1997: Monday at 9:00–9:30 PM
April 1997–May 1997: Monday at 8:30–9:00 PM
June 1997–September 1997: Monday at 9:30–10:00 PM
July 1997–June 1998: Wednesday at 8:30–9:00 PM
April 1998–August 10, 1998: Monday at 9:30–10:00 PM

Seasons: 10

Episodes: 247

Ratings History: 1988–1989 (not in Top 30), 1989–1990 (27), 1990–1991 (6), 1991–1992 (3), 1992–1993 (4), 1993–1994 (9), 1994–1995 (16), 1995–1996 (18), 1996–1997 (not in Top 30), 1997–1998 (not in Top 30)

Grant Shaud, Pat Corley, Joe Regalbuto, Candice Bergen, Faith Ford, and Charles Kimbrough. *CBS/Photofest ©CBS*

Overview

Perhaps former vice president Dan Quayle should have spent more time learning how to spell words like "*potato*" (which he famously directed a child to misspell in a notoriously comic caught-on-camera moment in a classroom) and less time watching *Murphy Brown* on television. If he had ignored the show's starring title character, Candice Bergen, he wouldn't have put his foot in his mouth—again!—and turned it into one of the most talked-about hits in the history of the small screen.

The Moral Majority was dead and buried during the 1992 presidential election campaign, but Quayle resurrected its memory by complaining about the decision of the title character to have a baby sans husband or active father. He deemed it a violation of family values. *Murphy Brown* deemed it a breakthrough for realism and the notion that a family can come in many variations and that its strength is love and compassion rather than form. The staff felt strongly enough about it to create a two-part episode to launch the 1992–1993 season entitled "You Say Potatoe, I Say Potato" (a not-so-subtle slam against Quayle), in which Brown spotlights the diverse American family in a special edition of her news magazine show, *FYI*.

Not that *Murphy Brown* wasn't already quite popular. It had already catapulted to number three in the Nielsen ratings the previous season in the midst of a seven-year run in the Top 30. But the polarizing controversy—many among the Religious Right sided with Quayle—transformed it from a well-watched sitcom into a cultural phenomenon.

The daughter of legendary ventriloquist Edgar Bergen and former actress Frances Bergen delivered punch lines with an icy stare and the sensitivity of a punch in the face. She proved in her sexiness in the role that warmth and the traditional vulnerability often associated with femininity isn't a prerequisite to beauty. Brown was a recovering alcoholic returning to *FYI* after drying out at the Betty Ford Clinic. She was supported by an excellent cast of youthful comparative unknowns who created their signature roles in *Murphy Brown*.

Among those characters were vapid, dull *FYI* anchorman Jim Dial (Charles Kimbrough); Murphy's platonic best friend, Frank Fontana (Joe Regalbuto), a neurotic and comic-tragic figure; and perky Corky Sherwood (Faith Ford), who had earned her job only because she was a reigning Miss America (because the winner was forced to relinquish her crown) and was no Walter Cronkite as a serious journalist. In one humorous twist, she married writer Will Forrest (whom she later divorced), and her last name became, of course, Sherwood-Forrest. Brilliant-yet-naïve yuppie producer Miles Silverberg (Grant Shaud) added a strong comic element to the show as the target of Murphy's witty insults.

One and all played brilliantly off the title character, who was so motivated to make her show and life a success that she sought to control her colleagues with an intimidating, sarcastic, and overbearing approach. It's no wonder that she lost every secretary she hired; ninety-three came and went during the run of the show. The running joke became so prevalent that in an episode of *Seinfeld*, the eccentric Kramer is shown doing that job on *Murphy Brown*. He, too, was asked with great emphasis not to return.

The show got a bit of fresh air outside the newsroom with a story line revolving around Murphy's home life. The most intriguing side character there was house painter Eldin Bernecky (Robert Pastorelli), who never finished his work on her town house (like the outrageously inept Monroe Brothers in *Green Acres*), despite hanging around at all hours of the day and night. Eldin saw his role to be equally his employer's life coach and, in fact, he eventually served as a daycare provider for baby boy, Avery, despite the fact that he had gained tremendous wealth after selling one of his paintings for a million bucks. He left the show in 1994 to study painting in Spain. The characters also spent time away from the workplace at a neighborhood bar run by a man named Phil (Pat Corley), who rivaled Eldin as an advisor before supposedly dying in 1996.

Several other story line and cast changes were on the horizon by that time. Some of them centered on the blossoming personal relationship between Corky and Miles, whose elopement in 1995 caused a dilemma for the writers a year later when Shaud decided to leave the show. They explained his departure as a decision to take a job in New York and leave Corky in Washington. The loss of Shaud resulted in the addition of Lily Tomlin to the cast as inexperienced executive producer replacement Kay Carter-Shepley.

The topical and strong left-leaning political nature of *Murphy Brown* prevents it from translating well in today's society, which perhaps can explain its limited exposure in syndication. Two issues touched upon on the show that have remained relevant revolved around the title character revealing she had breast cancer. Brown again caused controversy by admitting she had smoked marijuana to counteract the nausea associated with chemotherapy. Attacks from the right of the political spectrum notwithstanding, the number of American women undergoing mammograms at that time increased by an amazing 30 percent.

Murphy first announced she was retiring in the series finale, which aired on May 18, 1998, but after a traumatic experience in which under anesthesia she dreamed she was having an argument in heaven with God (played by veteran comedian Alan King), she decided to stay on the job. That wasn't the only shocker. Phil returned to the bar, announcing he had faked his death because he knew too much about the Whitewater scandal and the CIA had provided him with a new identity. That outfit whisked him away again for his inside knowledge of the President Clinton affair with Monica Lewinsky. And Eldin returned from Spain not only because of concern for Murphy, but also to paint a mural depicting the fall of the communist system in the Soviet Union.

Some believed *Murphy Brown* had worn out its welcome well before that point, but it can be argued that its social and political impact was as vast as any sitcom since *All in the Family*. There was little doubt, however, about its imbalance to the left, leading to charges from the right that the show merely fed into what was perceived as Hollywood's liberal bias.

Shining Stars of Journalism

Many of the premier television journalists and talk show hosts in the United States appeared as themselves in episodes of *Murphy Brown*. Among them were Mike Wallace, Leeza Gibbons, Linda Ellerbee, Joan Lunden, Lesley Stahl, Larry King, and Connie Chung. The most notable, however, was legendary Walter Cronkite, who also made a brief appearance on *The Mary Tyler Moore Show* in the 1970s.

Bergen's Big Break

Candice Bergen earned limited fame as a movie actress before blossoming in *Murphy Brown*. Her most notable previous role was in the controversial 1971 film *Carnal Knowledge*, which also stars Jack Nicholson, Ann-Margret, and singer-turned-actor Art Garfunkel. Bergen played a married mother who sought to pump life into her flagging sexual relationship with her husband by making love in every room in their apartment. The movie was criticized by some for its strong sexual content.

Did You Know?

Candice Bergen declined further Emmy nominations as Murphy Brown after winning five for Outstanding Lead Actress. She had been nominated seven times through 1994.

They Said It

> **Murphy:** [arguing with a Russian journalist] Oh yeah? Well I can't take ANYTHING you say seriously with that stupid accent. You sound like you should be 'plottink beeg trabble for moose and skvirrel'!

> **Kay:** Oh, good morning, my little worker ants! That's just a figure of speech; I would never compare you to insects. At least not after that sensitivity training seminar those maggots at the network forced me to attend.

Major Awards

EMMY AWARD WINS (18)

1989 (4): Outstanding Lead Actress in a Comedy Series (Candice Bergen); Outstanding Guest Actress in a Comedy Series (Colleen Dewhurst for "Mama Said"); Outstanding Writing in a Comedy Series (Diane English for the pilot, "Respect"); Outstanding Editing for a Series, Multi-Camera Production (Tucker Wiard for "Respect")

1990 (3): Outstanding Comedy Series; Outstanding Lead Actress in a Comedy Series (Candice Bergen); Outstanding Guest Actor in a Comedy Series (Jay Thomas for "Heart of Gold")

1991 (5): Outstanding Guest Actor in a Comedy Series (Jay Thomas for "Gold Rush"); Outstanding Guest Actress in a Comedy Series (Colleen Dewhurst for "Bob and Murphy and Ted and Avery"); Outstanding Writing in a Comedy Series (Gary Dontzig and Steven Peterman for "Jingle Hell, Jingle Hell, Jingle All the Way"); Outstanding Editing for a Series, Multi-Camera Production (Tucker Wiard for "On Another Plane"); Outstanding Costume Design for a Series (Bill Hargate for "Eldin Imitates Life")

1992 (3): Outstanding Comedy Series; Outstanding Lead Actress in a Comedy Series (Candice Bergen); Outstanding Individual Achievement in Directing in a Comedy Series (Barnet Kellman for "Birth 101")

1994 (2): Outstanding Lead Actress in a Comedy Series (Candice Bergen); Outstanding Guest Actor in a Comedy Series (Martin Sheen for "Angst for the Memories")

1995 (1): Outstanding Lead Actress in a Comedy Series (Candice Bergen)

EMMY AWARD NOMINATIONS, IN ADDITION TO WINS (44)

1989 (7): Outstanding Comedy Series; Outstanding Supporting Actor in a Comedy Series (Joe Regalbuto); Outstanding Supporting Actress in a Comedy Series (Faith Ford); Outstanding Directing in a Comedy Series (Barnet Kellman for the pilot, "Respect"); Outstanding Art Direction for a Series (Roy Christopher and Steve Rostine for "Mama Said"); Outstanding Costume Design for a Series (Bill Hargate for "Soul Man"); Outstanding Editing for a Series, Multi-Camera Production (Jerry Davis for "It's How You Play the Game")

1990 (9): Outstanding Supporting Actor in a Comedy Series (Charles Kimbrough); Outstanding Supporting Actress in a Comedy Series (Faith Ford); Outstanding Guest Actor in a Comedy Series (Darren McGavin for "Brown Like Me"); Outstanding Guest Actress in a Comedy Series (Morgan Fairchild for "TV or Not TV"); Outstanding Writing in a Comedy Series (Diane English for "Brown Like Me"); Outstanding Directing in a Comedy Series (Barnet Kellman for "Brown Like Me"); Outstanding Costume Design for a Series (Bill Hargate for "Brown Like Me"); Outstanding Editing for a Series, Multi-Camera Production (Tucker Wiard for "The Strike"); Outstanding Sound Mixing for a Comedy Series or a Special (John Hicks, David E. Fluhr, and Rick Himot for "The Strike")

1991 (8): Outstanding Comedy Series; Outstanding Lead Actress in a Comedy Series (Candice Bergen); Outstanding Supporting Actress in a Comedy Series (Faith Ford); Outstanding Guest Actor in a Comedy Series (Alan Oppenheimer for "Strike Two"); Outstanding Writing in a Comedy Series (Diane English for "On Another Plane"); Outstanding Directing in a Comedy Series (Barnet Kellman for "On Another Plane"); Outstanding Art Direction for a Series (Roy Christopher and Steve Rostine for "Retreat"); Outstanding Sound Mixing for a Comedy Series or a Special (John Hicks, David E. Fluhr, and Rick Himot for "On Another Plane")

1992 (6): Outstanding Supporting Actor in a Comedy Series (Jay Thomas); Outstanding Supporting Actress in a Comedy Series (Faith Ford); Outstanding Individual Achievement in Writing in a Comedy Series (Diane English and Korby Siamis for "Uh-Oh: Part II"); Outstanding Individual Achievement in Writing in a Comedy Series (Steven Peterman and Gary Dontzig for "Come Out, Come Out, Wherever You Are"); Outstanding Individual Achievement in Directing in a Comedy Series (Lee Shallat-Chemel for "Send in the Clowns"); Outstanding Individual Achievement in Editing for a Series, Multi-Camera Production (Tucker Wiard for "Send in the Clowns")

1993 (6): Outstanding Comedy Series; Outstanding Lead Actress in a Comedy Series (Candice Bergen); Outstanding Individual Achievement in Directing in a Comedy Series (Peter Bonerz for "You Say Potatoe, I Say Potato"); Outstanding Individual Achievement in Editing for a Series, Multi-Camera Production (Tucker Wiard for "The World According to Avery"); Outstanding Individual Achievement in Hairstyling for a Series (Judy Crown for "A Year to Remember"); Outstanding Individual Achievement in Makeup for a Series (Rick Stratton and Patricia Messina for "One")

1994 (3): Outstanding Supporting Actress in a Comedy Series (Faith Ford); Outstanding Guest Actress in a Comedy Series (Marcia Wallace for "Anything but Cured"); Outstanding Individual Achievement in Editing for a Series, Multi-Camera Production (Robert Souders and Tucker Wiard for "Socks and the Single Woman")

1995 (2): Outstanding Guest Actor in a Comedy Series (Robert Pastorelli for "Eldin Bernecky"); Outstanding Guest Actor in a Comedy Series (Paul Reubens for "Andrew J. Lansing III")

1996 (1): Outstanding Individual Achievement in Editing for a Series, Multi-Camera Production (Tucker Wiard for "Up in Smoke")

1998 (2): Outstanding Guest Actress in a Comedy Series (Bette Midler for "Never Can Say Good-bye"); Outstanding Multi-Camera Picture Editing for a Series (Tucker Wiard for "Opus One")

GOLDEN GLOBE WINS (3)

1989 (1): Best Performance by an Actress in a TV Series, Musical/Comedy (Candice Bergen)

1990 (1): Best TV Series, Musical/Comedy

1992 (1): Best Performance by an Actress in a TV Series, Musical/Comedy (Candice Bergen)

GOLDEN GLOBE NOMINATIONS, IN ADDITION TO WINS (10)

1989 (1): Best TV Series, Musical/Comedy

1990 (1): Best Performance by an Actress in a TV Series, Musical/Comedy (Candice Bergen)

1991 (2): Best Performance by an Actress in a TV Series, Musical/Comedy (Candice Bergen); Best Performance by an Actress in a Supporting Role in a Series, Mini-Series, or Motion Picture Made for TV (Faith Ford)

1992 (2): Best TV Series, Musical/Comedy; Best Performance by an Actress in a Supporting Role in a Series, Mini-Series, or Motion Picture Made for TV (Faith Ford)

1993 (1): Best Performance by an Actress in a TV Series, Musical/Comedy (Candice Bergen)

1994 (1): Best Performance by an Actress in a TV Series, Musical/Comedy (Candice Bergen)

1995 (1): Best Performance by an Actress in a TV Series, Musical/Comedy (Candice Bergen)

1996 (1): Best Performance by an Actress in a TV Series, Musical/Comedy (Candice Bergen)

HUMANITAS PRIZE

1994: 30-Minute Category (Rob Bragin)
1998: 30-Minute Category (Marilyn Suzanne Miller)

PEABODY AWARD

1992: CBS

Further Reading

Bergen, Candice. *Knock Wood*. New York: Linden Press/Simon & Schuster, 1984.

"Dan Quayle vs. Murphy Brown." *Time Magazine*, January 1, 1992. Available online at www .time.com/time/magazine/article/0,9171,975627,00.html.

Klein, Allison. *What Would Murphy Brown Do? How the Women of Prime Time Changed Our Lives*. Berkeley, CA: Seal Press, 2006.

✷ 13 ✷

The Cosby Show

(1984–1992)

Cast: Bill Cosby (Dr. Heathcliff Huxtable), Phylicia Rashad (Clair Huxtable), Sabrina Le Beauf (Sondra Huxtable Tibideaux), Lisa Bonet (Denise Huxtable Kendall), Malcolm-Jamal Warner (Theodore Huxtable), Tempestt Bledsoe (Vanessa Huxtable), Keshia Knight Pulliam (Rudy Huxtable), Geoffrey Owens (Elvin Tibideaux), Joseph C. Phillips (Martin Kendall)

Created by: Writers Bill Cosby, Ed. Weinberger, and Michael Leeson

Network: NBC

First Air Date: September 20, 1984

Last Air Date: September 17, 1992

Broadcast History:

September 20, 1984–June 1982: Thursday at 8:00–8:30 PM

July 1992–September 17, 1992: Thursday at 8:30–9:00 PM

Seasons: 8

Episodes: 200

Ratings History: 1984–1985 (3), 1985–1986 (1), 1986–1987 (1), 1987–1988 (1), 1988–1989 (1), 1989–1990 (1), 1990–1991 (5), 1991–1992 (18)

Malcolm-Jamal Warner, Keshia Knight Pulliam, Bill Cosby, Tempestt Bledsoe, Phylicia Rashad, and Lisa Bonet. *NBC/Photofest ©NBC*

Overview

Educated and ethical major black characters had been sprinkled into the television scene well before *The Cosby Show* took America by storm in 1984. Such characters as Julia (Diahann Carroll on *Julia*), Benson (Robert Guillaume on *Soap* and *Benson*), and Florida Evans (Esther Rolle on *Maude* and *Good Times*) were highly principled and articulate. But such exceptions were vastly outnumbered by portrayals of lowbrow, clownish, or downright deceitful black characters, for example, Fred Sanford (Redd Foxx on *Sanford and Son*), J. J. Evans (Jimmie Walker on *Good Times*), and "Rerun" Stubbs (Fred Berry on *What's Happening*).

The result of greater professional economic opportunities for blacks during that era had yet to be translated onto the small screen. The huge majority of black families on television, with the "movin' on up" Jeffersons as one exception, struggled financially and resided in poor neighborhoods, despite the influx of blacks now solidly entrenched in the middle and even upper classes. Some complained that a sitcom needed to be created that would give black youth more positive role models and white viewers a chance to embrace complex, highbrow, moralistic black characters. Along came *The Cosby Show*, which tossed all negative black stereotypes out the window.

Bill Cosby had been the most important black entertainer since becoming the first major cast member of a television drama when he landed the role of Alexander

Scott in the detective drama *I Spy* in 1965, which earned him three Emmy Awards for Outstanding Continued Performance by an Actor in a Leading Role in a Dramatic Series. His stand-up comedy had also attracted a huge white following in an era when black entertainers struggled mightily to gain acceptance. That attraction allowed him to sway both black and white viewers to tune in to *The Cosby Show*. When they did, they watched a proud, self-actualized black family grow and love, and the audience loved the sophisticated, character-driven humor to the tune of five consecutive seasons ranked number one in the Nielsen ratings, matching *All in the Family* for the longest such run in the history of American television.

Cosby played husband and father Dr. Heathcliff Huxtable, whose love and respect for wife Clair (Phylicia Rashad) was apparent with every glance and playful moment. That Cliff was an obstetrician-gynecologist and Clair an attorney was the not-so-subtle first clue that this sitcom featuring a black family would be different from any before it. But the couple did not eschew their black heritage in living among the predominantly white upper crust. Their beautiful Brooklyn home that also served as Cliff's office was decorated with works created by notable African American artists. Such highly respected black musicians as Stevie Wonder, Sammy Davis Jr., and B. B. King appeared on the show, and episode themes sometimes delved into the importance of acknowledging and learning from both distant and recent black history.

The students of that history were the Huxtable kids, all of whom were deep and thoughtful characters searching for happiness. Perhaps the funniest of the group was scheming Theo (Malcolm-Jamal Warner), who often put play before work, which drew stern reactions from his father. But all the Huxtable kids were intriguing. The eldest was Sondra (Sabrina Le Beauf), who in a span of four years went from Princeton University senior to proud married woman to mother of twins Winnie and Nelson, named after the Mandelas, the couple most responsible for destroying apartheid in South Africa.

Stunningly attractive Denise (Lisa Bonet) was independent, intelligent, and proud. Her foray into college life was followed in the flash-in-the-pan spin-off *A Different World*, but her adventures had just begun. Denise moved to Africa to work as a photographer's assistant before returning home in 1989, shockingly married to a U.S. Navy lieutenant with a four-year-old daughter.

Vanessa (Tempestt Bledsoe) was a typical middle child with insecurities and jealousies of her older siblings. She, too, grew out of her youthful innocence and announced in the early 1990s she was marrying a maintenance worker at her college who was twelve years her senior. Even cute little Rudy (Keshia Knight Pulliam) was a teenager by the time the show was finally cancelled in 1992. One memorable episode spotlights Rudy's misery when pet goldfish Lamont dies. Cliff chastises her siblings for their insensitivity to her plight and forces an elaborate funeral for the pet in the bathroom. In the end, however, Rudy grows disinterested in the proceedings and leaves to watch television.

The Cosby Show was criticized by some for painting what was perceived as an unrealistic portrayal of black family life. They claimed that the show creators overshot realism in their attempt to bring to the small screen a more positive depiction of black characters by featuring a doctor and attorney as wise parental figures who always had time for their five children and were practically flawless in raising them. That was certainly a valid point, but it can be argued that, just as affirmative action was used to counterbalance discrimination and inequality in real-life America, the portrayals in this sitcom were intended to offset the negative ones that were so prevailing in black comedies of the 1970s.

The proof of the show's brilliance was in the ratings and its critical acclaim. *The Cosby Show* was ultimately one of the biggest successes in television history because of its lighthearted humor tinged with drama, as well as its sensitivity and the likeable and intriguing characters—and, of course, for the foresight of casting comedic genius Bill Cosby as the lead.

Critical Cosby

Bill Cosby became the center of both positive and negative attention for his criticism of what he considered to be negligent black parents and uneducated offspring. His 2004 rant at an NAACP event entitled "We Cannot Blame the White People Any Longer" was both applauded and condemned by blacks and whites. Cosby, who earned a doctorate in education, harkened back to the civil rights movement in making his point, saying the following:

> People marched and were hit in the face with rocks to get an education, and now we've got these knuckleheads walking around. . . . They're standing on the corner and they can't speak English. I can't even talk the way these people talk. . . . You can't be a doctor with that kind of crap coming out of your mouth. In fact, you will never get any kind of job making a decent living.
>
> We, as black folks, have to do a better job. We have to start holding each other to a higher standard. [This] is no longer the white person's problem. We have got to take the neighborhood back.

Did You Know?

Cliff Huxtable was rated as the "Greatest TV Dad of All Time" in a *TV Guide* list published in 2004. He beat out second-place Ben Cartwright (Lorne Greene on *Bonanza*). The second-ranked sitcom father was Danny Williams (Danny Thomas on *Make Room for Daddy*).

They Said It

Vanessa: Rudy, what are you gonna do in life with a fourth grade education?
Rudy: Teach third grade!

Theo: [to his father after receiving a D in school] You're a doctor and Mom's a lawyer, and you're both successful in everything and that's great!

But maybe I was born to be a regular person and have a regular life. If you weren't a doctor, I wouldn't love you less, because you're my dad. So rather than feeling disappointed because I'm not like you, maybe you should accept who I am and love me anyway, because I'm your son.

Cliff: Theo . . . that's the dumbest thing I've ever heard in my life! No wonder you get D's in everything! You're afraid to try because you're afraid your brain is going to explode and it's going to ooze out of your ears. Now I'm telling you, you are going to try as hard as you can. And you're going to do it because I said so. I am your father. I brought you into this world, and I'll take you out!

Denise: Olivia what are you doing? You know you're not supposed to touch any machines in this house. Now why did you put your crayons in the washer with Theo's pants?

Olivia: Because the label on the crayon said 'washable.'

Denise: Olivia, sweetheart, that means you can wash it off the walls, your skin, or your clothes.

Olivia: I wish someone had told me that.

Major Awards

EMMY AWARD WINS (6)

1985 (3): Outstanding Comedy Series; Outstanding Writing in a Comedy Series (Ed. Weinberger and Michael Leeson for the premiere episode); Outstanding Directing in a Comedy Series (Jay Sandrich for "The Younger Woman")

1986 (3): Outstanding Guest Performer in a Comedy Series (Roscoe Lee Browne for "The Card Game"); Outstanding Directing in a Comedy Series (Jay Sandrich for "Denise's Friend"); Outstanding Editing for a Series, Multi-Camera Production (Henry Chan for "Full House")

EMMY AWARD NOMINATIONS, IN ADDITION TO WINS (23)

1985 (5): Outstanding Lead Actress in a Comedy Series (Phylicia Rashad); Outstanding Writing in a Comedy Series (Earl Pomerantz for "Good-bye Mr. Fish"); Outstanding Live and Tape Sound Mixing and Sound Effects for a Series (Rich Jacob, Alan Patapoff, David E. Fluhr, and Mauren Teller for "Presentation"); Outstanding Live and Tape Sound Mixing and Sound Effects for a Series (Alan Patapoff and Craig Porter for "Good-bye Mr. Fish"); Outstanding Technical Direction/Electronic Camerawork/Video Control for a Series (various individuals for "Presentation")

1986 (12): Outstanding Comedy Series; Outstanding Lead Actress in a Comedy Series (Phylicia Rashad); Outstanding Supporting Actor in a Comedy Series (Malcolm-Jamal Warner); Outstanding Supporting Actress in a Comedy Series

(Lisa Bonet); Outstanding Supporting Actress in a Comedy Series (Keshia Knight Pulliam); Outstanding Writing in a Comedy Series (John Markus for "Denise's Friend"); Outstanding Writing in a Comedy Series (Carmen Finestra, John Markus, and Matt Williams for "Theo's Holiday"); Outstanding Guest Performer in a Comedy Series (Earle Hyman for "Happy Anniversary"); Outstanding Guest Performer in a Comedy Series (Danny Kaye for "The Dentist"); Outstanding Guest Performer in a Comedy Series (Clarice Taylor for "Happy Anniversary"); Outstanding Guest Performer in a Comedy Series (Stevie Wonder for "A Touch of Wonder"); Outstanding Sound Mixing for a Comedy Series or a Special (Rich Jacob, Alan Patapoff, and Craig Porter for "Happy Anniversary")

1987 (4): Outstanding Comedy Series; Outstanding Directing in a Comedy Series (Jay Sandrich for "I Know That You Know"); Outstanding Editing for a Series, Multi-Camera Production (Henry Chan for "I Know That You Know"); Outstanding Sound Mixing for a Comedy Series or a Special (Rich Jacob, Alan Patapoff, Craig Porter, and Maureen Teller for "I Know That You Know")

1988 (1): Outstanding Guest Performer in a Comedy Series (Eileen Heckart for "Autumn Gifts")

1989 (1): Outstanding Guest Performer in a Comedy Series (Sammy Davis Jr. for "No Way Baby")

GOLDEN GLOBE WINS (3)

1985 (2): Best TV Series, Musical/Comedy; Best Performance by an Actor in a TV Series, Musical/Comedy (Bill Cosby)

1986 (1): Best Performance by an Actor in a TV Series, Musical/Comedy (Bill Cosby)

GOLDEN GLOBE NOMINATIONS, IN ADDITION TO WINS (3)

1986 (1): Best TV Series, Musical/Comedy

1987 (2): Best TV Series, Musical/Comedy; Best Performance by an Actor in a TV Series, Musical/Comedy (Bill Cosby)

HUMANITAS PRIZE

1985: 30-Minute Category (John Markus)
1986: 30-Minute Category (John Markus)

HUMANITAS PRIZE NOMINATIONS

1986: 30-Minute Category (Matt Williams)
1987: 30-Minute Category (Gary Kott)
1989: 30-Minute Category (John Markus, Carmen Finestra, and Gary Kott)

PEABODY AWARD

1987: NBC

Further Reading

Cosby, Bill. *Cosbyology: Essays and Observations from the Doctor of Comedy.* New York: Hyperion, 2002.

———. *I Didn't Ask to Be Born (But I'm Glad I Was).* New York: Center Street Publishing, 2011.

Fuller, Linda K. *The Cosby Show: Audiences, Impact, and Implications (Contributions to the Study of Popular Culture).* Westport, CT: Praeger, 1992.

✳ **14** ✳

The Simpsons

(1989–)

Voices: Dan Castellaneta (Homer Simpson and Grandpa Simpson), Julie Kavner (Marge Simpson and Patty and Selma), Nancy Cartwright (Bart Simpson), Yeardley Smith (Lisa Simpson and Maggie Simpson), Harry Shearer (Ned Flanders, Charles Montgomery Burns, and Smithers), Hank Azaria (Chief Clancy Wiggun and Apu), Marcia Wallace (Edna Krabappel)

Created by: Executive producer and writer Matt Groening

Network: FOX

First Air Date: December 17, 1989

Broadcast History:
> December 17, 1989–August 1990: Sunday at 8:30–9:00 PM
> August 1990–July 1994: Thursday at 8:00–8:30 PM
> August 1994: Sunday at 8:00–9:00 PM
> September 1994–October 1994: Sunday at 8:00–8:30 PM
> October 1994–December 1994: Sunday at 8:00–9:00 PM
> December 1994–July 1998: Sunday at 8:00–8:30 PM
> January 1995–February 1995: Sunday at 7:00–7:30 PM
> August 1998: Sunday at 8:00–9:00 PM
> August 1998–August 2004: Sunday at 8:00–8:30 PM
> February 2003–March 2003: Sunday at 8:30–9:00 PM
> November 2003: Sunday at 8:30–9:00 PM
> March 2004–May 2004: Sunday at 8:30–9:00 PM
> November 2004: Sunday at 8:00–8:30 PM
> January 2005–March 2005: Sunday at 9:30–10:00 PM
> March 2005–April 2005: Sunday at 9:00–9:30 PM
> May 2005–August 2005: Sunday at 8:30–9:00 PM
> September 2006–November 2006: Sunday at 7:00–7:30 PM
> April 2007–May 2007: Sunday at 8:30–9:00 PM

Seasons: 23

Episodes: 516 (through 2012)

Ratings History: 1989–1990 (30), 1990–1991 (not in Top 30), 1991–
1992 (not in Top 30), 1992–1993 (30), 1993–1994 (not in Top 30),
1994–1995 (not in Top 30), 1995–1996 (not in Top 30), 1996–1997
(not in Top 30), 1997–1998 (not in Top 30), 1998–1999 (not in Top
30), 1999–2000 (not in Top 30), 2000–2001 (21), 2001–2002 (30),
2002–2003 (25), 2003–2004 (not in Top 30), 2004–2005 (not in Top
30), 2005–2006 (not in Top 30), 2006–2007 (not in Top 30), 2007–
2008 (not in Top 30), 2008–2009 (not in Top 30), 2009–2010 (not
in Top 30), 2010–2011 (not in Top 30), 2011–2012 (not in Top 30)

Homer, Snowball II, Lisa, Maggie, Santa's Little Helper, Bart, and Marge. *FOX/Photofest
TM FOX*

Overview

It was 1989, and the newfangled Fox television network needed a jump-start. It had begun prime-time broadcasting two years earlier but had yet to challenge the big boys with any hit show. Not even *Married . . . with Children* had attracted a wide-ranging audience. The programming department decided to take a chance on transforming what had been a bumper between sketches on its *The Tracey Ullman Show* to full-fledged status on Sunday nights. It was called *The Simpsons*, and it was to be the first major prime-time animated show since what was by that time, literally and figuratively, the archaic *Flintstones*.

Yeah. Good call. *The Simpsons* is still going strong twenty-four years later. The creation of young Washington State graduate Matt Groening emerged as the most successful animated show in the history of American television. Its comedic strength is in its characters. The five members of the Simpson clan living in the fictional town of Springfield (state unknown) have become household names. There is dopey, beer-swigging simpleton dad Homer (voiced by Dan Castellaneta); sensible, caring, blue-haired mother Marge (Julie Kavner); precocious son Bart (Nancy Cartwright); wise-beyond-her-years daughter Lisa (Yeardley Smith); and baby Maggie (also Yeardley Smith), who has been sucking on her pacifier for more than two decades. Of course, none of the Simpsons or their many hilarious friends, relatives, or colleagues have aged a bit, and fans of the show wouldn't want it any other way.

In a case of delicious irony, the lazy nitwit Homer holds the job of safety inspector at a nuclear power plant. Of course, there would be no more Springfield if his care-lessness caused a meltdown, so that plotline has never been explored, but suffice it to say that Homer is far more interested in downing brews at nearby Moe's Tavern than keeping his hometown safe from himself.

Bart is too young to frequent Moe's Tavern, but he makes many a phony phone call to the establishment, much to the annoyance of the proprietor, who always realizes too late that he had been duped. In one typical exchange, Bart requests Al Coholic. Moe asks if there is an Al Coholic in his bar, and his patrons laugh. Moe wises up and calls Bart a "yellow-bellied rat jackass." Later in the same episode, Bart calls for Oliver Clothesoff, and the fun starts again. It's no wonder Bart drives everyone around him crazy, as he skateboards his way in and out of jams with a life-be-damned attitude one can only imagine would change if he ever grew up. Some real-life adults might consider such a troublemaking underachiever a bad influence on young boys, who certainly adore him. T-shirts and other paraphernalia sporting such Bart catchphrases as "Don't have a cow, man!" and "Ay, Caramba!" flew off the shelves as he emerged as a full-fledged phenomenon.

The females of the family have proved far more levelheaded—someone had to keep the guys in line. Environmentalist Lisa actually cares deeply about those with whom she shares the planet. Her brilliance in the classroom and as a saxophone prodigy would draw greater attention if her brother and father were not so busy get-ting themselves and everyone around them in trouble, and her mother isn't always so busy cleaning up the mess.

The hilarity doesn't end with the Simpsons themselves. The ever-expanding cast of recurring characters has been entertaining viewers for more than two decades. Perhaps the funniest—and certainly the most evil—is scheming, unfeeling Charles

Montgomery Burns (Harry Shearer), who plays Homer's boss at the nuclear plant. Then there are Marge's outrageously negative, chain-smoking twin sisters Patty and Selma (Kavner), who make no secret of their hatred for Homer. Then there is deeply religious neighbor Ned Flanders (Shearer), defender of all he perceives as moral in Springfield. And Homer's crusty father, Grandpa Simpson (Castellaneta), is the town historian. Then there is . . . well . . . you get the idea. Dozens of unique supporting characters have helped make *The Simpsons* easily the most successful animated program ever.

There are even hilarious animated TV characters within the animated TV show. Bart's favorite is Krusty the Clown, who shows to the kiddies at home the ultraviolent cat and mouse cartoon *Itchy and Scratchy*, which features the former (the mouse) delightfully turning Scratchy into a bloody, mangled mess or simply blowing him up.

Everything is fair game for *The Simpsons*, which pokes fun at many aspects of pop culture and modern society. One episode that clearly parodies thriller film *Cape Feare* features madman Sideshow Bob, whose threatening tone is voiced perfectly by *Cheers* and *Frasier* star Kelsey Grammer, getting paroled from prison and stalking Bart. The boy, who has always lived by his wits, survives only because he says his last request was to have Sideshow Bob sing the entire score of the comic opera *H.M.S. Pinafore*. That buys enough time for the boat they are in to run aground and for the police to arrive to arrest Sideshow Bob.

The Simpsons has not blossomed into an American institution through one-dimensional humor or characterizations. The depth and breadth of both have made it one of the most brilliant sitcoms of all time. The show elicits laughs through comedy that ranges from slapstick, as displayed on *Itchy and Scratchy*, to sociopolitical, as can be taken from its satirical takes on such issues as gun control, homosexuality, religion, and television itself. Its wide-ranging characters appeal to viewers of almost every demographic because everyone is bound to embrace the personality and humor of someone on *The Simpsons*.

Gobs of Great Guests

The number of famous actors, musicians, and athletes who have lent their talents as guest voices on *The Simpsons* is mind-boggling. The following sections serve as a *partial* alphabetical list, separated into categories.

ACTORS

Ed Asner, Alec Baldwin, Anne Bancroft, Drew Barrymore, Halle Berry, Ernest Borgnine, Steve Carell, Glenn Close, Willem Dafoe, Ted Danson, Zooey Deschanel, Danny DeVito, Kirk Douglas, Jodie Foster, Mel Gibson, Kelsey Grammer, Larry Hagman, Tom Hanks, Valerie Harper, Neil Patrick Harris, Dustin Hoffman, Ron Howard, Helen Hunt, James Earl Jones, Cloris Leachman, Jack Lemmon, Penny Marshall, Bob Newhart, Paul Newman, Mickey Rooney, Susan Sarandon, Meryl Streep, Elizabeth Taylor, Marisa Tomei, Kathleen Turner, Betty White

COMEDIANS

Mel Brooks, George Burns, George Carlin, Johnny Carson, Ellen DeGeneres, Phil Hartman, Bob Hope, Jay Leno, David Letterman, Jon Lovitz, Steve Martin

MUSICIANS

Aerosmith, Tony Bennett, Johnny Cash, David Crosby, the Dixie Chicks, Lady Gaga, George Harrison, Michael Jackson, Mick Jagger, Elton John, Little Richard, Paul McCartney, Metallica, Bette Midler, Moody Blues, Willie Nelson, Ted Nugent, Dolly Parton, Katy Perry, Tom Petty, R.E.M., Keith Richards, Kid Rock, Linda Ronstadt, Sonic Youth, Britney Spears, Ringo Starr, Sting, James Taylor, The Who, Hank Williams Jr.

ATHLETES

Kareem Abdul-Jabbar, Andre Agassi, Troy Aikman, Wade Boggs, Terry Bradshaw, Tom Brady, Jose Canseco, Roger Clemens, Joe DiMaggio, Joe Frazier, Ken Griffey Jr., LeBron James, Eli Manning, Peyton Manning, Dan Marino, Don Mattingly, Joe Montana, Joe Namath, Pete Sampras, Steve Sax, Johnny Unitas, Serena Williams, Venus Williams

OTHERS

Buzz Aldrin, Lance Armstrong, Dick Clark, Bob Costas, Hugh Hefner, Larry King, Stephen King, John Madden, Rupert Murdoch, Dan Rather, Ryan Seacrest, Gore Vidal

Did You Know?

Show creator Matt Groening named several characters after close relatives. His parents were named Homer and Marge. His sisters were Lisa and Maggie. He named his sons Homer and Abe.

They Said It

Homer: Kids, just because I don't care doesn't mean I'm not listening.

Lisa: Dad, just for once don't you want to try something new?
Homer: Oh Lisa, trying is just the first step toward failure.

Krustyburger manager: We need more secret sauce. Put this mayonnaise in the sun.

Homer: You don't like your job, you don't strike. You go in every day and do it really half-assed. That's the American way.

Sherri: Hey, Bart, our dad says your dad is incompetent.
Bart: What does incompetent mean?
Terri: It means he spends more time yakking and scarfing down doughnuts than doing his job.
Bart: Oh, okay. I thought you were putting him down.

Krusty the Clown: Kids, we need to talk for a moment about Krusty Brand Chew Goo Gum Like Substance. We all knew it contained spider eggs, but the hantavirus? That came out of left field. So if you're experiencing numbness and/or comas, send five dollars to Antidote, PO Box . . ."

Major Awards

EMMY AWARD WINS (28)

1990 (1): Outstanding Animated Program for Programming One Hour or Less (for "Life in the Fast Lane")
1991 (1): Outstanding Animated Program for Programming One Hour or Less (for "Homer vs. Lisa and the 8th Commandment")
1992 (6): Outstanding Voice-Over Performance (Nancy Cartwright for "Separate Vocations"); Outstanding Voice-Over Performance (Dan Castellaneta for "Lisa's Pony"); Outstanding Voice-Over Performance (Julie Kavner for "I Married Marge"); Outstanding Voice-Over Performance (Jackie Mason for "Like Father, Like Clown"); Outstanding Voice-Over Performance (Yeardley Smith for "Lisa the Greek"); Outstanding Voice-Over Performance (Marcia Wallace for "Bart the Lover")
1993 (1): Outstanding Voice-Over Performance (Dan Castellaneta for "Mr. Plow")
1995 (1): Outstanding Animated Program for Programming One Hour or Less (for "Lisa's Wedding")
1997 (2): Outstanding Animated Program for Programming One Hour or Less (for "Homer's Phobia"); Outstanding Individual Achievement in Music and Lyrics (Alf Clausen and Ken Keeler for the song "We Put the Spring in Springfield" for "Bart after Dark")
1998 (3): Outstanding Animated Program for Programming One Hour or Less (for "Trash of the Titans"); Outstanding Voice-Over Performance (Hank Azaria); Outstanding Individual Achievement in Music and Lyrics (Alf Clausen and Ken Keeler for the song "You're Checking In [A Musical Tribute to the Betty Ford Center]" for "The City of New York vs. Homer Simpson")
2000 (1): Outstanding Animated Program for Programming One Hour or Less (for "Behind the Laughter")
2001 (2): Outstanding Animated Program for Programming Less Than One Hour (for "Homr"); Outstanding Voice-Over Performance (Hank Azaria for "Worst Episode Ever")

2003 (2): Outstanding Animated Program for Programming Less Than One Hour (for "Three Gays of the Condo"); Outstanding Voice-Over Performance (Hank Azaria for "Moe Baby Blues")

2004 (1): Outstanding Voice-Over Performance (Dan Castellaneta for "Today I Am a Clown")

2006 (2): Outstanding Animated Program for Programming Less Than One Hour (for "The Seemingly Never-Ending Story"); Outstanding Voice-Over Performance (Kelsey Grammer for "The Italian Bob")

2008 (1): Outstanding Animated Program for Programming Less Than One Hour (for "Eternal Moonshine of the Simpson Mind")

2009 (1): Outstanding Voice-Over Performance (Dan Castellaneta for "Father Knows Worst")

2010 (2): Outstanding Voice-Over Performance (Anne Hathaway for "Once upon a Time in Springfield"); Outstanding Individual Achievement in Animation (Charles Ragins for "Postcards from the Wedge")

2013 (1): Outstanding Individual Achievement in Animation (Paul Wee, Character Animation, "Treehouse of Horror XXIII")

EMMY AWARD NOMINATIONS, IN ADDITION TO WINS (48)

1990 (4): Outstanding Animated Program for Programming One Hour or Less (for "Simpsons Raosting on an Open Fire"); Outstanding Achievement in Main Title Theme Music (Danny Elfman); Outstanding Editing for a Mini-Series or a Special, Single Camera Production (Ric Eisman and Brian K. Roberts for "Simpsons Roasting on an Open Fire"); Outstanding Sound Mixing for a Comedy Series or a Special (Brad Brock, Jim Fitzpatrick, Gary Montgomery, and Brad Sherman for "Call of the Simpsons")

1991 (1): Outstanding Sound Mixing for a Comedy Series or a Special (Brad Brock, Jim Fitzpatrick, and Gary Montgomery for episode "Homer vs. Lisa and the 8th Commandment")

1992 (3): Outstanding Animated Program for Programming One Hour or Less (for "Radio Bart"); Outstanding Individual Achievement in Music Composition for a Series, Dramatic Underscore (Alf Clausen for "Treehouse of Horror II"); Outstanding Individual Achievement in Sound Mixing for a Comedy Series or a Special (Brad Brock, Peter Cole, Anthony D'Amico, and Gary Gegan for "Treehouse of Horror II")

1993 (2): Outstanding Individual Achievement in Music Composition for a Series, Dramatic Underscore (Alf Clausen for "Treehouse of Horror III"); Outstanding Individual Achievement in Sound Mixing for a Comedy Series or a Special (Brad Brock, Anthony D'Amico, Greg Orloff, and R. Russell Smith for "Treehouse of Horror III")

1994 (2): Outstanding Individual Achievement in Music Composition for a Series, Dramatic Underscore (Alf Clausen episode "Cape Feare"); Outstanding Individual Achievement in Music and Lyrics (Alf Clausen and Greg Daniels for the song "Who Needs the Kwik-E Mart?" for "Homer and Apu")

1995 (3): Outstanding Individual Achievement in Music Composition for a Series, Dramatic Underscore (Alf Clausen for "Treehouse of Horror IV"); Outstanding Individual Achievement in Music and Lyrics (Alf Clausen and John Swartzwelder for the song "We Do [The Stonecutter's Song]" for "Homer the Great"); Outstanding Individual Achievement in Sound Mixing for a Comedy Series or a Special (Ronny Cox, Anthony D'Amico, Greg Orloff, and R. Russell Smith for "Bart vs. Australia")

1996 (2): Outstanding Animated Program for Programming One Hour or Less (for "Treehouse of Horror VI"); Outstanding Individual Achievement in Music and Lyrics (Alf Clausen, Bill Oakley, and Josh Weinstein for the song "Señor Burns" for "Who Shot Mr. Burns?")

1997 (2): Outstanding Music Direction (Alf Clausen for "Simpsoncalifragilisticexpiali-i[Annoyed Grunt]cious"); Outstanding Individual Achievement in Sound Mixing for a Comedy Series or a Special (Ronny Cox, Greg Orloff, and R. Russell Smith for "The Brother from Another Series")

1998 (2): Outstanding Individual Achievement in Music Composition for a Series, Dramatic Underscore (Alf Clausen for "Treehouse of Horror VIII"); Outstanding Music Direction (Alf Clausen for "All Singing, All Dancing")

1999 (2): Outstanding Animated Program for Programming One Hour or Less (for "Viva Ned Flanders"); Outstanding Individual Achievement in Music Composition for a Series, Dramatic Underscore (Alf Clausen for "Treehouse of Horror IX")

2001 (1): Outstanding Individual Achievement in Music Composition for a Series, Dramatic Underscore (Alf Clausen for "Simpson Safari")

2002 (2): Outstanding Animated Program for Programming Less Than One Hour (for "She of Little Faith"); Outstanding Individual Achievement in Music and Lyrics (Alf Clausen and Jon Vitti for the song "Ode to Branson" for "The Old Man and the Key")

2003 (1): Outstanding Individual Achievement in Music and Lyrics (Alf Clausen, Ian Maxtone-Graham, and Ken Keeler for the song "Everybody Hates Ned Flanders" for "Dude, Where's My Ranch?")

2004 (3): Outstanding Animated Program for Programming Less Than One Hour (for "The Way We Weren't"); Outstanding Individual Achievement in Music Composition for a Series, Dramatic Underscore (Alf Clausen for "Treehouse of Horror XIV"); Outstanding Individual Achievement in Music and Lyrics (Alf Clausen and Dana Gould for the song "Vote for a Winner" for "The President Wore Pearls")

2005 (3): Outstanding Animated Program for Programming Less Than One Hour (for "Future-Drama"); Outstanding Individual Achievement in Music Composition for a Series, Dramatic Underscore (Alf Clausen for "Treehouse of Horror XV"); Outstanding Individual Achievement in Music and Lyrics (Alf Clausen and Carolyn Omine for the song "Always My Dad" for "A Star Is Torn")

2007 (1): Outstanding Animated Program for Programming Less Than One Hour (for "The Haw-Hawed Couple")

2008 (1): Outstanding Individual Achievement in Music Composition for a Series, Dramatic Underscore (Alf Clausen for "Treehouse of Horror XVIII")

2009 (4): Outstanding Animated Program for Programming Less Than One Hour (for "Gone Maggie Gone"); Outstanding Voice-Over Performance (Hank Azaria for "Eeny Teeny Maya, Moe"); Outstanding Voice-Over Performance (Harry Shearer for "The Burns and the Bees"); Outstanding Individual Achievement in Music Composition for a Series, Dramatic Underscore (Alf Clausen for "Gone Maggie Gone")

2010 (3): Outstanding Animated Program for Programming Less Than One Hour (for "Once Upon a Time in Springfield"); Outstanding Voice-Over Performance (Hank Azaria for "Moe Letter Blues"); Outstanding Voice-Over Performance (Dan Castellaneta for "Thursdays with Abie")

2011 (3): Outstanding Animated Program for Programming Less Than One Hour (for "Angry Dad: The Movie"); Outstanding Voice-Over Performance (Dan Castellaneta for "Donnie Fatso"); Outstanding Individual Achievement in Music Composition for a Series, Dramatic Underscore (Alf Clausen for "Treehouse of Horror XXI")

2012 (2): Outstanding Animated Program for Programming Less Than One Hour (for "Holidays of Future Passed"); Outstanding Voice-Over Performance (Hank Azaria for "Moe Goes from Rags to Riches")

2013 (1): Outstanding Animated Program (for episode "Treehouse of Horror XXIII")

GOLDEN GLOBE NOMINATION (1)

2003 (1): Best TV Series, Musical/Comedy

HUMANITAS PRIZE NOMINATIONS

2009: 30-Minute Category (John Frink)
2010: 30 Minute-Category (Kevin Curran)

PEABODY AWARD

1997: 20th Century Fox Television and Gracie Films

Further Reading

Clark, Kenneth R. "The Simpsons Prove Cartoons Not Just for Kids." *Chicago Tribune*, January 14, 1990, p. 3–4.

Groening, Matt, and Ray Richmond. *Simpsons World: The Ultimate Episode Guide, Seasons 1-20*. New York: HarperDesign, 2010.

Ortved, John. *The Simpsons: An Uncensored, Unauthorized History*. London: Faber & Faber, 2009.

Turner, Chris: *Planet Simpson: How a Cartoon Masterpiece Defined a Generation*. Cambridge, MA: Da Capo Press, 2005.

✴ 15 ✴

30 Rock

(2006–2013)

Cast: Tina Fey (Liz Lemon), Alec Baldwin (Jack Donaghy), Tracy Morgan (Tracy Jordan), Jane Krakowski (Jenna Maroney), Jack McBrayer (Kenneth Parcell), Scott Adsit (Pete Hornberger), Judah Friedlander (Frank Rossitano), Keith Powell (Toofer), Katrina Bowden (Cerie), Kevin Brown (Dot Com), Grizz Chapman (Grizz), John Lutz (J. D. Lutz), Maulik Pancholy (Jonathan)

Created by: Executive producer, writer, and lead actress Tina Fey

Network: NBC

First Air Date: October 11, 2006

Broadcast History:
    October 11, 2006–November 2006: Wednesday at 8:00–8:30 PM
    November 2006–March 2007: Thursday at 9:30–10:00 PM
    April 2007: Thursday at 9:00–9:30 PM
    October 2007–December 2007: Thursday at 8:30–9:00 PM
    December 2007: Thursday at 9:00 PM
    January 2008–April 2008: Thursday at 8:30–9:00 PM
    April 2008–May 2008: Thursday at 9:30–10:00 PM
    October 2008–May 2009: Thursday at 9:30–10:00 PM
    October 2009–May 2010: Thursday at 9:30–10:00 PM
    January 2010: Thursday at 9:00–9:30 PM
    April 2010: Thursday 8:30–9:00 PM
    September 2010–December 2010: Thursday at 8:30–9:00 PM
    January 2011–May 2011: Thursday at 10:00–10:30 PM
    April 2011: Thursday at 10:30 PM
    January 2012–March 2012: Thursday at 8:00–8:30 PM
    January 2012: Thursday at 9:00–9:30 PM
    March 2012–May 2012: Thursday at 8:30–9:00 PM
    March 2012: Thursday at 9:00–9:30 PM
    October 2012–January 2013: Thursday at 8:00–8:30 PM
    October 2012: Wednesday at 8:00–8:30 PM

Seasons: 7

Episodes: 138

Ratings History: Never in Top 30

Alec Baldwin, Tina Fey, and Tracy Morgan. *NBC/Photofest ©NBC; Photographer: Paul Drinkwater*

Overview

Some things are unexplainable, like the old what came first, the chicken or the egg question. The terrible ratings for *30 Rock* certainly falls into that category. The gap between the interest of the American viewer and the critical acclaim for this brilliant sitcom made the Grand Canyon look like a pothole. The sitcom spent its seven seasons buried between 69 (2008–2009) and 130 (2011–2012) in the Nielsen ratings, yet it was given its due at the Emmy Awards, snagging Outstanding Comedy Series honors every year from 2007 to 2009, and earning nominations in the same category after each of its other four seasons. Four different actors from the program won Emmys in its first three years.

Tina Fey, creator of *30 Rock*, used her experiences as head writer for *Saturday Night Live* to write this program, which spotlighted the cast of a live comedy sketch series called *The Girlie Show*, mostly behind the scenes. Part of the humor was that the program within the program ran on NBC. Fey played the same role in the sitcom as Liz Lemon, who created the comedy to provide a vehicle for off-kilter actress friend Jenna Maroney (Jane Krakowski). But Liz was in for far more than she bargained for, as her new boss at the network signed arrogant, abhorrent crackpot Jack Donaghy (Alec Baldwin) to oversee the production, giving him the silly title of vice president of East Coast television and microwave programming.

Liz could accomplish little with Jack meddling in every aspect of the operation. He ruined her plan to spotlight Jenna in the show by hiring mentally unbalanced Tracy Jordan (Tracy Morgan) to star, and even changing the name of the sketch comedy to TGS with Tracy Jordan. Jordan had hardly earned the opportunity through his movie career, which featured roles in such disasters as *Grandma Be Trippin'* and *Who Dat Ninja?*, and his emotional instability always had his colleagues on edge.

Critics claimed that *30 Rock* had little heart and that Fey made no statement with her comedy series, but fans of the show had no problem with a sitcom that worked to make them laugh with one punch line after another. They didn't watch to see strong and positive emotional bonds develop between the characters. The humor revolved around absurd personalities that led to conflicts and jokes. Perhaps the fact that the characters were not particularly relatable played a role in the poor ratings, but ridiculous people are not generally relatable to a more sane public. On the other hand, few Americans could relate to silly, exaggerated characters like Barney Fife (*The Andy Griffith Show*) or Ted Baxter (*The Mary Tyler Moore Show*), but they have remained two of the most popular characters in the history of television. Those on *30 Rock* were not as overstated, but their traits were nevertheless embellished into unreality. And the history of the medium has proven that there's nothing wrong with that, even in an era of more realistic sitcoms.

One attraction of *30 Rock* was versatility in the comedic styles of its cast members. There were the cutting, derisive put-downs from Jack; the butchering of the English language and physical humor from Tracy; and the long-winded illogical answers to questions. Other characters, including happy-go-lucky NBC page Kenneth Parcell (Jack McBrayer), producer Pete Hornberger (Scott Adsit), and sarcastic writer Frank Rossitano (Judah Friedlander), brought unique and humorous qualities to the show.

So did the sight gags and parodies. One of the latter lampooned iconic 1950s sitcom *The Honeymooners* and the physical intimidation from husband Ralph Kramden to his wife, which would never be allowed on modern television, for example, when he threatened to punch her in the face ("To the moon, Alice!"). In the *30 Rock* parody, entitled "The Lovebirds," Baldwin exaggerates the intent of the Kramden line and adds graphic detail for effect. "You're a real cut-up!," he screams at Fey after she talks back to him. "In fact, one of these days, I'm gonna cut you up into pieces and feed you to the neighbor's dog!"

The show was cancelled in January 2013, to great media fanfare, and those who loved it were left to wonder just how long it would have remained on the air had more people felt the same way. After all, most shows with ratings like those earned by *30 Rock* would have been dead and buried within two or three seasons. Some complained that NBC was to blame for placing *30 Rock* in competition against such hugely popular reality shows as *Dancing with the Stars* and *American Idol*. Fans of *30 Rock* wished it had remained on the air. They also had a message for those who never tuned in: Your loss.

The Perfect Palin

Show creator and star Tina Fey had been toiling as head writer and comedian on *Saturday Night Live* for a decade when one spot-on impression of a famous politician made her a household name. Fey nailed the look, speech, and mannerisms of vice presidential candidate Sarah Palin so perfectly in various parodies that the latter joined Fey to open the show on October 18, 2008.

They Said It

Jack: All of my summer replacement shows were big hits: 'America's Next Top Pirate,' 'Are You Stronger Than a Dog?,' 'MILF Island.'
Liz: MILF Island?
Jack: Twenty-five super-hot moms, fifty eighth-grade boys, no rules.
Liz: Oh yeah, didn't one of those women turn out to be a prostitute?
Jack: That doesn't mean she's not a wonderful, caring MILF.

Jack: Lemon, I'm impressed. You're beginning to think like a businessman.
Liz: A businesswoman.
Jack: I don't think that's a word.

Jack: Have you ever considered becoming the celebrity face of the Republican Party?
Tracy: What? Hell no! Black people supporting Republicans? Does hot support cold? Does rain support the Earth?
Jack: Now, that misperception is precisely why the GOP needs better celebrities. And a black celebrity, such as yourself, would really make us look good. Now, do you like lower taxes?
Tracy: If I paid taxes, I sure would.

Major Awards

EMMY AWARD WINS (16)

2007 (2): Outstanding Comedy Series; Outstanding Guest Actress in a Comedy Series (Elaine Stritch for "Hiatus")
2008 (7): Outstanding Comedy Series; Outstanding Lead Actor in a Comedy Series (Alec Baldwin); Outstanding Lead Actress in a Comedy Series (Tina Fey); Outstanding Guest Actor in a Comedy Series (Tim Conway for "Subway Hero"); Outstanding Writing for a Comedy Series (Tina Fey for "Cooter"); Outstanding Casting for a Comedy Series (Jennifer McNamara); Outstanding Sound Mixing for a Comedy or Drama Series (Half-Hour) and Animation (Griffin Richardson, Bill Marino, and Tony Pipitone for "Episode 210")
2009 (5): Outstanding Comedy Series; Outstanding Lead Actor in a Comedy Series (Alec Baldwin); Outstanding Writing for a Comedy Series (Matt Hubbard for "Reunion"); Outstanding Casting for a Comedy Series (Jennifer McNamara); Outstanding Picture Editing for a Comedy Series, Single or Multi-Camera (Ken Eluto for "Apollo, Apollo")
2013 (2): Outstanding Writing for a Comedy Series (Tina Fey and Tracey Wigfield for episode "Last Lunch"); Outstanding Casting for a Comedy Series

EMMY AWARD NOMINATIONS, IN ADDITION TO WINS (93)

2007 (8): Outstanding Lead Actor in a Comedy Series (Alec Baldwin); Outstanding Lead Actress in a Comedy Series (Tina Fey); Outstanding Writing for a Comedy

Series (Robert Carlock for "Jack-Tor"); Outstanding Writing for a Comedy Series (Tina Fey for "Tracy Does Conan"); Outstanding Directing for a Comedy Series (Scott Ellis for "The Break-up"); Outstanding Casting for a Comedy Series (Jennifer McNamara); Outstanding Original Main Title Theme Music (Jack Richmond for "Hard Ball"); Outstanding Sound Mixing for a Comedy or Drama Series (Half-Hour) and Animation (Griffin Richardson for "Corporate Crush")

2008 (11): Outstanding Guest Actor in a Comedy Series (Will Arnett); Outstanding Guest Actor in a Comedy Series (Steve Buscemi for "The Collection"); Outstanding Guest Actor in a Comedy Series (Rip Torn); Outstanding Guest Actress in a Comedy Series (Edie Falco); Outstanding Guest Actress in a Comedy Series (Carrie Fisher for "Rosemary's Baby"); Outstanding Guest Actress in a Comedy Series (Elaine Stritch for "Ludachristmas"); Outstanding Writing for a Comedy Series (Jack Burditt for "Rosemary's Baby"); Outstanding Directing for a Comedy Series (Michael Engler for "Rosemary's Baby"); Outstanding Cinematography for a Half-Hour Series (Vanja Cernjul for "Rosemary's Baby"); Outstanding Picture Editing for a Comedy Series, Single or Multi-Camera (Ken Eluto for "Cooter"); Outstanding Special Class, Short-Format Live-Action Entertainment Programs (Eric Gurian, Jack McBrayer, Carole Panick, Josh Silberman, and Andrew Singer for "30 Rock's Kenneth the Web Page")

2009 (19): Outstanding Lead Actress in a Comedy Series (Tina Fey); Outstanding Supporting Actor in a Comedy Series (Jack McBrayer); Outstanding Supporting Actor in a Comedy Series (Tracy Morgan); Outstanding Supporting Actress in a Comedy Series (Jane Krakowski); Outstanding Guest Actor in a Comedy Series (Alan Alda for "Mamma Mia"); Outstanding Guest Actor in a Comedy Series (Jon Hamm for "The Bubble"); Outstanding Guest Actor in a Comedy Series (Steve Martin for "Gavin Volure"); Outstanding Guest Actress in a Comedy Series (Jennifer Aniston for "The One with the Cast of Night Court"); Outstanding Guest Actress in a Comedy Series (Elaine Stritch for "Christmas Special"); Outstanding Writing for a Comedy Series (Jack Burditt and Robert Carlock for "Kidney Now!"); Outstanding Writing for a Comedy Series (Robert Carlock for "Apollo, Apollo"); Outstanding Writing for a Comedy Series (Ron Weiner for "Mamma Mia"); Outstanding Directing for a Comedy Series (Todd Holland for "Generalissimo"); Outstanding Directing for a Comedy Series (Beth McCarthy-Miller for "Reunion"); Outstanding Directing for a Comedy Series (Millicent Shelton for "Apollo, Apollo"); Outstanding Cinematography for a Half-Hour Series (Mathew Clark for "Apollo, Apollo"); Outstanding Sound Mixing for a Comedy or Drama Series (Half-Hour) and Animation (Griffin Richardson and Tony Pipitone for "Kidney Now!"); Outstanding Special Class, Short-Format Live-Action Entertainment Programs (Eric Gurian, Jack McBrayer, William Sell, Josh Silberman, and Tracey Wigfield for "30 Rock's Kenneth the Web Page"); Outstanding Creative Achievement in Interactive Media, Fiction (for "The 30 Rock Digital Experience")

2010 (15): Outstanding Comedy Series; Outstanding Lead Actor in a Comedy Series (Alec Baldwin); Outstanding Lead Actress in a Comedy Series (Tina Fey); Outstanding Supporting Actress in a Comedy Series (Jane Krakowski); Outstanding Guest Actor in a Comedy Series (Jon Hamm for "Anna Howard Shaw Day");

Outstanding Guest Actor in a Comedy Series (Will Arnett for "Into the Crevasse"); Outstanding Guest Actress in a Comedy Series (Elaine Stritch for "The Moms"); Outstanding Writing for a Comedy Series (Tina Fey and Kay Cannon for "Lee Marvin vs. Derek Jeter"); Outstanding Writing for a Comedy Series (Matt Hubbard for "Anna Howard Shaw Day"); Outstanding Directing for a Comedy Series (Don Scardino for "I Do, I Do"); Outstanding Casting for a Comedy Series (Jennifer McNamara); Outstanding Cinematography for a Half-Hour Series (Mathew Clark for "Season Four"); Outstanding Costumes for a Series (Tom Broecker, Joanna Brett, and Remy Pearce for "I Do, I Do"); Outstanding Picture Editing for a Comedy Series, Single or Multi-Camera (Ken Eluto for "Dealbreakers Talk Show #0001"); Outstanding Sound Mixing for a Comedy or Drama Series (Half-Hour) and Animation (Griffin Richardson, Bill Marino, and Tony Pipitone for "Argus")

2011 (14): Outstanding Comedy Series; Outstanding Lead Actor in a Comedy Series (Alec Baldwin); Outstanding Lead Actress in a Comedy Series (Tina Fey); Outstanding Supporting Actress in a Comedy Series (Jane Krakowski); Outstanding Guest Actor in a Comedy Series (Matt Damon for "Double-Edged Sword"); Outstanding Guest Actor in a Comedy Series (Will Arnett for "Plan B"); Outstanding Guest Actress in a Comedy Series (Elizabeth Banks for "Double-Edged Sword"); Outstanding Writing for a Comedy Series (Matt Hubbard for "Reaganing"); Outstanding Directing for a Comedy Series (Beth McCarthy-Miller for "Live Show"); Outstanding Casting for a Comedy Series (Jennifer McNamara); Outstanding Music Composition for a Series, Original Dramatic Score (Jeff Richmond for "100"); Outstanding Picture Editing for a Comedy Series, Single or Multi-Camera (Meg Reticker for "100"); Outstanding Technical Direction, Camerawork, Video Control for a Series (for "Live Show: West Coast"); Outstanding Special Class, Short-Format Live-Action Entertainment Programs (Eric Gurian, Clint Koltveit, and William Sell)

2012 (13): Outstanding Comedy Series; Outstanding Lead Actor in a Comedy Series (Alec Baldwin); Outstanding Lead Actress in a Comedy Series (Tina Fey); Outstanding Guest Actor in a Comedy Series (Jon Hamm for "Live from Studio 6H"); Outstanding Guest Actor in a Comedy Series (Will Arnett for "Idiots Are People Three"); Outstanding Guest Actress in a Comedy Series (Elizabeth Banks for "The Return of Avery Jessup"); Outstanding Guest Actress in a Comedy Series (Margaret Cho for "The Return of Avery Jessup"); Outstanding Art Direction for a Multi-Camera Series (Jennifer Greenberg, Keith Raywood, and Teresa Mastropierro for "Live from Studio 6H"); Outstanding Music Composition for a Series, Original Dramatic Score (Jeff Richmond for "The Tuxedo Begins"); Outstanding Single-Camera Picture Editing for a Comedy Series (Ken Eluto for "The Tuxedo Begins"); Outstanding Single-Camera Picture Editing for a Comedy Series (Meg Reticker for "Leap Day"); Outstanding Sound Mixing for a Comedy or Drama Series (Half-Hour) and Animation (Robert Palladino, Martin Brumbach, Josiah Gluck, and William Taylor for "Live from Studio 6H"); Outstanding Technical Direction, Camerawork, Video Control for a Series (for "Live from Studio 6H: West Coast Version")

2013 (13): Outstanding Comedy Series; Outstanding Lead Actor in a Comedy Series (Alec Baldwin); Outstanding Lead Actress in a Comedy Series (Tina Fey); Outstanding Supporting Actress in a Comedy Series (Jane Krakowski); Outstanding Guest Actor in a Comedy Series (Will Forte as Paul); Outstanding Guest Actress in a Comedy Series (Elaine Stritch as Colleen Donaghy); Outstanding Writing for a Comedy Series (Jack Burditt and Robert Carlock for episode "Hogcock!"); Outstanding Directing for a Comedy Series (Beth McCarthy-Miller for episode "Hogcock! / Last Lunch"); Outstanding Single-Camera Picture Editing for a Comedy Series; Outstanding Original Music and Lyrics (for song "Rural Juror"); Outstanding Sound Mixing for a Comedy or Drama Series (Half-Hour) and Animation; Outstanding Special Class—Short-Format Live-Action Entertainment Programs (for the Webisodes); Outstanding Special Class—Short-Format Nonfiction Programs (for The Final Season)

GOLDEN GLOBE WINS (6)

2007 (1): Best Performance by an Actor in a TV Series, Musical/Comedy (Alec Baldwin)
2008 (1): Best Performance by an Actress in a TV Series, Musical/Comedy (Tina Fey)
2009 (3): Best TV Series, Musical/Comedy; Best Performance by an Actor in a TV Series, Musical/Comedy (Alec Baldwin); Best Performance by an Actress in a TV Series, Musical/Comedy (Tina Fey)
2010 (1): Best Performance by an Actor in a TV Series, Musical/Comedy (Alec Baldwin)

GOLDEN GLOBE NOMINATIONS, IN ADDITION TO WINS (11)

2008 (2): Best TV Series, Musical/Comedy; Best Performance by an Actor in a TV Series, Musical/Comedy (Alec Baldwin)
2010 (2): Best TV Series, Musical/Comedy; Best Performance by an Actress in a TV Series, Musical/Comedy (Tina Fey)
2011 (3): Best TV Series, Musical/Comedy; Best Performance by an Actor in a TV Series, Musical/Comedy (Alec Baldwin); Best Performance by an Actress in a TV Series, Musical/Comedy (Tina Fey)
2012 (2): Best Performance by an Actor in a TV Series, Musical/Comedy (Alec Baldwin); Best Performance by an Actress in a TV Series, Musical/Comedy (Tina Fey)
2013 (2): Best Performance by an Actor in a TV Series, Musical/Comedy (Alec Baldwin); Best Performance by an Actress in a TV Series, Musical/Comedy (Tina Fey)

HUMANITAS PRIZE NOMINATION

2009: 30-Minute Category (Robert Carlock)

PEABODY AWARD

2009: Universal Media Studios, Broadway Video Television, and Little Stranger (production company)

Further Reading

Fey, Tina. *Bossypants*. New York: Reagan Arthur/Back Bay, 2011.

McFarlane, Mhairi. "30 Rock Is the Best Show on Television." *Guardian*, February 7, 2008. Available online at www.guardian.co.uk/culture/tvandradioblog/2008/feb/07/30rockisthebestshowonte.

Wisnewski, J. Jeremy. *30 Rock and Philosophy: We Want to Go There*. New York: John Wiley, 2010.

✳ **16** ✳

Everybody Loves Raymond

(1996–2005)

Cast: Ray Romano (Ray Barone), Patricia Heaton (Debra Barone), Brad Garrett (Robert Barone), Doris Roberts (Marie Barone), Peter Boyle (Frank Barone), Madylin Sweeten (Ally Barone), Sawyer Sweeten (Michael Barone), Sullivan Sweeten (Geoffrey Barone), Georgia Engel (Pat MacDougall), Monica Horan (Amy MacDougall), Fred Willard (Hank MacDougall)

Created by: Executive producer and writer Philip Rosenthal

Network: CBS

First Air Date: September 13, 1996

Last Air Date: September 12, 2005

Broadcast History:
September 13, 1996–February 1997: Friday at 8:30–9:00 PM
March 1997–August 1998: Monday at 8:30–9:00 PM
August 1998–September 1998: Monday at 9:00–10:00 PM
September 1998–June 2005: Monday at 9:00–9:30 PM
April 1999–May 1999: Wednesday at 8:00–8:30 PM
May 2004: Wednesday at 9:30–10:00 PM
July 2005–September 12, 2005: Monday at 8:30–9:00 PM

Seasons: 9

Episodes: 210

Ratings History: 1996–1997 (not in Top 30), 1997–1998 (30), 1998–1999 (11), 1999–2000 (12), 2000–2001 (5), 2001–2002 (4), 2002–2003 (7), 2003–2004 (9), 2004–2005 (9)

Brad Garrett, Peter Boyle, Doris Roberts, Ray Romano, and Patricia Heaton. *CBS/ Photofest ©CBS*

Overview

Many people like to stay close to their parents. For some, that means within driving range, while for others that means phoning them often. Only for those still tied to the umbilical cord does it mean living across the street from them.

Successful sportswriter Ray Barone (Ray Romano) was an independent man, but his parents not only lived across the street from him, they took advantage of their proximity to burst in at any time to make his life and that of his wife miserable. Romano played the lead role in the wonderfully casted, creatively written *Everybody Loves Raymond*, which thrived as a Monday night staple on CBS. The unique personalities and pronounced frailties of the characters made this one of the finest all-around sitcoms ever produced.

The series was a direct reflection on Romano's stand-up comedy routine, in which he joked about his real life as a father of three living across the street from his parents and brother, a former police officer, in Queens. Ray played a friendly, but spineless, selfish, and somewhat dense husband and father who spent every waking moment either fouling up the relationships between family members or working to undo those mistakes, for example, the time he taped a football game over his wedding, much to the horror and anger of wife Debra (Patricia Heaton). His exasperated spouse reacted angrily with great justification to his self-centered actions, which included, for instance, playing a round of golf rather than taking care of their three young children, but she provided tough love and most often found a way to straighten Ray out before the half-hour was up.

Debra could not, however, straighten out her meddling mother-in-law Marie, played in award-winning fashion by Doris Roberts, who wore out a path to the dais at the Emmys. Marie insulted Debra as a matter of course, uttering subtle put-downs about her cooking, mothering, housekeeping, and treatment of her beloved Raymond (who could do little wrong) with a condescending smile on her face. A gourmet Italian cook, she made it clear in her understated brilliance that she would love to have her little boy back eating at her dinner table. Not that Marie was a pain in the butt only to Debra. She also slighted husband Frank (Peter Boyle) at every opportunity and, quite often, with good reason. He spent most of his days and nights lounging around watching television and snacking, although he did find time to utter "holy crap!" when he was surprised and steal the code to Ray's answering machine so he could monitor his calls.

Rounding out the main cast was Brad Garrett, who brilliantly played the hulking, depressed, and hilarious police officer Robert Barone. He tried in vain to hide his jealousy of Ray's success in landing an attractive wife and happiness. Every setback for Ray prompted a sense of satisfaction for Robert, who also believed with validation that his mother liked his brother more than she did him. Robert felt ashamed that he was forced to live with his parents until he finally moved out in favor of his own apartment in 1998 and eventually married longtime girlfriend Amy (Monica Horan), who seemed overwhelmed by the constant bickering in the Barone home but managed to relate better to Marie than the prideful Debra ever could. Debra fought back against Marie, leading to a power struggle between the two for the approval of Ray, who yearned for everyone to simply get along. But that wasn't destined to happen. Neither was approval of the last-season marriage between Robert and Amy by her conservative parents Pat and Hank, played by sitcom veterans Georgia Engel (*The Mary Tyler Moore Show*) and Fred Willard (*Fernwood Tonight*).

No sitcom is flawless, and some complained about the frequent disappearing act of the three Barone children, including twin boys Michael and Geoffrey, who were a mere two years old when the show was launched. The kids gave Ray yet another opportunity to display his fumbling ineptitude in anything practical in life. Although he loved them, he struggled in his role as a father, just as he did in every aspect of his personal life, because he was driven more by immediate gratification than improving himself as a human being.

But then, all the major characters, except poor Debra, who must have felt like a straight woman in a vaudeville show, were badly flawed. The millions of viewers who made *Everybody Loves Raymond* one of the top-rated shows on television and one of the biggest hits in syndication wouldn't have had it any other way.

"Heaton" Up the Airwaves

Patricia Heaton knew all about the life of sportswriters when she played the wife of one on *Everybody Loves Raymond*. Her real-life father Chuck was a highly accomplished sportswriter with the *Cleveland Plain Dealer*. Heaton began her career in the theater before landing major roles in failed sitcoms *Someone Like Me* and *Women of the House* in the mid-1990s. Her success in *Everybody Loves Raymond* was followed by her biggest disappointment when the strongly promoted *Back to You*, in which she played a coanchor alongside fellow sitcom heavyweight Kelsey Grammer, was cancelled after seventeen episodes.

Did You Know?

Iconic late-night talk show host David Letterman served as an executive producer of *Everybody Loves Raymond*. His role was recognized by star Ray Romano, who introduced and thanked Letterman at the 35th Annual Kennedy Center Honors in December 2012.

They Said It

Ray: [after his twins have knocked his golf clubs down the stairs] Yeah . . . you won't be smiling when we send you a postcard from Disneyland.

Debra: [to daughter Ally] Honey, show daddy what you drew.
Ray: That's okay, I can figure it out. Um, let's see. A big wall of red?
Ally: No.
Debra: Ally told me that was a picture of you in hell.

Ray: This coming from the guy who once threw a shoe at a swan.
Frank: It's called protecting your sandwich!

Robert: I'm a cop and live with my parents. I'm on a constant diet of human suffering.

Major Awards

EMMY AWARD WINS (15)

2000 (1): Outstanding Lead Actress in a Comedy Series (Patricia Heaton)
2001 (3): Outstanding Lead Actress in a Comedy Series (Patricia Heaton); Outstanding Supporting Actress in a Comedy Series (Doris Roberts); Outstanding Multi-Camera Sound Mixing for a Series or a Special (Brentley Walton, Doug Gray, Anthony Constantini, and Rick Himot for "Italy")
2002 (3): Outstanding Lead Actor in a Comedy Series (Ray Romano); Outstanding Supporting Actor in a Comedy Series (Brad Garrett); Outstanding Supporting Actress in a Comedy Series (Doris Roberts)
2003 (5): Outstanding Comedy Series; Outstanding Supporting Actor in a Comedy Series (Brad Garrett); Outstanding Supporting Actress in a Comedy Series (Doris

Roberts); Outstanding Writing for a Comedy Series (Tucker Cawley for "Baggage"); Outstanding Multi-Camera Sound Mixing for a Series or a Special (Rick Himot, Kathy Oldham, and Brentley Walton for "She's the One")

2005 (3): Outstanding Comedy Series; Outstanding Supporting Actor in a Comedy Series (Brad Garrett); Outstanding Supporting Actress in a Comedy Series (Doris Roberts)

EMMY AWARD NOMINATIONS, IN ADDITION TO WINS (54)

1999 (6): Outstanding Comedy Series; Outstanding Lead Actor in a Comedy Series (Ray Romano); Outstanding Lead Actress in a Comedy Series (Patricia Heaton); Outstanding Supporting Actor in a Comedy Series (Peter Boyle); Outstanding Supporting Actress in a Comedy Series (Doris Roberts); Outstanding Directing for a Comedy Series (Will Mackenzie for "Robert's Date")

2000 (8): Outstanding Comedy Series; Outstanding Lead Actor in a Comedy Series (Ray Romano); Outstanding Supporting Actor in a Comedy Series (Brad Garrett); Outstanding Supporting Actor in a Comedy Series (Peter Boyle); Outstanding Supporting Actress in a Comedy Series (Doris Roberts); Outstanding Writing for a Comedy Series (Ray Romano and Philip Rosenthal for "Bad Moon Rising"); Outstanding Directing for a Comedy Series (Will Mackenzie for "The Christmas Picture"); Outstanding Cinematography for a Multi-Camera Series (Mike Berlin for "Robert's Rodeo")

2001 (5): Outstanding Comedy Series; Outstanding Lead Actor in a Comedy Series (Ray Romano); Outstanding Supporting Actor in a Comedy Series (Peter Boyle); Outstanding Cinematography for a Multi-Camera Series (Mike Berlin and Alessio Gelsini Toressi for "Italy"); Outstanding Multi-Camera Picture Editing for a Series (Patricia Barnett for "Italy")

2002 (8): Outstanding Comedy Series; Outstanding Lead Actress in a Comedy Series (Patricia Heaton); Outstanding Supporting Actor in a Comedy Series (Peter Boyle); Outstanding Guest Actress in a Comedy Series (Katherine Helmond); Outstanding Writing for a Comedy Series (Jennifer Crittenden for "Marie's Sculpture"); Outstanding Writing for a Comedy Series (Philip Rosenthal for "Angry Family"); Outstanding Multi-Camera Picture Editing for a Series (Patricia Barnett for "Talk to Your Daughter"); Outstanding Multi-Camera Sound Mixing for a Series or a Special (Brentley Walton, Doug Gray, Anthony Constantini, and Rick Himot for "It's Supposed to Be Fun")

2003 (8): Outstanding Lead Actor in a Comedy Series (Ray Romano); Outstanding Lead Actress in a Comedy Series (Patricia Heaton); Outstanding Supporting Actor in a Comedy Series (Peter Boyle); Outstanding Guest Actor in a Comedy Series (Fred Willard); Outstanding Guest Actress in a Comedy Series (Georgia Engel); Outstanding Writing for a Comedy Series (Mike Royce for "Counseling"); Outstanding Cinematography for a Multi-Camera Series (Mike Berlin for "It's Just a Formality"); Outstanding Multi-Camera Picture Editing for a Series (Patricia Barnett for "She's the One")

2004 (9): Outstanding Comedy Series; Outstanding Lead Actress in a Comedy Series (Patricia Heaton); Outstanding Supporting Actor in a Comedy Series (Peter Boyle); Outstanding Supporting Actor in a Comedy Series (Brad Garrett); Outstanding Supporting Actress in a Comedy Series (Doris Roberts); Outstanding Guest Actor in a Comedy Series (Fred Willard); Outstanding Guest Actress in a Comedy Series (Georgia Engel); Outstanding Multi-Camera Picture Editing for a Series (Patricia Barnett for "Golf for It"); Outstanding Multi-Camera Sound Mixing for a Series or a Special (Kathy Oldham, John Bickelhaupt, and Brentley Walton for "The Model")

2005 (10): Outstanding Lead Actor in a Comedy Series (Ray Romano); Outstanding Lead Actress in a Comedy Series (Patricia Heaton); Outstanding Supporting Actor in a Comedy Series (Peter Boyle); Outstanding Guest Actor in a Comedy Series (Fred Willard); Outstanding Guest Actress in a Comedy Series (Georgia Engel); Outstanding Writing for a Comedy Series (Philip Rosenthal, Ray Romano, Rory Rosegarten, Stu Smiley, Tucker Cawley, Lew Schneider, Steve Skrovan, Jeremy Stevens, Lisa Helfrich, Mike Royce, Mike Scully, Hollie Gailen, Ken Ornstein, Aaron Shure, Tom Caltabiano, and Leslie Caveny for "Finale"); Outstanding Directing for a Comedy Series (Gary Halvorson for "Finale"); Outstanding Cinematography for a Multi-Camera Series (Mike Berlin for "Pat's Secret"); Outstanding Multi-Camera Picture Editing for a Series (Patricia Barnett for "The Faux Pas"); Outstanding Multi-Camera Sound Mixing for a Series or a Special (Kathy Oldham, John Bickelhaupt, and Brentley Walton for "Boys' Therapy")

GOLDEN GLOBE NOMINATIONS (2)

2000 (1): Best Performance by an Actor in a TV Series, Musical/Comedy (Ray Romano)
2001 (1): Best Performance by an Actor in a TV Series, Musical/Comedy (Ray Romano)

HUMANITAS PRIZE

2001: 30-Minute Category (Jennifer Crittenden)

HUMANITAS PRIZE NOMINATION

1999: 30-Minute Category (Eric Cohen)

Further Reading

Brownfield, Paul. "Would We Ever Stop Laughing?" *Los Angeles Times*, March 4, 1999. Available online at http://articles.latimes.com/1999/mar/04/entertainment/ca-13719.

Roberts, Doris. *Are You Hungry, Dear? Life, Laughs, and Lasagna*. New York: St. Martin's Griffin, 2004.

Romano, Ray, and Philip Rosenthal. *Everybody Loves Raymond: Our Family Album*. New York: Pocket Books, 2004.

✴ 17 ✴

The Jack Benny Program

(1950–1965)

Cast: Jack Benny (Jack Benny), Eddie "Rochester" Anderson (Rochester), Don Wilson (Don Wilson), Dennis Day (Dennis Day), Mary Livingstone (Mary Livingstone)

Created by: Star Jack Benny

Network: CBS (1950–1964), NBC (1964–1965)

First Air Date: October 28, 1950

Last Air Date: April 16, 1965

Broadcast History:
October 28 1950–June 1959: Sunday at 7:30–8:00 PM
October 1959–June 1960: Sunday at 10:00–10:30 PM
October 1960–June 1962: Sunday at 9:30–10:00 PM
September 1962–September 1964: Tuesday at 9:30–10:00 PM
September 1964–September 1965: Friday at 9:30–10:00 PM

Seasons: 15

Episodes: 244

Ratings History: 1950–1951 (not in Top 30), 1951–1952 (9), 1952–1953 (12), 1953–1954 (16), 1954–1955 (7), 1955–1956 (5), 1956–1957 (10), 1957–1958 (10), 1958–1959 (28), 1959–1960 (not in Top 30), 1960–1961 (not in Top 30), 1961–1962 (not in Top 30), 1962–1963 (11), 1963–1964 (12), 1964–1965 (not in Top 30)

Jack Benny and Eddie "Rochester" Anderson. *CBS/Photofest ©CBS*

Overview

The funniest cheapskate in the history of American entertainment emerged as one of its first television stars. Jack Benny brought the radio show in which he first appeared in the early days of the Great Depression to the new medium in 1950. Although his program did not rival *I Love Lucy* in the hearts and minds of viewers, it remained a hit through most of its run.

Benny tested the television waters the first two seasons with a series of specials that aired occasionally on what would become a familiar Sunday night slot. The program then appeared just once a month from October 1952 to September 1953, and only every other week through June 1960, after which it was shown weekly. His immensely popular radio show remained on the air until 1955.

The visual brilliance of Benny's understated comedy enhanced his transition from radio to television. The incredulous stare, pause for effect, trademark hand to the cheek, and facial expression as he uttered his irritated "Well!" could now be seen by the millions of Americans who had only the opportunity to listen to him on the radio, which they had done faithfully for the previous two decades. A sense of familiarity with Benny and his routines attracted viewers who were thankful that his show maintained virtually the same format in its evolution to television.

Benny's portrayal of a tightwad, which he created in vaudeville and honed in film and radio and a career as a stand-up comedian, was in direct contrast to his real-life generosity. He was actually an accomplished violinist; his musical incompetence in front of television audiences was merely for humorous effect. His persona had been perfected through decades of work before the television show that ostensibly showed the "real Jack Benny" hit the air.

The Jack Benny Program featured elements typical to variety shows rather than sitcoms, including the opening stand-up routine provided by its star. This was not uncommon to that genre during the early days of television; George Burns and Gracie Allen did the same in front of live audiences before and after the sitcom portion of their 1950s sitcom.

Benny remained true to his radio show in casting as well. Among the stalwarts who also made the switch to the new medium was gravelly voiced Eddie "Rochester" Anderson, who continued to portray his valet. Anderson displayed greater depth and pride than many of the subservient, stereotypical black characters of his era. Despite playing the role of Benny's underling, their friendship was apparent in front of the camera, and scripts often called for Anderson to outwit his employer. Confirmation of the enlightened attitude toward African Americans came in the periodic appearances of actor Roy Glenn, who played a refined, well-spoken black man and friend of Anderson.

Anderson was far less often a butt of Benny's jokes than announcer and friend Don Wilson, whose portly frame was often the target of humor and whose distinctive voice and genial personality graced the program until its demise in 1965. That ended a long and productive professional relationship between Benny and Wilson that began in 1934.

The only other actor that appeared on a semiregular basis was Dennis Day, another longtime friend who joined the radio show five years later than Anderson and also remained with the cast until the television program was cancelled. Day, whose character remained in his early twenties on the show, despite the fact that he left it at forty-nine, provided versatility, a variety of accents for skits, and an occasional singing performance to the show.

Benny's real-life wife did not play a significant part in the program. Mary Livingstone, who married Benny in 1927, portrayed a wise-cracking girlfriend unafraid to fault Benny for his vanity and for being a skinflint. But Livingstone suffered from a severe case of stage fright, which limited her appearances.

Perhaps the most noteworthy bit actor that appeared on *The Jack Benny Program* was Mel Blanc, better known as the voice of such beloved Warner Bros. cartoon characters as Bugs Bunny, Daffy Duck, and Porky Pig. Blanc had lent his talents to Benny's radio show before following him to television. He voiced the engine of Benny's trademark Maxwell automobile, which its stingy owner was still driving despite the fact that it had gone out of production in 1925. Blanc also played the role of Professor Le Blanc, his exasperated and finally broken violin instructor. The extent of teacher frustration was illuminated in a 1964 episode, in which his psychiatrist called Benny with the news that Le Blanc was bitterly muttering and repeating the name of his student. It was revealed that Le Blanc had lost his mind because he could not lose his hearing and was forced to listen to Benny play the violin.

Benny said good night to his audience at the end of every show, but he did not do so for good until the fifteen-year run ended in 1965. *The Jack Benny Program* remains the longest-running nonanimated sitcom in American television history, losing out only to *The Simpsons*.

Stars That Briefly Shined Brightly

Perhaps no sitcom has attracted more famous guest stars than *The Jack Benny Program*. Luminaries throughout show business made appearances on the show as themselves. The following are the twelve most notable:

George Burns (10 episodes)
Jimmy Stewart (8 episodes)
Bob Hope (6 episodes)
Ed Sullivan (2 episodes)
Milton Berle (2 episodes)
Carol Burnett (2 episodes)
Johnny Carson (2 episodes)
Danny Thomas (2 episodes)
Barbara Stanwyck (2 episodes)
Jayne Mansfield (2 episodes)
Humphrey Bogart (1 episode)
Marilyn Monroe (1 episode, only TV appearance)

Many future sitcom, drama, or variety show stars bolstered their credentials by taking on roles in *The Jack Benny Program*. Included are the following:

Bea Benaderet (Blanche Morton in *The George Burns and Gracie Allen Show*, Kate Bradley in *Petticoat Junction*)
Richard Deacon (Mel Cooley on *The Dick Van Dyke Show*)
Barbara Pepper (Doris Ziffel on *Green Acres*)
Howard McNear (Floyd the Barber on *The Andy Griffith Show*)
Jack Albertson (Ed Brown on *Chico and the Man*)
Bernie Kopell (Siegfried on *Get Smart*, Jerry Bauman on *That Girl*)
Harvey Korman (various roles on *The Carol Burnett Show*)
Raymond Burr (Perry Mason on *Perry Mason*, Robert T. Ironside on *Ironside*)
Nancy Kulp (Jane Hathaway on *The Beverly Hillbillies*)
Alan Hale Jr. (the Skipper on *Gilligan's Island*)
Robert Wagner (Alexander Mundy on *It Takes a Thief*, Jonathan Hart on *Hart to Hart*)

The Unforgettable Burt Mustin

Few character actors enjoyed more storied careers than Burt Mustin, who appeared in two episodes of *The Jack Benny Program* in its last season at the age of eighty. Mustin had already earned repeating roles in such sitcoms as *Leave it to Beaver*, *The Many Loves of Dobie Gillis*, and *The Andy Griffith Show* when he played opposite Benny, but his career was far from over. He remained active for more than a decade, landing significant roles in both *All in the Family* and *Phyllis* at the age of ninety-two.

Did You Know?

In 1977, CBS aired four episodes of *The Jack Benny Program* that had been filmed in the early 1960s.

They Said It

> **Jack:** What do you think of this card I wrote for Don? 'To Don from Jackie, Oh golly, oh shucks. I hope that you like it; it cost forty bucks.'
> **Rochester:** It would have been hard to rhyme a dollar ninety-eight.

> **Thug:** Look, bud, I said, 'Your money or your life.'
> **Jack:** I'm thinking it over.

Major Awards

EMMY AWARD WINS (7)

1958 (1): Best Continuing Performance (Male) in a Series by a Comedian, Singer, Host, Dancer, M.C., Announcer, Narrator, Panelist, or any Person who Essentially Plays Himself (Jack Benny)

1959 (3): Best Comedy Series; Best Actor in a Leading Role (Continuing Character) in a Comedy Series (Jack Benny); Best Writing of a Single Program of a Comedy Series (George Balzer, Hal Goldman, Al Gordon, and Sam Perrin for episode with Ernie Kovacs)

1960 (2): Outstanding Directorial Achievement in Comedy (Ralph Levy and Bud Yorkin); Outstanding Writing Achievement in Comedy (George Balzer, Hal Goldman, Al Gordon, and Sam Perrin)

1961 (1): Outstanding Program Achievement in the Field of Humor

EMMY AWARD NOMINATIONS, IN ADDITION TO WINS (13)

1955 (2): Best Variety Series Including Musical Variety; Best Written Comedy Material (George Balzer, Milt Josefsberg, Sam Perrin, and John Tackaberry)

1956 (2): Best Comedy Series; Best Comedy Writing (George Balzer, Hal Goldman, Al Gordon, and Sam Perrin)

1957 (3): Best Series, Half Hour or Less; Best Continuing Performance by a Comedian in a Series (Jack Benny); Best Comedy Writing, Variety or Situation Comedy (George Balzer, Hal Goldman, Al Gordon, and Sam Perrin)

1958 (2): Best Comedy Series; Best Comedy Writing (George Balzer, Hal Goldman, Al Gordon, and Sam Perrin)

1959 (1): Best Direction of a Single Program of a Comedy Series (Seymour Berns for episode with Gary Cooper)

1960 (1): Outstanding Program Achievement in the Field of Humor

1963 (2): Outstanding Directorial Achievement in Comedy (Fred DeCordova); Outstanding Writing Achievement in Comedy (George Balzer, Hal Goldman, Al Gordon, and Sam Perrin)

GOLDEN GLOBE NOMINATION (1)

1964 (1): Best TV Show

Further Reading

Benny, Jack, and Joan Benny. *Sunday Nights at Seven: The Jack Benny Story.* New York: Warner Books, 1990.

Leannah, Michael. *Well! Reflections on the Life and Career of Jack Benny.* Duncan, OK: Bear-Manor Media, 2007.

✳ **18** ✳

Family Ties

(1982–1989)

Cast: Meredith Baxter-Birney (Elyse Keaton), Michael Gross (Steven Keaton), Michael J. Fox (Alex P. Keaton), Justine Bateman (Mallory Keaton), Tina Yothers (Jennifer Keaton), Brian Bonsall (Andrew Keaton), Marc Price (Irwin "Skippy" Handelman), Scott Valentine (Nick Moore), Tracy Pollan (Ellen Reed), Courteney Cox (Lauren Miller)

Created by: Producer and writer Garry David Goldberg

Network: NBC

First Air Date: September 22, 1982

Last Air Date: September 17, 1989

Broadcast History:
> September 22, 1982–March 1983: Wednesday at 9:30–10:00 PM
> March 1983–August 1983: Monday at 8:30–9:00 PM
> August 1983–December 1983: Wednesday at 9:30–10:00 PM
> January 1984–August 1987: Thursday at 8:30–9:00 PM
> August 1987–September 1987: Sunday at 8:00–9:00 PM
> September 1987–September 17, 1989: Sunday at 8:00–8:30 PM

Seasons: 7

Episodes: 180

Ratings History: 1982–1983 (not in Top 30), 1983–1984 (not in Top 30), 1984–1985 (5), 1985–1986 (2), 1986–1987 (2), 1987–1988 (17), 1988–1989 (not in Top 30)

Clockwise from top left: Michael J. Fox, Justine Bateman, Tina Yothers, Meredith Baxter-Birney, and Michael Gross. *NBC/Photofest ©NBC*

Overview

The social and political landscape had completed an unsavory 180-degree turn for many Baby Boomers when *Family Ties* debuted in September 1982. Many of the folks who were burning draft cards or bras a decade earlier had voted for president the same Ronald Reagan they once viewed as a dangerous, right-wing radical.

The times were indeed a-changin', but one fictional couple living in Columbus, Ohio, that maintained their left-wing beliefs was the Keatons. Wife Elyse (Meredith Baxter-Birney), a former folk singer who worked as an architect, and husband Steven (Michael Gross), who managed a public television station, sought to instill a set of morals and values they embraced in the 1960s into their three (eventually four) children. The trouble was, the oldest considered Reagan a god and wealth the Holy Grail, the middle one was far too superficial, and the youngest was, well, too young to understand.

The former was ultraconservative Alex (Michael J. Fox), whose bible was the *Wall Street Journal* and who laughed condescendingly when his parents regaled him with stories about their hippie days or involvement in the antiwar movement or other social and political causes of the previous generation. He dressed in a suit and tie and looked down upon those he considered his intellectual inferior—which included just about everyone. He was especially critical of sister Mallory (Justine Bateman), whose mediocre grades were a source of humor for him. Mallory indeed spent far more time and energy worrying about the social aspects of school than academic pursuits. Alex sought to groom smart-as-a-whip younger sister Jennifer (Tina Yothers) into a mini-me, but she proved far too independent a thinker and embraced the freedom of childhood.

The ideological conflict between Alex and his parents, as well as sibling rivalries and jealousies, never weakened the love that permeated the Keaton family. Viewers understood that Alex, in his own warped way, criticized Mallory because he loved her and wanted her to maximize her potential. He could never divorce himself emotionally from his parents despite his rejection of their views on life. He even learned, on occasion, that their idealism could tug at his heartstrings a lot more effectively when dealing with others than the cold, hard reality in which he believed he lived.

The familial relationships cultivated by series creator Gary David Goldberg and a slew of talented writers emerged quickly as the strength of the show. It took most viewers time to gain an appreciation of *Family Ties*, but when they did, they were hooked. The sitcom remained out of the Top 30 in the Nielsen ratings in its first two seasons before skyrocketing to number five in its third year and number two in each of the next two. By that time, an addition had joined the family, as Elyse had given birth to son Andrew, who fit in seamlessly despite a spate of jealousy experienced by Jennifer, who no longer received the attention as the youngest sibling to which she had grown accustomed. Alex groomed little Andrew in his own image; the two even shared the experience of watching *Wall Street Week* on TV.

Every character contributed humor in his or her own way. There were the understated comments from the parents, sarcastic put-downs from Alex, straight-faced expressions of ignorance from Mallory, and deadpan delivery from Jennifer. The personalities of the side characters, however, proved far less intriguing, with one notable exception. Perpetually confused family friend and neighbor Irwin "Skippy" Handelman (Marc Price), whose crush on the indifferent Mallory was never reciprocated, delivered plenty of laughs. One had to marvel at how well Skippy bounced back emotionally from the many rejections he received from the girl of his dreams.

The story line shifted in the fourth season when Alex enrolled at local Leland College (which seemed unrealistic considering his ambition and brilliant academic record) and began dating rather bland ballerina student Ellen Reed (Tracy Pollan). Far more intriguing a character was sculptor and high school dropout Nick Moore (Scott Valentine), who began a romance with Mallory and maintained it for the duration of the show. The Keaton parents were slow to accept Nick, despite his artistic side, because he seemed to lack any practicality or plan for his life.

Although the show was lighthearted for the most part, the writers occasionally tackled dark and controversial issues when creating plot lines. One episode features an uncle molesting Mallory. Another revolves around Alex seeing a therapist after a close friend is killed in a car accident. Such issues as censorship, teen pregnancy, Alzheimer's disease, and alcoholism were also spotlighted.

Despite still-strong ratings, *Family Ties* was cancelled in 1989, after Fox had emerged as a big-screen star in *Back to the Future* and *Teen Wolf*. His character left Columbus to take a job with a Wall Street investment firm, much to the chagrin of Elyse, who was saddened by the thought of losing her first-born child. But perhaps it was for the best that one of the finest sitcoms ever produced left the air before it grew stale. That allowed its legacy to be a portrayal of the 1960s generation gap in reverse and one very funny show.

On Their Way to Stardom

Two young actors that later shot to stardom appeared on *Family Ties*, one as a regular and the other who portrayed a troubled uncle. The former was Courteney Cox, who played Lauren Miller, a psychology student and girlfriend of Alex in the last two seasons of the series. Cox, who was just twenty-three years old when her first appearance aired, gained far greater fame as Monica Geller in the hit 1990s sitcom *Friends*. The latter was Tom Hanks, who blossomed into an Oscar-winning actor. In *Family Ties*, he played troubled alcoholic Uncle Ned. Hanks had already starred in short-lived sitcom *Bosom Buddies*.

They Said It

Andrew: Alex is reading me *Robin Hood*, where he robs from the poor and gives to the rich.
Steven: That's not Robin Hood. That's Ronald Reagan.

Mallory: [panicked] The light bulb is out in my bedroom! What are we going to do?

Elyse: Alex was offended by our political magazines and ripped them up.
Alex: You have no proof.
Elyse: Yes we do. We found your rattle on the floor next to the evidence.
Alex: It could have been Mallory's.
Elyse: It was your Nixon rattle.

Major Awards

EMMY AWARD WINS (5)

1986 (1): Outstanding Lead Actor in a Comedy Series (Michael J. Fox)
1987 (3): Outstanding Lead Actor in a Comedy Series (Michael J. Fox); Outstanding Writing in a Comedy Series (Gary David Goldberg and Alan Unger for "A, My Name Is Alex"); Outstanding Technical Direction/Electronic Camerawork/Video Control for a Series (Paul Basta, Eric Clay, Tom Dasbach, Richard Price, John Repcynski, and Parker Roe for "A, My Name Is Alex")
1989 (1): Outstanding Lead Actor in a Comedy Series (Michael J. Fox)

EMMY AWARD NOMINATIONS, IN ADDITION TO WINS (14)

1984 (2): Outstanding Comedy Series; Outstanding Lighting Direction (Electronic) for a Series (Mikel Neiers for "Birthday Boy")
1985 (2): Outstanding Comedy Series; Outstanding Lead Actor in a Comedy Series (Michael J. Fox)
1986 (3): Outstanding Comedy Series; Outstanding Supporting Actress in a Comedy Series (Justine Bateman); Outstanding Writing in a Comedy Series (Michael Weithorn for "The Real Thing: Part II")
1987 (4): Outstanding Comedy Series; Outstanding Supporting Actress in a Comedy Series (Justine Bateman); Outstanding Directing in a Comedy Series (Will Mackenzie for "A, My Name Is Alex"); Outstanding Editing for a Series, Multi-Camera Production (Gary Anderson and Jon Bellis for "Band on the Run")
1989 (3): Outstanding Lead Actor in a Comedy Series (Michael J. Fox); Outstanding Lighting Direction (Electronic) for a Comedy Series (Robert F. Lieu for "Alex Doesn't Live Here Anymore"); Outstanding Technical Direction/Camera/Video for a Series (Parker Roe, Paul Basta, Rick Caswell, Richard Price, Hank Geving, and Eric Clay for "Alex Doesn't Live Here Anymore")

GOLDEN GLOBE WIN (1)

1989 (1): Best Performance by an Actor in a TV Series, Musical/Comedy (Michael J. Fox)

GOLDEN GLOBE NOMINATIONS, IN ADDITION TO WIN (7)

1986 (2): Best TV Series, Musical/Comedy; Best Performance by an Actor in a TV Series, Musical/Comedy (Michael J. Fox)
1987 (3): Best TV Series, Musical/Comedy; Best Performance by an Actor in a TV Series, Musical/Comedy (Michael J. Fox); Best Performance by an Actress in a

Supporting Role in a Series, Mini-Series, or Motion Picture Made for TV (Justine Bateman)

1988 (2): Best TV Series, Musical/Comedy; Best Performance by an Actor in a TV Series, Musical/Comedy (Michael J. Fox)

HUMANITAS PRIZE

1984: 30-Minute Category (Gary David Goldberg and Ruth Bennett)
1987: 60-Minute Category (Gary David Goldberg and Alan Unger)

HUMANITAS PRIZE NOMINATIONS

1984: 30-Minute Category (Ruth Bennett)
1985: 30-Minute Category (Marc Lawrence), 30-Minute Category (Gary David Goldberg and Alan Unger)
1987: 30-Minute Category (Ruth Bennett)

Further Reading

Patterson, Thom. "What Would Alex P. Keaton Do?" *CNN*, November 1, 2006. Available online at http://edition.cnn.com/2006/POLITICS/11/01/alexpkeaton/.
Stewart, Susan. "The Parents Ate Sprouts; the Kid Stole the Show." *New York Times*, February 25, 2007. Available online at www.nytimes.com/2007/02/25/arts/television/25stew.html?_r=0.

✳ 19 ✳

Modern Family

(2009–)

Cast: Ed O'Neill (Jay Pritchett), Sofia Vergara (Gloria Delgado-Pritchett), Ty Burrell (Phil Dunphy), Jesse Tyler Ferguson (Mitchell Pritchett), Eric Stonestreet (Cameron Tucker), Julie Bowen (Claire Dunphy), Rico Rodriguez (Manny Delgado), Nolan Gould (Luke Dunphy), Sarah Hyland (Haley Dunphy), Ariel Winter (Alex Dunphy), Aubrey Anderson-Emmons (Lily Tucker-Pritchett)

Created by: Executive producers and writers Steven Levitan and Christopher Lloyd

Network: ABC

First Air Date: September 23, 2009

Broadcast History:
September 23, 2009: Wednesday at 9:00–9:30 PM

Seasons: 3

Episodes: 85 (through January 23, 2013)

Ratings History: 2009–2010 (not in Top 30), 2010–2011 (24), 2011–2012 (17)

Overview

No sitcom since *All in the Family* has made a more indelible mark on critics upon its arrival than *Modern Family*. The only show ever to earn Outstanding Comedy Series Emmys in each of its first three seasons was aptly named. Television had indeed completed a 180-degree turn from its depictions of American families in the 1950s and early 1960s (with such rare exceptions as *The Andy Griffith Show*) as boasting a mom and pop and their offspring—all Caucasian and heterosexual, of course.

Ed O'Neill, Sarah Hyland, Eric Stonestreet, Jesse Tyler Ferguson, Ariel Winter, Julie Bowen, Sofia Vergara, Nolan Gould, Rico Rodriguez, and Ty Burrell. *ABC/Photofest* ©*ABC*

Yes, times had changed by 2009, when *Modern Family* hit the airwaves featuring one traditional family, one married couple of two divorcees in which the white husband is old enough to be his Hispanic wife's father, and another of two gay men who have adopted a Vietnamese daughter. The show uses humor and its title to bring awareness and acceptance to the fact that American families, particularly in an era in which homosexuals are fighting for the right to marry, come in all forms.

Modern Family, which features a single-camera, mockumentary style of filming, follows the relationships between branches of an extended family tree. The eldest is Jay, played by Ed O'Neill, who gained fame as the self-absorbed husband Al Bundy on *Married . . . with Children*. This sixty-something divorcee is married to thirty-something Colombian stunner Gloria (Sofia Vergara), who has with her teenage son Manny (Rico Rodriguez) and who gave birth to Jay's baby son, Fulgencio.

Jay's adult daughter Claire Dunphy (Julie Bowen) from his first marriage is a homemaker wed to real estate agent Phil (Ty Burrell), who prides himself on being hip to the modern lingo and gadgetry. The traditional couple takes care of three kids—independent, confident, but gullible, teenage girl Haley (Sarah Hyland), likeable girl genius Alex (Ariel Winter), and mischievous Luke (Nolan Gould), who (to borrow a line from Linda Ronstadt) travels to the beat of a different drum, getting his head stuck in the banister and bouncing around on a trampoline in his underwear.

The gay couple consists of Jay's redheaded attorney son Mitchell (Jesse Tyler Ferguson), a worrier whose mellowness and uptight personality are counterbalanced by the carefree attitude of his trained clown partner Cameron (Eric Stonestreet). His trophy for bass catching rests next to Mitchell's award for distinguished service in the field of environmental law. Their vast differences are further explored in their parenting of adopted daughter Lily (Aubrey Anderson-Emmons).

Modern Family wasted little time in attracting premier guest stars, including Fred Willard (*Fernwood Tonight* and *Everybody Loves Raymond*) as Phil's father, Shelley Long (*Cheers*) as Jay's ex-wife, and Nathan Lane (*The Birdcage* and *The Producers*) as a showy homosexual friend of Cameron and Mitchell. The show thrives on straight situation comedy that plays off the personalities of its characters. Two such examples in one episode occur as little Lily spits out the "F" word as a flower girl at a wedding, and, meanwhile, Jay fears that his dog is suicidal. But perhaps the funniest moment in the early history of the sitcom revolves around Manny accompanying Phil to an alley in an episode in which he plans on picking up a baseball card autographed by Joe DiMaggio from a stranger. Thanks to fears about kidnapping expressed by his mother and brother, Manny grows paranoid that the man from whom the ball is to be purchased could whisk him away or even kill him, and he waits nervously in the car while Phil meets the seller. When Phil doesn't bring enough money to buy the card, the dealer points at a turkey in the car and insists that he is "takin' the Butterball." Manny, who is sitting beside the bird, thinks the man is referring to him, so he pulls out a stun gun and takes a shot, accidentally hitting Phil, who crumples and ruins the valuable card as he spazzes out from the zapping.

Few shows can make a statement while emerging as one of the premier sitcoms of a generation. *All in the Family* and *The Cosby Show* immediately come to mind, the former for its exploration of social and political issues previously uncharted, and the latter for its departure from the negatively stereotypical black family life as portrayed in the media. *Modern Family* might not be a breakthrough program at the same level, but its title certainly represents a new and open examination of what the definition of a family really is, while delivering some of the finest humor of any sitcom produced in the twenty-first century.

Rising Star

Modern Family cocreator and writer Steve Levitan had been one of the more successful television writers in Hollywood when he started work on the show. He was a mere twenty-eight years old when he began crafting episodes for the popular sitcom *Wings*. He later contributed to *Frasier* and *Just Shoot Me* (which he created), before turning his attention to *Modern Family*. Levitan toiled as both a writer and producer on each of those shows.

Did You Know?

In 2010, *Modern Family* became the first ABC sitcom to win an Outstanding Comedy Series Emmy since *The Wonder Years* in 1988.

They Said It

Claire: Okay, I checked the rest of the computers in the house—I didn't find any more porn.
Phil: That was hardly porn. It was a topless woman on a tractor. You know what they call that in Europe? A cereal commercial.

Cameron: There's a fish in nature that swims around with its babies in its mouth. That fish would look at Mitchell's relationship with his mother and say, 'That's messed up.'

Haley: Why are you guys yelling at us? We were way upstairs. Just text me.

Major Awards

EMMY AWARD WINS (18)

2010 (6): Outstanding Comedy Series; Outstanding Supporting Actor in a Comedy Series (Eric Stonestreet); Outstanding Writing for a Comedy Series (Steven Levitan and Christopher Lloyd for the pilot); Outstanding Casting for a Comedy Series (Jeff Greenberg); Outstanding Picture Editing for a Comedy Series, Single or Multi-Camera (Ryan Case for the pilot); Outstanding Sound Mixing for a Comedy or Drama Series (Half-Hour) and Animation (Stephen Tibbo, Brian R. Harman, and Dean Okrand for "En Garde")

2011 (5): Outstanding Comedy Series; Outstanding Supporting Actor in a Comedy Series (Ty Burrell); Outstanding Supporting Actress in a Comedy Series (Julie Bowen); Outstanding Directing for a Comedy Series (Michael Spiller for "Halloween"); Outstanding Writing for a Comedy Series (Jeffrey Richman and Steven Levitan for "Caught in the Act")

2012 (5): Outstanding Comedy Series; Outstanding Supporting Actor in a Comedy Series (Eric Stonestreet); Outstanding Supporting Actress in a Comedy Series (Julie Bowen); Outstanding Directing in a Comedy Series (Steven Levitan for "Baby On Board"); Outstanding Sound Mixing for a Comedy or Drama Series (Half-Hour) and Animation (Stephen Tibbo, Brian R. Harman, and Dean Okrand for "Dude Ranch")

2013 (2): Outstanding Comedy Series; Outstanding Directing in a Comedy Series (Gail Mancuso for episode "Arrested")

EMMY AWARD NOMINATIONS, IN ADDITION TO WINS (39)

2010 (8): Outstanding Supporting Actor in a Comedy Series (Ty Burrell); Outstanding Supporting Actor in a Comedy Series (Jesse Tyler Ferguson); Outstanding Supporting Actress in a Comedy Series (Sofia Vergara); Outstanding Supporting Actress in a Comedy Series (Julie Bowen); Outstanding Guest Actor in a Comedy Series (Fred Willard); Outstanding Directing for a Comedy Series (Jason Winer for the pilot); Outstanding Art Direction for a Single Camera Series (Richard Berg and Amber Marie-Angelique Haley for "Moon Landing"); Outstanding Picture Editing for a Comedy Series, Single or Multi-Camera (Jonathan Maxwell Schwartz for "Family Portrait")

2011 (12): Outstanding Supporting Actor in a Comedy Series (Ed O'Neill); Outstanding Supporting Actor in a Comedy Series (Jesse Tyler Ferguson); Outstanding Supporting Actor in a Comedy Series (Eric Stonestreet); Outstanding Supporting Actress in a Comedy Series (Sofia Vergara); Outstanding Guest Actor in a Comedy Series (Nathan Lane); Outstanding Directing for a Comedy Series (Gail Mancuso for episode "Slow Down Your Neighbors"); Outstanding Directing for a Comedy Series (Steven Levitan for "See You Next Fall"); Outstanding Art Direction for a Single-Camera Series (Richard Berg and Amber Marie-Angelique Haley for "Halloween"); Outstanding Casting for a Comedy Series (Jeff Greenberg); Outstanding Picture Editing for a Comedy Series, Single or Multi-Camera (Jonathan Maxwell Schwartz for "Slow Down Your Neighbors"); Outstanding Picture Editing for a Comedy Series, Single or Multi-Camera (Ryan Case for "Halloween"); Outstanding Sound Mixing for a Comedy or Drama Series (Half-Hour) and Animation (Stephen Tibbo, Brian R. Harman, and Dean Okrand for "Halloween")

2012 (9): Outstanding Supporting Actor in a Comedy Series (Ed O'Neill); Outstanding Supporting Actor in a Comedy Series (Jesse Tyler Ferguson); Outstanding Supporting Actor in a Comedy Series (Ty Burrell); Outstanding Supporting Actress in a Comedy Series (Sofia Vergara); Outstanding Guest Actor in a Comedy Series (Greg Kinnear for episode "Me? Jealous?"); Outstanding Directing in a Comedy Series (Jason Winer for episode "Virgin Territory"); Outstanding Casting for a Comedy Series (Jeff Greenberg); Outstanding Single-Camera Picture Editing for a Comedy Series (Steven A. Rasch for "Election Day"); Outstanding Picture Editing for a Comedy Series, Single or Multi-Camera (Ryan Case for "Leap Day")

2013 (10): Outstanding Supporting Actor in a Comedy Series (Jesse Tyler Ferguson); Outstanding Supporting Actor in a Comedy Series (Ed O'Neill); Outstanding Supporting Actor in a Comedy Series (Ty Burrell); Outstanding Supporting Actress in a Comedy Series (Sofia Vergara); Outstanding Supporting Actress in a Comedy Series (Julie Bowen); Outstanding Guest Actor in a Comedy Series (Nathan Lane); Outstanding Casting for a Comedy Series; Outstanding Single-Camera Picture Editing for a Comedy Series; Outstanding Sound Mixing for a Comedy or Drama Series (Half-Hour) and Animation; Outstanding Stunt Coordination for a Comedy Series or a Variety Program

GOLDEN GLOBE WIN (1)

2012 (1): Best TV Series, Musical/Comedy

GOLDEN GLOBE NOMINATIONS, IN ADDITION TO WIN (8)

2011 (3): Best TV Series, Musical/Comedy; Best Performance by an Actor in a Supporting Role in a Series, Mini-Series, or Motion Picture Made for Television (Eric Stonestreet); Best Performance by an Actress in a Supporting Role in a Series, Mini-Series, or Motion Picture Made for Television (Sofia Vergara)

2012 (2): Best Performance by an Actor in a Supporting Role in a Series, Mini-Series, or Motion Picture Made for Television (Eric Stonestreet); Best Performance by an Actress in a Supporting Role in a Series, Mini-Series, or Motion Picture Made for Television (Sofia Vergara)

2013 (3): Best TV Series, Musical/Comedy; Best Performance by an Actor in a Supporting Role in a Series, Mini-Series, or Motion Picture Made for Television (Eric Stonestreet); Best Performance by an Actress in a Supporting Role in a Series, Mini-Series, or Motion Picture Made for Television (Sofia Vergara)

HUMANITAS PRIZE

2011: 30-Minute Category (Abraham Higginbotham)
2012: 30-Minute Category (Abraham Higginbotham and Dan O'Shannon)

Further Reading

McNamara, Mary. "'Modern Family.'" *Los Angeles Times*, September 23, 2009. Available online at http://articles.latimes.com/2009/sep/23/entertainment/et-modernfamily23.

Writers of *Modern Family*, The. *Modern Family: Wit and Wisdom from America's Favorite Family*. New York: Hyperion, 2012.

✯ **20** ✯

Leave It to Beaver

(1957–1963)

Cast: Barbara Billingsley (June Cleaver), Hugh Beaumont (Ward Cleaver), Jerry Mathers (Theodore "Beaver" Cleaver), Tony Dow (Wally Cleaver), Ken Osmond (Eddie Haskell), Sue Randall (Miss Landers), Rusty Stevens (Larry Mondello), Frank Bank (Clarence "Lumpy" Rutherford)

Created by: Joe Connelly and Bob Mosher

Network: CBS (1957–1958) and ABC (1958–1963)

First Air Date: October 4, 1957

Last Air Date: June 20, 1963

Broadcast History:
    October 4, 1957–March 1958: Friday at 7:30–8:00 PM
    March 1958–September 1958: Wednesday at 8:00–8:30 PM
    October 1958–June 1959: Thursday at 7:30–8:00 PM
    July 1959–September 1959: Thursday at 9:00–9:30 PM
    October 1959–September 1962: Saturday at 8:30–9:00 PM
    September 1962–September 1963: Thursday at 8:30–9:00 PM

Seasons: 6

Episodes: 234

Ratings History: Never in Top 30

Overview

For any male Baby Boomer raised with a brother, the dialogue and interaction between characters Beaver and Wally Cleaver in *Leave It to Beaver* rang true and delivered a satisfying sense of nostalgia. The good-natured and combative banter, as well as love

Clockwise from top: Tony Dow, Hugh Beaumont, Jerry Mathers, and Barbara Billingsley. *ABC/Photofest ©ABC*

and affection they showed for one another, reflected the relationships of millions of real-life brothers in the 1950s and early 1960s.

And unlike other rather staid family sitcoms of the era, this one was edgy within the social and political constraints of its time. One might look no further than the two-faced, incorrigible Eddie Haskell (Ken Osmond), who greeted Cleaver parents Ward (Hugh Beaumont) and June (Barbara Billingsley) with sugary praise and phony friendliness, only to arrive in the boys' bedroom seconds later and acknowledge the sight of Beaver (Jerry Mathers) with a customary "How ya doin', squirt?" Sometimes he was caught in his deceitfulness by the Cleaver parents, for example, in the following line from a scene in which he insists to best friend Wally (Tony Dow) that Beaver should not hang out with them on a trip to the theater: "Wally, if your dumb brother tags along, I'm gonna . . . oh, good afternoon, Mrs. Cleaver. I was just telling Wallace how pleasant it would be for Theodore to accompany us to the movies."

Undaunted by such embarrassing moments, Eddie often embarked on some devious plan to make life miserable for one or both of the brothers. Eddie, Wally, Beaver, and such friends as Lumpy Rutherford (Frank Bank) and Larry Mondello (Rusty Stevens) were characters that brought realism to the small screen, which is why the show remains a syndication staple. Even Ward and June seemed like real-life parents that watched over the first wave of Baby Boomer kids.

Like "The Swamp" in *M*A*S*H*, where the love/hate relationships between the doctors blossomed, the bedroom shared by Wally and Beaver allowed viewers to get a sense of their fears about school, relationships, and dad "hollerin'" at them or for one of their many indiscretions. They worried constantly about someone making fun of them or—as they expressed it—"giving them the business." They were humorous because they did stupid and silly things that kids tend to do, unlike the children in many 1970s and 1980s sitcoms who were supposed to elicit laughs for acting and speaking like little adults. Kids are funny because they are kids. Those who wrote for Mathers and Ron Howard (Opie in *The Andy Griffith Show*) understood that.

Viewers of other family shows of the era believed that the children were truly learning life lessons when their fathers pointed out an error in judgment or action. And even though the scenes in which Ward cited the mistakes made by Beaver and how they should be corrected appeared sincere, the assumption remained that the boy was going to make an equally heinous blunder in the next episode. The intelligence of children in other family sitcoms of the 1950s and early 1960s was apparent. It was never even implied in the case of Beaver Cleaver, which added to the show's sense of realism. Wally and Beaver seemed real and uncontrolled by their parents, although they feared and respected their father. The kids in competing family sitcoms most often appeared as extensions of their parents. *Leave It to Beaver* was the first sitcom to focus on the kids (hence the title) rather than the parents, despite the blossoming into stardom of Ricky Nelson on *The Adventures of Ozzie and Harriet*.

Not that Billingsley and Beaumont were given minor roles; they were mentioned first in the opening credits. But their relationships with one another and their children were far less intriguing than that of the Wally and Beaver. They were often clueless as to the whereabouts of their kids and what their offspring were perpetrating behind their backs. Beaver, in particular, discovered too late that his best option would have been confiding in his father about whatever mess he had gotten himself into, a fact Ward inevitably explained to him. But Beaver would not have been Beaver had he showed at the same time and same channel a week later that he had grown not a lick from the experience.

On the other hand, Wally showed significant emotional growth as he reached his teenage years. He developed healthy relationships with girls, protected Beaver from Eddie and Lumpy, and gained a greater understanding of the importance of education. The show even touched upon subjects like alcoholism, which proved to be a bit of a breakthrough. Other programs before and after embraced drunkenness as a subject of humor, but rarely spotlighted it as a serious disease.

Although *Leave It to Beaver* received neither critical acclaim nor high ratings during its six-year run, it remains one of the most beloved comedies in the history of American television for its character interaction and the sense of nostalgia and realism it provides for those who lived through the era in which it aired.

The Other Famous Madge of the 1960s

The most legendary Madge of the 1960s was a manicurist that soaked her client's fingers in Palmolive dishwashing liquid in one of the most famous television advertising campaigns ever. The second most famous might have been Madge Blake, who played the permanently freaked-out mother of Beaver's friend, Larry Mondello. Two years after the cancellation of *Leave It to Beaver*, she landed the part of clueless Aunt Harriet, who could never figure out the true identity of millionaire Bruce Wayne and faithful ward Dick Grayson in the hit series *Batman*.

They Said It

June: Wally, where are you going?
Wally: I'm going over to slug Eddie.
June: That's no way to talk. This is Sunday.
Wally: You're right. I'll wait 'til tomorrow and slug him in the cafeteria.

Eddie: Your father doesn't like me.
Wally: Why would you say that?
Eddie: On account of the way he looks at me when he opens the door. Sometimes I think he'd be happier to see Khrushchev standing there.

Mr. Foster [teacher]: [reading out grades to his class] Miss Rogers, A; Mr. Haskell, B-plus; Mr. Cleaver, A-minus; Mr. Rutherford, F.
Lumpy Rutherford: An F, Mr. Foster?
Mr. Foster: Yes, Mr. Rutherford. It's the lowest grade they allow me to give.

Major Awards

EMMY AWARD NOMINATIONS (2)

1958 (2): Best New Program Series of the Year; Best Teleplay Writing Half Hour or Less (Joe Connelly and Bob Mosher for "Beaver Gets Spelled")

Further Reading

Applebaum, Irwyn. *The World According to Beaver: The Official Leave It to Beaver Book*. New York: Bantam, 1984.
Shepard, Richard. "'Busy Beaver' and His Brother." *New York Times*, October 30, 1960, Section 2, p. 15.

✳ **21** ✳

The Golden Girls

(1985–1992)

Cast: Bea Arthur (Dorothy Zbornak), Betty White (Rose Nylund), Rue McClanahan (Blanche Devereaux), Estelle Getty (Sophia Petrillo)

Created by: Executive producer and writer Susan Harris

Network: NBC

First Air Date: September 14, 1985

Last Air Date: September 14, 1992

Broadcast History:
> September 14, 1985–July 1991: Saturday at 9:00–9:30 PM
> August 1991–September 1991: Saturday at 8:00–8:30 PM
> September 1991–September 14, 1992: Saturday at 8:30–9:00 PM

Seasons: 7

Episodes: 180

Ratings History: 1985–1986 (7), 1986–1987 (5), 1987–1988 (4), 1988–1989 (6), 1989–1990 (6), 1990–1991 (10), 1991–1992 (30)

Overview

Nearly forty years had passed since the first television comedies had hit the airwaves when *The Golden Girls* debuted on NBC on September 14, 1985. Forty years had come and gone without a sitcom spotlighting a group of aging adults. Perhaps television producers and writers shied away from featuring that demographic because they believed viewers would not laugh at a reminder of their own mortality. Perhaps they believed story lines and plot lines would be lacking for characters careening toward old age. Perhaps they felt a show about golden agers simply wouldn't be funny.

Estelle Getty, Bea Arthur, Rue McClanahan, and Betty White. *NBC/Photofest ©NBC*

The Golden Girls was about golden agers, and it was very funny. It was so funny that it captured a wide enough audience to open at number seven in the Nielsen ratings and remain in the Top 10 in each of the next five seasons. It remained a Saturday night staple for seven years. The credits belong to the network; show creator Susan Harris, who had distinguished herself for her willingness to take chances by creating the satirical sitcom *Soap* in the 1970s; and one of the finest casts of main characters ever assembled. It's no wonder that the four "golden girls" appeared in all 180 episodes and no one else in more than 25.

The only problem in casting was figuring out which of the four would play what role. The original intent was to have Betty White portray the sex-starved Blanche Devereaux. After all, White had played a similar character with tremendous humor, realism, and acclaim as Sue Ann Nivens on *The Mary Tyler Moore Show*. But that part went instead to Rue McClanahan, who had shown her propensity to play a woman of rather loose morals in a memorable wife-swapping episode of *All in the Family* in the early 1970s. McClanahan nailed the character with a distinct southern accent and charm. White instead garnered the role of painfully naïve, gullible, and a bit ditzy widow Rose Nylund, which, when compared to her performance in *The Mary Tyler Moore Show*, showed her incredible range as an actress.

The only problem with the Bea Arthur role as the blunt, but caring, Dorothy Zbornak was convincing her to take it after she had initially turned it down. The character was much like Maude, with less emphasis on feminism and a bit more detectable sensitivity. Dorothy was particularly concerning of elderly mother Sophia Petrillo, played by Estelle Getty (who was actually the second-youngest of the four main cast members). The caustic, insulting eighty-something Sophia, who had moved in with the three others after a fire had destroyed her retirement home, was no warm, tender grandmotherly type.

The four characters soon interacted their way into the hearts and minds of American viewers, as well as critics. Each earned an Emmy Award within the first three seasons, by which time *The Golden Girls* had also been twice voted Outstanding Comedy Series. All but McClanahan had reached her sixties, a fact that motivated Harris to place the characters in the retirement haven of Miami.

Each of the golden girls developed unique personalities and traits that strongly distinguished one from the others. The plot lines created for them by Harris, who contributed as a writer to all the episodes, allowed all to display their comedic talents. That each of the characters was single provided story line opportunities that showed off their vulnerabilities in their relationships with men and, particularly in the case of Blanche, their aggressiveness in pursuing the opposite sex. Among those who played suitors were aging actors Dick Van Dyke (*The Dick Van Dyke Show*), Herb Edelman (*The Good Guys*), Hal Linden (*Barney Miller*), and Robert Culp (*I Spy*). Even entertainment icon Mickey Rooney and Jack Gilford, who helped create a new generation of Cracker Jack lovers through his television commercials, took on such roles.

Not all was well on the set, however. Rumors of a personality conflict between Arthur and White was thought to have played a role in the former wanting to leave the show. She stuck around long enough to have Dorothy marry Blanche's uncle Lucas (Leslie Nielsen) in the final episode, which proved to be only the final episode of *The Golden Girls*. The other three continued in a renamed series entitled *The Golden Palace*, in which they ran a hotel in Miami Beach, but the chemistry without Arthur was lacking, and it soon became apparent that the concept had run its course. That sitcom bit the dust after one season.

In didn't matter in the scope of television history. *The Golden Girls* continued to be a hit in syndication because of its warmth and humor. Its millions of fans remain indebted to NBC and Harris for taking a chance on four aging women.

Burned Coco

The pilot of *The Golden Girls* didn't include the Sophia character, but rather a gay cook named Coco (Charles Levin). Susan Harris had earned the distinction of creating the first gay character on television in Jodie Dallas (Billy Crystal in *Soap*). The addition of Sophia resulted in the subtraction of Coco.

The Amazing Betty White

The career of Betty White as a sitcom regular reached an incredible sixty years in 2013, when she continued her fourth season on the TV Land original series *Hot in Cleveland* at the age of ninety-one. Her first regular part in a sitcom was as the title character in *Life with Elizabeth* (1953–1955). In between, she landed major roles in

The Mary Tyler Moore Show and *The Golden Girls*, as well as several less successful television comedies.

White's talent in creating unique and humorous characters, as well as her love for late husband and *Password* game show host Allen Ludden and staunch animal rights activism, has made her one of the most beloved entertainment icons ever. Millions of fans of the medium have marveled at her ability to remain active and sharp into her early nineties.

Did You Know?

Andrew Gold wrote *The Golden Girls* theme song, "Thank You for Being a Friend." Gold had already been established as a prolific singer-songwriter in the 1970s. His biggest hit was "Lonely Boy," which was released as a single in 1977 and reached number seven on the Billboard charts.

They Said It

Rebecca: [to mother Blanche] I'm havin' this baby in a birthin' center. They emphasize natural childbirth without any painkillers.
Blanche: Honey, I know I told you where babies come from, but did I ever mention where they come from.

Dorothy: [on Sophia] You'll have to excuse my mother. She suffered a slight stroke a few years ago, which rendered her totally annoying.

Blanche: I treat my body like a temple.
Sophia: Yeah, open to everyone, day or night.

Rose: Now, I know no one wants to hear any of my stories right now.
Dorothy: That's always a safe bet, Rose.
Rose: But you need to hear about my cousin Ingmar. He was different. He used to do bird imitations.
Blanche: Well, what's wrong with that?
Rose: Well, let's just say you wouldn't want to park your car under their oak tree.

Major Awards

EMMY AWARD WINS (11)

1986 (4): Outstanding Comedy Series; Outstanding Lead Actress in a Comedy Series (Betty White); Outstanding Writing in a Comedy Series (Barry Fanaro and Mort Nathan for "A Little Romance"); Outstanding Technical Direction/Electronic

Camerawork/Video Control for a Series (Randy Baer, Victor Bugdadi, Gerry Bucci, Dale Carlson, Steve Jones, and Donna J. Quante)

1987 (3): Outstanding Comedy Series; Outstanding Lead Actress in a Comedy Series (Rue McClanahan); Outstanding Directing in a Comedy Series (Terry Hughes for "Isn't It Romantic?")

1988 (3): Outstanding Lead Actress in a Comedy Series (Bea Arthur); Outstanding Supporting Actress in a Comedy Series (Estelle Getty); Outstanding Technical Direction/Electronic Camerawork/Video Control for a Series (Jack Chisholm, Steve Jones, Bob Kaufman, Ritch Kenney, O. Tamburri, and Ken Tamburri)

1992 (1): Outstanding Technical Direction/Camera/Video for a Series (Dave Heckman, Chester Jackson, Randy Johnson, Steve Jones, Ritch Kenney, Bob Keys, John O'Brien, Richard Steiner, and Ken Tamburri)

EMMY AWARD NOMINATIONS, IN ADDITION TO WINS (57)

1986 (11): Outstanding Lead Actress in a Comedy Series (Rue McClanahan); Outstanding Lead Actress in a Comedy Series (Bea Arthur); Outstanding Supporting Actress in a Comedy Series (Estelle Getty); Outstanding Writing in a Comedy Series (Susan Harris for the pilot); Outstanding Directing in a Comedy Series (Jim Drake for "The Heart Attack"); Outstanding Directing in a Comedy Series (Terry Hughes for "A Little Romance"); Outstanding Editing for a Series, Multi-Camera Production (Harold McKenzie); Outstanding Art Direction for a Series (Edward Stephenson); Outstanding Costume Design for a Series (Judy Evans); Outstanding Lighting Direction (Electronic) for a Series (Alan K. Walker); Outstanding Sound Mixing for a Comedy Series or a Special (Terri Lynn Fraser, Alan Patapoff, Craig Porter, and Ken Quayle)

1987 (11): Outstanding Lead Actress in a Comedy Series (Betty White); Outstanding Lead Actress in a Comedy Series (Bea Arthur); Outstanding Supporting Actress in a Comedy Series (Estelle Getty); Outstanding Guest Performer in a Comedy Series (Herb Edelman for "The Stan Who Came to Dinner"); Outstanding Guest Performer in a Comedy Series (Lois Nettleton for "Isn't It Romantic?"); Outstanding Guest Performer in a Comedy Series (Nancy Walker for "Long Day's Journey into Marinara"); Outstanding Writing in a Comedy Series (Jeffrey Duteil for "Isn't It Romantic?"); Outstanding Editing for a Series, Multi-Camera Production (Herb McKenzie); Outstanding Sound Mixing for a Comedy Series or a Special (Richard Burns, Ed Epstein, Alan Patapoff, and Craig Porter); Outstanding Sound Mixing for a Comedy Series or a Special (Edward L. Moskowitz, John Orr, Alan Patapoff, and Craig Porter); Outstanding Technical Direction/Electronic Camerawork/Video Control for a Series (Jack Chisholm, Bob Kaufman, Ritch Kenney, O. Tamburri, Ken Tamburri, and Carol A. Wetovich)

1988 (9): Outstanding Comedy Series; Outstanding Lead Actress in a Comedy Series (Betty White); Outstanding Lead Actress in a Comedy Series (Rue McClanahan); Outstanding Guest Performer in a Comedy Series (Herb Edelman for "The Audit"); Outstanding Guest Performer in a Comedy Series (Geraldine Fitzgerald for "Mother's Day"); Outstanding Directing in a Comedy Series (Terry Hughes for "Old Friends"); Outstanding Editing for a Series, Multi-Camera Production (Jim McElroy); Outstanding Lighting Direction (Electronic) for a Comedy Series (Alan K. Walker); Outstanding Sound Mixing for a Comedy Series or a Special (Edward L. Moskowitz, Alan Patapoff, and Craig Porter)

1989 (10): Outstanding Comedy Series; Outstanding Lead Actress in a Comedy Series (Betty White); Outstanding Lead Actress in a Comedy Series (Rue McClanahan); Outstanding Lead Actress in a Comedy Series (Bea Arthur); Outstanding Supporting Actress in a Comedy Series (Estelle Getty); Outstanding Guest Actor in a Comedy Series (Jack Gilford for "Sophia's Wedding"); Outstanding Directing in a Comedy Series (Terry Hughes for "Brother Can You Spare That Jacket?"); Outstanding Lighting Direction (Electronic) for a Comedy Series (Alan K. Walker); Outstanding Sound Mixing for a Comedy Series or a Special (Edward L. Moskowitz, Alan Patapoff, and Craig Porter); Outstanding Technical Direction/Camera/Video for a Series (Chester Jackson, Steve Jones, Ritch Kenney, John D. O'Brien, O. Tamburri, and Ken Tamburri)

1990 (8): Outstanding Comedy Series; Outstanding Lead Actress in a Comedy Series (Betty White); Outstanding Supporting Actress in a Comedy Series (Estelle Getty); Outstanding Guest Actor in a Comedy Series (Jerry Orbach for "Cheaters"); Outstanding Guest Actor in a Comedy Series (Dick Van Dyke for "Love Under the Big Top"); Outstanding Directing in a Comedy Series (Terry Hughes for "Triple Play"); Outstanding Lighting Direction (Electronic) for a Comedy Series (Alan K. Walker); Outstanding Technical Direction/Camera/Video for a Series (Dave Heckman, Chester Jackson, Randy Johnson, Steve Jones, Ritch Kenney, and O. Tamburri)

1991 (6): Outstanding Comedy Series; Outstanding Lead Actress in a Comedy Series (Betty White); Outstanding Supporting Actress in a Comedy Series (Estelle Getty); Outstanding Guest Actress in a Comedy Series (Brenda Vaccaro for "Ebbtide's Revenge"); Outstanding Lighting Direction (Electronic) for a Comedy Series (Alan K. Walker); Outstanding Technical Direction/Camera/Video for a Series (Dave Heckman, Chester Jackson, Randy Johnson, Steve Jones, Ritch Kenney, and Kenneth Tamburri)

1992 (2): Outstanding Lead Actress in a Comedy Series (Betty White); Outstanding Supporting Actress in a Comedy Series (Estelle Getty)

GOLDEN GLOBE WINS (4)

1986 (2): Best TV Series, Musical/Comedy; Best Performance by an Actress in a TV Series, Musical/Comedy (Estelle Getty)
1987 (1): Best TV Series, Musical/Comedy
1988 (1): Best TV Series, Musical/Comedy

GOLDEN GLOBE NOMINATIONS, IN ADDITION TO WINS (17)

1986 (3): Best Performance by an Actress in a TV Series, Musical/Comedy (Bea Arthur); Best Performance by an Actress in a TV Series, Musical/Comedy (Betty White); Best Performance by an Actress in a TV Series, Musical/Comedy (Rue McClanahan)

1987 (4): Best Performance by an Actress in a TV Series, Musical/Comedy (Bea Arthur); Best Performance by an Actress in a TV Series, Musical/Comedy (Betty White); Best Performance by an Actress in a TV Series, Musical/Comedy (Rue McClanahan); Best Performance by an Actress in a TV Series, Musical/Comedy (Estelle Getty)

1988 (3): Best Performance by an Actress in a TV Series, Musical/Comedy (Bea Arthur); Best Performance by an Actress in a TV Series, Musical/Comedy (Betty White); Best Performance by an Actress in a TV Series, Musical/Comedy (Rue McClanahan)

1989 (3): Best TV Series, Musical/Comedy; Best Performance by an Actress in a TV Series, Musical/Comedy (Bea Arthur); Best Performance by an Actress in a TV Series, Musical/Comedy (Betty White)

1990 (1): Best TV Series, Musical/Comedy

1991 (1): Best TV Series, Musical/Comedy

1992 (2): Best TV Series, Musical/Comedy; Best Performance by an Actress in a Supporting Role in a Series, Mini-Series, or Motion Picture Made for TV (Estelle Getty)

Further Reading

Huryk, Harry. *The Golden Girls: The Ultimate Trivia Book*. Lulu.com, 2009.

McClanahan, Rue. *My First Five Husbands . . . and the Ones Who Got Away*. New York: Three Rivers Press, 2008.

Patterson, Troy. "Four Old Women Share an Apartment: Why The Golden Girls Was Sitcom Genius." *Slate*, August 29, 2009. Available online at www.slate.com/articles/arts/television/2009/04/four_old_women_share_an_apartment.html.

✳ **22** ✳

Will & Grace

(1998–2006)

Cast: Eric McCormack (Will Truman), Debra Messing (Grace Adler),
 Megan Mullally (Karen Walker), Sean Hayes (Jack McFarland),
 Shelley Morrison (Rosario Salazar)

Created by: Executive producers and writers David Kohan and Max
 Mutchnick

Network: NBC

First Air Date: September 21, 1998

Last Air Date: May 18, 2006

Broadcast History:
 September 21, 1998–November 1998: Monday at 9:30–10:00 PM
 December 1998–March 1999: Tuesday at 9:30–10:00 PM
 April 1999–May 1999: Thursday at 8:30–9:00 PM
 May 1999–July 1999: Thursday at 9:30–10:00 PM
 June 1999–September 1999: Tuesday at 9:30–10:00 PM
 August 1999–August 2003: Thursday at 9:00–9:30 PM
 May 2000: Tuesday at 8:30–9:00 PM
 August 2000–September 2000: Thursday at 8:30–9:00 PM
 January 2002: Thursday at 8:30–9:00 PM
 August 2002–September 2002: Thursday at 9:30–10:00 PM
 August 2003–September 2003: Thursday at 8:30–9:00 PM
 September 2003–January 2004: Thursday at 9:00–9:30 PM
 February 2004–April 2004: Thursday at 8:30–9:00 PM
 April 2004–July 2004: Thursday at 9:00–9:30 PM
 July 2004–September 2004: Thursday at 8:00–8:30 PM
 September 2004–December 2004: Thursday at 8:30–9:00 PM
 December 2004–January 2005: Thursday at 9:30–10:00 PM
 February 2005–June 2005: Thursday at 8:30–9:00 PM
 March 2005–May 2005: Tuesday at 8:00–8:30 PM
 July 2005: Thursday at 9:30–10:00 PM
 July 2005–December 2005: Thursday at 8:30–9:00 PM
 January 2006–May 18, 2006: Thursday at 8:00–8:30 PM

Seasons: 8

Episodes: 193

Ratings History: 1998–1999 (not in Top 30), 1999–2000 (not in Top 30), 2000–2001 (14), 2001–2002 (9), 2002–2003 (11), 2003–2004 (13), 2004–2005 (not in Top 30), 2005–2006 (not in Top 30)

Overview

Gay characters and themes had been part of American television comedy for nearly four decades before *Will & Grace* premiered in 1998. The third episode of the groundbreaking sitcom *All in the Family* in 1971 is highlighted by bigoted Archie Bunker claiming that a visitor to his home was a "queer" and a "fag." Several years later, Billy Crystal

Sean Hayes, Debra Messing, Eric McCormack, and Megan Mullally. *NBC/Photofest* ©*NBC*

embarked on playing the first openly homosexual sitcom character on *Soap*. Frequent references and minor roles to gays followed in the 1980s and 1990s. But it took this marvelously crafted sitcom to fearlessly go where none had gone before in developing well-rounded and funny major gay characters. *Will & Grace* did not revolve its comedy strictly around the issues of homosexuality, but the emotional and motivational differences between the two gay men and two straight women on the show were explored for humorous effect, as were the contrasting personalities of the gay men themselves.

The talents of the four main cast members and the intrigue provided by their characters left little need for others; only one other actor appeared in more than twenty-five of the 177 episodes. The show revolved around various relationships forged by title characters Will Truman (Eric McCormack), a gay attorney, and interior designer Grace Adler (Debra Messing), longtime friends who decided to share a Manhattan apartment.

The other gay man and straight woman on the show brought striking contrast. Will's friend Jack McFarland (Sean Hayes) was downright flaming, as was sung in *The Mary Tyler Moore Show* theme song, "with every glance and every little movement you show it." Unlike the subtleness of his friend, Jack's gestures and body language screamed out his sexual orientation. The flightiness in his personal life was matched by that of his professional life as he bounced from one job to another. Jack worked as an actor, acting teacher, dancer, salesman, waiter, student nurse, and even talk show host. Then there was Grace's business assistant and socialite Karen Walker (Megan Mullally), who wore her heterosexuality on her sleeve. Mullally brought humor to the show with her girlish voice and outrageous remarks.

Grace bounced from one man to another without satisfaction. She eventually agreed to give in to Will's requests to have his baby, but fate took her in a different turn when she met pretty boy Dr. Leo Markus (Harry Connick Jr.) on the way to the fertility clinic. She fell in love with him and they were married in 2002, but he turned out to be a two-timer. Grace discovered his infidelity, leading to their divorce.

Jack, Will, and Karen experienced their own personal traumas. Despite his staunch homosexuality, Jack married Karen's El Salvadoran housekeeper Rosario Salazar (Shelley Morrison) to prevent her deportation. Jack later discovered that he was the father of a teenage boy through a sperm bank and was forced to learn fatherhood on the job while putting up with the kid's spirited mother, played by Rosie O'Donnell. Karen was led to believe that her wealthy husband Stan, who remained unseen throughout the run of the show, had died, but he then turned up in her life again, whereupon they divorced.

The final season proved explosive as the tight-knit group split apart. Grace remarried Leo after learning she was pregnant with his baby, a decision that led to a fallout with Will, who shacked up with boyfriend Vince (Bobby Cannavale) and finally got the baby he had so desired through adoption. The title characters reconciled in an epilogue that revealed that Grace's daughter married Will's son. Meanwhile, Karen and Jack traded places financially, as the former lost all her money and the latter gained an inheritance when his tiny boyfriend was killed by a gust of wind that blew him off the balcony of their apartment in a freak accident.

Some fans of the show believe that the strange twists in the last year resulted in the loss of a sense of realism that *Will & Grace* had brought to the small screen. Its thoughtful, yet humorous, portrayal of both gay and straight life made it an important, even a breakthrough, sitcom in American television history. Critics claimed that the erratic and dramatic story lines that accompanied the final season somehow lessened its impact.

Messing Around

Debra Messing was nominated eleven times for either a Golden Globe or Emmy as female lead in *Will & Grace* and won just once. She was shut out of the former despite six nominations but did win the latter in 2003. Despite her youth (she was only thirty when *Will & Grace* debuted), Messing was a veteran sitcom actor by the time the show premiered in 1998. She had already played Jerry's love interest in two episodes of *Seinfeld* and earned regular roles in the TV series *Ned & Stacey* and *Prey*. At the end of her second appearance on *Seinfeld*, her character revealed to the Jewish title character that she was an anti-Semitic racist. Megan Mullally also acted in an episode of *Seinfeld* as George Costanza's girlfriend.

Did You Know?

Actor John Barrowman auditioned for the role of Will but lost out to Eric McCormack. Ironically, Barrowman is an admitted homosexual, while McCormack is straight.

They Said It

Karen: Good Lord. I can't believe I'm at a public pool. Why doesn't somebody just pee directly on me?

Will: [seeking a way to escape crazy neighbors] Come on, Jack, let's try the back door.
Jack: Will Truman! Coming on to me at a time like this!

Major Awards

EMMY AWARD WINS (16)

2000 (3): Outstanding Comedy Series; Outstanding Supporting Actor in a Comedy Series (Sean Hayes); Outstanding Supporting Actress in a Comedy Series (Megan Mullally)
2001 (3): Outstanding Lead Actor in a Comedy Series (Eric McCormack); Outstanding Art Direction for a Multi-Camera Series (Glenda Rovello and Melinda Ritz for "Lows in the Mid-Eighties"); Outstanding Cinematography for a Multi-Camera Series (Tony Askins for "Sons and Lovers")
2002 (2): Outstanding Art Direction for a Multi-Camera Series (Glenda Rovello and Melinda Ritz for "Cheatin' Trouble Blues"); Outstanding Cinematography for a Multi-Camera Series (Tony Askins for "A Chorus Lie")

2003 (4): Outstanding Lead Actress in a Comedy Series (Debra Messing); Outstanding Guest Actor in a Comedy Series (Gene Wilder); Outstanding Art Direction for a Multi-Camera Series (Glenda Rovello and Melinda Ritz for "23"); Outstanding Cinematography for a Multi-Camera Series (Tony Askins for "23")

2005 (2): Outstanding Guest Actor in a Comedy Series (Bobby Cannavale); Outstanding Cinematography for a Multi-Camera Series (Tony Askins for "Friends with Benefits")

2006 (2): Outstanding Supporting Actress in a Comedy Series (Megan Mullally); Outstanding Guest Actor in a Comedy Series (Leslie Jordan)

EMMY AWARD NOMINATIONS, IN ADDITION TO WINS (67)

1999 (1): Outstanding Directing for a Comedy Series (James Burrows for the pilot)

2000 (8): Outstanding Lead Actor in a Comedy Series (Eric McCormack); Outstanding Lead Actress in a Comedy Series (Debra Messing); Outstanding Guest Actress in a Comedy Series (Debbie Reynolds); Outstanding Directing for a Comedy Series (James Burrows for "Homo for the Holidays"); Outstanding Art Direction for a Multi-Camera Series (Glenda Rovello and Melinda Ritz for "Ben? Her?"); Outstanding Casting for a Comedy Series (Tracy Lilienfield); Outstanding Cinematography for a Multi-Camera Series (Tony Askins for "Acting Out"); Outstanding Multi-Camera Picture Editing for a Series (Peter Chakos for "Ben? Her?")

2001 (9): Outstanding Comedy Series; Outstanding Lead Actress in a Comedy Series (Debra Messing); Outstanding Supporting Actor in a Comedy Series (Sean Hayes); Outstanding Supporting Actress in a Comedy Series (Megan Mullally); Outstanding Writing for a Comedy Series (Jeff Greenstein for "Lows in the Mid-Eighties); Outstanding Directing for a Comedy Series (James Burrows for "Lows in the Mid-Eighties"); Outstanding Casting for a Comedy Series (Tracy Lilienfield); Outstanding Costumes for a Series (Lori Eskowitz and Mary Walbridge for "Lows in the Mid-Eighties"); Outstanding Multi-Camera Picture Editing for a Series (Peter Chakos for "Lows in the Mid-Eighties")

2002 (11): Outstanding Comedy Series; Outstanding Lead Actress in a Comedy Series (Debra Messing); Outstanding Supporting Actor in a Comedy Series (Sean Hayes); Outstanding Supporting Actress in a Comedy Series (Megan Mullally); Outstanding Guest Actor in a Comedy Series (Michael Douglas for "Fagel Attraction"); Outstanding Guest Actress in a Comedy Series (Glenn Close for "Hocus Focus"); Outstanding Directing for a Comedy Series (James Burrows for "A Chorus Lie"); Outstanding Casting for a Comedy Series (Tracy Lilienfield); Outstanding Costumes for a Series (Lori Eskowitz and Mary Walbridge for "A Moveable Feast"); Outstanding Multi-Camera Picture Editing for a Series (Peter Chakos for "A Chorus Lie"); Outstanding Multi-Camera Sound Mixing for a Series or a Special (Peter Damski, Todd Grace, and Craig Porter for "Fagel Attraction")

2003 (8): Outstanding Comedy Series; Outstanding Lead Actor in a Comedy Series (Eric McCormack); Outstanding Supporting Actor in a Comedy Series (Sean Hayes); Outstanding Supporting Actress in a Comedy Series (Megan Mullally);

Outstanding Directing for a Comedy Series (James Burrows for "23"); Outstanding Casting for a Comedy Series (Tracy Lilienfield); Outstanding Multi-Camera Picture Editing for a Series (Peter Chakos for "Marry Me a Little, Marry Me a Little More"); Outstanding Multi-Camera Sound Mixing for a Series or a Special (Peter Damski, Todd Grace, and Craig Porter for "23")

2004 (9): Outstanding Comedy Series; Outstanding Supporting Actor in a Comedy Series (Sean Hayes); Outstanding Supporting Actress in a Comedy Series (Megan Mullally); Outstanding Guest Actor in a Comedy Series (John Cleese); Outstanding Guest Actress in a Comedy Series (Eileen Brennan); Outstanding Art Direction for a Multi-Camera Series (Glenda Rovello and Melinda Ritz for "I Do, Oh, No, You Di-in't"); Outstanding Cinematography for a Multi-Camera Series (Tony Askins for "Ice Cream Balls"); Outstanding Multi-Camera Picture Editing for a Series (Peter Chakos for "Looking for Mr. Good Enough"); Outstanding Multi-Camera Sound Mixing for a Series or Special (Peter Damski, Todd Grace, and Craig Porter for "Looking for Mr. Good Enough")

2005 (13): Outstanding Comedy Series; Outstanding Lead Actor in a Comedy Series (Eric McCormack); Outstanding Supporting Actor in a Comedy Series (Sean Hayes); Outstanding Supporting Actress in a Comedy Series (Megan Mullally); Outstanding Guest Actor in a Comedy Series (Alec Baldwin); Outstanding Guest Actor in a Comedy Series (Victor Garber for "Saving Grace Again"); Outstanding Guest Actor in a Comedy Series (Jeff Goldblum); Outstanding Guest Actress in a Comedy Series (Blythe Danner); Outstanding Directing for a Comedy Series (James Burrows for "It's a Dad, Dad, Dad, Dad World"); Outstanding Art Direction for a Multi-Camera Series (Glenda Rovello and Melinda Ritz for "The Birds and the Bees"); Outstanding Casting for a Comedy Series (Tracy Lilienfield); Outstanding Multi-Camera Picture Editing for a Series (Peter Chakos for "It's a Dad, Dad, Dad, Dad World"); Outstanding Multi-Camera Sound Mixing for a Series or a Special (Peter Damski, Kathy Oldham, and Craig Porter for "Friends with Benefits" and "Kiss and Tell")

2006 (8): Outstanding Lead Actress in a Comedy Series (Debra Messing); Outstanding Supporting Actor in a Comedy Series (Sean Hayes); Outstanding Guest Actor in a Comedy Series (Alec Baldwin); Outstanding Guest Actress in a Comedy Series (Blythe Danner); Outstanding Art Direction for a Multi-Camera Series (Glenda Rovello and Melinda Ritz for "The Finale"); Outstanding Hairstyling for a Series (Luke O'Connor and Tim Burke for "The Finale"); Outstanding Makeup for a Series (Nonprosthetic) (Patricia Bunch, Karen Kawahara, Farah Bunch, and Greg Cannomfor for "The Finale"); Outstanding Multi-Camera Picture Editing for a Series (Peter Chakos for "The Finale")

GOLDEN GLOBE NOMINATIONS (27)

2000 (4): Best TV Series, Musical/Comedy; Best Performance by an Actor in a TV Series, Musical/Comedy (Eric McCormack); Best Performance by an Actress in a TV Series, Musical/Comedy (Debra Messing); Best Performance by an Actor in a Supporting Role in a Series, Mini-Series, or Motion Picture Made for TV (Sean Hayes)

2001 (5): Best TV Series, Musical/Comedy; Best Performance by an Actor in a TV Series, Musical/Comedy (Eric McCormack); Best Performance by an Actress in a TV Series, Musical/Comedy (Debra Messing); Best Performance by an Actor in a Supporting Role in a Series, Mini-Series, or Motion Picture Made for TV (Sean Hayes); Best Performance by an Actress in a Supporting Role in a Series, Mini-Series, or Motion Picture Made for TV (Megan Mullally)

2002 (5): Best TV Series, Musical/Comedy; Best Performance by an Actor in a TV Series, Musical/Comedy (Eric McCormack); Best Performance by an Actress in a TV Series, Musical/Comedy (Debra Messing); Best Performance by an Actor in a Supporting Role in a Series, Mini-Series, or Motion Picture Made for TV (Sean Hayes); Best Performance by an Actress in a Supporting Role in a Series, Mini-Series, or Motion Picture Made for TV (Megan Mullally)

2003 (5): Best TV Series, Musical/Comedy; Best Performance by an Actor in a TV Series, Musical/Comedy (Eric McCormack); Best Performance by an Actress in a TV Series, Musical/Comedy (Debra Messing); Best Performance by an Actor in a Supporting Role in a Series, Mini-Series, or Motion Picture Made for TV (Sean Hayes); Best Performance by an Actress in a Supporting Role in a Series, Mini-Series, or Motion Picture Made for TV (Megan Mullally)

2004 (5): Best TV Series, Musical/Comedy; Best Performance by an Actor in a TV Series, Musical/Comedy (Eric McCormack); Best Performance by an Actress in a TV Series, Musical/Comedy (Debra Messing); Best Performance by an Actor in a Supporting Role in a Series, Mini-Series, or Motion Picture Made for TV (Sean Hayes); Best Performance by an Actress in a Supporting Role in a Series, Mini-Series, or Motion Picture Made for TV (Megan Mullally)

2005 (3): Best TV Series, Musical/Comedy; Best Performance by an Actress in a TV Series, Musical/Comedy (Debra Messing); Best Performance by an Actor in a Supporting Role in a Series, Mini-Series, or Motion Picture Made for TV (Sean Hayes)

Further Reading

Colucci, Jim. *Will & Grace: Fabulously Uncensored.* New York: Time, Inc., Home Entertainment, 2004.

Marshall, Corinne. *The Q Guide to Will and Grace: Stuff You Didn't Even Know You Wanted to Know . . . about Will, Grace, Jack, Karen, and Lots of Guest Stars.* New York: Alyson Books, 2008.

Schiappa, Edward, Peter B. Gregg, and Dean E. Hewes. "Can One TV Show Make a Difference? Will & Grace and the Parasocial Contact Hypothesis." *Journal of Homosexuality* 51, no. 51 (2006): 14–37. Available online at www.comm.umn.edu/department/pch/wg.pdf.

✦ 23 ✦

The Larry Sanders Show

(1992–1998)

Cast: Garry Shandling (Larry Sanders), Jeffrey Tambor (Hank Kingsley), Wallace Langham (Phil), Rip Torn (Arthur), Penny Johnson (Beverly Barnes), Janeane Garofalo (Paula), Linda Doucett (Darlene Chapinni), Bobby Figueroa (Bandleader)

Created by: Dennis Klein and Garry Shandling

Network: HBO

First Air Date: August 15, 1992

Last Air Date: May 1, 1998

Broadcast History:
August 15, 1992–November 1992: Saturday at 10:00–10:30 PM
June 1993–November 1999: Wednesday at 10:00–10:30 PM
March 1998–May 1, 1998: Sunday at 10:00–10:30 PM

Seasons: 6

Episodes: 89

Ratings History: Never in Top 30

Overview

It was *30 Rock* before *30 Rock*, *Murphy Brown* on steroids. It was *The Larry Sanders Show*, otherwise known as *The Garry Shandling Show*, otherwise known as the funniest show within a show ever produced. This sitcom revolved around a neurotic, insecure, slightly twisted talk show host (Garry Shandling) and his two minions, who worked feverishly to keep him out of trouble on and off the set. Shandling is ideally cast, he had

158

Jeffrey Tambor, Rip Torn, and Garry Shandling. *HBO/Photofest ©HBO*

often substituted for Johnny Carson on *The Tonight Show.* The action could be manic and the plot lines absurd, but the humor was far more character-driven than physical.

Larry couldn't have lasted a month as host of his talk show, whose real-life guests included dozens of the biggest stars in Hollywood, if not for the behind-the-scenes scrambling of executive producer Artie (Rip Torn), who went to great lengths to pull Larry out of the proverbial quicksand. Far less effective, but equally passionate about saving the talk show host from himself, was bumbling announcer and on-air sidekick Hank Kingsley (Jeffrey Tambor), who wore both his emotions and his intentions on his sleeve.

In one memorable episode, it is claimed in a newspaper article that Larry has impregnated a waitress from Montana. She arrives at his office to confront him and later pays a surprise visit to his house while he is trying to make time with actress Mimi

Rogers, thereby ruining that relationship. Larry first contends that he has never previously met the woman, and he then admits that he may have spoken with her, but when witnesses emerge offering that they had seen him in the car with her, he concedes that there was sexual activity, but no intercourse. Meanwhile, Hank is toiling feverishly to put out the fire. He calls the reporter and tells him it was a nonstory and that a far better one is the bullying he was forced to endure as a child. Much to the relief of one and all, Artie finally reports that the woman admitted she was impregnated by another man, but that she did indeed fool around with Larry in a Denny's parking lot.

The theme of Larry trying to deceive his way out of trouble was established early in the series. One episode in the first season, which received an Emmy nomination for writing, revolves around an incident in which he denies accidentally knocking a woman into a magazine rack in a supermarket after the incident is splashed on tabloid headlines and she threatens to sue. The store cameras confirm his guilt, leading network public relations man Norman Litkey (David Paymer) to try to take advantage of his belief that any publicity is good publicity and announce happily that CNN plans on airing the video. The embarrassed and upset talk show host locks himself in his office and refuses to emerge until wife Jeannie (Megan Gallagher) arrives and threatens to reveal his nickname for his penis to his colleagues.

Such plot lines confirmed that the strength of the show extended beyond the performances of the major cast members to the creative writing of Shandling and cocreator Dennis Klein, who had displayed his talents for penning offbeat stories for the highly acclaimed sitcom *Buffalo Bill*, which also featured the personal and professional life of a talk show host. Also contributing to the attractive qualities of *The Larry Sanders Show* were the contrasts in taping—crisp and shiny in shooting the talk show and mildly grainy filming of offstage scenes.

The series finale aired just fourteen days before the last episode of *Seinfeld* and attracted 2.5 million viewers—quite a ratings coup for a cable network like HBO. It received far more positive reviews than did the *Seinfeld* series finale, which was criticized for its rehashing of previous events on the show. Jerry Seinfeld was also the last of the dozens of the stars of the entertainment world to appear on the talk show within the sitcom.

Its millions of fans were thirsting for the show to continue beyond the eighty-nine episodes that were produced, but it went off the air in 1998. One was left to wonder how *The Larry Sanders Show*, whose ratings were shackled by its cable home, preventing it from ever reaching the Top 30 in the Nielsens, would have fared had it aired on network television, but the elimination of profanity would have weakened the sense of comic reality that made the show so appealing.

In the lens of television history, it will remain one of the most creative and humorous sitcoms ever produced. It comes as little surprise that it earned an Emmy nomination for Outstanding Comedy Series for five consecutive years.

Ugly Spat between Former Friends

The Larry Sanders Show was marred by a long, bitter, and public battle between star Garry Shandling and coproducer Brad Grey. Shandling filed a conflict of interest lawsuit against Grey for $100 million that alleged he had improperly taken advantage of their relationship to benefit other business interests. Grey countersued for $10 million, claiming "aberrant and irresponsible behavior" from Shandling. The disputes were finally settled in 1999—a year after the show was cancelled—with terms undisclosed.

They Said It

Arthur: Your fly is undone.
Larry: Oh, thanks.
Arthur: Just doing my job.
Larry: It's your job to look at my crotch?
Arthur: I consider it one of my perks.

Arthur: You'll have to forgive Hank. His heart's in the right place, but he keeps his brain in a box at home.

Arthur: You finally got to do a sketch with the great Carol Burnett.
Larry: It wasn't a sketch. It was a massive spastic fuck-up.
Arthur: Tomato, tomahto!

Hank: [giving a tour] And if you stop by here, you can say hello to my good friend, Larry Sanders. [knocks on his door] Hey now, Larry.
Larry: Fuck off, Hank.
Hank: [returning to tour] And over here . . .

Major Awards

EMMY AWARD WINS (3)

1996 (1): Outstanding Supporting Actor in a Comedy Series (Rip Torn)
1998 (2): Outstanding Writing for a Comedy Series (Peter Tolan and Garry Shandling for "Flip"); Outstanding Directing for a Comedy Series (Todd Holland for "Flip")

EMMY AWARD NOMINATIONS, IN ADDITION TO WINS (53)

1993 (8): Outstanding Comedy Series; Outstanding Lead Actor in a Comedy Series (Garry Shandling); Outstanding Supporting Actor in a Comedy Series (Jeffrey Tambor); Outstanding Supporting Actor in a Comedy Series (Rip Torn); Outstanding Guest Actor in a Comedy Series (Dana Carvey for "Guest Host"); Outstanding Guest Actress in a Comedy Series (Carol Burnett for "The Spider Episode"); Outstanding Individual Achievement in Writing in a Comedy Series (Garry Shandling and Dennis Klein for "The Hey Now Episode"); Outstanding

Individual Achievement in Writing in a Comedy Series (Garry Shandling, Peter Tolan, Paul Simms, and Rosie Shuster for "The Spider Episode")

1994 (4): Outstanding Comedy Series; Outstanding Supporting Actor in a Comedy Series (Rip Torn); Outstanding Individual Achievement in Writing in a Comedy Series (Drake Sather, Maya Forbes, Garry Shandling, Victor Levin, and Paul Simms for "Larry's Agent"); Outstanding Individual Achievement in Directing in a Comedy Series (Todd Holland for "Life behind Larry")

1995 (6): Outstanding Comedy Series; Outstanding Lead Actor in a Comedy Series (Garry Shandling); Outstanding Supporting Actor in a Comedy Series (Rip Torn); Outstanding Individual Achievement in Writing for a Comedy Series (Garry Shandling and Peter Tolan for "The Mr. Sharon Stone Show"); Outstanding Individual Achievement in Writing for a Comedy Series (Peter Tolan for "Hank's Night in the Sun"); Outstanding Individual Achievement in Directing for a Comedy Series (Todd Holland for "Hank's Night in the Sun")

1996 (11): Outstanding Comedy Series; Outstanding Lead Actor in a Comedy Series (Garry Shandling); Outstanding Supporting Actor in a Comedy Series (Jeffrey Tambor); Outstanding Supporting Actress in a Comedy Series (Janeane Garofalo); Outstanding Guest Actor in a Comedy Series (Mandy Patinkin for "Eight"); Outstanding Guest Actress in a Comedy Series (Rosie O'Donnell for "Eight"); Outstanding Individual Achievement in Writing for a Comedy Series (Peter Tolan for "Arthur After Hours"); Outstanding Individual Achievement in Writing for a Comedy Series (Maya Forbes, Steve Levitan, and Garry Shandling for "Roseanne's Return"); Outstanding Individual Achievement in Writing for a Comedy Series (Jon Vitti for "Hank's Sex Tape"); Outstanding Individual Achievement in Directing for a Comedy Series (Todd Holland for "Arthur After Hours"); Outstanding Individual Achievement in Directing for a Comedy Series (Michael Lehmann for "I Was a Teenage Lesbian")

1997 (16): Outstanding Comedy Series; Outstanding Lead Actor in a Comedy Series (Garry Shandling); Outstanding Supporting Actor in a Comedy Series (Jeffrey Tambor); Outstanding Supporting Actor in a Comedy Series (Rip Torn); Outstanding Supporting Actress in a Comedy Series (Janeane Garofalo); Outstanding Guest Actor in a Comedy Series (David Duchovny for "Everybody Loves Larry"); Outstanding Guest Actress in a Comedy Series (Ellen DeGeneres for "Ellen, Or Isn't She?"); Outstanding Writing for a Comedy Series (Judd Apatow, John Markus, and Garry Shandling for "Ellen, Or Isn't She?"); Outstanding Writing for a Comedy Series (Peter Tolan for "My Name Is Asher Kingsley"); Outstanding Writing for a Comedy Series (Jon Vitti for "Everybody Loves Larry"); Outstanding Directing for a Comedy Series (Todd Holland for "Everybody Loves Larry"); Outstanding Directing for a Comedy Series (Alan Myerson for "Ellen, Or Isn't She?"); Outstanding Editing for a Series, Multi-Camera Production (Sean Lambert and Leslie Tolan for "Everybody Loves Larry"); Outstanding Editing for a Series, Multi-Camera Production (Paul Anderson and Leslie Tolan for "My Name Is Asher Kingsley"); Outstanding Lighting Direction (Electronic) for a Comedy Series (Peter Smokler for "Ellen, Or Isn't She?"); Outstanding Sound

Mixing for a Comedy Series or a Special (John Bickelhaupt, Ed Golya, and Edward L. Moskowitz for "Ellen, Or Isn't She?")

1998 (8): Outstanding Comedy Series; Outstanding Lead Actor in a Comedy Series (Garry Shandling); Outstanding Supporting Actor in a Comedy Series (Jeffrey Tambor); Outstanding Supporting Actor in a Comedy Series (Rip Torn); Outstanding Writing for a Comedy Series (Richard Day, Alex Gregory, and Peter Huyck for "Putting the 'Gay' Back in Litigation"); Outstanding Lighting Direction (Electronic) for a Comedy Series (Peter Smokler for "Flip"); Outstanding Multi-Camera Picture Editing for a Series (Paul Anderson, Sean Lambert, and Leslie Tolan for "Flip"); Outstanding Sound Mixing for a Comedy Series or a Special (John Bickelhaupt, Ed Golya, and Edward L. Moskowitz for "Flip")

GOLDEN GLOBE NOMINATIONS (3)

1995 (1): Best Performance by an Actor in a TV Series, Musical/Comedy (Garry Shandling)

1996 (1): Best Performance by an Actor in a TV Series, Musical/Comedy (Garry Shandling)

1997 (1): Best TV Series, Musical/Comedy

PEABODY AWARD

1994: HBO
1999: HBO

Further Reading

Shandling, Garry, and David Rensin. *Confessions of a Late Night Talk Show Host.* New York: Simon & Schuster, 1998.
Tucker, Ken. "The Larry Sanders Show." *Entertainment Weekly Online*, June 4, 1983. Available online at www.ew.com/ew/article/0,,306821,00.html.

✳ **24** ✳

Friends

(1994–2004)

Cast: Jennifer Aniston (Rachel Green), Courteney Cox (Monica Geller), Lisa Kudrow (Phoebe Buffay), Matt LeBlanc (Joey Tribbiani), Matthew Perry (Chandler Bing), David Schwimmer (Dr. Ross Geller), James Michael Tyler (Gunther)

Created by: Executive producers and writers Marta Kauffman and David Crane

Network: NBC

First Air Date: September 22, 1994

Last Air Date: July 8, 2004

Broadcast History:
    September 1994–February 1995: Thursday at 8:30–9:00 PM
    February 1995–August 1995: Thursday at 9:30–10:00 PM
    August 1995–July 2004: Thursday at 8:00–8:30 PM
    November 1999: Monday at 8:00–8:30 PM
    April 2002–May 2002: Thursday at 8:30–9:00 PM
    November 2003: Thursday at 8:30–9:00 PM
    April 2004–May 2004: Thursday at 8:30–9:30 PM

Seasons: 10

Episodes: 238

Ratings History: 1994–1995 (8), 1995–1996 (3), 1996–1997 (4), 1997–1998 (4), 1998–1999 (2), 1999–2000 (5), 2000–2001 (5), 2001–2002 (1), 2002–2003 (2), 2003–2004 (4)

Jennifer Aniston, David Schwimmer, Courteney Cox, Matt LeBlanc, Lisa Kudrow, and Matthew Perry. *Warner Bros./Photofest ©Warner Bros.*

Overview

What *Seinfeld* was to Baby Boomers, *Friends* was to Generation Xers. They both spotlighted unique and humorous characters (although the traits and idiosyncrasies of those on *Seinfeld* were exaggerated for effect) hanging around their New York apartments discussing their personal lives, but the latter appealed to a younger audience. There were significant differences. *Seinfeld* billed itself as a show about nothing. *Friends* was about something—relationships, relationships, and more relationships. The humor revolved around the personalities in the tight-knit group. The mix of three women and three men allowed cocreators and writers Marta Kauffman and David Crane to explore both platonic and more advanced relationships between them.

Kauffman and Crane had teamed up as writers for such moderately successful shows as *Veronica's Closet* and *Dream On* before striking it rich with *Friends*, one of the most popular sitcoms of its era. It seemed that the six extremely attractive twenty-somethings were paired in every imaginable combination that precluded homosexuality and were, more or less, just out to make the most of their social lives in The Big Apple, although the more down-to-earth assistant chef Monica Geller (Courteney Cox) sought to keep the others in line and did seek out Mr. Right. The obsessive-compulsive "den mother" for her *Friends* friends later eventually realized that "Mr. Right" was fellow regular Chandler Bing (Matthew Perry), whom she married at the end of season seven after having dated an older man, dentist Richard Burke (Tom Selleck). The rather sarcastic Chandler proved he was motivated more by striving for inner peace and happiness than greed by quitting his corporate job as a statistical analyst for work as a junior copywriter at an ad agency, which allowed him to maximize his sense of humor.

By the time Monica and Chandler tied the knot, paleontologist and paleontology professor Ross Geller (Monica's brother, played by David Schwimmer) and fashion designer wannabe Rachel Green (Jennifer Aniston) had already been married and divorced. The two had ended an earlier affair, after which Ross married British grouch Emily, but disaster struck at the wedding when he accidentally blurted out Rachel's name during the ceremony. With that relationship doomed, Ross and Rachel set out to reinvent theirs. Their wedding at the conclusion of the 1998–1999 season was the result of a wild, drunken weekend in Vegas, and soon thereafter they were divorced by mutual consent. But their relationship was far from over. She began cohabitating after she gave birth to his baby, a girl named Emma whom they decided to raise together as single parents. The comedic soap opera just went on and on.

The ditzy blonde role in the show was embraced in unique fashion by masseuse and musician Phoebe Buffay (Lisa Kudrow), whose attempts at singing her one folk song creation ("Smelly Cat") at the coffee shop in which she and her friends spent countless hours (Central Perk) proved historically bad. The friendly Phoebe maintained her good nature and optimism throughout the show despite the fact that her professional outlook remained more bleak than that of the others. Even dopey soap opera actor Joey Tribbiani (Matt LeBlanc), who greeted one and all with his signature line, "How you doin'?," landed a gig on *Days of Our Lives*, where the manly man, ironically, played the part of a guy with a woman's brain.

Phoebe finally found personal happiness in the final season of the show, when the group began to break apart. She married pianist Mike Hannigan (Paul Rudd), while Chandler and Monica, who realized much to their dismay that they could not conceive, adopted twins Erica and Jack and planned a move to the suburbs. Rachel nearly wrecked her marriage by embarking on an affair. On the verge of taking off for Paris (where she had landed a job) without her husband, she decided against leaving and stayed with Ross. Joey was also on the move—to Hollywood for his own sitcom.

Friends has been criticized by some for its narcissistic characters with whom it was difficult to empathize. Fans of the show claim that the writers never asked for empathy from their characters, just laughs, and they earned enough laughs to maintain Nielsen ratings that hovered in the top eight throughout its ten-year run and peaked at number one in season eight. The show was also destined for tremendous success in syndication.

The Rembrandts' Brush with Fame

The iconic *Friends* theme song entitled "I'll Be There for You" was recorded by a California band called The Rembrandts. It brought them more fame and fortune than they could have imagined, but it also tore them apart. American radio stations were flooded with requests for the song, but its forty-second length precluded it from being released as a single. Their record company sent the group to Los Angeles to record a full-length version, which soared to number one on the charts for eleven straight weeks. It was placed on an album, which sold 2 million copies.

The band, however, was far from thrilled with the ride to the top. Singer Danny Wilde explained that the jingle-jangle upbeat tune bucked against the more serious, alternative music they pursued on the album. He added that the band's split in 1997 was the result of the frustration associated with "I'll Be There for You" being their only recognized song.

One Spin-Off, One Flop

Friends spawned one spin-off, but it didn't last long. *Joey* featured Matt LeBlanc as an actor trying to make it in Hollywood. The show debuted on NBC in the fall of 2004 and lasted until December 2005. NBC gave it another shot in March 2006, but cancelled it after one episode. The sitcom featured several hot blondes and Joey dating actresses and producers while landing work on an action show about skiing called *Deep Powder.*

Did You Know?

Courteney Cox appeared in the 1984 music video that showed Bruce Springsteen in concert singing "Dancing in the Dark." Springsteen pulled the short-haired Cox out of the audience to dance with him onstage.

They Said It

Ross: What are you doing?
Chandler: Making chocolate milk. You want some?
Ross: No, thanks. I'm 29.

Joey: I hate Pottery Barn, too! They kicked me out of there just because I sat on a bed.
Chandler: You took off your pants and climbed under the sheets!

Monica: Oh my god. How cute is the new eye doctor.
Rachel: So cute I'm thinking about jamming this pen in my eye.

Ross: What are you doing tonight?
Chandler: Why, do you have a lecture?
Ross: No.
Chandler: Free as a bird, what's up?

Major Awards

EMMY AWARD WINS (6)

1996 (1): Outstanding Individual Achievement in Directing for a Comedy Series (Michael Lembeck for "The One after the Super Bowl")

1998 (1): Outstanding Supporting Actress in a Comedy Series (Lisa Kudrow)

2000 (1): Outstanding Guest Actor in a Comedy Series (Bruce Willis)

2002 (2): Outstanding Comedy Series; Outstanding Lead Actress in a Comedy Series (Jennifer Aniston)

2003 (1): Outstanding Guest Actress in a Comedy Series (Christina Applegate for "The One with Rachel's Other Sister")

EMMY AWARD NOMINATIONS, IN ADDITION TO WINS (56)

1995 (9): Outstanding Comedy Series; Outstanding Supporting Actor in a Comedy Series (David Schwimmer); Outstanding Supporting Actress in a Comedy Series (Lisa Kudrow); Outstanding Guest Actress in a Comedy Series (Christina Pickles for "The One Where Nana Dies Twice"); Outstanding Individual Achievement in Writing for a Comedy Series (Jeff Greenstein and Jeff Strauss for "The One Where Underdog Gets Away"); Outstanding Individual Achievement in Directing for a Comedy Series (James Burrows for "The One with the Blackout"); Outstanding Individual Achievement in Art Direction for a Series (John Shaffner and Greg J. Grande for "The One Where Rachel Finds Out"); Outstanding Individual Achievement in Editing for a Series, Multi-Camera Production (Andy Zall for "The One with Two Parts: Part Two"); Outstanding Individual Achievement in Main Title Theme Music (Allee Willis and Michael Skloff)

1996 (2): Outstanding Comedy Series; Outstanding Guest Actress in a Comedy Series (Marlo Thomas for "The One with the Lesbian Wedding")

1997 (1): Outstanding Supporting Actress in a Comedy Series (Lisa Kudrow)

1999 (6): Outstanding Comedy Series; Outstanding Supporting Actress in a Comedy Series (Lisa Kudrow); Outstanding Writing for a Comedy Series (Alexa Junge for "The One Where Everybody Finds Out"); Outstanding Directing for a Comedy Series (Michael Lembeck for "The One Where Everyone Finds Out"); Outstanding Costume Design for a Series (Debra McGuire for "The One with All the Thanksgivings"); Outstanding Sound Mixing for a Comedy Series or a Special (Dana Mark McClure, Charlie McDaniel, Kathy Oldham, and John Bickelhaupt for "The One with All the Thanksgivings")

2000 (7): Outstanding Comedy Series; Outstanding Supporting Actress in a Comedy Series (Jennifer Aniston); Outstanding Supporting Actress in a Comedy Series (Lisa Kudrow); Outstanding Guest Actor in a Comedy Series (Tom Selleck); Outstanding Directing for a Comedy Series (Michael Lembeck for "The One That Could Have Been"); Outstanding Multi-Camera Picture Editing for a Series

(Stephen Prime for "The One with the Proposal"); Outstanding Sound Mixing for a Comedy Series or a Special (Dana Mark McClure, Charlie McDaniel, Kathy Oldham, and John Bickelhaupt for "The One with Chandler and Monica's Wedding")

2001 (5): Outstanding Supporting Actress in a Comedy Series (Jennifer Aniston); Outstanding Supporting Actress in a Comedy Series (Lisa Kudrow); Outstanding Guest Actor in a Comedy Series (Gary Oldman); Outstanding Guest Actress in a Comedy Series (Susan Sarandon for "The One with Joey's New Brain"); Outstanding Art Direction for a Multi-Camera Series (John Shaffner, Joe Stewart, and Greg J. Grande for "The One Where Rachel Finds Out")

2002 (8): Outstanding Lead Actor in a Comedy Series (Matt LeBlanc); Outstanding Lead Actor in a Comedy Series (Matthew Perry); Outstanding Guest Actor in a Comedy Series (Brad Pitt for "The One with the Rumor"); Outstanding Art Direction for a Multi-Camera Series (John Shaffner, Joe Stewart, and Greg J. Grande for "The One Where Rachel Has a Baby"); Outstanding Casting for a Comedy Series (Leslie Litt and Barbara Miller); Outstanding Cinematography for a Multi-Camera Series (Nick McLean for "The One with the Rumor"); Outstanding Multi-Camera Picture Editing for a Series (Kenny Tintorri for "The One with the Halloween Party"); Outstanding Multi-Camera Sound Mixing for a Series or a Special (Dana Mark McClure, Charlie McDaniel, Kathy Oldham, and John Bickelhaupt for "The One Where Rachel Has a Baby")

2003 (10): Outstanding Comedy Series; Outstanding Lead Actor in a Comedy Series (Matt LeBlanc); Outstanding Lead Actress in a Comedy Series (Jennifer Aniston); Outstanding Guest Actor in a Comedy Series (Hank Azaria); Outstanding Art Direction for a Multi-Camera Series (John Shaffner, Joe Stewart, and Greg J. Grande for "The One in Barbados"); Outstanding Casting for a Comedy Series (Leslie Litt and Barbara Miller); Outstanding Cinematography for a Multi-Camera Series (Nick McLean for "The One in Barbados"); Outstanding Multi-Camera Picture Editing for a Series (Stephen Prime for "The One in Barbados"); Outstanding Multi-Camera Picture Editing for a Series (Kenny Tintorri for "The One with Ross's Inappropriate Song"); Outstanding Multi-Camera Sound Mixing for a Series or a Special (Dana Mark McClure, Charlie McDaniel, and John Bickelhaupt for "The One in Barbados")

2004 (8): Outstanding Lead Actor in a Comedy Series (Matt LeBlanc); Outstanding Lead Actress in a Comedy Series (Jennifer Aniston); Outstanding Guest Actor in a Comedy Series (Danny DeVito); Outstanding Guest Actress in a Comedy Series (Christina Applegate); Outstanding Cinematography for a Multi-Camera Series (Nick McLean for "The One with Phoebe's Wedding"); Outstanding Multi-Camera Picture Editing for a Miniseries, a Movie, or a Special (Sven Nilsson, Stephen Prime, Todd Felker, and Kenny Tintorri for "Friends: The One before the Last One—10 Years of Friends"); Outstanding Multi-Camera Picture Editing for a Series (Stephen Prime for :The Last One"); Outstanding Multi-Camera Sound Mixing for a Series or a Special (Dana Mark McClure, Charlie McDaniel, and John Bickelhaupt for "The Last One")

GOLDEN GLOBE WIN (1)

2003 (1): Best Performance by an Actress in a TV Series, Musical/Comedy (Jennifer Aniston)

GOLDEN GLOBE NOMINATIONS, IN ADDITION TO WIN (9)

1996 (2): Best TV Series, Musical/Comedy; Best Performance by an Actress in a Supporting Role in a Series, Mini-Series, or Motion Picture Made for TV (Lisa Kudrow)
1997 (1): Best TV Series, Musical/Comedy
1998 (1): Best TV Series, Musical/Comedy
2002 (2): Best TV Series, Musical/Comedy; Best Performance by an Actress in a Supporting Role in a Series, Mini-Series, or Motion Picture Made for Television (Jennifer Aniston)
2003 (2): Best TV Series, Musical/Comedy; Best Performance by an Actor in a TV Series, Musical/Comedy (Matt LeBlanc)
2004 (1): Best Performance by an Actor in a TV Series, Musical/Comedy (Matt LeBlanc)

Further Reading

Johnson, Lauren. *Friends: The One about the #1 Sitcom.* New York: NAL Trade, 2003.
Smith, Sean. *Aniston: The Unauthorized Biography.* London: Macmillan UK, 2008.
Wild, David. *Friends 'Til the End: The Official Celebration of All Ten Years.* New York: Time, Inc., Home Entertainment, 2004.

✶ **25** ✶

The Odd Couple

(1970–1975)

Cast: Tony Randall (Felix Unger), Jack Klugman (Oscar Madison), Al
  Molinaro (Murray Greshler), Penny Marshall (Myrna Turner)

Created by: Executive producer Garry Marshall

Network: ABC

First Air Date: September 24, 1970

Last Air Date: March 7, 1975

Broadcast History:
  September 1970–January 1971: Thursday at 9:30–10:00 PM
  January 1971–June 1973: Friday at 9:30–10:00 PM
  June 1973–January 1974: Friday at 8:30–9:00 PM
  January 1974–September 1974: Friday at 9:30–10:00 PM
  September 1974–January 1975: Thursday at 8:00–8:30 PM
  January 1975–March 1975: Friday at 9:30–10:00 PM

Seasons: 5

Episodes: 114

Ratings History: Never in Top 30

Overview

You want an actor to play a slob like Oscar Madison? Hire Jack Klugman. You want an
actor to play a neurotic neatnik like Felix Unger? Hire Tony Randall. It's that simple.
If the basis of sitcom humor is conflict and contrast, creator Garry Marshall struck it
rich by placing these two stars together in front of a camera in the TV adaptation of
The Odd Couple.

Jack Klugman and Tony Randall. *ABC/Photofest ©ABC*

The precedent was set in 1965, when the namesake Neil Simon play, directed by Mike Nichols (who later won an Oscar for his work as director of the iconic film *The Graduate*), debuted on Broadway. It featured Walter Matthau as slovenly sportswriter Oscar and Art Carney (of *Honeymooners* fame) as Felix. Klugman eventually replaced Matthau, who had earned a Tony Award for Best Actor.

Then came the 1968 film starring Matthau and Jack Lemmon, which was not only a hit at the box office, but also earned a Golden Globe nomination for Best Motion Picture, a notable feat for a straight comedy. The popularity of the play and movie motivated Marshall to give it a shot on the small screen. The result was a show that earned greater critical acclaim than viewership. *The Odd Couple* was no bomb—it hung around for five years—but it never rose higher than number thirty-six in the Nielsen ratings.

As explained in the opening theme music, the seeds of the domestic arrangement between sloppy Oscar and fastidious Felix were planted when the latter was asked to leave his home—a request made by his wife—and showed up at the apartment of his old friend. Oscar gave Felix a place to live and spent much of the next five television seasons regretting it. He regretted it every time Felix annoyed him by making a honking noise to clear his sinuses, walking behind his cigar-smoking roommate while spraying an air freshener, or butting into his personal life. Felix was appalled when he peered into Oscar's bedroom to find clothes and garbage strewn about, even on the lamp, or when Oscar chased after women with only a good time in mind, and he would invariably stare at him with pity and disgust, shake his head, and utter his trademark, "Oscar, Oscar, Oscar."

The show continued to evolve while Klugman and Randall managed to maintain the traits and idiosyncrasies that created conflict. Scenes in the early episodes mirror those of the movie with Oscar and his poker-playing buddies sitting around the table yammering about their wives and jobs. Invariably included was the hilarious Murray Greshler (Al Molinaro), also known as Murray the Cop, whose naïve gullibility and sweetness proved a contrast to the portrayals of police officers, even in sitcoms, as sharp-minded, tough, and downright mean. But the show began creating its own identity when it followed the new trend of dumping the laugh track in favor of taping in front of a live studio audience, and main character story lines beyond professional and personal lives were expanded to include more scenes outside the apartment.

Such developments marked an end to the roles of the flighty Pigeon sisters Gwendolyn (Carol Shelly) and Cecily (Monica Evans), both of whom left the show after one season. The addition to the cast of the talented Penny Marshall, who played Oscar's befuddled assistant, Myrna Turner, proved as the sister of show creator Garry Marshall that nepotism wasn't always a motivating factor in casting and gave *The Odd Couple* another heavyweight comic character.

Many of its most memorable and funniest moments revolved around celebrity appearances. In one episode, the pair lands on the game show *Password*, and Felix famously gives Oscar the clue "Aristophanes" for the word *bird* because the Greek author, who lived in the fourth century B.C., wrote a play called *The Birds*. *The Odd Couple* continued to take advantage of pop culture phenomena in 1973, the year in which the horror film *The Exorcist* scared the hell out of millions of Americans, with an episode in which Felix seeks to exorcise a demon he is convinced has made a home in the air conditioner. Writers also used Oscar's renown as a sportswriter for the fictional *New York Herald* to arrange appearances of such real-life personalities as controversial sportscaster Howard Cosell, as well as tennis hustler Bobby Riggs and superstar Billie Jean King two months after their famed on-court "Battle of the Sexes." The pair appears in an episode entitled "The Pig Who Came to Dinner." (Riggs had been cast well before the show as a male chauvinist pig, although his disrespect for women was contrived for publicity purposes.)

The writers managed to keep fresh the relationships between Oscar and Felix and the women in their lives. Felix enjoyed the company of girlfriend Miriam Welby (Elinor Donahue), but continued to pine for ex-wife Gloria (Janis Hansen). He finally reconciled with her in the final season and marries her in the last episode, leading Oscar to revel in reestablishing his live-alone bachelor status with a messy celebration. Oscar, forever the opposite of Felix, preferred the single life, although he got along well with ex-wife Blanche, played by Klugman's real spouse, Brett Somers.

In the end, the answer was "yes, but barely" in answering the following question offered in the opening narration: "Can two divorced men share an apartment without driving each other crazy?" Felix and Oscar managed to maintain their sanity despite their maddening habits and contrasting personality traits. It was either a testament to their strength or an unrealistic necessity in keeping a sitcom on the air. Either way, it was pretty darn funny.

The Inimitable John Fiedler

Viewers could close their eyes and recognize actor John Fiedler by his unmistakable high-pitched voice. Fiedler played the role of Vinnie in *The Odd Couple* movie (which was assumed by Larry Gelman on TV) before making several appearances on the sitcom. Fiedler generally portrayed meek, insecure characters. He worked with Jack Klugman as a fellow juror in the 1957 film *Twelve Angry Men*, but his most recognized part was as Emil Peterson, a patient of psychologist Robert Hartley who was overwhelmed by life in *The Bob Newhart Show*.

If At First You *Do* Succeed, Try, Try Again

The success of *The Odd Couple* motivated ABC to give the premise another shot in October 1982, under the same name with black main characters played by *Sanford and Son* standout Desmond Wilson as Oscar and *Barney Miller* regular Ron Glass as Felix. Many of the same characters were brought back, including the Pigeon sisters and buddies Murray and Speed. The show was gone by June 1983.

They Said It

> **Felix:** What are you doing?
> **Oscar:** Sterilizing the wound.
> **Felix:** [incredulous] With beer?
> **Oscar:** It's got alcohol in it.

> **Felix:** Everyone things I'm a hypochondriac. It makes me sick.

Major Awards

EMMY AWARD WINS (3)

1971 (1): Outstanding Continued Performance by an Actor in a Leading Role in a Comedy Series (Jack Klugman)
1973 (1): Outstanding Continued Performance by an Actor in a Leading Role in a Comedy Series (Jack Klugman)
1975 (1): Outstanding Lead Actor in a Comedy Series (Tony Randall)

EMMY AWARD NOMINATIONS, IN ADDITION TO WINS (12)

1971 (4): Outstanding Series, Comedy; Outstanding New Series; Outstanding Continued Performance by an Actor in a Leading Role in a Comedy Series (Jack Klugman); Outstanding Continued Performance by an Actor in a Leading Role in a Comedy Series (Tony Randall)
1972 (3): Outstanding Series, Comedy; Outstanding Continued Performance by an Actor in a Leading Role in a Comedy Series (Jack Klugman); Outstanding Continued Performance by an Actor in a Leading Role in a Comedy Series (Tony Randall)
1973 (1): Outstanding Continued Performance by an Actor in a Leading Role in a Comedy Series (Tony Randall)
1974 (3): Outstanding Comedy Series; Best Lead Actor in a Comedy Series (Jack Klugman); Best Lead Actor in a Comedy Series (Tony Randall)
1975 (1): Outstanding Lead Actor in a Comedy Series (Jack Klugman)

GOLDEN GLOBE WIN (1)

1974 (1): Best TV Actor, Musical/Comedy (Jack Klugman)

GOLDEN GLOBE NOMINATION, IN ADDITION TO WIN (1)

1972 (1): Best TV Actor, Musical/Comedy (Jack Klugman)

Further Reading

Gross, Edward A. *The 25th Anniversary Odd Couple Companion: Still Odd after All These Years.* Las Vegas, NV: Pioneer, 1989.
Klugman, Jack, with Burton Rocks. *Tony and Me: A Story of Friendship.* West Linn, OR: Good Hill Press, 2005.
Randall, Tony, and Michael Mindlin. *Which Reminds Me.* Beverly Hills, CA: New Millennium Press, 1989.

✴ **26** ✴

The George Burns and Gracie Allen Show

(1950–1958)

Cast: George Burns (George Burns), Gracie Allen (Gracie Allen), Bea Benaderet (Blanche Morton), Harry von Zell (announcer), Larry Keating (Harry Morton), Ronnie Burns (Ronnie Burns)

Created by: Stars George Burns and Gracie Allen

Network: CBS

First Air Date: October 12, 1950

Last Air Date: September 22, 1958

Broadcast History:
October 12, 1950–March 1953: Thursday at 8:00–8:30 PM
March 1953–September 22, 1958: Monday at 8:00–8:30 PM

Seasons: 8

Episodes: 291

Ratings History: 1950–1951 (not in Top 30), 1951–1952 (not in Top 30), 1952–1953 (not in Top 30), 1953–1954 (20), 1954–1955 (26), 1955–1956 (27), 1956–1957 (28), 1957–1958 (not in Top 30)

Overview

The success of the American sitcom owes a debt of gratitude to *The George Burns and Gracie Allen Show*. It set trends that writers of future programs used as a basis of humor, and it was simply one of the funniest ever. The surreal foundation for the comedy laid the groundwork for other offbeat shows. For star George Burns, it was part sitcom and part stand-up routine. He was alone among the characters who acknowledged the studio audience. The others were also unaware that the Beverly Hills home of Burns

176

Gracie Allen and George Burns. *CBS/Photofest ©CBS*

and wife Gracie Allen rested on a stage in a theater. And Burns could witness the plans of his fellow character unfold downstairs from a television upstairs.

The program blazed new trails in a fairly new medium. It was the first to portray the home lives of its stars and feature a cast member (in this case Burns) breaking out of character and the scene in which he is involved to speak directly to a live audience. That added to the surreal feel of the playlike atmosphere of the proceedings.

The roots of the bubble-headed blonde character later embraced by such actresses as Eva Gabor (*Green Acres*) and Suzanne Somers (*Three's Company*) were planted by the costar of this show—the inimitable Allen. Allen uttered the most humorous lines delivered during the eight-year run of the program in all confidence as she consistently misinterpreted the meaning of the simplest of comments spoken by others. In one such exchange in a 1951 episode, tax man Ralph Hanley announces his arrival to help the couple with their taxes. "Oh we're glad," she replies. "We got tired of paying them all ourselves."

Burns and Allen followed the same formula for success on TV as Jack Benny. Their comic timing and smooth on-camera relationship were polished and perfected in vaudeville, film, and radio. Although they played themselves, the personalities of their characters had little basis in reality. The sharpness of the real-life Allen belied her ditzy persona.

George served as both narrator and levelheaded straight man to his wife, whose antics often involved neighbor Blanche Morton (Bea Benaderet). Husband Harry Morton, whose role was played by four different actors during the eight-year run of the show, became angry and frustrated by the various schemes concocted by the women, while Burns remained calm as he learned about them through his magic upstairs television. He reacted in typical Burns fashion, grinning and pulling out his trademark cigar before explaining in humorous dialogue to his appreciative audience his plans to put out the figurative fire inevitably started by Gracie.

The writing for the television show remained true to its radio roots. The absurdity of the Allen character alone precluded the need for off-the-wall story lines and humor based on newsworthy events of the time. The plots revolved around simple pursuits, for example, preparing for a dinner party, while the comedy centered on how the scatter-brained Gracie zigged (dragging Blanche along with her) as the rest of her world zagged in reacting to such mundane endeavors. The use of Gracie as the empty-headed spouse and George as her straight man had been established long before the birth of television.

It comes as little surprise when considering the surreal nature of the show that one of the writers in its early years was Paul Henning, who later created the bizarre 1960s sitcom and cult classic *Green Acres*. The writing talent beyond Henning was evident from the start. Among the chief contributors was Sid Dorfman, who later wrote episodes of the brilliant 1970s show *M*A*S*H*, as well as Keith Fowler, who years later lent his talents to *The Addams Family*.

Each show ended with a short bit from the costars in front of the audience that concluded with Burns asking his wife, "Say good night, Gracie," and her replying simply, "Good night." Her last "good night" meant good night for one of the most popular sitcoms of its day. Failing health forced Allen to retire in 1958, after which the name of the program was changed to *The George Burns Show*, and it moved from CBS to NBC. Although it featured the same characters sans Gracie, the focus shifted to George as a theatrical producer and Blanche as his secretary. Among the story lines was Blanche working to keep her boss from becoming involved with the many sexy starlets that crossed his path and remain true to Gracie, who was often mentioned in the dialogue. The morphed sitcom, which later featured a variety show within nearly every episode, failed to maintain the same viewership without the comedic genius of Gracie Allen. It lasted five months before the network pulled the plug.

Heeeeere's Fred!

No one directed more episodes of *The George Burns and Gracie Allen Show* than Fred De Cordova. He arrived on the scene in 1953, and directed 120 episodes through 1958. But De Cordova gained greater fame as producer and executive producer of *The Tonight Show Starring Johnny Carson*. He served in the former capacity for 1,407 shows from 1970 to 1983, and as the latter for 442 shows from 1975 to 1992. De Cordova had also produced *The Smothers Brothers Show* in 1965 and 1966. He left before that program was tossed off the air, despite its number-one Nielsen rating, due to its overt antiwar stand.

Imagine *Her* State of the Union Addresses

Gracie Allen embarked on a run for the presidency in 1940, in a publicity stunt. She claimed to have been sitting in her Beverly Hills home when she suddenly exclaimed, "You know, I'm tired of knitting this sweater. I think I'll run for president." Her campaign was taken far more seriously than anyone could have imagined. It was plugged on several of the most popular radio programs of the day, including *The Jack Benny Program*, *The Texaco Star Theater*, and *Fibber McGee and Molly*. She even gave interviews and press conferences. First Lady Eleanor Roosevelt invited her to speak at the Women's National Press Club in Washington. When asked about the $43 billion national debt, she exclaimed that she was quite proud of it and that the American people should be as well. "Why, it's the biggest in the world," she crowed.

Allen was endorsed by Harvard University and conducted a whistle-stop speaking tour from Los Angeles to Omaha, where, in May, she was finally given the Surprise Party nomination for president by acclamation. Her acceptance speech was aired live by NBC, the network that carried *The Jack Benny Show*. Allen fell a tad short of unseating Franklin Roosevelt, but she did garner a few thousand votes.

They Said It

> **Gracie:** Well, you see one Christmas my father caught a wild turkey, and he fed him corn and chestnuts. But then we didn't have the heart to kill him so we let him get away.
> **George:** Oh, I see.
> **Gracie:** But the turkey liked the food so well that he came back each year. And that way we always had . . .
> **George:** A turkey for Christmas dinner?
> **Gracie:** Yes.

Major Awards

EMMY AWARD NOMINATIONS (11)

1952 (1): Best Comedy Show
1953 (1): Best Situation Comedy
1954 (2): Best Situation Comedy; Best Supporting Actress in a Regular Series (Bea Benaderet)
1955 (3): Best Situation Comedy Series; Best Actress Starring in a Regular Series (Gracie Allen); Best Supporting Actress in a Regular Series (Bea Benaderet)
1956 (1): Best Actress, Continuing Performance (Gracie Allen)
1957 (1): Best Continuing Performance by a Comedienne in a Series (Gracie Allen)

1958 (1): Best Continuing Performance (Female) in a Series by a Comedienne, Singer, Hostess, Dancer, M.C., Announcer, Narrator, Panelist, or Any Person Who Essentially Plays Herself (Gracie Allen)

1959 (1): Best Actress in a Leading Role (Continuing Character) in a Comedy Series (Gracie Allen)

Further Reading

Blythe, Cheryl, and Susan Sackett. *Say Goodnight, Gracie! The Story of Burns and Allen.* New York: Dutton, 1986.

Burns, George. *Gracie: A Love Story.* New York: G.P. Putnam's Sons, 1988.

✳ **27** ✳

Barney Miller

(1975–1982)

Cast: Hal Linden (Captain Barney Miller), Max Gail (Detective Stan "Wojo" Wojciehowicz), Ron Glass (Detective Ron Harris), Steve Landesberg (Detective Arthur Dietrich), Ron Carey (Officer Carl Levitt), Jack Soo (Detective Nick Yemana), Abe Vigoda (Detective Phil Fish), James Gregory (Inspector Frank Luger), Gregory Sierra (Sergeant Chano Amenguale)

Created by: Producer and writer Danny Arnold and writer Theodore J. Flicker

Network: ABC

First Air Date: January 23, 1975

Last Air Date: September 9, 1982

Broadcast History:
January 23, 1975–January 1976: Thursday at 8:00–8:30 PM
January 1976–December 1976: Thursday at 8:30–9:00 PM
December 1976–March 1982: Thursday at 9:00–9:30 PM
March 1982–April 1982: Friday at 8:30–9:00 PM
April 1982–September 9, 1982: Thursday at 9:00–9:30 PM

Seasons: 8

Episodes: 170

Ratings History: 1974–1975 (not in Top 30), 1975–1976 (not in Top 30), 1976–1977 (17), 1977–1978 (17), 1978–1979 (15), 1979–1980 (20), 1980–1981 (not in Top 30), 1981–1982 (not in Top 30)

Ron Glass, Max Gail, Hal Linden, Ron Carey, Steve Landesberg, and Jack Soo. *ABC/ Photofest ©ABC*

Overview

If not for Danny Arnold and John Rich, *Barney Miller* would never have graced the airwaves, and that would have been a shame—despite the fact that Arnold and Rich clashed professionally. Arnold already had such producing and writing credits in his pocket as the highly popular *Bewitched* and the critically acclaimed *My World and Welcome to It* when he pitched a sitcom entitled *The Life and Times of Captain Barney Miller* to ABC that ran as a pilot in 1974 but was ultimately rejected. Rich, who had beefed up an already impressive resume by directing *All in the Family*, sought to resurrect the venture. ABC wised up to its potential and put it on the air.

Never mind that Arnold, who was tied so strongly to the project that he put his stamp on all areas of production, pushed Rich out after just two episodes. *Barney Miller* blossomed into one of the most critically and intellectually acclaimed sitcoms in the history of American television. The sophisticated humor never demeaned the characters or even the collection of unsavory prisoners placed behind bars at the 12th Precinct in the Greenwich Village section of New York City.

This was no ordinary cop show. It featured one of the best and deepest casts ever assembled, although none of its members had previously gained fame on the small screen. The lead actor was Hal Linden, who managed a seamless transition from Broadway to television. Linden played the title role, a tough, but fair, captain who tried to sympathize with the plight of the accused. But the surprise star was Abe Vigoda, who played slouched-over, grouchy detective Phil Fish with such aplomb that he earned a spin-off simply known as *Fish*.

Each significant cast member crafted a unique and attractive character. Ron Glass brought a still all-too-rare refinement to an African American role in the 1970s as Detective Ron Harris, whose wide-ranging knowledge of all things trivial marveled his colleagues. Irascible detective Stanley Wojciehowicz (Max Gail) had a likeable guy-next-door quality, despite a prodigious temper. Detective Nick Yemana (Jack Soo) entertained viewers and his fellow cops with a quick wit and poker-faced delivery. Sergeant Chano Amenguale (Gregory Sierra, who showed his versatility by playing a Jewish vigilante in *All in the Family* and a Puerto Rican detective in this show) was sarcastic and sometimes unsympathetic to criminals.

Plot lines not only revolved around their relationships, but the stories behind the parade of con artists, whores, muggers, thieves, and just plain wackos that had been rounded up and tossed into the slammer. The personal lives of the main characters quickly become secondary to their interrelationships and those between the cops and criminals. Barney's wife Elizabeth (Barbara Barrie) began the show as a regular but was written out after the first season.

The second year brought two more notable characters in diminutive officer Carl Levitt (Ron Carey), who expressed his desire to become a detective in no uncertain terms, and the intellectual and overanalytical detective Arthur Dietrich (Steve Landesberg). The loss of Vigoda and Soo, who died in 1979, resulted in the addition of James Gregory, who portrayed mean-spirited inspector Frank Luger.

Barney Miller paved the way for other sitcoms that eschewed the notion of spotlighting both the home and professional lives of their main characters. The depth of its characterization and intriguing nature of the story lines and plot lines proved strong enough to carry the show. It can be argued that the depth of its cast prevented any of the actors from winning individual awards. The show snagged two Golden Globes and one Emmy for Outstanding Comedy Series. Yet, Linden, Vigoda, Gail, and Landesberg never took home the prize, despite consistent nominations. To fans of the show, however, it doesn't matter. They will remember *Barney Miller* as a show that raised the level of comic erudition in television programming.

Soo What?

The respect fellow cast members had for Jack Soo, who died of cancer of the esophagus in 1979, was put into action on an episode that same year. In that installment, they express their feelings for Soo individually and unscripted as clips of his portrayal of Detective Nick Yemana are interspersed. They raise their coffee cups in honor of him at the end of the episode, concluding a long-running joke about the terrible java he made (quite unintentionally) for his fellow cops.

Did You Know?

Both Ron Carey and Steve Landesberg made guest appearances as crooks before landing full-time roles on the show.

They Said It

Nick: Then Fish runs in the alley, and he leaps over us like one of those, what do you call those things in Africa that run and leap in the air?
Ron: Slaves.

Barney: So Dietrich, big plans for the weekend?
Arthur: No, I'm staying home. I've gotten involved in the New Celibacy Movement.
Barney: Oh, yeah? What's that?
Arthur: It's a movement for people who are fed up with the whole shallow dating scene.
Barney: Couldn't get a date, huh?
Arthur: Not a single one.

Nick: I'm not Chinese, you know.
Captain Donnelly: That doesn't matter, detective.
Nick: Now it doesn't matter, but in 1942 . . .

Major Awards

EMMY AWARD WINS (3)

1979 (1): Outstanding Directing in a Comedy or Comedy-Variety or Music Series (Noam Pitlik for "The Harris Incident")
1980 (1): Outstanding Writing in a Comedy Series (Bob Colleary for "Photographer")
1982 (1): Outstanding Comedy Series

EMMY AWARD NOMINATIONS, IN ADDITION TO WINS (29)

1976 (6): Outstanding Comedy Series; Outstanding Lead Actor in a Comedy Series (Hal Linden); Outstanding Continuing Performance by a Supporting Actor in a Comedy Series (Abe Vigoda); Outstanding Single Performance by a Supporting Actor in Comedy or Drama Series (Roscoe Lee Browne for "The Escape Artist"); Outstanding Writing in a Comedy Series (Danny Arnold and Chris Heyward for "The Hero"); Outstanding Achievement in Video Tape Editing for a Series (Fred Golan, Homer Powell, and Paul Schatzkin for "Happy New Year")
1977 (4): Outstanding Comedy Series; Outstanding Lead Actor in a Comedy Series (Hal Linden); Outstanding Continuing Performance by a Supporting Actor in a Comedy Series (Abe Vigoda); Outstanding Writing in a Comedy Series (Tony Sheehan and Danny Arnold for "Quarantine: Part 2")
1978 (4): Outstanding Comedy Series; Outstanding Lead Actor in a Comedy Series (Hal Linden); Outstanding Single Performance by a Supporting Actor in Comedy or Drama Series (Abe Vigoda for "Goodbye, Mr. Fish: Part II"); Outstanding

Single Performance by a Supporting Actor in Comedy or Drama Series (Larry Gelman for "Goodbye, Mr. Fish: Part II")

1979 (3): Outstanding Comedy Series; Outstanding Lead Actor in a Comedy Series (Hal Linden); Outstanding Performance by a Supporting Actor in a Comedy or Comedy-Variety or Music Series (Max Gail)

1980 (4): Outstanding Comedy Series; Outstanding Lead Actor in a Comedy Series (Hal Linden); Outstanding Supporting Actor in a Comedy or Variety or Music Series (Max Gail); Outstanding Supporting Actor in a Comedy or Variety or Music Series (Steve Landesberg)

1981 (4): Outstanding Comedy Series; Outstanding Lead Actor in a Comedy Series (Hal Linden); Outstanding Supporting Actor in a Comedy or Variety or Music Series (Steve Landesberg); Outstanding Directing in a Comedy Series (Noam Pitlik for "Liquidation")

1982 (4): Outstanding Lead Actor in a Comedy Series (Hal Linden); Outstanding Supporting Actor in a Comedy or Variety or Music Series (Steve Landesberg); Outstanding Supporting Actor in a Comedy or Variety or Music Series (Ron Glass); Outstanding Writing in a Comedy Series (Frank Dungan, Jeff Stein, and Tony Sheehan for "Landmark: Part 3")

GOLDEN GLOBE WINS (2)

1976 (1): Best TV Show, Musical/Comedy
1977 (1): Best TV Show, Musical/Comedy

GOLDEN GLOBE NOMINATIONS, IN ADDITION TO WINS (5)

1976 (1): Best TV Actor, Musical/Comedy (Hal Linden)
1977 (1): Best TV Actor, Musical/Comedy (Hal Linden)
1978 (2): Best TV Series, Musical/Comedy; Best TV Actor, Musical/Comedy (Hal Linden)
1981 (1): Best Performance by an Actor in a TV Series, Musical/Comedy (Hal Linden)

HUMANITAS PRIZE NOMINATION

1978: 30-Minute Category (Reinhold Weege)

Further Reading

"Hal Linden Biography (1931–)." *Film Reference.* Available online at www.filmreference.com/film/73/Hal-Linden.html.

✷ 28 ✷
The Office
(2005–2013)

Cast: Steve Carell (Michael Scott), Rainn Wilson (Dwight Schrute), John Krasinski (Jim Halpert), Jenna Fischer (Pam Beesly), Leslie David Baker (Stanley Hudson), Brian Baumgartner (Kevin Malone), Angela Kinsey (Angela Martin), Phyllis Smith (Phyllis Lapin-Vance), Kate Flaherty (Meredith Palmer), Creed Bratton (Creed Bratton), B. J. Novak (Ryan Howard), Oscar Nuñez (Oscar Martinez), Mindy Kaling (Kelly Kapoor), Ed Helms (Andy Bernard), Paul Lieberstein (Toby Flenderson), Craig Robinson (Darryl Philbin), Ellie Kemper (Kelly Erin Hannon)

Created by: Executive producers Ricky Gervais and Stephen Merchant

Network: NBC

First Air Date: March 24, 2005

Last Air Date: May 16, 2013

Broadcast History:
March 24, 2005: Thursday at 9:30–10:00 PM
March 2005–April 2005: Tuesday at 9:30–10:00 PM
September 2005–December 2005: Tuesday at 9:30–10:00 PM
January 2006–May 2006: Thursday at 9:30–10:00 PM
September 2006–May 2007: Thursday at 8:30–9:00 PM
September 2007–May 16, 2013: Thursday at 9:00–9:30 PM

Seasons: 9

Episodes: 174

Ratings History: Never in Top 30

Back row, from left: Rainn Wilson, Jenna Fischer, B. J. Novak, Steve Carell; front: John Krasinski. *NBC/Photofest ©NBC; Photographer: Mitchell Haaseth*

Overview

First-time viewers of *The Office* likely found it as confusing as a first day on the job at the Dunder Mifflin Paper Company. It might have even made you want to quit—watching, that is. The quick cutaways. The focus on individual characters speaking directly into the camera. The long, pregnant pauses between lines. The documentary style. For a character-driven sitcom, the stuttering timing of the filming made it difficult to maintain the interest of viewers long enough to keep them from flipping the channel. It's no wonder *The Office* hadn't ascended past number fifty-two in the Nielsen ratings through 2012.

But those who stuck around long enough to gain an understanding of the characters and their personalities and motivations were hooked. The critics were similarly impressed. The brilliance of the show resulted in an Outstanding Comedy Series Emmy nomination in each of its first six seasons and a win in its debut year of 2006.

The story line indeed revolved around the employees of the Dunder Mifflin Paper Company in Scranton, Pennsylvania. It was a typical office, with cubicles, staplers, paper clips, and copy machines, but there was nothing typical about the personnel. The unfortunate head of the screwy crew was regional manager Michael Scott (Steve Carell), who worked in vain (except for in his own mind) to be funny and hip to his underlings. He had no filter from his brain to his mouth to prevent inappropriate cracks, particularly to women and accounting department worker Oscar Martinez (Oscar Nuñez), who often bore the brunt of his improper jokes as both Hispanic and gay.

Dunder Mifflin might have gone out of business if not for the salesmanship of Dwight Schrute (Rainn Wilson), but his fellow employees would likely have traded a few sales for the right to kick him to the curb, or at least kick him in the butt. His lacking in the social graces and expressed feelings of superiority either annoyed or amused his colleagues, especially receptionist Pam Beesly (Jenna Fischer), who was most often in his line of fire. Wilson certainly understood the distaste for his character, calling Dwight in one episode commentary a "fascist nerd."

The quick pace of the show thrived on the large number of character contributors beyond Michael and Dwight. Salesman and eventual comanager Jim Halpert (John Krasinski) sought to win the affection of Pam by aiding and abetting in pranks played against disliked Dwight. The two later wed and became parents to a baby girl. Shady Ryan Howard (B. J. Novak) began as merely a temp, but he rose in the corporate hierarchy until his fraudulent activities cost him his job and forced him to return to the same position in which he began in the Scranton office. Nervous neat freak Angela Martin (Angela Kinsey) and immature goofball Kevin Malone (Brian Baumgartner) brought contrast and conflict to the accounting department. Salesman Stanley Hudson (Leslie David Baker) spent much of his time figuring out crossword puzzles rather than working or angrily fielding Michael's jokes about his African American heritage. Saleswoman Phyllis Lapin-Vance (Phyllis Smith) brought a rare selflessness and kindness to Dunder Mifflin, while outgoing customer service representative Kelly Kapoor (Mindy Kaling) was the promiscuous boozer of the bunch.

The wide-ranging personalities and motivations resulted in intriguing relationships and story lines, but they were so numerous and transient that they were difficult to grasp for viewers not in on the show from the beginning. Cast changes caused some to lose identity with the sitcom, which continued to struggle to attract an audience worthy of its unique and attractive qualities. Even Carell bolted after the seventh season and was replaced as the top banana by noted movie actor James Spader, who played the role of CEO Robert California, leading to the promotion of Dwight into Michael's old position.

Many fans of *The Office* considered it among the funniest shows on television. The show attracted enough viewers to remain on the air for nine years through the 2012–2013 season. The numbers slipped dramatically in 2011 and 2012, but a new generation of fans finally had an opportunity to pick up on what was once a fresh sitcom from the beginning through syndication.

Vice President Schrute?

Republican senator John McCain, who ran an unsuccessful presidential campaign in 2008, was a fan of *The Office*. During his run for the nomination, he offered to *The Daily Show* host Jon Stewart that Dwight Schrute would be his vice presidential candidate (some might claim that would have proven to be a wiser choice than Sarah Palin). Rainn Wilson was quick to reply during a visit to *The Tonight Show with Jay Leno*. He listed his demands needed to place his character into that high office. Included among them was the right to pilot Air Force One, an Iron Man suit, and the appointment of Dunder Mifflin boss Michael Scott as "ambassador" to Hawaii.

Did You Know?

The city of Scranton has embraced being the city in which the fictional Dunder Mifflin Paper Company is located. The company logo sits on a lamppost in front of the city hall in that Pennsylvania town.

They Said It

Michael: You don't call retarded people retards. It's bad taste. You call your friends retards when they're acting retarded.

Jan's lawyer: [representing her in a wrongful termination lawsuit] How long have you known Ms. Levinson?
Michael: Six years and two months.
Jan's lawyer: And you were directly under her the entire time?
Michael: That's what she said.
Jan's lawyer: Excuse me?
Michael: [slowly] That's what she said.

Major Awards

EMMY AWARD WINS (5)

2006 (1): Outstanding Comedy Series
2007 (2): Outstanding Writing for a Comedy Series (Greg Daniels for "Gay Witch Hunt"); Outstanding Single Camera Picture Editing for a Comedy Series (David Rogers and Dean Holland for "The Job")
2009 (1): Outstanding Directing for a Comedy Series (Jeffrey Blitz for "Stress Relief")
2013 (1): Outstanding Single-Camera Picture Editing for a Comedy Series (David Rogers, Claire Scanlon for episode "Finale")

EMMY AWARD NOMINATIONS, IN ADDITION TO WINS (39)

2006 (4): Outstanding Lead Actor in a Comedy Series (Steve Carell); Outstanding Writing for a Comedy Series (Michael Schur for "Christmas Party"); Outstanding Single-Camera Picture Editing for a Comedy Series (David Rogers for "Christmas Party"); Outstanding Single-Camera Picture Editing for a Comedy Series (Dean Holland for episode "Booze Cruise")

2007 (7): Outstanding Comedy Series; Outstanding Lead Actor in a Comedy Series (Steve Carell); Outstanding Supporting Actor in a Comedy Series (Rainn Wilson); Outstanding Supporting Actress in a Comedy Series (Jenna Fischer); Outstanding Writing for a Comedy Series (Michael Schur for "The Negotiation"); Outstanding Directing for a Comedy Series (Ken Kwapis for "Gay Witch Hunt"); Outstanding Sound Mixing for a Comedy or Drama Series (Half-Hour) and Animation (Benjamin Patrick, John W. Cook II, and Peter J. Nusbaum for "The Coup")

2008 (8): Outstanding Comedy Series; Outstanding Lead Actor in a Comedy Series (Steve Carell); Outstanding Supporting Actor in a Comedy Series (Rainn Wilson); Outstanding Writing for a Comedy Series (Lee Eisenberg and Greg Stupnitsky for "Dinner Party"); Outstanding Directing for a Comedy Series (Paul Feig for "Good-bye, Toby"); Outstanding Directing for a Comedy Series (Paul Lieberstein for "Money: Part I and Part II"); Outstanding Picture Editing for a Comedy Series (Single or Multi-Camera) (David Rogers and Dean Holland for "Good-bye, Toby"); Outstanding Sound Mixing for a Comedy or Drama Series (Half-Hour) and Animation (Benjamin Patrick, John W. Cook II, and Peter J. Nusbaum for "Local Ad")

2009 (9): Outstanding Comedy Series; Outstanding Lead Actor in a Comedy Series (Steve Carell); Outstanding Supporting Actor in a Comedy Series (Rainn Wilson); Outstanding Picture Editing for a Comedy Series (Single or Multi-Camera) (David Rogers and Dean Holland for "Stress Relief"); Outstanding Picture Editing for a Comedy Series (Single or Multi-Camera) (Claire Scanlon for "Dream Team"); Outstanding Picture Editing for a Comedy Series (Single or Multi-Camera) (Stuart Bass for "Two Weeks"); Outstanding Sound Mixing for a Comedy or Drama Series (Half-Hour) and Animation (Benjamin Patrick, John W. Cook II, and Peter J. Nusbaum for "The Michael Scott Paper Co."); Outstanding Casting for a Comedy Series (Allison Jones); Outstanding Creative Achievement in Interactive Media-Fiction

2010 (4): Outstanding Comedy Series; Outstanding Lead Actor in a Comedy Series (Steve Carell); Outstanding Writing for a Comedy Series (Greg Daniels and Mindy Kaling for "Niagara"); Outstanding Sound Mixing for a Comedy or Drama Series (Half-Hour) and Animation (Benjamin Patrick, John W. Cook II, and Peter J. Nusbaum for "Niagara")

2011 (4): Outstanding Comedy Series; Outstanding Lead Actor in a Comedy Series (Steve Carell); Outstanding Writing for a Comedy Series (Greg Daniels for "Good-bye, Michael"); Outstanding Sound Mixing for a Comedy or Drama Series (Half-Hour) and Animation (Benjamin Patrick, John W. Cook II, and Peter J. Nusbaum for "Andy's Play")

2013 (3): Outstanding Writing for a Comedy Series (Greg Daniels for episode "Finale"); Outstanding Sound Mixing for a Comedy or Drama Series (Half-Hour) and Animation; Outstanding Special Class—Short-Format Nonfiction Programs (for "The Farewells")

GOLDEN GLOBE WIN (1)

2006 (1): Best Performance by an Actor in a TV Series, Musical/Comedy (Steve Carell)

GOLDEN GLOBE NOMINATIONS, IN ADDITION TO WIN (7)

2007 (1): Best Performance by an Actor in a TV Series, Musical/Comedy (Steve Carell)

2008 (1): Best Performance by an Actor in a TV Series, Musical/Comedy (Steve Carell)

2009 (2): Best TV Series, Musical/Comedy; Best Performance by an Actor in a TV Series, Musical/Comedy (Steve Carell)

2010 (2): Best TV Series, Musical/Comedy; Best Performance by an Actor in a TV Series, Musical/Comedy (Steve Carell)

2011 (1): Best Performance by an Actor in a TV Series, Musical/Comedy (Steve Carell)

Further Reading

Sepinwall, Alan. "Review: 'The Office' Struggles to Find Its Center Post-Steve Carell." *Hitfix. com*, November 10, 2011. Available online at www.hitfix.com/blogs/whats-alan-watching/posts/review-the-office-struggles-to-find-its-center-post-steve-carell.

Wisnewski, J. Jeremy, Ed. *The Office and Philosophy: Scenes from the Unexamined Life*. Malden, MA: Wiley-Blackwell, 2008.

29

Get Smart

(1965–1970)

Cast: Don Adams (Maxwell Smart, Agent 86), Barbara Feldon (Agent 99), Edward Platt (Thaddeus, "The Chief"), Bernie Kopell (Siegfried)

Created by: Mel Brooks and Buck Henry

Network: NBC (1965–1969), CBS (1969–1970)

First Air Date: September 18, 1965

Last Air Date: September 11, 1970

Broadcast History:
    September 18, 1965–September 1968: Saturday at 8:30–9:00 PM
    September 1968–September 1969: Saturday at 8:00–8:30 PM
    September 1969–September 11, 1970: Friday at 7:30–8:00 PM

Seasons: 5

Episodes: 138

Ratings History: 1965–1966 (12), 1966–1967 (22), 1967–1968 (not in Top 30), 1968–1969 (not in Top 30), 1969–1970 (not in Top 30)

Overview

Throughout much of the twentieth century, movies contributed most of the catchphrases in the American lexicon. Television eventually stole that distinction. And until *Seinfeld* rolled around, the sitcom that foisted more catchphrases onto a very willing public was *Get Smart*.

Scatterbrained super-secret agent Maxwell Smart, played in award-winning fashion by Don Adams, uttered every one of them in his distinctive nasal voice. They were

Don Adams. *CBS/Photofest ©CBS*

repeated by millions of viewers as *Get Smart* exploded onto the scene as an immedi-ate hit in 1965. One can still recall Smart delivering such lines as "Sorry about that, Chief," "Would you believe . . .," and "Missed it by *that* much" with precision timing.

This imaginative sitcom was the brainchild of creative comedy writers Mel Brooks and Buck Henry. Its premise of an inept secret agent stumbling his way through cases took advantage of the success of James Bond movies and spy thriller shows like *The Man from U.N.C.L.E. Get Smart* featured the title character teamed with beautiful and forever unnamed Agent 99 (Barbara Feldon) working for C.O.N.T.R.O.L., a government spy agency headed by "The Chief" (Edward Platt). The show not only spoofed spy movies and TV programs, but also the modern gadgetry featured in them. The most humorous *Get Smart* contraption was the Cone of Silence, which hovered above The Chief's desk and descended over him and Smart to keep their talks top secret. The only problem was that it either malfunctioned or gave off an echo that made their discussions loud and clear from the outside. But the most memorable prop was Smart's shoe phone, which provided a ridiculous image whenever he used it.

The on-screen rapport between the Max and 99 characters proved to be a key to the success of the show. Their growing romantic interest was passed off as quite realistic and led to their eventual marriage. The two spies battled the forces working for K.A.O.S., specifically the inane and fiendish Siegfried (Bernie Kopell), who had earned the ridiculous title of vice president of public relations and terror at that evil organization.

Side characters also proved memorable. Among them was hapless Agent 13 (Dave Ketchum), who, despite his six-foot, two-inch frame, was stationed and stuffed into such spots as an ice machine, a mailbox, a locker, and the inside of a sofa. Another was the robot Hymie, who was built by K.A.O.S., transformed into an ally by Smart, and took orders quite literally. Told by The Chief to "knock that stuff off" as he made annoying computing noises while filing papers into his memory bank, he swept the papers off the desk.

The contrasts between the silliness of Smart, the quick thinking of Agent 99, and the dead serious and easily frustrated nature of The Chief helped make the show a success. So did the genius of Brooks and Henry, who wrote the vast majority of the episodes and created deliciously implausible plot lines that spoofed social and political trends, for instance, when many of the nation's teenagers (as well as two C.O.N.T.R.O.L. agents) fell under the spell of the Groovy Guru (Larry Storch) and couldn't stop dancing. The Guru planned to incite them to riot by broadcasting a special song performed by a rock group called The Sacred Cows.

The popularity of *Get Smart* fell after it surged to number twelve in the Nielsen ratings its first season. It fell to number twenty-two its second year and then permanently out of the Top 30. Like other sitcoms, particularly in the 1960s, that depended on outrageous premises and silly devices to elicit laughs, TV viewers eventually tired of seeing the same shticks repeated time and again. They no longer found humor in Smart talking on his shoe phone or The Chief frustrated by the Cone of Silence.

Despite its inability to maintain its place as one of the most popular shows of its time, *Get Smart* remains one of the most memorable sitcoms in American television history. It spawned an albeit disastrous and deservedly short-lived namesake series on Fox in 1995, and a far more successful 2008 movie featuring a star-studded cast of Steve Carell, Anne Hathaway, and Alan Arkin. Although Carell didn't play the Smart character with the absurdity of his predecessor, he did capture the essence of the role. It was a tall task. Adams, after all, earned three Emmys for his portrayal of Maxwell Smart.

Oh, Henry!

Get Smart cocreator and writer Buck Henry earned a reputation for boasting one of the most inventive minds in American entertainment. He not only won an Emmy for penning a two-part 1967 episode entitled "Ship of Fools," he also won an Academy Award the following year for writing the screenplay for *The Graduate*, which is still considered one of the greatest achievements in the history of American cinema. Henry was far less accomplished as an actor, although he was a semiregular alongside the likes of John Belushi, Dan Aykroyd, Gilda Radner, and Bill Murray in the early years of *Saturday Night Live*.

Did You Know?

Barbara Feldon married Burt Nodella, who won two Emmy Awards as producer of *Get Smart*.

They Said It

> **Smart:** [interrogating the evil Mohammed Khan] You think you've got me, but I have you surrounded by the entire mounted 17th Bengal Lancers.
> **Khan:** I don't believe you.
> **Smart:** Would you believe the 1st Bengal Lancers?
> **Khan:** No.
> **Smart:** How about Gunga Din on a donkey?

> **Smart:** The old bulletproof-cummerbund-in-the-tuxedo trick.
> **Smart:** The old microphone-in-the-squeegee trick.
> **Smart:** The old Professor-Peter-Peckinpah-all-purpose-anti-personnel-Peckinpah-pocket-pistol-under-the-toupee trick.
> **Smart:** [putting his forefinger and thumb an inch apart after a K.A.O.S. agent, who jumped out of a window, fell past a truckload of mattresses] Missed it by that much.

> **Shtarker [K.A.O.S. agent]:** [to sidekick Siegfried] Are you crazy? This is radioactive material. One wrong move . . . and it's ka-frickin'-boom!
> **Siegfried:** This is K.A.O.S. We don't 'ka-frickin'-boom' here.

Major Awards

EMMY AWARD WINS (7)

1967 (2): Outstanding Continued Performance by an Actor in a Leading Role in a Comedy Series (Don Adams); Outstanding Writing Achievement in Comedy (Buck Henry and Leonard Stern for "Ship of Spies")

1968 (3): Outstanding Comedy Series; Outstanding Continued Performance by an Actor in a Leading Role in a Comedy Series (Don Adams); Outstanding Directorial Achievement in Comedy (Bruce Bilson for "Maxwell Smart, Private Eye")

1969 (2): Outstanding Comedy Series; Outstanding Continued Performance by an Actor in a Leading Role in a Comedy Series (Don Adams)

EMMY AWARD NOMINATIONS, IN ADDITION TO WINS (7)

1966 (4): Outstanding Comedy Series; Outstanding Continued Performance by an Actor in a Leading Role in a Comedy Series (Don Adams); Outstanding Writing Achievement in Comedy (Mel Brooks and Buck Henry for "Mr. Big"); Outstanding Directorial Achievement in Comedy (Paul Bogart for "Diplomat's Daughter")

1967 (1): Outstanding Comedy Series

1968 (1): Outstanding Continued Performance by an Actress in a Leading Role in a Comedy Series (Barbara Feldon)

1969 (1): Outstanding Continued Performance by an Actress in a Leading Role in a Comedy Series (Barbara Feldon)

GOLDEN GLOBE NOMINATIONS (2)

1966 (2): Best TV Show; Best TV Star, Male (Don Adams)

Further Reading

Adams, Don, and Bill Dana. *Would You Believe . . .?* New York: Bantam Books: 1982.

Green, Joey. *The Get Smart Handbook.* New York: Collier Books, 1993.

✴ 30 ✴

Family Guy

(1999–2002, 2005–)

Voices: Peter Griffin, Stewie Griffin, Brian the Dog, Glenn Quagmire (Seth MacFarlane); Lois Griffin (Alex Borstein); Meg Griffin (Mila Kunis); Chris Griffin (Seth Green); Officer Joe Swanson (Patrick Warburton); Cleveland Brown (Mike Henry)

Created by: Executive producer, writer, and voice Seth MacFarlane

Network: FOX

First Air Date: April 6, 1999

Broadcast History:
January 1999–May 1999: Sunday at 8:30–9:00 PM
September 1999–August 2000: Thursday at 9:00–9:30 PM
July 2001–November 2003: Thursday at 8:30–9:00 PM
May 2005: Sunday at 9:00–9:30 PM

Seasons: 11

Episodes: 201

Ratings History: Never in Top 30

Overview

Those who consider themselves television anarchists and believe nothing should be censored can take heart at what passes through on *Family Guy*. You want gross? How about frequent farts, belches, and one marathon barfing session resulting from the chugging of syrup of ipecac. You want sexually inappropriate? How about a major character who lusts after teenage girls and another named Herbert the Pervert, who seeks to seduce small boys? How about a pot-smoking dog shown in bed after having

Brian, Meg, Chris, Peter, Lois, and Stewie. *FOX/Photofest ©FOX*

had intercourse with humans? You want just plain wrong? How about a father offering his teenage son crystal meth, then pulling his own eye out? How about joking about dead babies? How about a barbershop quartet dancing around the bed of a man with end-stage AIDS and singing a song entitled "You Have AIDS"?

Indeed, viewers must temporarily divorce themselves from their morality to find such *Family Guy* bits funny. But not every moment is disgusting or reprehensible. The vast majority is simply ridiculous.

The most popular animated sitcom since the turn of the twenty-first century spotlights a beyond dysfunctional family living in fictional Quahog, Rhode Island. Show creator Seth MacFarlane voices outrageously insensitive, stupid, lazy, and obese husband and father Peter Griffin, who somehow manages to stay employed as a safety inspector at the Happy-Go-Lucky Toy Company, until his boss chokes to death on a roll at Peter's house. When he isn't fighting bloody battles with gigantic chickens, he is feeding the insecurities of his two teenagers, the miserable and awkward Meg (Mila Kunis) and overweight and underachieving son Chris (Seth Green), who seems destined to follow in his father's footsteps as an uncaring, unfeeling loser. All of this would be quite sad if the writers would work to convince viewers to care about the characters rather than just laugh at them. Viewers roar at how Meg's loneliness and unhappiness are ignored, or even exacerbated, by everyone in her family because the entire show is so silly in the first place.

How silly? How about an evil, narcissistic baby with a British accent named Stewie (MacFarlane) whose love/hate relationship with his mother, Lois (Alex Borstein), causes him to alternately yearn to be nursed by her and plan her murder and the end of the world? How about an alcoholic, talking dog named Brian (MacFarlane) who is the family intellectual? How about the revelation that sex addict neighbor Glenn Quagmire (MacFarlane) was Jack the Ripper in a previous life? How about paraplegic police officer Joe Swanson (Patrick Warburton) claiming that he lost his legs trying to prevent the Grinch from stealing Christmas from an orphanage? How about Peter accidentally killing his adopted father Francis (Charles Durning) on Meg's seventeenth birthday, when he dressed up as a clown, got drunk, fell off a unicycle he attempted to ride down the stairs, and landed on top of his dad, whose last words at the hospital were, "Peter . . . you're a fat stinking drunk!"?

And how about those cutaways? *Family Guy* features several in each show that flash back to absurd moments in the lives of the Griffins or notable people, real or fictional, in the present time or history. In one episode, perhaps the funniest makes light of what, in reality, would have been a torturous childhood for *Peanuts* character Charlie Brown. He is depicted as a crack addict and drug dealer who shows up to a *Peanuts* reunion with a drug-addled prostitute. Another pokes fun at former president George W. Bush, as he is spotted by Brian hiding in a tree house to avoid taking action during Hurricane Katrina. "You gotta come down and deal with this," Brian says. "Don't make me do stuff," Bush answers.

Family Guy premiered after the 1999 Super Bowl and nearly cracked the Top 30 in the Nielsen ratings in its first season. It was cancelled in April 2002, but resurrected after strong DVD sales and a fan campaign to return it to the air. Its popularity grew after it was brought back, and, since May 2005, it remains a Sunday night staple.

Few shows in the history of television have proven more controversial than *Family Guy*, although it rarely attempts to make a strong social or political statement. Critics simply hate it for what they perceive as bad taste. Fans simply love it because it makes them laugh and, well, because of what some of *them* perceive as bad taste.

(Johnny) Bravo, Seth!

Family Guy creator Seth MacFarlane established himself as one of the most successful among the new wave of cartoon writers well before the show hit the air. He wrote for such popular animated programs as *Dexter's Laboratory* and *Johnny Bravo* and later penned episodes of *American Dad* and *Family Guy* spin-off *The Cleveland Show*. It was also amazing that he remained alive on September 11, 2001. A mix-up by his travel agent forced him to miss his morning flight, which was hijacked by terrorists and crashed into the World Trade Center in New York, killing every passenger onboard.

Another Side of Family Guy

Millions of *Family Guy* viewers were shocked by a deadly serious and thoughtful episode that aired in the spring of 2010. It features Brian and Stewie locked in a bank vault and the former's admission that he is suicidal after the latter discovers that the dog owns a gun. The two talk at length about the revelation. Brian states that his life has become meaningless and purposeless, leading Stewie to call Brian selfish for wanting to kill himself. Stewie expresses his love for Brian and adds that he would be angry at him for doing himself in because he would be losing the creature that brought him so much joy.

Did You Know?

Adam West, who played Batman in the campy, flash in the pan 1960s TV series, voices the mayor of Quahog in *Family Guy*.

They Said It

> **Peter:** [talking to Sunday school children] And when you die, you go to a wonderful place called heaven. [the kids gasp with joy and Peter laughs]. Nah, I'm just jackin' ya. You'll all rot in the ground. [the kids look horrified]

> **Stewie:** Up! Stewie wants to go uppie! Mmm . . . mama's skin's so soft.
> **Lois:** Oh, aren't you affectionate tonight. Well, let me give you a kiss.
> **Stewie:** Another! Another! Mama has candy kisses!
> **Brian:** [leaving the table in disgust] All right, that's enough.
> **Lois:** Stewie . . . did you unhook mommy's bra?

> **Peter:** Huh, I wonder what Scooby and the gang are up to?
> **TV Announcer:** [as the Scooby-Doo theme plays] We now return to *The Scooby-Doo Murder Files*.
> **Fred Jones:** Gee whiz, gang. Looks like the killer gutted the victim, strangled him with his own intestines, and then dumped the body in the river.
> **Velma:** Jinkies! What a mystery!

> **Peter:** Brian, there's a message in my Alpha Bits. It says "OOOOO.
> **Brian:** Peter, those are Cheerios.

Major Awards

EMMY AWARD WINS (5)

2000 (1): Outstanding Voice-Over Performance (Seth MacFarlane)
2002 (1): Outstanding Music and Lyrics (Seth MacFarlane and Walter Murphy for the song "You've Got a Lot to See" for "Brian Wallows and Peter's Swallows")
2007 (1): Outstanding Individual Achievement in Animation (Steve Fonti for "No Chris Left Behind")
2010 (1): Outstanding Individual Achievement in Animation (Greg Colton for "Road to the Multiverse")

2011 (1): Outstanding Sound Mixing for a Comedy or Drama Series (Half-Hour) and Animation (Patrick Clark and James F. Fitzpatrick for "Road to the North Pole")

EMMY AWARD NOMINATIONS, IN ADDITION TO WINS (14)

2000 (2): Outstanding Animated Program (for Programming One Hour or Less); Outstanding Music and Lyrics (Ron Jones and Chris Sheridan for the song "We Only Live to Kiss Your Ass" for "Peter, Peter Caviar Eater")

2005 (1): Outstanding Animated Program (for Programming Less Than One Hour)

2006 (1): Outstanding Animated Program (for Programming Less Than One Hour)

2007 (1): Outstanding Original Music and Lyrics (Danny Smith and Walter Murphy for "Peter's Two Dads")

2008 (2): Outstanding Animated Program (for Programming One Hour or More); Outstanding Music Composition for a Series (Ronald Neal Jones for "Lois Kills Stewie")

2009 (2): Outstanding Comedy Series; Outstanding Voice-Over Performance (Seth MacFarlane for "I Dream of Jesus")

2010 (1): Outstanding Original Music and Lyrics (Seth MacFarlane and Walter Murphy for the song "Down's Syndrome Girl" for "Extra Large Medium")

2011 (2): Outstanding Music Composition for a Series (Original Dramatic Score) (Walter Murphy for "And Then There Were Fewer"); Outstanding Original Music and Lyrics (Ron Jones, Seth MacFarlane, and Danny Smith for the song "Christmastime Is Killing Us" for "Road to the North Pole")

2013 (2): Outstanding Voice-Over Performance (Seth MacFarlane for episode "Brian's Play"); Outstanding Voice-Over Performance (Alex Borstein for episode "Lois Comes out of Her Shell")

Further Reading

Callahan, Steve, Ed. *Family Guy: The Official Episode Guide, Seasons 1-3*. New York: It Books, 2005.

"Debate: Family Guy Has an Explicit Liberal Agenda That Ruins the Show." *Debate.org*. Available online at www.debate.org/debates/Family-Guy-has-an-explicit-liberal-agenda-that -ruins-the-show/1/.

✴ **31** ✴

Curb Your Enthusiasm

(2000–)

Cast: Larry David (Larry David), Jeff Garlin (Jeff Greene), Cheryl Hines (Cheryl David), Susie Essman (Susie Greene), Richard Lewis (Richard Lewis)

Created by: Larry David

Network: HBO

First Air Date: October 15, 2000

Broadcast History:
    October 2000–December 2000: Sunday at 10:00–10:30 PM
    September 2001–November 2001: Sunday at 10:00–10:30 PM
    September 2002–November 2002: Sunday at 10:00–10:30 PM
    January 2004–March 2004: Sunday at 10:00–10:30 PM
    September 2005–December 2005: Sunday at 10:00–10:30 PM
    September 2007–November 2007: Sunday at 10:00–10:30 PM
    September 2009–November 2009: Sunday at 10:00–10:30 PM
    July 2011–November 2011: Sunday at 10:00–10:30 PM

Seasons: 8

Episodes: 80

Ratings History: Never in Top 30

Overview

Lesson learned from George Costanza: Schmucks can be very popular on television. Larry David should know. He created the funniest jackass in television history when he created arguably the funniest show in television history: *Seinfeld*. So he executed a personality transplant, extracting the same negative traits from George and placing

Larry David and Cheryl Hines. *HBO/Photofest ©HBO*

them in himself. Voila! Perhaps the most embraced TV jackass of the twenty-first century. *Curb Your Enthusiasm* was born.

David plays himself as a fictionalized (thank goodness!) character on the show, which features largely improvised dialogue and premiered two years after *Seinfeld* was cancelled. He works as a semiretired television writer and producer in Los Angeles, and eventually New York. He is self-absorbed and vengeful, often taking umbrage over perceived slights that are usually justified anyway because everyone on the show, aside from wife Cheryl (Cheryl Hines), either hates him or is at least suspect of his intentions. Among them is unscrupulous manager Jeff Greene (Jeff Garlin), who is suspicious of Larry and his best friend at the same time. Beyond suspicion and into the realm of abhorrence is Jeff's vulgar wife Susie (Susie Essman), who saves her most intense hatred and choicest swear words for the main character.

And for good reason. Larry is not only thoughtless, but often mindless. And when he does something stupid, he compounds matters by lying about it or arguing in defense rather than sincerely apologizing. He is, in fact, wholly insincere, as is cited in one episode in which his Christian wife invites her religious family to stay with him during Christmas. Rather than welcoming them and attempting to get himself into the holiday spirit, Larry sulks and then thoughtlessly eats gingerbread cookies arranged as part of a manger scene, leading to the following verbal confrontation with Cheryl and her family members:

> **Becky [Cheryl's sister]:** You ate the baby Jesus and his mother, Mary!
> **Larry:** I thought they were animals!

Becky: Jesus Christ is not an animal!
Larry: I-I-I thought . . . he was a monkey! . . . I thought that was all part of the zoo.
Becky: [concluding sadly] You just swallowed our Lord and Savior!

Curb Your Enthusiasm uses Larry to create humor from breaches in the social graces and conversational etiquette. Much like *Seinfeld*, the "show about nothing," this sitcom utilizes the cad of a main character to lampoon such social amenities as tipping at restaurants, the use of a car pool lane when driving alone, or the amount of caviar that is proper to place on a cracker. But far more sensitive issues are also fair game. No subjects are off-limits—not even homosexuality, the Holocaust, terrorism, or the "N" word. In one episode, a Jewish Holocaust survivor and a contestant on the reality show *The Survivor* are arguing bitterly over who has endured the greater torture. In another, Larry hires a new restaurant a chef who is inflicted with Tourette syndrome and begins loudly tossing around profanity in front of a full house of patrons.

The appearance of guest stars playing themselves has strengthened the authenticity of a sitcom based around Hollywood. A number of premier players in the entertainment world have been attracted to the show, including Ted Danson, Dustin Hoffman, Martin Scorsese, Hugh Hefner, Wanda Sykes, Ben Stiller, Christian Slater, Rob Reiner, Michael York, Mary Steenburgen, Rosie O'Donnell, Michael J. Fox, and Mel Brooks. Frequent appearances of *Seinfeld* cast members Jerry Seinfeld, Julia Louis-Dreyfus, and Jason Alexander have also added to the realism and the humor. Their inclusion, which included a *Seinfeld* reunion show in the seventh season, provided a treat to viewers who recognized and appreciated the similarities between the two beloved television comedies.

The story lines remain in the backseat to the episode plot lines revolving around Larry's relationships with family, friends, and others whom fate has tragically placed in his path. He subscribes to a set of questionable principles to which he holds so firmly that his ego, stubbornness, and insulting manner take over when he believes they have been violated. The result is conflict that he often exacerbates as he attempts to smooth it over during the course of the half hour.

Although the plot lines take center stage on *Curb Your Enthusiasm*, the writers have developed wider stories that have provided opportunities to create humorous scenarios for individual episodes. By the second season, Cheryl had grown weary of Larry's professional dormancy, so he sought another television vehicle that at first was to star Louis-Dreyfus and Alexander, but he rubbed enough people the wrong way to ruin the project. He later invested in a restaurant business, got handed the lead role from Brooks in the smash hit play *The Producers*, embarked on a search for his biological parents after becoming convinced he was adopted, and caused Cheryl to leave him and move to New York.

While the status of *Seinfeld* as arguably the most popular modern sitcom during its run and in syndication has played a role in the success of *Curb Your Enthusiasm*, one must wonder just how high the latter would soar in the ratings if it were on network television rather than HBO. The profanity used well for effect precludes any opportunity for the show to air anywhere but on cable, so such a scenario can only be speculated on. Suffice it to say that Larry David takes the concept of a show about nothing in only a slightly different direction and creates one that some believe is even funnier. The seven Emmy Award nominations for Outstanding Comedy Series speak for themselves.

Hines Plays Catch-up in Television Comedy

Cheryl Hines studied theater and television production at the University of Central Florida, but she knew little about comedy until she moved to Los Angeles and joined the improvisational Groundlings Theater. Her first instructor in that troupe was *Friends* star Lisa Kudrow, who helped her learn how to improvise and write comedy sketches. Her experiences proved invaluable in playing Larry David's wife in the largely improvisational *Curb Your Enthusiasm*. It also helped her land the major role of Dallas Royce in the sitcom *Suburgatory*, which was nominated for a People's Choice Award in 2012 for Favorite New TV Comedy.

Did You Know?

Curb Your Enthusiasm featured an episode with basketball superstar Shaquille O'Neal. It revolves around events after he is tripped during a game by Larry David, who becomes a sports villain for his actions. To make up for his indiscretion, Larry brings Shaq a tape of the entire *Seinfeld* collection. O'Neal states that his favorite episode of that show was "The Contest," which involves the four major characters seeing who can go the longest without sexually gratifying themselves.

They Said It

Donald: You know what you are? You're a self-loathing Jew.
Larry: Hey, I may loathe myself, but it has nothing to do with the fact that I'm Jewish.

Larry: OK, Wanda . . .
Wanda Sykes: Oh, you know who I am, OK. I thought I would have to turn around and show you my big ass.
Larry: OK, you completely misinterpreted that . . .
Wanda: How am I supposed to interpret it? You shouted out 'Hey, big ass Wanda.'
Larry: I didn't say big ass, I was just saying hello.
Wanda: Is that how you say hello?
Larry: Uh, well . . .
Wanda: 'Hey big ass' or 'Hey assy' or 'Hey I know your ass.' What is that? That's not how you say hello.
Larry: Perhaps not.

Richard Lewis: You're looking at my girlfriend's breasts!
Larry: First of all, Richard, they're not breasts. They're not breasts, they're just big chemical balls, OK?

Major Awards

EMMY AWARD WINS (2)

2003 (1): Outstanding Directing for a Comedy Series (Robert B. Weide for "Krazee-Eyez Killa")

2012 (1): Outstanding Single-Camera Picture Editing for a Comedy Series (Steven A. Rasch for "Palestinian Chicken")

EMMY AWARD NOMINATIONS, IN ADDITION TO WINS (35)

2002 (2): Outstanding Comedy Series; Outstanding Directing for a Comedy Series (Robert B. Weide for "The Doll")

2003 (8): Outstanding Comedy Series; Outstanding Lead Actor in a Comedy Series (Larry David); Outstanding Supporting Actress in a Comedy Series (Cheryl Hines); Outstanding Directing for a Comedy Series (Larry Charles for "The Nanny from Hell"); Outstanding Directing for a Comedy Series (David Steinberg for "Mary, Joseph, and Larry"); Outstanding Directing for a Comedy Series (Bryan Gordon for "The Special Section"); Outstanding Casting for a Comedy Series (Marla Garlin, Richard Hicks, and Ronnie Yeskel); Outstanding Single-Camera Picture Editing for a Comedy Series (Jonathan Corn for "Krazee-Eyez Killa")

2004 (7): Outstanding Comedy Series; Outstanding Lead Actor in a Comedy Series (Larry David); Outstanding Directing for a Comedy Series (Larry Charles for "The Survivor"); Outstanding Directing for a Comedy Series (Robert B. Weide for "The Car Pool Lane"); Outstanding Directing for a Comedy Series (Bryan Gordon for "The 5 Wood"); Outstanding Casting for a Comedy Series (Allison Jones); Outstanding Single-Camera Picture Editing for a Comedy Series (Jonathan Corn for "The Survivor")

2006 (6): Outstanding Comedy Series; Outstanding Lead Actor in a Comedy Series (Larry David); Outstanding Supporting Actress in a Comedy Series (Cheryl Hines); Outstanding Directing for a Comedy Series (Robert B. Weide for "The Christ Nail"); Outstanding Casting for a Comedy Series (Allison Jones); Outstanding Single-Camera Picture Editing for a Comedy Series (Steven A. Rasch for "The Ski Lift")

2008 (4): Outstanding Comedy Series; Outstanding Guest Actor in a Comedy Series (Shelley Berman for "The Rat Dog"); Outstanding Casting for a Comedy Series (Allison Jones); Outstanding Picture Editing for a Comedy Series (Single or Multi-Camera) (Steven A. Rasch for "The Bat Mitzvah")

2010 (4): Outstanding Comedy Series; Outstanding Lead Actor in a Comedy Series (Larry David); Outstanding Picture Editing for a Comedy Series (Single or Multi-Camera) (Steven A. Rasch for "The Bare Midriff"); Outstanding Picture Editing for a Comedy Series (Single or Multi-Camera) (Roger Nygard and Jonathan Corn for "The Table Read")

2012 (4): Outstanding Comedy Series; Outstanding Lead Actor in a Comedy Series (Larry David); Outstanding Guest Actor in a Comedy Series (Michael J. Fox for "Larry vs. Michael J. Fox"); Outstanding Directing in a Comedy Series (Robert B. Weide for "Palestinian Chicken")

GOLDEN GLOBE WIN (1)

2003 (1): Best TV Series, Musical/Comedy

GOLDEN GLOBE NOMINATIONS, IN ADDITION TO WIN (4)

2003 (1): Best Performance by an Actor in a TV, Musical/Comedy (Larry David)
2005 (1): Best Performance by an Actor in a TV Series, Musical/Comedy (Larry David)
2006 (2): Best TV Series, Musical/Comedy; Best Performance by an Actor in a TV Series, Musical/Comedy (Larry David)

Further Reading

Dolan, Deirdre. *Curb Your Enthusiasm: The Book*. New York: Gotham Books, 2006.
Hinckley, David. "'Curb Your Enthusiasm' Review: Larry David Goes beyond Offensive into Outrageous with Racial Jokes." *New York Daily News*, July 6, 2011. Available online at www .nydailynews.com/entertainment/tv-movies/curb-enthusiasm-review-larry-david-offensive -outrageous-racial-jokes-article-1.156098.
Levine, Josh. *Pretty Good, Pretty Good: Larry David and the Making of Seinfeld and Curb Your Enthusiasm*. Toronto: ECW Press, 2010.

✳ **32** ✳

Roseanne

(1988–1997)

Cast: Roseanne Barr (Roseanne Conner), John Goodman (Dan Conner), Laurie Metcalf (Jackie Harris), Michael Fishman (D. J. Conner), Sara Gilbert (Darlene Conner), Alicia Goranson (Becky Conner), Johnny Galecki (David Healy), Natalie West (Crystal Anderson-Conner), Glenn Quinn (Mark Healy), Sarah Chalke (Becky Conner-Healy)

Created by: Executive producer and writer Matt Williams

Network: ABC

First Air Date: October 18, 1988

Last Air Date: August 26, 1997

Broadcast History:
October 18, 1988–February 1989: Tuesday at 8:30–9:00 PM
February 1989–February 1994: Tuesday at 9:00–9:30 PM
September 1994–March 1995: Wednesday at 9:00–9:30 PM
March 1995–May 1995: Wednesday at 8:00–8:30 PM
May 1995–July 1995: Wednesday at 9:30–10:00 PM
August 1995–September 1995: Tuesday at 8:30–9:00 PM
September 1995–August 26, 1997: Tuesday at 8:00–8:30 PM

Seasons: 9

Episodes: 222

Ratings History: 1988–1989 (2), 1989–1990 (1), 1990–1991 (3), 1991–1992 (2), 1992–1993 (2), 1993–1994 (4), 1994–1995 (10), 1995–1996 (16), 1996–1997 (not in Top 30)

Top: Sara Gilbert, Alicia Goranson, and Laurie Metcalf; bottom: Michael Fishman, Roseanne Barr, and John Goodman. *ABC/Photofest ©ABC*

Overview

It took a quarter-century to obliterate the traditional family sitcom of the 1950s and early 1960s. Then along came *Roseanne* to bury it once and for all. Other shows chipped away at it, but there were always those nurturing parents to remind viewers that the genre hadn't strayed all that far from the Nelsons and Cleavers. Yeah, mom and dad Conner loved each other and their kids, but would Harriet Nelson or June Cleaver have told their annoying brats to "go play in traffic"? Roseanne did. She ran the ultimate dysfunctional family; forget *Married . . . with Children*, which aired at the same time but lacked the sense of realism that made *Roseanne* far more viable.

And make no mistake about it—Roseanne (Roseanne Barr) ran that family. She and husband Dan (John Goodman) were the funniest blue-collar couple since Edith and Archie Bunker. In a medium in which attractiveness sells, nobody seemed to care that both were rotund and slovenly. The dysfunctional, sarcastic, and bickering Conners were everything that the traditional television family was not, except for the deep feelings of affection they felt for one another (although you had to go pretty deep), and American viewers watched in droves. The show remarkably soared to number two in the Nielsen ratings in its debut season, secured the top spot the following year, and remained in the top four in each of the next four years.

The sitcom spotlighted the high-spirited and playful relationship between Roseanne and Dan, as well as daughters Becky (Alicia Goranson 1988–1992 and 1995–1996, Sarah Chalke 1993–1997) and Darlene (Sara Gilbert) and son D. J. (Michael Fishman). The dismissive jibes at one another were most often accompanied by a smile, but the conflicts, particularly between the pretty, popular, boy-crazy Becky and the socially awkward and frustrated Darlene, boasted an intensity and realism rarely seen on TV sitcoms of any era. The struggles of the Conners to make ends meet in their Lankford, Illinois, home made them seem like a family viewers knew, only a lot funnier.

Money was indeed scarce. Roseanne toiled at various low-paying jobs, including one in a plastics plant and another as a lounge waitress. She shared the same financial battles as younger sister Jackie Harris (Laurie Metcalf), who worked in the same plant before landing a job as a cop. They finally teamed up to open their own coffee shop in 1992. Dan gained his independence and found the opportunity to embrace his passion by opening up a motorcycle shop after fighting perpetual unemployment as a contractor doing various odd jobs. One and all always found a way, however, to fight bureaucracy, which was one major theme of the show. But it was the private moments inside the home, the dialogue and interaction that revealed the feelings of the characters about themselves and one another, that proved most humorous and satisfying.

All good things must come to an end, and this one did prematurely and unintentionally. The story lines strayed dramatically after real-life Roseanne got pregnant and gave birth on the show to Jerry Garcia Conner (her tribute to the recently departed *Grateful Dead* lead singer, whose spirit visited her in the delivery room). Meanwhile, Jackie and husband Fred (Michael O'Keefe) separated and then divorced.

Roseanne deteriorated by the end of its run. Dan suffered a heart attack at Darlene's wedding reception and then separated from his wife after an argument. The drastic turn smacked of unrealism considering the deep love and affection they had shown for one another throughout; the writers could have found a better way to placate Goodman, who yearned to lessen his workload on the show. The two got back together when the Conners won $108 million in the lottery, adding to the ridiculousness. Dan embarked on an affair, which caused a second breakup. The "about time" series finale features the birth of Darlene's first child and a Roseanne of the future explaining that Dan had died of a second heart attack. And then, to top it all off, she reveals that nothing that happened in the entire last season had really happened. It was all a hallucination of sorts.

It was, as Roseanne might say, a bummer of a way to end a sitcom that exuded optimism and positivity and nurtured an "us against the world" relationship that helped maintain a tight-knit family and marital relationship. After all, those insults tossed about the Conner home were good-natured.

Who's Who?

Roseanne cast members came and went in record numbers. There were two Beckys (Alicia Goranson and Sarah Chalke), two actresses playing Dan's mother Audrey (Ann Wedgeworth and Debbie Reynolds), two D. J.s (Sal Barone in the pilot and Michael

Fishman), three actors playing Crystal's son (Josh C. Williams, Luke Edwards, and Kristopher Kent Hill), and two actors playing D. J.'s friend Todd (Troy Davidson and Adam Hendershott).

Did You Know?

Roseanne Barr's real-life husband, Tom Arnold, appeared on the show periodically between 1989 and 1994 as Dan's buddy Arnie.

They Said It

Jackie: [on living on a tight budget] It could be done. I was watching this National Geographic special on desert people. Bedouins can live for three days on one fig.
Roseanne: Well, that don't do me no good. My family can't live three days on one Bedouin.

Darlene: You guys think we don't get your corny little sex jokes?
Roseanne: Hey, you kids *are* our corny little sex joke.

Becky: No one could eat this crud.
Dan: Hey, if you don't finish your crud, you're not gonna get any crap for dessert.

Major Awards

EMMY AWARD WINS (4)

1992 (1): Outstanding Supporting Actress in a Comedy Series (Laurie Metcalf)
1993 (2): Outstanding Lead Actress in a Comedy Series (Roseanne Barr); Outstanding Supporting Actress in a Comedy Series (Laurie Metcalf)
1994 (1): Outstanding Supporting Actress in a Comedy Series (Laurie Metcalf)

EMMY AWARD NOMINATIONS, IN ADDITION TO WINS (21)

1989 (4): Outstanding Lead Actor in a Comedy Series (John Goodman); Outstanding Achievement in Music and Lyrics (Dan Foliart and Howard Pearl for the song "I'll Never Change My Mind" for "Radio Days"); Outstanding Art Direction for a Series (Garvin Eddy for "Lover's Lanes"); Outstanding Editing for a Series, Multi-Camera Production (Marco Zappia for "Toto, We're Not in Kansas Anymore")
1990 (2): Outstanding Lead Actor in a Comedy Series (John Goodman); Outstanding Lighting Direction (Electronic) for a Comedy Series (Daniel Flannery for "Boo")

1991 (1): Outstanding Lead Actor in a Comedy Series (John Goodman)

1992 (3): Outstanding Lead Actor in a Comedy Series (John Goodman); Outstanding Lead Actress in a Comedy Series (Roseanne Barr); Outstanding Individual Achievement in Writing in a Comedy Series (Jennifer Heath and Amy Sherman for "A Bitter Pill to Swallow")

1993 (3): Outstanding Lead Actor in a Comedy Series (John Goodman); Outstanding Supporting Actress in a Comedy Series (Sara Gilbert); Outstanding Individual Achievement in Lighting Direction (Electronic) for a Comedy Series (Daniel Flannery for "Halloween IV")

1994 (4): Outstanding Lead Actor in a Comedy Series (John Goodman); Outstanding Lead Actress in a Comedy Series (Roseanne Barr); Outstanding Supporting Actress in a Comedy Series (Sara Gilbert); Outstanding Individual Achievement in Lighting Direction (Electronic) for a Comedy Series (Daniel Flannery for "White Trash Christmas")

1995 (4): Outstanding Lead Actor in a Comedy Series (John Goodman); Outstanding Lead Actress in a Comedy Series (Roseanne Barr); Outstanding Supporting Actress in a Comedy Series (Laurie Metcalf); Outstanding Individual Achievement in Hairstyling for a Series (Pixie Schwartz for "Skeletons in the Closet")

GOLDEN GLOBE WINS (3)

1993 (3): Best TV Series, Musical/Comedy; Best Performance by an Actor in a TV Series, Musical/Comedy (John Goodman); Best Performance by an Actress in a TV Series, Musical/Comedy (Roseanne Barr)

GOLDEN GLOBE NOMINATIONS, IN ADDITION TO WINS (11)

1989 (3): Best TV Series, Musical/Comedy; Best Performance by an Actor in a TV Series, Musical/Comedy (John Goodman); Best Performance by an Actress in a TV Series, Musical/Comedy (Roseanne Barr)

1990 (1): Best Performance by an Actor in a TV Series, Musical/Comedy (John Goodman)

1991 (2): Best Performance by an Actor in a TV Series, Musical/Comedy (John Goodman); Best Performance by an Actress in a TV Series, Musical/Comedy (Roseanne Barr)

1992 (1): Best Performance by an Actress in a TV Series, Musical/Comedy (Roseanne Barr)

1993 (1): Best Performance by an Actress in a Supporting Role in a Series, Mini-Series, or Motion Picture Made for TV (Laurie Metcalf)

1994 (2): Best TV Series, Musical/Comedy; Best Performance by an Actress in a TV Series, Musical/Comedy (Roseanne Barr)

1995 (1): Best Performance by an Actress in a Supporting Role in a Series, Mini-Series, or Motion Picture Made for TV (Laurie Metcalf)

HUMANITAS PRIZE

1993: 30-Minute Category (Rob Ulin)

HUMANITAS PRIZE NOMINATIONS

1992: 30-Minute Category (Chuck Lorre, Jeff Abugov, and Michael Poryes)
1993: 30-Minute Category (Amy Sherman)
1995: 30-Minute Category (Rob Ulin and Kevin Abbott)
1997: 30-Minute Category (Drew Ogier)

PEABODY AWARD

1993: NBC

Further Reading

Barr, Roseanne. "And I Should Know." *New York Magazine*, May 15, 2011. Available online at http://nymag.com/arts/tv/upfronts/2011/roseanne-barr-2011-5/.
———. *My Life as a Woman*. New York: Harper & Row, 1989.
Stransky, Tanner. "A 'Roseanne' Family Reunion." *Entertainment Weekly*, October 31, 2008. Available online at www.ew.com/ew/article/0,,20235368,00.html.

✷ 33 ✷

Father Knows Best

(1954–1960)

Cast: Robert Young (Jim Anderson), Jane Wyatt (Margaret Anderson), Elinor Donahue (Betty "Princess" Anderson), Billy Gray (James "Bud" Anderson), Lauren Chapin (Kathy "Kitten" Anderson)

Created by: Ed James

Network: CBS (1954–1955, 1958–1960), NBC (1955–1958)

First Air Date: October 3, 1954

Last Air Date: May 23, 1960

Broadcast History:
October 3, 1954–March 1955: Sunday at 10:00–10:30 PM
August 1955–September 1958: Wednesday at 8:30–9:00 PM
September 1958–September 1960: Monday at 8:30–9:00 PM

Seasons: 6

Episodes: 202

Ratings History: 1954–1955 (not in Top 30), 1955–1956 (not in Top 30), 1956–1957 (not in Top 30), 1957–1958 (17), 1958–1959 (14), 1959–1960 (6)

Overview

The success of *Father Knows Best* is a tribute to the power of the viewer. The show appeared doomed just a few weeks after its debut when sponsor Kent Cigarettes grew dissatisfied with its poor ratings and declined to extend its twenty-six-week contract. Fearing the sitcom would be pulled from the air, hard-core fans sent letters of protest claiming that it was a wonderful family program and that the problem was the 10:00 p.m. time slot,

214

Clockwise from bottom left: Lauren Chapin, Elinor Donahue, Robert Young, Billy Gray, and Jane Wyatt. *NBC/Photofest ©NBC*

which prevented kids from watching on school nights. Proof of its worthiness to remain on the air came in the form of a Sylvania Award for outstanding family entertainment.

The complaints fell on deaf ears at CBS and the cigarette company. Despite urgings from television critics to keep *Father Knows Best* on the air, it was cancelled in March 1955. Soon the Scott Paper Company, impressed with the positive response to the program, came to the rescue and moved it to NBC at a more reasonable time of 8:30 p.m. It gained an audience year after year, peaking at number six in the Nielsen ratings in its final season. By that time, CBS, which had seen the errors of its ways, had bought the show back from NBC. Only a severe case of burnout for star Robert Young prevented *Father Knows Best* from embarking on a longer run. Young could not be blamed. He had played one of the iconic fathers in American entertainment for more than a decade, starting with the namesake radio show (although the title of that program had a question mark in it), which ran for six years before it moved to television.

Father Knows Best embodied the innocuous, wholesome family sitcoms in the 1950s and early 1960s, but what it lacked in edginess it made up for in the pleasantness and compassion of the characters. Father and insurance agent Jim Anderson (Young) and mother Margaret (Jane Wyatt) were both sensible parents. The former, who traded in his sports jacket for his trademark sweater upon returning from work, gave sage advice to his three kids. His love for them could be felt in every episode, despite an occasional show of temper generally calmed by his wife. Jim made each child feel special, as he referred to daughters Betty (Elinor Donahue) and Kathy (Lauren Chapin) as "Princess" and "Kitten," respectively, and son James (Billy Gray) as "Bud." Viewers followed Betty and James through high school and into a local college that allowed them to remain at home throughout the run of the show.

The desire of Young to leave the role that had made him famous forced CBS to stop creating new episodes of *Father Knows Best* at the peak of its popularity, but the network knew a goldmine when they saw it. They continued airing reruns into September 1962, after which ABC picked it up for another season. The show boasts the distinction of having been shown on all three major networks. Only the shortsightedness of CBS and its sponsor in 1955 allowed NBC to get into the act.

From Anderson to Flintstone

One of two voices that portrayed the wife of Jim Anderson in the radio version of *Father Knows Best* was Jean Vander Pyl. She later gained greater fame as the voice of Wilma Flintstone in *The Flintstones*, the first prime-time animated series.

House Call from Robert Young

Robert Young played arguably the most beloved doctor in the history of American television when he assumed the role of Marcus Welby in the namesake drama that ran on ABC from 1969 to 1976, but his life was filled with turmoil before and after playing that part. Young began his career as a busy movie actor in the 1930s and 1940s. His charming, but nonthreatening, persona landed him roles alongside the most notable actresses of their times, including Joan Crawford, Katharine Hepburn, and Claudette Colbert. But he also struggled with alcoholism and suffered a nervous breakdown in 1966, from which it took him four years to recover. Young, who served as a spokesman for Sanka coffee for five years, overcame his drinking problem thanks greatly to Alcoholics Anonymous. Severe depression, heart problems, and Alzheimer's led him to attempt suicide in 1991. He died in 1998, at the age of ninety-one.

Did You Know?

Elinor Donahue played the role of Andy Taylor's first girlfriend in the first year of *The Andy Griffith Show*. She portrayed what was referred to as "lady druggist" Ellie Walker for one season. She later played Felix Unger's girlfriend Miriam Welby on *The Odd Couple.*

They Said It

> **Bud:** How many people were in your class, dad?
> **Jim:** Oh, 2 to 300, I guess.
> **Bud:** How many are left?

Major Awards

EMMY AWARD WINS (6)

1957 (1): Best Continuing Performance by an Actor in a Dramatic Series (Robert Young)

1958 (2): Best Continuing Performance by an Actor in a Dramatic or Comedy Series (Robert Young); Best Continuing Performance by an Actress in a Dramatic or Comedy Series (Jane Wyatt)

1959 (2): Best Actress in a Leading Role (Continuing Character) in a Comedy Series (Jane Wyatt); Best Direction of a Single Program of a Comedy Series (Peter Tewksbury for "Medal for Margaret")

1960 (1): Outstanding Performance by an Actress in a Series Lead or Support (Jane Wyatt)

EMMY AWARD NOMINATIONS, IN ADDITION TO WINS (13)

1956 (1): Best Actor, Continuing Performance (Robert Young)

1957 (1): Best Series, Half Hour or Less; Best Editing of a Film for Television (Richard Fantl for "Betty's Birthday")

1958 (4): Best Comedy Series; Best Comedy Writing (Roswell Rogers and Paul West); Best Direction, Half Hour or Less (Peter Tewksbury); Best Teleplay Writing, Half Hour or Less (Roswell Rogers for "Margaret Hires a Gardener")

1959 (5): Best Comedy Series; Best Actor in a Leading Role (Continuing Character) in a Comedy Series (Robert Young); Best Supporting Actor (Continuing Character) in a Comedy Series (Billy Gray); Best Supporting Actress (Continuing Character) in a Comedy Series (Elinor Donahue); Best Writing of a Single Program of a Comedy Series (Roswell Rogers for "Medal for Margaret")

1960 (2): Outstanding Program Achievement in the Field of Humor; Outstanding Writing Achievement in Comedy (Dorothy Rogers and Roswell Rogers)

Further Reading

Leibman, Nina. *Living Room Lectures: The Fifties Family in Film and Television.* Austin: University of Texas Press, 1995.

✳ **34** ✳

Arrested Development

(2003–2006, 2013–)

Cast: Portia de Rossi (Lindsay Bluth Funke), Jason Bateman (Michael Bluth), David Cross (Tobias Funke), Jeffrey Tambor (George Bluth Sr.), Michael Cera (George-Michael Bluth), Will Arnett (George Oscar "GOB" Bluth), Alia Shawkat (Maeby Funke), Jessica Walter (Lucille Bluth), Ron Howard (narrator), Tony Hale (Buster Bluth)

Created by: Executive producer, director (six episodes), and writer Mitchell Hurwitz

Network: FOX

First Air Date: November 2, 2003

Last Air Date: November 10, 2006

First Air Date (second run): May 4, 2013

Broadcast History:
    November 2003–April 2004: Sunday at 9:30–10:00 PM
    June 2004–April 2005: Sunday at 8:30–9:00 PM
    June 2004: Sunday at 9:30–10:00 PM
    June 2004–April 2005: Sunday at 8:30–9:00 PM
    February 2005: Friday at 8:00–10:00 PM
    July 2005–August 2005: Friday at 8:00–10:00 PM
    September 2005–October 2005: Monday at 8:00–8:30 PM
    December 2005–June 2006: Monday at 8:00–9:00 PM

Seasons: 4

Episodes: 53 (2003–2006)

Ratings History: Never in Top 30

Clockwise from bottom left: Alia Shawkat, David Cross, Portia de Rossi, Jessica Walter, Tony Hale, Jeffrey Tambor, Michael Cera, Will Arnett, and Jason Bateman. *20th Century Fox/Photofest ©20th Century Fox*

Overview

In a bygone era, the mere premise of many sitcoms proved to be the basis for their humor. There was a Martian and a talking horse and a witch and a flying nun and a couple of ghoulish families. But the genre evolved toward more realistic, character-driven programming that often tried to make a social or political statement.

Then there is *Arrested Development*, which uses its premise for a comedic base. The difference is that it is a semitragedy that show creator Mitchell Hurwitz and his writers transformed into one of the funniest shows of its generation. That rather sad notion is the arrest of a wealthy family patriarch that results in the freezing of his assets, transforming a rich family into a struggling one overnight. Bingo. A once comfortable family is comfortable no more, causing panic among its members and exposing the neurotic and borderline psychotic tendencies of each, as well as the dysfunctionality of the family itself. Add the narration of iconic actor and director Ron Howard, and the foundation for one weird sitcom was set.

How weird? What about the following conversation between matriarch Lucille Bluth (Jessica Walter) and a surgeon who played a recurring role known only as "The Literal Doctor" about the status of son Buster (Tony Hale):

> **Lucille:** [the family is waiting for news on Buster from a very literal doctor] How's my son?
> **The Literal Doctor:** He's going to be all right.
> **Lindsay Funke:** Finally some good news from this guy.
> **George Michael Bluth:** There's no other way to take that.
> **The Literal Doctor:** That's a great attitude. I got to tell you, if I was getting this news, I don't know that I'd take it this well.
> **Lucille:** But you said he was all right.
> **The Literal Doctor:** Yes, he's lost his left hand. So he's going to be 'all right.'

All that is not all right with *Arrested Development* is its ratings, which have never approached the level of its critical acclaim. The show earned an Emmy nomination for Outstanding Comedy Series in three of its four seasons on the air, snagging the prize in 2004. It enjoys a core following and is considered by many the downright funniest and most offbeat sitcom of the new millennium.

The spotlight character is Michael Bluth (Jason Bateman), who seeks to maintain his own sanity and his real estate business in Orange County while teaching his family members to live within their means after his father, George Sr. (Jeffrey Tambor), was sent up the river for illegal accounting practices. While the elder Bluth uses his time behind bars to dabble in Judaism and record inspirational tapes, blue-blood socialite wife Lucille tries to survive emotionally and financially living in a penthouse she can no longer afford.

Sons George Oscar (known as GOB and played by Will Arnett) and Buster help set the tone for the wacky comedy. The former is a wolf with women and a failed magician (although he prefers the term *illusionist*) whose every trick proves to be hilariously disastrous. The latter should have his picture resting next to the term *Oedipus complex* in the dictionary, perhaps because he spent nearly a year in Lucille's womb.

Phony adopted sister Lindsay (Portia de Rossi) masquerades as a social and political activist who truly cares, but her involvement is motivated by raising her status and massaging her ego. She could have taken pride in having married a psychiatrist named Tobias Funke (David Cross) if he hadn't lost his license for giving CPR to a man who was not having a heart attack and embarked in vain on an acting career. He claims himself to be the world's first "analrapist," an unfortunate word describing his supposed dual skills as an analyst and therapist. And that is the least of his problems. He also has a phobia about being naked that even follows him into the shower. Most kids rebel against the strictness of their parents. Their teenage daughter Maeby (Alia

Shawkat) rebels against their permissiveness and doting. That does not prevent Michael's son George-Michael Bluth (Michael Cera), who takes pride in his successful banana-stand business, from being in love with her. So what if she's his cousin?

The story lines are as bizarre as the characters, and the show has taken the form of an implausible and loony soap opera. Among the most elaborate feature George Bluth Sr., who escapes from prison by faking a heart attack, nearly has his mistress killed when his family yacht explodes, uses his company to build mini palaces for Saddam Hussein, and hides out in GOB's Aztec tomb while the media embarks on a wild goose chase looking for him in Iraq. Meanwhile, Buster avoids military service when his hand is bitten off by a seal, and Tobias paints himself blue in a vain attempt to join the Blue Man Group.

Combined with the wild characterizations, the story lines and episode plot lines make this one of the craziest sitcoms in television history. It has returned the American sitcom to an absurdity and unrealism little seen in the modern era. It was a welcome change from the somewhat staid and sophisticated fare that began to permeate the airwaves in the late 1970s. The best of that ilk boasted a fine brand of humor in its own right, but *Arrested Development* proves that zaniness is still a viable style for a TV sitcom.

Terrific Tambor

Jeffrey Tambor, who plays the embattled George Bluth Sr. in *Arrested Development*, is among the most underrated and versatile actors of his time. His career was launched by his role as an emotionally distressed and mentally unstable attorney in the classic 1979 film *And Justice for All*, in which he performs alongside Al Pacino. He landed a recurring role in the cop drama *Hill Street Blues* and a starring part in *The Larry Sanders Show* before hooking up with *Arrested Development*. Tambor earned six Emmy nominations for his performances in the two sitcoms but has never snagged the coveted trophy.

They Said It

> **Michael:** [to his family after his father has been given a jail sentence] They're going to keep dad in jail until this thing gets sorted out. [silence] Also, I've been told that the company's expense accounts have been frozen. [everyone gasps] Interesting. I would have expected that after 'They're keeping dad in jail.'

Major Awards

EMMY AWARD WINS (6)

2004 (5): Outstanding Comedy Series; Outstanding Writing for a Comedy Series (Mitchell Hurwitz for the pilot); Outstanding Directing for a Comedy Series (Joe

Russo and Anthony Russo for the pilot); Outstanding Casting for a Comedy Series (Deborah Barylski and Geraldine Leder); Outstanding Single-Camera Picture Editing for a Comedy Series (Lee Haxall for the pilot)

2005 (1): Outstanding Writing for a Comedy Series (Mitchell Hurwitz and James Vallely for "The Righteous Brothers")

EMMY AWARD NOMINATIONS, IN ADDITION TO WINS (17)

2004 (2): Outstanding Supporting Actor in a Comedy Series (Jeffrey Tambor); Outstanding Art Direction for a Multi-Camera Series (Denny Dugally, Charisse Cardenas, and Ellen Brill for the pilot)

2005 (8): Outstanding Comedy Series; Outstanding Lead Actor in a Comedy Series (Jason Bateman); Outstanding Supporting Actor in a Comedy Series (Jeffrey Tambor); Outstanding Supporting Actress in a Comedy Series (Jessica Walter); Outstanding Writing for a Comedy Series (Barbara Feldman for "Sad Sack"); Outstanding Writing for a Comedy Series (Brad Copeland for "Sword of Destiny"); Outstanding Casting for a Comedy Series (Allison Jones); Outstanding Single-Camera Picture Editing for a Comedy Series (Richard Bramwell for "Mother Boy XXX")

2006 (4): Outstanding Comedy Series; Outstanding Supporting Actor in a Comedy Series (Will Arnett); Outstanding Writing for a Comedy Series (Chuck Tatham, James Vallely, Richard Day, and Mitchell Hurwitz for "Development Arrested"); Outstanding Single-Camera Picture Editing for a Comedy Series (Stuart Bass for "The Ocean Walker")

2013 (3): Outstanding Lead Actor in a Comedy Series (Jason Bateman); Outstanding Single-Camera Picture Editing for a Comedy Series; Outstanding Music Composition for a Series (Original Dramatic Score)

GOLDEN GLOBE WIN (1)

2005 (1): Best Performance by an Actor in a TV Series, Musical/Comedy (Jason Bateman)

GOLDEN GLOBE NOMINATIONS, IN ADDITION TO WIN (2)

2004 (1): Best TV Series, Musical/Comedy
2005 (1): Best TV Series, Musical/Comedy

Further Reading

Stanley, Allesandra. "A Quick End to the Cult Series That Lived Up to Its Name." *New York Times*, February 10, 2006, p. B30.

✳ **35** ✳

The Wonder Years

(1988–1993)

Cast: Fred Savage (Kevin Arnold), Daniel Stern (Kevin Arnold the narrator), Dan Lauria (Jack Arnold), Alley Mills (Norma Arnold), Jason Hervey (Wayne Arnold), Josh Saviano (Paul Pfeiffer), Danica McKellar (Winnie Cooper), Olivia d'Abo (Karen Arnold)

Created by: Executive producers and writers Carol Black and Neal Marlens

Network: ABC

First Air Date: March 15, 1988

Last Air Date: September 1, 1993

Broadcast History:
March 15, 1988–April 1988: Tuesday at 8:30–9:00 PM
October 1988–February 1989: Wednesday at 9:00–9:30 PM
February 1989–August 1990: Tuesday at 8:30–9:00 PM
August 1990–August 1991: Wednesday at 8:00–8:30 PM
August 1991–February 1992: Wednesday at 8:30–9:00 PM
March 1992–September 1, 1993: Wednesday at 8:00–8:30 PM

Seasons: 6

Episodes: 115

Ratings History: 1988–1989 (22), 1989–1990 (8), 1990–1991 (30), 1991–1992 (not in Top 30), 1992–1993 (not in Top 30)

Clockwise from bottom left: Jason Hervey, Dan Lauria, Olivia d'Abo, Alley Mills, and Fred Savage. *ABC/Photofest ©ABC*

Overview

Take *Leave It to Beaver* and inject it with social and political themes considered taboo in the late 1950s and early 1960s and what do you have? *The Wonder Years.* The eras of the two shows were close chronologically but light years apart historically. *Leave It to Beaver* was a modern-day show that completed its run in 1963. *The Wonder Years* looked back at an era that began in 1968. Those four years in between were marred by major U.S. troop involvement in the Vietnam War, riots in the inner cities, protests on college campuses, and the assassinations of Martin Luther King Jr. and Robert Kennedy. The turbulence of the late 1960s was touched upon with great poignancy on a show that was unafraid to explore the inner feelings of a boy growing up during that era. But the relationship between lead character Kevin Arnold (Fred Savage) and older brother Wayne (Jason Hervey) was eerily similar to, although far more contentious than, that of Wally and The Beaver. The significant difference was that Wally was a model older brother, and Wayne was a rat.

The Wonder Years provided a unique, fanciful first-person look at growing up in the 1960s and early 1970s from the view of Kevin, who was twelve years old when the show was launched and whose memories were voiced lovingly and passionately as an adult by Daniel Stern. Although the traumatic events of the era influenced his thoughts and the show itself—sister Karen (Olivia d'Abo) was a full-fledged bead-wearing hippie who eventually married and moved to Alaska—his primary motivations were driven by more personal pursuits. Kevin sought to survive the emotional torment heaped upon him by his unfeeling brother and transform his friendship with the girl of his dreams, Winnie Cooper (Danica McKellar), into a romance.

Little help was forthcoming from his parents. Neither impatient father Jack (Dan Lauria) nor mother Norma (Alley Mills) satisfied his emotional needs. The former was especially distant, opting for relaxation of both mind and body upon returning home from a hard day's work rather than involvement in the daily business of fatherhood. When it came to figuring out life, Kevin was virtually on his own, and he did so quite thoughtfully. The experiences of each episode, it seemed, influenced him for the rest of his life.

One rare glance into the inner Jack came in a first-season episode entitled "My Father's Office," which was ranked twenty-seventh in the *TV Guide* all-time list of sitcom episodes. In this episode, Jack allows his son to accompany him to work. Kevin soon realizes, much to his disappointment, that Jack is not as important on the job as he perceived him to be, but instead rather ordinary. He learns of the pressure his father is under and gains an understanding of why he is so distant at home. Jack later finds more personal satisfaction when he quits that job to open his own furniture-making business.

The only friendly and close male character for Kevin was nerdy best buddy Paul Pfeiffer (Josh Saviano), with whom he could share his feelings and motivations. But it was his on-again, off-again romance with Winnie that provided the greatest sense of wonderment on *The Wonder Years*. Viewers continued to follow the volatile relationship until the very end. In the final episode, Stern explains that Jack had died after leaving his job, Wayne was working at his father's former business, Winnie had gone to Paris to study art, and Kevin had married another woman and had a son. But Winnie remains his first love; when she returns from Europe and Kevin meets her at the airport, he is left to wonder what could have been.

Even those not a fan of *The Wonder Years* must concede that it was among the most creative and imaginative sitcoms ever produced. It interspersed news clips and music from the era for greater authenticity and a reminder to viewers just how different the world was twenty years earlier.

A Savage Start

While most kids were taking Flintstones vitamins, Fred Savage was hawking Pac-Man vitamins in a television commercial as he boldly proclaimed, "Good-bye Fred, hello Pac-Man." He received steady work before hitting it big time as a sick boy being read to by his grandfather in the popular 1986 film *The Princess Bride*. His performance in that movie, however, did not land him the part of Kevin Arnold in *The Wonder Years*. It was his role alongside Judge Reinhold in the far less acclaimed *Vice Versa* that got him noticed by the casting crew. He soon committed himself to a career in show business, moving with his family to Los Angeles. Savage has since worked extensively as an actor, director, and producer of various television programs and landed a bit role in the film comedy *Austin Powers in Goldmember*.

They Said It

> **Kevin [the narrator]:** All of our young lives we search for someone to love. Someone that makes us complete. We choose partners and change partners. We dance to a song of heartbreak and hope. All the while wondering if somewhere, somehow, there's someone perfect who might be searching for us.

Major Awards

EMMY AWARD WINS (4)

1988 (1): Outstanding Comedy Series
1989 (1): Outstanding Directing in a Comedy Series (Peter Baldwin for "Our Miss White")
1990 (2): Outstanding Writing in a Comedy Series (Bob Brush for "Good-bye"); Outstanding Directing in a Comedy Series (Michael Dinner for "Good-bye")

EMMY AWARD NOMINATIONS, IN ADDITION TO WINS (24)

1988 (1): Outstanding Writing in a Comedy Series (Carol Black and Neal Marlens for the pilot)
1989 (13): Outstanding Comedy Series; Outstanding Lead Actor in a Comedy Series (Fred Savage); Outstanding Guest Actor in a Comedy Series (Robert Picardo for "Loosiers"); Outstanding Guest Actress in a Comedy Series (Maxine Stuart for "Coda"); Outstanding Writing in a Comedy Series (Matthew Carlson for "Pottery Will Get You Nowhere"); Outstanding Writing in a Comedy Series (Todd W. Langen for "Coda"); Outstanding Writing in a Comedy Series (David M. Stern for "Loosiers"); Outstanding Writing in a Comedy Series (Michael Weithorn for "Our Miss White"); Outstanding Directing in a Comedy Series (Steve Miner for "Birthday Boy"); Outstanding Directing in a Comedy Series (Michael Dinner for "How I'm Spending My Summer Vacation"); Outstanding Costume Design for a Series (Scilla Andreen for "Birthday Boy"); Outstanding Editing for a Series, Single Camera Production (Stuart Bass for "Loosiers"); Outstanding Sound Mixing for a Comedy Series or a Special (Agamemnon Andrianos, David John West, Ray West, and John L. Mack for "Birthday Boy")
1990 (5): Outstanding Comedy Series; Outstanding Lead Actor in a Comedy Series (Fred Savage); Outstanding Guest Actor in a Comedy Series (David Huddleston for "The Powers That Be"); Outstanding Editing for a Series, Single Camera Production (Michael Vejar for "Good-bye"); Outstanding Sound Mixing for a Comedy Series or a Special (Agamemnon Andrianos, David John West, Ray West, and John L. Mack for "St. Valentine's Day Massacre")
1991 (3): Outstanding Comedy Series; Outstanding Directing in a Comedy Series (Peter Baldwin for "The Ties That Bind—Thanksgiving"); Outstanding Sound Mixing for a Comedy Series or a Special (Agamemnon Andrianos, David John West, Nello Torri, and John L. Mack for "Little Debbie")

1992 (1): Outstanding Sound Mixing for a Comedy Series or a Special (Agamemnon Andrianos, David John West, Nello Torri, and Craig Hunter for "Grandpa's Car")
1993 (1): Outstanding Sound Mixing for a Comedy Series or a Special (Agamemnon Andrianos, David John West, Nello Torri, and John L. Mack for "Summer")

GOLDEN GLOBE WIN (1)

1989 (1): Best TV Series, Musical/Comedy

GOLDEN GLOBE NOMINATIONS, IN ADDITION TO WIN (3)

1990 (2): Best TV Series, Musical/Comedy; Best Performance by an Actor in a TV Series, Musical/Comedy (Fred Savage)
1991 (1): Best Performance by an Actor in a TV Series, Musical/Comedy (Fred Savage)

HUMANITAS PRIZE

1989: 30-Minute Category (Matthew Carlson)
1990: 30-Minute Category (Todd W. Langen)
1991: 30-Minute Category (Bob Brush)

HUMANITAS PRIZE NOMINATIONS

1988: 30-Minute Category (Carol Black and Neal Marlens)
1990: 30-Minute Category (David M. Stern)
1991: 30-Minute Category (Mark B. Perry)
1992: 30-Minute Category (Craig Hoffman)
1993: 30-Minute Category (Sy Rosen)

PEABODY AWARD

1990: ABC

Further Reading

O'Connor, John. "Wonder Years: A New Series on ABC." *New York Times*, January 30, 1988. Available online at www.nytimes.com/1988/01/30/arts/tv-wonder-years-a-new-series-on -abc.html.
Weinstein, Steve. "Reeling in the Bittersweet 'Wonder Years': With Rising Costs, Aging Cast, Series Comes to a Close." *Los Angeles Times*, May 12, 1993. Available online at http://articles .latimes.com/1993-05-12/entertainment/ca-34310_1_kevin-arnold.

36

Soap

(1977–1981)

Cast: Katherine Helmond (Jessica Tate), Richard Mulligan (Burt Campbell), Cathryn Damon (Mary Campbell), Rod Roddy (Announcer), Ted Wass (Danny Dallas), Billy Crystal (Jodie Dallas), Robert Mandan (Chester Tate), Jennifer Salt (Eunice Tate), Jimmy Baio (Billy Tate), Diana Canova (Corinne Tate-Flotsky), Arthur Peterson (The Major), Jay Johnson (Bob Campbell), Jay Johnson (Chuck Campbell), Robert Guillaume (Benson DuBois), Donnelly Rhodes (Dutch Leitner)

Created by: Producer and writer Susan Harris

Network: ABC

First Air Date: September 13, 1977

Last Air Date: April 20, 1981

Broadcast History:
September 13, 1977–March 1978: Tuesday at 9:30–10:00 PM
September 1978–March 1979: Thursday at 9:30–10:00 PM
September 1979–March 1980: Thursday at 9:30–10:00 PM
October 1980–January 1981: Wednesday at 9:30–10:00 PM
March 1981–April 20, 1981: Monday at 10:00–11:00 PM

Seasons: 4

Episodes: 85

Ratings History: 1977–1978 (13), 1978–1979 (19), 1979–1980 (25), 1980–1981 (not in Top 30)

Seated: Cathryn Damon, Katherine Helmond, Robert Mandan, and Diana Canova; standing: Billy Crystal, Richard Mulligan, Ted Wass, Robert Guillaume, Jennifer Salt, and Arthur Peterson. *ABC/Photofest ©ABC*

Overview

Networks rarely make the same mistake twice. They all passed on the soap opera satire *Mary Hartman, Mary Hartman* in 1976, forcing creator Norman Lear to sell it into syndication. ABC was not about to pass on *Soap*, despite its controversial nature. Protests followed its launch, but so did banter about it in the homes and around the watercoolers throughout the United States, leading to sensational ratings. Despite some affiliates refusing to run it, others scheduling it past prime time, and some sponsors boycotting it, ABC was rewarded when *Soap* debuted at number thirteen in the Nielsen ratings.

Why all the hubbub? Because many of the ABC affiliates were aghast by its emphasis on sex and infidelity after watching a two-episode screening. *Newsweek* writer Harry F. Waters even claimed, with no basis, in fact, that one plot line spotlighted the seduction of a Catholic priest in a confessional. Only the green light given by ABC programming head Fred Silverman ensured its survival.

It's no wonder that folks tuned in to *Soap* when it debuted on September 13, 1977. Whereas the more morose *Mary Hartman, Mary Hartman* exaggerated the drama associated with soap operas to create humor and tension, this show took a lighthearted approach in satirizing the genre for maximum laughs. Not that writers like show creator Susan Harris didn't take outrageous liberties with story lines—how about a possessed baby for starters?

No subject was taboo on *Soap*, which followed the travails of the affluent Tate family and the working class Campbells. Those concerned that infidelity would be a hot topic on the show had their worst fears realized as airheaded wife Jessica Tate (Katherine Helmond) and husband Chester (Robert Mandan) seemed to sleep with everyone in their fictional Connecticut town of Dunn's River and beyond before they mercifully divorced. Jessica's whacko father, referred to only as "The Major," remained in uniform for good reason; he believed that World War II was still being waged. That the Tate kids were a mess was a foregone conclusion. Son Billy (Jimmy Baio, cousin of *Happy Days* star Scott Baio) embarked on a love affair with his teacher, joined a religious cult, and became a general in the army of South American revolutionary "El Puerco," while daughter Eunice (Jennifer Salt) fell in love with and married a convicted murderer. The only sanity in that household came from wisecracking butler Benson (Robert Guillaume), who rescued Billy from the cult and whose appeal as a character landed him a popular spin-off series that forced him to leave the show in 1979.

The Campbells were no less dysfunctional. Husband Burt (Richard Mulligan) could certainly be blamed for murdering his son Peter, but it was merely an accident when he killed the first husband of alcoholic wife Mary (Cathryn Damon). And it wasn't his fault that he was abducted by aliens and a look-alike Burt Campbell was returned to Earth, resulting in a baby born to him and Mary that could fly. If that wasn't enough, his ventriloquist son Chuck (Jay Johnson) believed his dummy Bob to be real, and Mary's son Danny (Ted Wass) was a gangster given the task of killing Burt. One might speculate that the only reason he couldn't bring himself to carry it out was that Mulligan was such an integral part of the show.

Then there was Mary's son Jodie, played by Billy Crystal, who not only emerged as the most successful actor from the show, but also proved to be a trailblazer in portraying the first openly gay television character. One might think that was enough of a distinction, but not on this sitcom. His journey on the show ends with him identifying himself as an old Jewish man named Julius Kassendorf after a failed hypnotherapy session.

Despite the story lines that piqued the moral outrage of mostly religious groups, the furor died down after the first season and *Soap* settled in as one of the most popular shows on television. Its 9:30 p.m. time slot allowed adults to watch it before at least some of their kids had crashed for the night. The novelty eventually wore off, as it dropped in the Nielsen ratings each year following its initial season, but it remained in the Top 25 in each of its first three years, which was a testament to its appeal.

Tennis, Anyone?

The first major controversy on *Soap* revolved around the murder of womanizer tennis instructor Billy Campbell, who was played by Robert Urich. Urich was among the most accomplished actors in the cast, having already landed the role of Officer Jim

Street in the crime drama *S.W.A.T.* Urich left the show to play a leading role in the series *Tabitha*, a quasi-spin-off of *Bewitched* featuring the Stephens's daughter that lasted just twelve episodes. He later starred in far more successful series, *Vega$* and *Spenser for Hire*.

Did You Know?

Rod Roddy, the longtime announcer for popular game show *The Price Is Right*, served in the same role on *Soap*.

They Said It

Jodie: Plato was gay.
Jessica: Mickey Mouse's dog was gay?
Jodie: Goofy was his lover.

Billy: Why can't anybody in this family talk in front of me? For years I went around thinking a surprise party was being planned for me!

Ingrid Svenson: You think I'm finished?
Jessica: No, Swedish.

Eunice: Tell mother I won't be home this evening. I'm flying to Washington to cover Congressman McCallum's press conference.
Benson: And then she's gonna cover McCallum.

Major Awards

EMMY AWARD WINS (4)

1978 (1): Outstanding Art Direction for a Comedy Series (Edward Stephenson for "#1")
1979 (1): Outstanding Supporting Actor in a Comedy or Comedy-Variety or Music Series (Robert Guillaume)
1980 (2): Outstanding Lead Actor in a Comedy Series (Richard Mulligan); Outstanding Lead Actress in a Comedy Series (Cathryn Damon)

EMMY AWARD NOMINATIONS, IN ADDITION TO WINS (13)

1978 (5): Outstanding Comedy Series; Outstanding Lead Actress in a Comedy Series (Katherine Helmond); Outstanding Lead Actress in a Comedy Series (Cathryn Damon); Outstanding Directing in a Comedy Series (Jay Sandrich for "#24");

Outstanding Achievement in Video Tape Editing for a Series (Gary Anderson for "#2")

1979 (2): Outstanding Lead Actress in a Comedy Series (Katherine Helmond); Outstanding Directing in a Comedy or Comedy-Variety or Music Series (Jay Sandrich for "#27")

1980 (2): Outstanding Comedy Series; Outstanding Lead Actress in a Comedy Series (Katherine Helmond)

1981 (4): Outstanding Comedy Series; Outstanding Lead Actor in a Comedy Series (Richard Mulligan); Outstanding Lead Actress in a Comedy Series (Katherine Helmond); Outstanding Lead Actress in a Comedy Series (Cathryn Damon)

GOLDEN GLOBE WIN (1)

1981 (1): Best Performance by an Actress in a TV Series, Musical/Comedy (Katherine Helmond)

GOLDEN GLOBE NOMINATION, IN ADDITION TO WIN (1)

1981 (1): Best TV Series, Musical/Comedy

Further Reading

Crystal, Billy. *700 Sundays*. New York: Grand Central Publishing, 2006.
"Mature Adult 'Soap' Rocks ABCs Boat." *Time Magazine*, September 18, 1977, p. 13.

✶ 37 ✶

Happy Days

(1974–1984)

Cast: Ron Howard (Richie Cunningham), Henry Winkler (Arthur "Fonzie" Fonzarelli), Tom Bosley (Howard Cunningham), Marion Ross (Marion Cunningham), Erin Moran (Joanie Cunningham), Anson Williams (Warren "Potsie" Weber), Donny Most (Ralph Malph), Pat Morita (Matsuo "Arnold" Takahashi), Al Molinaro (Alfred Delvecchio), Scott Baio (Charles "Chachi" Arcola), Lynda Goodfriend (Lori Beth Allen Cunningham), Cathy Silvers (Jenny Piccalo), Ted McGinley (Roger Phillips)

Created by: Executive producer Garry Marshall

Network: ABC

First Air Date: January 15, 1974

Last Air Date: July 12, 1984

Broadcast History:
January 15, 1974–January 1983: Tuesday at 8:00–8:30 PM
September 1983–May 1984: Saturday at 8:30–9:00 PM
June 1984–July 12, 1984: Thursday at 8:00–8:30 PM

Seasons: 11

Episodes: 255

Ratings History: 1974–1975 (not in Top 30), 1975–1976 (11), 1976–1977 (1), 1977–1978 (2), 1978–1979 (3), 1979–1980 (17), 1980–1981 (15), 1981–1982 (18), 1982–1983 (28), 1983–1984 (not in Top 30)

Clockwise from top left: Henry Winkler, Tom Bosley, Anson Williams, Marion Ross, Ron Howard, Erin Moran, and Donny Most. *ABC/Photofest ©ABC*

Overview

What can accurately be called the Nostalgia Movement began with a 1973 film entitled *American Graffiti*, which critics have rated as one of the best ever. It depicts with great realism and sentimentality the thoughts, feelings, and actions of several high school seniors in the early 1960s, as they wax philosophic about their futures and embark on adventures one fateful night to the most memorable tunes of the era. It features a brilliant young cast, led by Richard Dreyfuss, Ron Howard, Harrison Ford, Cindy Williams, and Mackenzie Phillips. Only Howard, through his years playing the unforgettable Opie in *The Andy Griffith Show*, had already gained fame. The others were budding stars.

And only Howard would land in the bandwagon when a program began airing that took advantage of the nostalgia craze started by *American Graffiti* (although the pilot for the show had already been shot before the movie was released). Show creator Garry Marshall jumped back a few years into the 1950s, when rock and roll was in its infancy, to nail the ideal time frame for a sitcom about teenagers living in a far more innocent and carefree era in the nation's history. It was a time of a burgeoning suburbia in which Americans embraced the notion of strong families and the importance of friendship.

These were indeed happy days, hence the title of one of the biggest hits in American television history. The biggest star of the show, which was set in Milwaukee, was supposed to be Howard, who played sensible Richie Cunningham, but a surprising bit character named Arthur Fonzarelli emerged not only as a costar, but as a household name better known as "Fonzie." Replete with leather jacket, greased-back hair, and a harem of pretty girls following him around, the greaser played by Henry Winkler took the country by storm. One still recalls "The Fonz" about to take comb to hair and then putting it down as he stared at himself in the mirror and uttered his trademark line: "Aaaaaaaaaay!" Why mess with perfection, right? The switch from a laugh track to filming before a studio audience allowed fans to cheer Fonzie upon his arrival and gave *Happy Days* a theater feel and energy.

Despite the emergence of Fonzie as an integral player (he eventually moved into the Cunningham attic), the early years of the show still revolved around Richie. They spotlighted equally his family and personal life with intriguing and humorous characters and colorful personalities. Howard Cunningham (Tom Bosley) was an understanding, lenient father, conservative yet cool enough to earn the nickname "Mr. C" from Fonzie. Wife and mother Marion (Marion Ross) never played the role of subservient to her husband, as did the spouses of star characters in the sitcoms of that era. And little sister Joanie (Erin Moran) performed her role with realism and spirit, particularly before she reached high school age.

That realism extended to the trio of Richie and best buddies Ralph Malph (Donny Most) and Potsie Weber (Anson Williams). Their interaction and dialogue rang authentic as they joyfully careened through their teenage years with a sense that, indeed, more serious times in their lives lay ahead, while displaying personalities unique to their characters. Ralph was the clown of the group who worked to mask his insecurities. Potsie didn't feel compelled to mask insecurities; he seemingly had none.

The quintessential 1950s environment required music and a hangout. Such tunes as "Blueberry Hill" (Fats Domino), "Splish Splash" (Bobby Darin), and "Chantilly Lace" (The Big Bopper) blared from the jukebox at Arnold's Drive-In, whose namesake proprietor (Pat Morita) welcomed the teenagers that patronized his business. It was where Fonzie was in his element. No need for him to put money in the jukebox; he simply slammed his magical fist on it and it played.

One and all remained happy on *Happy Days*, but as the 1950s turned into the 1960s, the show itself took a fall so profound that the precipitous drop gave birth to an insult used forever more about the moments programs take a turn for the worse from which they never recover. It jumped the shark. The line came quite literally from an episode in which Fonzie jumped a shark while water skiing; it wasn't enough that a greaser from Milwaukee could water ski in the first place.

New characters brought new and unrealistic story lines, including the appearance of an alien named Mork (Robin Williams) that spawned spin-off *Mork & Mindy* and a relationship between Fonzie's nephew "Chachi" Arcola (Scott Baio) and Joanie that led to another (*Joanie Loves Chachi*). The 1950s feel was replaced with a modern flavor that killed the charm of *Happy Days*. Soon Howard and Most had quit the show, and largely unappealing characters like Jenny Piccalo (Cathy Silvers, daughter of comedian Phil Silvers) and Roger Phillips (Ted McGinley) joined the cast. When Fonzie took a job as an auto mechanic instructor at the school and became an adopted father, it was time to pull the plug, which was mercifully done in 1984.

Television viewers with a "glass half-empty" outlook will recall with sadness the last several seasons of a once-great show. The "glass half-full" types will only remember the *Happy Days* that made them happy.

Chuck Was There, Chuck Was Gone

There were three Cunningham kids when *Happy Days* hit the airwaves in 1974. Two years later, there were two. Older brother Chuck was gone and never mentioned again. Seen mostly dribbling a basketball around, Chuck was played by Gavan O'Herlihy in nine episodes of the first season, and Randolph Roberts in just two episodes of the second. He never made another appearance.

Before "Schlemiel, Schlimazel, Hasenpfeffer Incorporated"

Happy Days spawned several spin-offs, but only one highly successful one. The occasional appearances of Cindy Williams (who costarred in *American Graffiti*) and future top-flight director Penny Marshall (sister of show creator Garry Marshall) led to their pairing in *Laverne and Shirley*, which was launched in 1976.

Did You Know?

Suzi Quatro, who played a singer with the unforgettable name of Leather Tuscadero in seven episodes of *Happy Days*, was a star rocker in Great Britain and Australia, with such hits as "Can the Can" and "48 Crash."

They Said It

Marion: Richie just hasn't got the appetite that Chuck has.
Howard: Marion, Argentina hasn't got the appetite that Chuck has.

Fonzie: [after Marion yelled at him and stormed out of the room] I'm gonna hit her.
Howard: No, you're not gonna hit my wife.
Fonzie: [to Richie] Then I'll hit you!
Howard: You're not gonna hit my son.
Fonzie: Then I'll hit you.
Richie: You're not gonna hit my father either.
Fonzie: Well I gotta hit somebody. You know where Potsie is?

Richie: There must be girls somewhere that think of us as men.
Potsie: There are, but Joanie's friends are too short.

Major Awards

EMMY AWARD WIN (1)

1978 (1): Outstanding Film Editing in a Comedy Series (Ed Cotter for "Richie Almost Dies")

EMMY AWARD NOMINATIONS, IN ADDITION TO WIN (8)

1976 (1): Outstanding Lead Actor in a Comedy Series (Henry Winkler)
1977 (1): Outstanding Lead Actor in a Comedy Series (Henry Winkler)
1978 (3): Outstanding Lead Actor in a Comedy Series (Henry Winkler); Outstanding Continuing Performance by a Supporting Actor in a Comedy Series (Tom Bosley); Outstanding Directing in a Comedy Series (Jerry Paris for "Richie Almost Dies")
1979 (1): Outstanding Performance by a Supporting Actress in a Comedy or Comedy-Variety or Music Series (Marion Ross)
1981 (1): Outstanding Directing in a Comedy Series (Jerry Paris for "Hello Mrs. Arcola")
1984 (1): Outstanding Supporting Actress in a Comedy Series (Marion Ross)

GOLDEN GLOBE WINS (3)

1977 (1): Best TV Actor, Musical/Comedy (Henry Winkler)
1978 (2): Best TV Actor, Musical/Comedy (Henry Winkler); Best TV Actor, Musical/Comedy (Ron Howard)

GOLDEN GLOBE NOMINATIONS, IN ADDITION TO WINS (3)

1977 (1): Best TV Series, Musical/Comedy
1978 (1): Best TV Series, Musical/Comedy
1983 (1): Best Performance by an Actor in a Supporting Role in a Series, Mini-Series, or Motion Picture Made for TV (Anson Williams)

Further Reading

Marshall, Garry. *My Happy Days in Hollywood: A Memoir*. New York: Crown Archetype, 2012.
Rich, Frank. "HEROES: Fearless Fonz." *Time Magazine*, November 21, 1977. Available online at www.time.com/time/magazine/article/0,9171,915741,00.html.

✳ **38** ✳

The Big Bang Theory

(2007–)

Cast: Johnny Galecki (Dr. Leonard Hofstadter), Jim Parsons (Dr. Sheldon Cooper), Kaley Cuoco (Penny), Simon Helberg (Howard Wolowitz), Kunal Nayyar (Rajesh "Raj" Koothrappali), Melissa Rauch (Bernadette Rostenkowski), Mayim Bialik (Dr. Amy Farrah Fowler)

Created by: Executive producers and writers Chuck Lorre and Bill Prady

Network: CBS

First Air Date: September 24, 2007

Broadcast History:
September 24, 2007–November 2007: Monday at 8:30–9:00 PM
March 2008–May 2008: Monday at 8:00–8:30 PM
September 2008–May 2009: Monday at 8:00–8:30 PM
February 2009: Monday at 9:30–10:00 PM
September 2009–May 2010: Monday at 9:30–10:00 PM
May 2010: Monday at 9:00–9:30 PM
September 2010–May 2013: Thursday at 8:00–8:30 PM

Seasons: 6

Episodes: 125 (through January 2013)

Ratings History: 2007–2008 (not in Top 30), 2008–2009 (not in Top 30), 2009–2010 (12), 2010–2011 (13), 2011–2012 (8)

Jim Parsons, Johnny Galecki, and Kaley Cuoco. *CBS/Photofest ©CBS*

Overview

This show could have been more appropriately titled *Dorks to the 100th Power*. The characters are geeks on overdrive. Indeed, *The Big Bang Theory* creators Chuck Lorre and Bill Prady wisely embraced the comparatively recent American fascination with nerds and ran with it. They transformed that rather abstract captivation into one of the funniest shows of the twenty-first century. Their task and those of the major cast members was to develop unique, humorous, multidimensional characters that were not merely super intelligent. Each required personalities and motivations that would create conflict and give viewers a deep examination of their strengths and vulnerabilities.

Mission accomplished. But one could not have expected anything less, particularly from Lorre, who has established himself as one of the most prolific and successful sitcom writers of his generation with such credits as *My Two Dads*, *Roseanne*, *Grace under Fire*, *Cybill*, *Dharma and Greg*, and *Two and a Half Men* to his name.

The most outrageous personality on *The Big Bang Theory* belongs to wildly up-tight and neurotic Dr. Sheldon Cooper (Jim Parsons), a theoretical physicist with an Einsteinesque IQ of 187. He is conniving, emotionally distant, and obsessive to the point that he anguishes over the slightest variation from routine. His passion for comic books and *Star Trek*, the notoriously geek favorite television and movie series, is a running joke on the show. He eventually finds female companionship in Dr. Amy Fowler (Mayim Bialik), a brilliant, but insecure, neurobiologist whose attempts to forge a sexual relationship have been thwarted by the emotionally vacuous Sheldon. His compulsive behavior is particularly grating to roommate Dr. Leonard Hofstadter (Johnny Galecki), an experimental physicist whose vast intelligence and professional ambition are equaled by desires of sexual and romantic gratification not shared by Sheldon. Leonard, who is far more socially adept than his friend, eventually forges a relationship with beautiful, but intellectually limited, neighbor Penny (Kaley Cuoco), who is at once humored and annoyed by what she perceives as the pointless pursuits of the nerdy crowd into which she has fallen.

The irritation Penny endures does not compare to that of aerospace engineer Howard Wolowitz (Simon Helberg), who spends much of his time at the apartment of friends Leonard and Sheldon, who chastise him for his status as the only one in the group (aside from Penny, of course) that has not earned a doctorate. Howard often feels exasperated dealing with Leonard, but he gains no more satisfaction living with his unseen mother, with whom he constantly engages in shouting matches from separate rooms. His attempts to attract women are hindered by his inability to communicate respectfully; his inappropriate pickup lines result in revulsion and rejection. Howard finally finds some personal satisfaction in his relationship with eccentric Bernadette Rostenkowski (Melissa Rauch), a friend of Penny's whom he eventually marries.

The other member of the geeky quintet is physicist Dr. Rajesh Koothrappali (Kunal Nayyar), a thoroughly Americanized native of India who still embraces Hinduism and a belief in reincarnation. His obsession with comic books, which matches that of Sheldon, and his lack of confidence around or strong attraction to women, as well as his love for girlie books and movies, leads to intimations from his friends that he is gay.

The story lines, episode plot lines, and humor most often revolve around the passions of the four main male characters, including their scientific work, science fiction on television, movies and comic books, various superheroes, and games involving all of the aforementioned, sometimes created by themselves in their sheltered lives. As the sitcom has evolved, so have their professional and personal relationships, as female love interests, aside from those of Sheldon and Penny, have grown in prominence. The additions to the cast of Bialik and Rauch have opened up opportunities for the male characters to grow emotionally.

Just as the characters have grown, so has the popularity of the show. The ratings of *The Big Bang Theory* have climbed each year after remaining outside the Top 30 in its first two seasons. The show has become one of the most-watched programs of its era.

Battle of the Sexes

Although the men take center stage in *The Big Bang Theory*, two of the three major cast members with extensive experience in previous television sitcoms are women. The only exception is Johnny Galecki, who played David Healy on *Roseanne*. Kaley Cuoco gained fame as the cute, self-absorbed teenager Bridget Hennessy in *8 Simple Rules* from 2002 to 2005. Mayim Bialik starred as Blossom in the namesake show of the early to mid-1990s.

Did You Know?

It's no coincidence that two of the main characters were named Sheldon and Leonard. They were so named to honor legendary television producer Sheldon Leonard.

They Said It

Penny: [about Christy] I know how she is. She'll keep having sex with you as long as you buy her stuff.
Howard: Really?
Penny: Yeah.
Howard: Yay!

Leonard: How did you know my birthday's Saturday?
Penny: I did your horoscope, remember? I was going to do everybody's until Sheldon went on one of his typical psychotic rants.
Sheldon: For the record, that psychotic rant was a concise summation of the research of Bertram Forer, who, in 1948, proved conclusively through meticulously designed experiments that astrology is nothing but pseudoscientific hokum.
Penny: Blah, blah, blah, a typical Taurus.

Major Awards

EMMY AWARD WINS (5)

2010 (1): Outstanding Lead Actor in a Comedy Series (Jim Parsons)
2011 (1): Outstanding Lead Actor in a Comedy Series (Jim Parsons)
2013 (3): Outstanding Lead Actor in a Comedy Series (Jim Parsons); Outstanding Guest Actor in a Comedy Series (Bob Newhart); Outstanding Technical Direction, Camerawork, Video Control for a Series

EMMY AWARD NOMINATIONS, IN ADDITION TO WINS (21)

2009 (3): Outstanding Lead Actor in a Comedy Series (Jim Parsons); Outstanding Guest Actress in a Comedy Series (Christine Baranski for "The Maternal Capacitance"); Outstanding Art Direction for a Multi-Camera Series (John S. Shaffner and Ann Margaret Shea for "The Hofstadter Isotope")
2010 (4): Outstanding Guest Actress in a Comedy Series (Christine Baranski for "The Maternal Capacitance"); Outstanding Art Direction for a Multi-Camera Series (John S. Shaffner and Ann Margaret Shea for "The Gothowitz Deviation"); Outstanding Makeup for a Multi-Camera Series or Special (Non-Prosthetic) (Peggy Nichols, Ken Diaz, and Vikki McCarter for "The Electric Can Opener Fluctuation"); Outstanding Technical Direction, Camerawork, Video Control for a Series (John Pierre Dechene, James L. Hitchcock, Richard Price, Brian Armstong, Devin Atwood, and John D. O'Brien for "The Adhesive Duck Deficiency")
2011 (4): Outstanding Comedy Series; Outstanding Lead Actor in a Comedy Series (Johnny Galecki); Outstanding Art Direction for a Multi-Camera Series (John S. Shaffner, Francoise Cherry-Cohen, and Ann Margaret Shea for "The Love Car Displacement"); Outstanding Picture Editing for a Comedy Series (Single or Multi-Camera) (Peter John Chakos for "The Agreement Dissection")

2012 (5): Outstanding Comedy Series; Outstanding Lead Actor in a Comedy Series (Jim Parsons); Outstanding Supporting Actress in a Comedy Series (Mayim Bialik); Outstanding Multi-Camera Picture Editing for a Comedy Series (Peter John Chakos for "The Countdown Reflection"); Outstanding Technical Direction, Camerawork, Video Control for a Series (John Pierre Dechene, James L. Hitchcock, Richard Price, Brian Armstong, and John D. O'Brien for "The Countdown Reflection")

2013 (5): Outstanding Comedy Series; Outstanding Supporting Actress in a Comedy Series (Mayim Bialik); Outstanding Art Direction for a Multi-Camera Series; Outstanding Multi-Camera Picture Editing for a Comedy Series; Outstanding Hairstyling for a Multi-Camera Series or Special

GOLDEN GLOBE WIN (1)

2011 (1): Best Performance by an Actor in a TV Series, Musical/Comedy (Jim Parsons)

GOLDEN GLOBE NOMINATIONS, IN ADDITION TO WIN (4)

2011 (1): Best TV Series, Musical/Comedy
2012 (1): Best Performance by an Actor in a TV Series, Musical/Comedy (Johnny Galecki)
2013 (2): Best TV Series, Musical/Comedy; Best Performance by an Actor in a TV Series, Musical/Comedy (Johnny Galecki)

Further Reading

Wyatt, Edward. "The Big Surprise of 'Big Bang': The Bigger Audience." *New York Times*, October 5, 2009, p. C1.

✳ **39** ✳

Green Acres

(1965–1971)

Cast: Eddie Albert (Oliver Wendell Douglas), Eva Gabor (Lisa Douglas), Tom Lester (Eb Dawson), Pat Buttram (Mr. Eustace Haney), Alvy Moore (Hank Kimball), Sid Melton (Alf Monroe), Mary Grace Canfield (Ralph Monroe), Hank Patterson (Fred Ziffel), Barbara Pepper (Doris Ziffel 1), Fran Ryan (Doris Ziffel 2), Arnold the Pig (Arnold Ziffel)

Created by: Producer and writer Jay Sommers

Network: CBS

First Air Date: September 15, 1965

Last Air Date: September 7, 1971

Broadcast History:
September 15, 1965–September 1968: Wednesday at 9:00–9:30 PM
September 1968–September 1969: Wednesday at 9:30–10:00 PM
September 1969–September 1970: Saturday at 9:00–9:30 PM
September 1970–September 7, 1971: Tuesday at 8:00–8:30 PM

Seasons: 6

Episodes: 170

Ratings History: 1965–1966 (11), 1966–1967 (6), 1967–1968 (15), 1968–1969 (19), 1969–1970 (not in Top 30), 1970–1971 (not in Top 30)

Eddie Albert and Eva Gabor. *CBS/Photofest ©CBS*

Overview

A chicken that laid square eggs. A pig whose painting "Nude at a Watering Trough" hangs proudly on the wall of his principal's office. A female carpenter named Ralph. Opening credits that were seen and commented on by the characters. Welcome to *Green Acres*, the loopiest, most surreal sitcom this side of Hooterville.

Executive producer Paul Henning, given carte blanche at CBS following the success of *The Beverly Hillbillies* and *Petticoat Junction*, brought one of the strangest sitcoms ever made to the small screen. In revamping his short-lived radio show *Granby's Green Acres*, creator Jay Sommers let his imagination run wild developing this show about New York attorney Oliver Wendell Douglas (Eddie Albert), who chucked what he disdainfully called the "rat race" of the Big Apple for the cherished and prideful life of a farmer. The problem is that he was one lousy farmer. And that was the least of his problems.

Oliver was surrounded by lunacy, from dingbat Hungarian wife Lisa (Eva Gabor), to goofball hired hand Eb Dawson (Tom Lester), to huckster Eustace Haney (Pat Buttram) trying to sell him broken-down Hoyt Clagwell products, to neighbor Fred Ziffel (Hank Patterson) treating his pig like a son, to a county agent named Hank Kimball (Alvy Moore) who couldn't even remember his own name. Then there were the daily annoyances for Oliver, for instance, climbing to the top of a telephone pole outside his bedroom because that's where the crack staff at the Hooterville Telephone Company placed his phone.

The plot lines were as bizarre as the characters. There was the one in which Hooterville blew up the bridge over Simpson's Swamp, seceded from the state, and installed the unsuspecting Oliver as ruler of the new kingdom. There was the one in which Arnold Ziffel inherited $1 million after proving he was an heir to a fortune by correctly forecasting snow in July with his tail. And there was the one in which a plane flight from Trans-Pixley Airlines was cancelled because the rubber band broke.

The premise of the show was a reversal of *The Beverly Hillbillies*, which featured a backwoods family striking it rich and hightailing it to one of the wealthiest communities in the country. Oliver, on the other hand, was a well-to-do lawyer living in a New York penthouse with his glamorous wife, who was far more sophisticated than goofy in the early episodes before becoming as off-the-wall as any of the Hooterville crackpots. The seemingly levelheaded Oliver, who had a passion for farming, showed he, too, was not playing with a full deck by purchasing from Haney a ramshackle dump in which to live, a Hoyt Clagwell tractor that fell apart upon ignition, a rooster that refused to crow, and other assorted goods and services that proved to be disasters. Although he finally caught on to Haney and rarely purchased anything else from him, he never grew as a farmer. In one of his few lucid moments, Hank Kimball said that Oliver's tomatoes looked like "olives that got sunburned."

It can be debated that Henning made a mockery of rural people and that such a story line would have been dismissed today as politically incorrect, but others believe Henning was making no statement at all; he was merely creating a bizarre world in which Oliver truly belonged, not because he gave up his life of wealth and comfort for one as a poor farmer, but because he made the transition as haphazardly as those he joined in Hooterville ran their lives.

Many *Green Acres* fans believe that the sitcom actually pulled a "reverse jump the shark" by becoming zanier and funnier as it went along, although it did fall out of the Top 30 in the Nielsen ratings in its last two seasons after remaining there in the first four. It bit the dust in 1971, when CBS purged its lineup of rural shows or, as Buttram noted, "killed everything with a tree in it." But the show lives on as a cult classic in the hearts and minds of those who still embrace it. And in the eyes of its fans, its greatness was confirmed by the words of Matt Groening, creator of *The Simpsons*, who said *Green Acres* influenced his upbringing and motivated him as a college student to attend a tribute honoring its cast. It must have been a surreal experience.

Pigs, Cows, Chickens, and Lisa Douglas

The Lisa Douglas character arrived in Hooterville as a socialite who knew nothing about farm life. Her desire throughout most of the episodes was to return to New York, but she did fall in love with the animals on the farm and in the community. Not only did she gain affection for Arnold the Pig and Douglas cow Eleanor, but also the chickens, each of which she gave names.

An urban legend was created that the first Arnold (there were many that came and went) was butchered and eaten by the cast. A book published in 1998, written by William Hedgepeth, entitled *The Hog Book*, makes the claim that the cooked creature wound up on the dinner table of trainer Frank Inn, but other reports claim that such a dastardly deed was never done.

They Said It

Oliver: [noting that Lisa is sweeping the carpet without having plugged in the vacuum] What's the matter with the vacuum?
Lisa: Nothing.
Oliver: It's not making any noise.
Lisa: Well, it only makes a noise when it's plugged in.
Oliver: Then what are you vacuuming?
Lisa: [with emphasis] I am not! It's not plugged in.

Lisa: [asking why Hank Kimball won't take Ralph Monroe, who is sweet on him, to the carpenter's ball] Why don't you want to take her? Don't you like her?
Hank: Aww, she's not too bad. . . . She's not too good either. Ah, well, she does have some nice, uh. . . . Well, they're not really nice, uh. . . . I'll say one thing for her: She's a mess!

Mr. Haney: How would like this gen-you-wine Eggslicer?
Oliver: Why, that's a harp, you . . .
Mr. Haney: Right you are: made by the famous harp-maker, Gustav Eggslicer!

Major Awards

None

Further Reading

Cox, Stephen. *The Hooterville Handbook: A Viewer's Guide to Green Acres.* New York: St. Martin's Griffin, 1994.

✳ **40** ✳

Malcolm in the Middle

(2000–2006)

Cast: Frankie Muniz (Malcolm Wilkerson), Jane Kaczmarek (Lois Wilkerson), Bryan Cranston (Hal Wilkerson), Justin Berfield (Reese Wilkerson), Erik Per Sullivan (Dewey Wilkerson), Christopher Masterson (Francis Wilkerson), Craig Lamar Traylor (Stevie Kenarban)

Created by: Executive producer and writer Linwood Boomer

Network: FOX

First Air Date: January 9, 2000

Last Air Date: August 6, 2006

Broadcast History:
    January 9, 2000–June 2002: Sunday at 8:30–9:00 PM
    January 2000: Tuesday at 8:30–9:00 PM
    November 2000: Wednesday at 8:00–8:30 PM
    July 2002–September 2002: Sunday at 9:00–10:00 PM
    November 2002: Sunday at 9:00–10:00 PM
    December 2002–August 2003: Sunday at 9:00–9:30 PM
    July 2003–August 2003: Sunday at 9:30–10:00 PM
    November 2003–July 2004: Sunday at 9:00–9:30 PM
    July 2004–August 2004: Sunday at 7:30–8:00 PM
    November 2004–May 2005: Sunday at 7:30–8:00 PM
    June 2005–September 2005: Sunday at 7:00–7:30 PM
    September 2005–June 2006: Friday at 8:30–9:00 PM
    June 2006–August 6, 2006: Sunday at 7:00–7:30 PM

Seasons: 7

Episodes: 151

Ratings History: 1999–2000 (28), 2000–2001 (not in Top 30), 2001–2002 (not in Top 30), 2002–2003 (not in Top 30), 2003–2004 (not in Top 30), 2004–2005 (not in Top 30), 2005–2006 (not in Top 30)

Clockwise from bottom: Frankie Muniz, Erik Per Sullivan, Jane Kaczmarek, Christopher Masterson, Bryan Cranston, and Justin Berfield. *FOX/Photofest ©FOX*

Overview

A glance at the acting credits of Linwood Boomer would give no clue as to why he embarked on creating the wonderfully offbeat *Malcolm in the Middle*. He appeared on such shows as *Hawaii Five-O*, *Little House on the Prairie*, and *Young and the Restless*. Not a comedy in the bunch. But he was motivated to write *Malcolm in the Middle* based on his upbringing as a highly intelligent boy attending a school for gifted children.

Boomer had already contributed as a writer and producer to the sitcoms *Silver Spoons* and *Night Court* by the time he got around to *Malcolm in the Middle*, a quirky and fresh midseason replacement in 1999 that drew humor from its surrealism and intriguing characters. The show focused on a dysfunctional middle-class family of six. The standout in the group of underachievers was the title character (Frankie Muniz), who rejected the expectations of his genius and hated the school for gifted kids he was forced to attend, but was treated as an outcast within his own family and by other children. Malcolm was set apart from the others through his frequent expression of his thoughts and fears directly to the camera. The sitcom ventured off further in relation to many of its contemporaries with his single-camera shooting and disuse of a laugh track.

The most manic of the characters was moody mother Lois (Jane Kaczmarek), who passed down discipline because someone had to; it wasn't going to be easygoing and dimwitted husband Hal (Bryan Cranston). Lois often took out her dissatisfaction with her professional life as a lowly worker at a grocery store on her family. Each of the actors playing the brothers crafted unique and captivating characterizations. Smart-aleck eldest son Francis (Christopher Masterson) was dispatched to military school but phoned in sage advice to his younger brothers as to how to stave off the wrath of their mother. Vacant and unintelligent Reese (Justin Berfield) was jealous of Malcolm's brilliance. And youngest son Dewey (Erik Per Sullivan) was just plain strange. His weird haircut and seeming awareness, despite his young age, that he was being screwed up for life by his parents made him one of the funniest characters on the show.

The sitcom was further enhanced by plot lines that brought out the personalities, motivations, and idiosyncrasies of the characters. That strategy was established by the second episode of the first season, in which Lois discovers the expensive red dress she bought for her wedding anniversary dinner with Hal partially burned and soaking in the toilet. While the kids work in vain to diffuse their furious mother, Hal is busy getting crocked with the staff of the restaurant at which he made reservations. Francis does his part to calm his mom by telling her to "let something go" for a change, advice she takes to heart. But disaster was always on the horizon in the Wilkerson family (the last name was never mentioned beyond the first episode). After Lois leaves for the restaurant with the kids, a drunken Hal arrives at home thinking that he was supposed to pick them all up. And when he lights his pipe, he sets the couch on fire, thereby giving the viewers a good idea as to how his wife's dress had been burned.

Story line changes kept *Malcolm in the Middle* fresh. Francis used an attorney to free him from the military school he detested, but his desire to become a logger was dashed and he was forced to work as a busboy at a restaurant. The silver lining was that he met driven Native American Piama Tananahaakna (Emy Coligado), whom he married and joined on a cross-country trip to find contentment. He eventually landed a job as a foreman on a dude ranch run by an inept German named Otto Mannkusser (Kenneth Mars).

Meanwhile, Malcolm sought to shed his image as a nerdy boy genius upon his arrival in high school, but to no avail, Lois gave birth to yet another boy, and Reese joined the army and was sent to Afghanistan before promptly going AWOL, motivating his mother to travel to the capital city of Kabul and fetch him.

Francis appeared infrequently in the last two seasons, which featured the brilliant Cloris Leachman added to the cast as Lois' crabby mother Ida. By the time the show was cancelled in 2006, Reese had hightailed it to Las Vegas to marry immigrant Raduca (Rheagan Wallace), who was motivated only by securing her work permit, and Malcolm was on his way to Harvard.

The realism that accompanied the dysfunctionality of the family was never compromised, despite the adventures each of its members experienced—even those of Francis, who eventually found stability and satisfaction as a data entry specialist. It was that sense of reality that brought identification with fans of the show. *Malcolm in the Middle* remains simply one of the most innovative and well-produced sitcoms of its era.

The Converted Dentist

Although Bryan Cranston starred as a husband and father in *Malcolm in the Middle*, many sitcom fans know him as having played memorable dentist Tim Whatley in five episodes of *Seinfeld*. The friend of Jerry and Elaine was portrayed as rather selfish. In one episode, Jerry suspects that Tim has converted to Judaism so he can tell Jewish jokes and not be considered anti-Semitic. Cranston broke from television comedy in 2008 to play chemist Walter White in the successful crime drama series *Breaking Bad*.

Did You Know?

Scenes from the 1966 sci-fi flick *One Million Years B.C.* are shown in the opening credits of *Malcolm in the Middle*. The movie starred emerging sex symbol Raquel Welch, who is seen in the credits of the sitcom in the claws of a huge prehistoric bird.

They Said It

Lois: [about Hal] He's battling his arch enemy.
Francis: Is the squirrel back again?

Lois: I just found out your family has a little nickname for me.
Hal: That's nice . . . what is it?
Lois: Lois Common Denominator.

Major Awards

EMMY AWARD WINS (7)

2000 (2): Outstanding Writing for a Comedy Series (Linwood Boomer for the pilot); Outstanding Directing for a Comedy Series (Todd Holland for the pilot)

2001 (2): Outstanding Writing for a Comedy Series (Alex Reid for "Bowling"); Outstanding Directing for a Comedy Series (Todd Holland for "Bowling")

2002 (1): Outstanding Guest Actress in a Comedy Series (Cloris Leachman)

2003 (1): Outstanding Single Camera Picture Editing for a Comedy Series (Mark Scheib and Steve Welch for "If Boys Were Girls")

2006 (1): Outstanding Guest Actress in a Comedy Series (Cloris Leachman for "Bride of Ida" and "Graduation")

EMMY AWARD NOMINATIONS, IN ADDITION TO WINS (26)

2000 (3): Outstanding Lead Actress in a Comedy Series (Jane Kaczmarek); Outstanding Guest Actress in a Comedy Series (Bea Arthur); Outstanding Casting for a Comedy Series (Ken Miller, Mary V. Black, Nikki Valko, and Susan Edelman)

2001 (6): Outstanding Comedy Series; Outstanding Lead Actor in a Comedy Series (Frankie Muniz); Outstanding Lead Actress in a Comedy Series (Jane Kaczmarek); Outstanding Guest Actress in a Comedy Series (Cloris Leachman for "Grandparents"); Outstanding Guest Actor in a Comedy Series (Robert Loggia for "Grandparents"); Outstanding Directing for a Comedy Series (Jeff Melman for "Flashback")

2002 (5): Outstanding Lead Actress in a Comedy Series (Jane Kaczmarek); Outstanding Supporting Actor in a Comedy Series (Bryan Cranston); Outstanding Guest Actress in a Comedy Series (Susan Sarandon for "Company Picnic: Part 1"); Outstanding Directing for a Comedy Series (Jeff Melman for "Christmas"); Outstanding Stunt Coordination (Bobby Porter for "Company Picnic")

2003 (3): Outstanding Lead Actress in a Comedy Series (Jane Kaczmarek); Outstanding Supporting Actor in a Comedy Series (Bryan Cranston); Outstanding Guest Actress in a Comedy Series (Cloris Leachman)

2004 (3): Outstanding Lead Actress in a Comedy Series (Jane Kaczmarek); Outstanding Guest Actress in a Comedy Series (Cloris Leachman); Outstanding Choreography (Fred Tallakson for "Dewey's Special Class")

2005 (3): Outstanding Lead Actress in a Comedy Series (Jane Kaczmarek); Outstanding Guest Actress in a Comedy Series (Cloris Leachman for "Ida Loses a Leg" and "Ida's Dance"); Outstanding Music and Lyrics (Charles Sydnor and Eric Kaplan for the song "The Married Bed" for "Dewey's Opera")

2006 (3): Outstanding Lead Actress in a Comedy Series (Jane Kaczmarek); Outstanding Supporting Actor in a Comedy Series (Bryan Cranston); Outstanding Choreography (Fred Tallakson for "Bomb Shelter")

GOLDEN GLOBE NOMINATIONS (7)

2001 (3): Best TV Series, Musical/Comedy; Best Performance by an Actor in a TV Series, Musical/Comedy (Frankie Muniz); Best Performance by an Actress in a TV Series, Musical/Comedy (Jane Kaczmarek)

2002 (2): Best Performance by an Actor in a TV Series, Musical/Comedy (Frankie Muniz); Best Performance by an Actress in a TV Series, Musical/Comedy (Jane Kaczmarek)

2003 (2): Best Performance by an Actress in a TV Series, Musical/Comedy (Jane Kaczmarek); Best Performance by an Actor in a Supporting Role in a Series, Mini-Series, or Motion Picture Made for Television (Bryan Cranston)

HUMANITAS PRIZE NOMINATION

2001: 30-Minute Category (Larry Strawther)

PEABODY AWARD

2001: FOX and Regency Television

Further Reading

Leonard, John. "The Littlest Freudian." *New York Magazine*, December 6, 2004. Available online at http://nymag.com/nymetro/arts/tv/reviews/10539/.

✷ **41** ✷

Bewitched

(1964–1972)

Cast: Elizabeth Montgomery (Samantha Stephens, Serena), Dick York (Darrin Stephens, 1964–1969), Dick Sargent (Darrin Stephens, 1969–1972), Agnes Moorehead (Endora), Erin Murphy (Tabitha Stevens), David White (Larry Tate), George Tobias (Abner Kravitz), Alice Pearce (Gladys Kravitz, 1964–1966), Sandra Gould (Gladys Kravitz, 1966–1972), Marion Lorne (Aunt Clara), Paul Lynde (Uncle Arthur)

Created by: Writer Sol Saks

Network: ABC

First Air Date: September 17, 1964

Last Air Date: July 1, 1972

Broadcast History:
September 17, 1964–January 1967: Thursday at 9:00–9:30 PM
January 1967–September 1971: Thursday at 8:30–9:00 PM
September 1971–January 1972: Wednesday at 8:00–8:30 PM
January 1972–July 1, 1972: Saturday at 8:00–8:30 PM

Seasons: 8

Episodes: 216

Ratings History: 1964–1965 (2), 1965–1966 (7), 1966–1967 (7), 1967–1968 (11), 1968–1969 (11), 1969–1970 (24), 1970–1971 (not in Top 30), 1971–1972 (not in Top 30)

Elizabeth Montgomery, Dick York, and Agnes Moorehead. *ABC/Photofest ©ABC*

Overview

If Elizabeth Montgomery had the power of Samantha Stephens, she could have willed every television viewer in America to tune into *Bewitched*. But even as a mere mortal, her cuteness and talent played the most significant role in making the sitcom one of the most-watched shows on television in the 1960s and beyond. Montgomery turned Stephens into a nose-twitching force, but one that only used her witchcraft to aid the career of husband Darrin (played more popularly by Dick York than replacement Dick

Sargent) and her community. The former motivation wasn't easy with her sly, scheming mother Endora (Agnes Moorehead) conjuring up spells to make both the personal and professional life miserable for the son-in-law she so despised.

The conflicts didn't stop there. For some reason unfathomable to real-life men, Darrin demanded that Samantha play the role of dutiful mortal wife and retire her witchcraft for good. That very strong request, which Samantha didn't try particularly hard to fulfill, came in the first episode when she revealed her powers to her stunned husband. Darrin I and Darrin II spent the next eight years toiling in vain to keep Samantha in check, unless they needed a nose twitch or two to extricate them from a particularly thorny situation.

Darrin was also forced to survive the sorcery of the other assorted eccentric relations, arguably the most entertaining of which were the inept Aunt Clara (Marion Lorne), who struggled to remember her incantations in casting spells or to remove those she did manage to place on her hapless victims, and madcap Uncle Arthur, played by the goofy and always entertaining Paul Lynde. Samantha's troublemaking, hedonistic cousin Serena (Montgomery) also popped in unannounced on occasion to turn the Stephens household upside down.

The hapless victim was most often Darrin. He was transformed through witchcraft into the world's biggest cheapskate, limited to speaking Spanish, rained upon, made to be universally disliked, given the biggest ego on the planet, slowly turned into a werewolf while entertaining clients, and transformed into a chimpanzee. Then there was the next season. The spells were most often cast by Endora, who sought to prove to the daughter she adored that marrying a mortal—especially the man she sneeringly referred to as "Derwood"—was a grave error in judgment. Darrin found it nearly impossible to explain such behavior to boss Larry Tate (David White) at the advertising agency where he was employed, but thanks to Samantha undoing the voodoo Endora did so well, everything always worked out in the end and Darren would wind up a hero. Larry would sometimes threaten to fire Darrin and then give him a raise in the same episode.

The strange happenings weren't limited to Darrin. Incantations by the collection of oddball witches and warlocks resulted in a huge ostrich and pink polka-dotted elephant running around the Stephens home, a person being turned into a chair, and Benjamin Franklin being summoned from the dead to fix a lamp. Even Julius Caesar was conjured up when Esmerelda (Alice Ghostley), who rivaled Aunt Clara in incompetence as a witch, tried to make a Caesar salad.

Taking in all the craziness as she peered through the window (hers or the Stephens's) was manic, perpetually freaked-out neighbor Gladys Kravitz, played by Emmy-winning Alice Pearce until her death in 1966, followed by Sandra Gould. Gladys would invariably race home and explain what she had seen to understated husband Abner, who merely marked her down as a nut.

Darrin could only hope that his kids didn't follow on their mom's broomstick, but how could the writers pass up such an opportunity? Daughter Tabitha (Erin Murphy) proved to be a witch with no self-control at that age, so she wreaked havoc as well by bringing her toys to life and generally ignoring the urgent requests from daddy not to twitch her little nose.

It can be argued that *Bewitched* was the finest of the escapist shows that peppered the television landscape in the 1960s and early 1970s. The ingenious plot lines and characters that literally popped in front of the cameras resulted in three Emmy wins, nineteen Emmy nominations, and four Golden Globe nominations. And Endora had nothing to do with it.

One Active Actress

Elizabeth Montgomery never shied away from expressing her liberal social and political views. She spoke out against U.S. involvement in the Vietnam War and during the Reagan administration narrated a documentary entitled *Coverup: Behind the Iran Contra Affair and the Panama Deception*, which won an Oscar. Montgomery later embraced gay rights causes and voiced her support of fellow *Bewitched* cast member Dick Sargent when he announced his homosexuality. The straight Montgomery served as grand marshal of a 1992 gay pride parade in Los Angeles.

Did You Know?

One of the first major acting roles for future movie star Richard Dreyfuss was as a former boyfriend of Samantha Stephens on a 1966 episode of *Bewitched*. The warlock turns himself into a dog in an attempt to break up her marriage. Dreyfuss was twenty-eight years old when he played the part.

They Incarnated It

Aunt Clara: Abba dabba dabba. Dabba dabba abba. Remedium, decapito, zippidaro! [Result: Darrin turned into a chimpanzee.]

Endora: Oh, wizards and warlocks of arts of the ages. Oh, pallets of paints and classical sages. This dreadful still-life just take it away. And bring me a landscape of Henri Monchet! [Result: Samantha's painting was replaced by a masterpiece.]

Samantha: From polliwogs come great big frogs, we'll never know quite how. It's easier to turn a bee into a purple cow. So, hark ye witches, now pay heed: Reverse this spell with haste and speed. With no regrets, man into toad, he'll hop the straight and narrow road. [Result: Samantha reunited a frog with the love of his life.]

Major Awards

EMMY AWARD WINS (3)

1966 (2): Outstanding Performance by an Actress in a Supporting Role in a Comedy (Alice Pearce); Outstanding Directorial Achievement in Comedy (William Asher)
1968 (1): Outstanding Performance by an Actress in a Supporting Role in a Comedy (Marion Lorne)

EMMY AWARD NOMINATIONS, IN ADDITION TO WINS (19)

1966 (3): Outstanding Comedy Series; Outstanding Continued Performance by an Actress in a Leading Role in a Comedy Series (Elizabeth Montgomery); Outstanding Performance by an Actress in a Supporting Role in a Comedy (Agnes Moorehead)

1967 (5): Outstanding Comedy Series; Outstanding Continued Performance by an Actress in a Leading Role in a Comedy Series (Elizabeth Montgomery); Outstanding Performance by an Actress in a Supporting Role in a Comedy (Agnes Moorehead); Outstanding Performance by an Actress in a Supporting Role in a Comedy (Marion Lorne); Outstanding Directorial Achievement in Comedy (William Asher)

1968 (4): Outstanding Comedy Series; Outstanding Continued Performance by an Actor in a Leading Role in a Comedy Series (Dick York); Outstanding Continued Performance by an Actress in a Leading Role in a Comedy Series (Elizabeth Montgomery); Outstanding Performance by an Actress in a Supporting Role in a Comedy (Agnes Moorehead)

1969 (3): Outstanding Comedy Series; Outstanding Continued Performance by an Actress in a Leading Role in a Comedy Series (Elizabeth Montgomery); Outstanding Performance by an Actress in a Supporting Role in a Comedy (Agnes Moorehead)

1970 (2): Outstanding Continued Performance by an Actress in a Leading Role in a Comedy Series (Elizabeth Montgomery); Outstanding Performance by an Actress in a Supporting Role in a Comedy (Agnes Moorehead)

1971 (2): Outstanding Performance by an Actress in a Supporting Role in a Comedy (Agnes Moorehead); Outstanding Achievement in Makeup (Rolf Miller for "Samantha's Old Man")

GOLDEN GLOBE NOMINATIONS (4)

1965 (1): Best TV Star, Female (Elizabeth Montgomery)
1967 (1): Best TV Star, Female (Elizabeth Montgomery)
1969 (1): Best TV Star, Female (Elizabeth Montgomery)
1971 (1): Best TV Actress, Musical/Comedy (Elizabeth Montgomery)

Further Reading

Pilato, Herbie J. *The Bewitched Book*. New York: Delta Publishing Group, 1992.
Pilato, Herbie J. *Twitch upon a Star: The Bewitched Life and Career of Elizabeth Montgomery*. Lanham, MD: Taylor Trade, 2012.
Piro, Rita E. *Elizabeth Montgomery: A Bewitching Life*. New York: Great Feats Press, 2006.

✴ **42** ✴

The Phil Silvers Show

(1955–1959)

Cast: Phil Silvers (Master Sergeant Ernie Bilko), Harvey Lembeck (Corporal Rocco Barbella), Herbie Faye (Private Sam Fender), Paul Ford (Colonel John Hall), Maurice Gosfield (Private Duane Doberman), Allan Melvin (Corporal Henshaw), Billy Sands (Private Dino Paparelli), Mickey Freeman (Private Zimmerman), Jimmy Little (Sergeant Grover), Bernard Fein (Private Gomez), Maurice Brenner (Private Irving Fleischman), Mickey Freeman (Private Fielding Zimmerman), Jack Healy (Private Mullen), Terry Carter (Private Sugie Sugarman), Karl Lucas (Private Stash Kadowski), Elizabeth Fraser (Sergeant Joan Hogan)

Created by: Producer and writer Nat Hiken

Network: CBS

First Air Date: September 20, 1955

Last Air Date: September 11, 1959

Broadcast History:
September 20, 1955–October 1955: Tuesday at 8:30–9:00 PM
November 1955–February 1958: Tuesday at 8:00–8:30 PM
February 1958–September 11, 1959: Friday at 9:00–9:30 PM

Seasons: 4

Episodes: 138

Ratings History: 1955–1956 (30), 1956–1957 (22), 1957–1958 (not in Top 30), 1958–1959 (not in Top 30)

Allan Melvin, Phil Silvers, and Harvey Lembeck. *CBS/Photofest ©CBS*

Overview

The contrast was striking. Here was a stage comedian of Russian Jewish descent, born and raised in Brooklyn, New York, and known for portraying fast-talking con men. Yet, he was playing an U.S. Army master sergeant at Fort Baxter, Kansas. Talk about a fish out of water! Welcome to Gomer Pyle in reverse. But it was that contrast and the vast talent that made *The Phil Silvers Show* funny.

Silvers played main character Ernie Bilko in a sitcom that should have featured the following disclaimer before each episode: Any similarity between the following show and real military life is patently ridiculous. The show featured Silvers at his impetuous, devious, calculating best as he repeatedly outwitted superior officer Colonel John Hall (Paul Ford). He overcame the boredom he perceived as being associated with living in the middle of nowhere and the shackles of an army existence by gambling and hatching money-making schemes.

Show creator Nat Hiken succeeded wildly in his first attempt at writing a sitcom. He had two comedy-variety programs (*All-Star Revue* and *The Martha Raye Show*) under his belt before approaching Silvers at the request of CBS programmer Hubbell Robinson. Silvers balked at first while waiting for theater opportunities that never arrived. His interest was piqued by the idea of playing his signature character bucking authority in an army camp. The rest was history.

The Phil Silvers Show never approached the popularity of other sitcoms featuring such old-school entertainers as Jack Benny and Danny Thomas, but its brilliance was confirmed by the spate of Emmy Awards it earned during the course of its four seasons on the air. And it was Silvers's colorful personality—loud, brash, and humorously obnoxious—that carried the day. Those who served both under and over him were no match for his conniving and ingenious ways.

Frequent guest appearances from some of the established and rising stars of television further spiced an already highly entertaining sitcom. Among those who later starred on other TV programs or movies were Tige Andrews (*The Detectives* and *Mod Squad*), George Kennedy (*Cool Hand Luke, Dallas,* and *Naked Gun*), David White (*Bewitched*), Jack Albertson (*Willy Wonka and the Chocolate Factory* and *Chico and the Man*), Al Lewis (*The Munsters*), and Dick Van Dyke (*Mary Poppins* and *The Dick Van Dyke Show*).

The Phil Silvers Show differed from other sitcoms that spotlighted stage comedians, for example, Benny and George Burns, in that Silvers did not play himself. That is, he didn't play himself in name, but his character embraced all the traits that made Silvers one of the premier entertainers of his generation.

"I Know Him, but What's His Name?"

One of the finest and most recognized character actors in the history of American television secured only one full-time role. Allan Melvin played Corporal Henshaw in 140 episodes of *The Phil Silvers Show*, but Melvin landed frequent or recurring roles in some of the most famous sitcoms ever, including (in chronological order) *The Dick Van Dyke Show, The Andy Griffith Show, Gomer Pyle, U.S.M.C., The Brady Bunch,* and *All in the Family*. Arguably his most memorable was as the boyfriend of housekeeper Alice, who waited in vain for him to pop the question on *The Brady Bunch*. Melvin also provided the voice for many cartoon characters, mostly notably the remarkably cheerful Magilla Gorilla.

They Said It

> **Eliott:** [reading Bilko's tax returns] On June 12, Benedict Arnold's birthday, he ran a 'Forgive and Forget' dance!

Major Awards

EMMY AWARD WINS (8)

1956 (4): Best Comedy Series; Best Actor, Continuing Performance (Phil Silvers); Best Comedy Writing (Nat Hiken, Barry E. Blitzer, Arnold Auerbach, Harvey Orkin, Vic Bogert, Arnie Rosen, Coleman Jacoby, Tony Webster, and Terry Ryan for "You'll Never Get Rich"); Best Director, Film Series (Nat Hiken for "You'll Never Get Rich")

1957 (2): Best Series, Half Hour or Less; Best Writing, Variety or Situation Comedy (Nat Hiken, Billy Friedberg, Tony Webster, Leonard Stern, Arnie Rosen, and Coleman Jacoby)

1958 (2): Best Comedy Series; Best Comedy Writing (Nat Hiken, Billy Friedberg, Phil Sharp, Terry Ryan, Coleman Jacoby, Arnie Rosen, Sydney Zelinka, A. J. Russell, and Tony Webster)

EMMY AWARD NOMINATIONS, IN ADDITION TO WINS (10)

1956 (1): Best Producer, Film Series (Nat Hiken for "You'll Never Get Rich")

1957 (2): Best Continuing Performance by a Comedian in a Series (Phil Silvers); Best Supporting Performance by an Actor (Paul Ford)

1958 (2): Best Continuing Performance by an Actor in a Leading Role in a Dramatic or Comedy Series (Phil Silvers); Best Continuing Supporting Performance by an Actor in a Dramatic or Comedy Series (Paul Ford)

1959 (5): Best Comedy Series; Best Actor in a Leading Role (Continuing Character) in a Comedy Series (Phil Silvers); Best Supporting Actor (Continuing Character) in a Comedy Series (Paul Ford); Best Supporting Actor (Continuing Character) in a Comedy Series (Maurice Gosfield); Best Writing of a Single Program of a Comedy Series (Billy Friedberg, Arnie Rosen, and Coleman Jacoby for "Bilko's Vampire")

Further Reading

Freeman, Mickey. *Bilko: Behind the Lines with Phil Silvers.* Waterville, ME: Thorndike Press, 2002.

Silvers, Phil, and Robert Saffron. *This Laugh Is on Me: The Phil Silvers Story.* New York: Prentice Hall, 1973.

✵ **43** ✵

The Bob Newhart Show

(1972–1978)

Cast: Bob Newhart (Robert Hartley), Suzanne Pleshette (Emily Hartley), Bill Daily (Howard Borden), Peter Bonerz (Jerry Robinson), Marcia Wallace (Carol Kester Bondurant), Jack Riley (Elliot Carlin)

Created by: Writers David Davis and Lorenzo Music

Network: CBS

First Air Date: September 16, 1972

Last Air Date: August 26, 1978

Broadcast History:
September 16, 1972–October 1976: Saturday at 9:30–10:00 PM
November 1976–September 1977: Saturday at 8:30–9:00 PM
September 1977–August 26, 1978: Saturday at 8:00–8:30 PM

Seasons: 6

Episodes: 142

Ratings History: 1972–1973 (16), 1973–1974 (12), 1974–1975 (17), 1975–1976 (26), 1976–1977 (not in Top 30), 1977–1978 (not in Top 30)

Overview

One assumed that the Bob Newhart persona honed onstage and spotlighted in Grammy-winning comedy albums in the early 1960s was not a fit for sitcom stardom. He was like your next-door neighbor. He was too soft-spoken. His comedic specialty was phone conversations, which didn't easily translate to the small screen. He hemmed and hawed and stammered. Heck, sitcoms were only thirty minutes, and some of that time was needed for commercials.

Bob Newhart and Suzanne Pleshette. *CBS/Photofest ©CBS*

Show creators David Davis and Lorenzo Music had a solution. They cast Newhart as psychologist Robert Hartley. Those with whom he worked professionally would make such outrageous claims that his stunned, yet thoughtful, reactions would be fitting and funny. Bingo. Newhart proved to be an ideal lead. His trademark delivery not only helped maintain *The Bob Newhart Show* as one of the most highly rated sitcoms on television, it also kept the show in good standing in the powerhouse Saturday night lineup on CBS—arguably the finest ever assembled. And it landed Newhart a highly successful series simply known as *Newhart* shortly thereafter.

Not only was Hartley surrounded by eccentric patients and colleagues at work, he and elementary school teacher wife Emily (Suzanne Pleshette), living comfortably in their plush high-rise Chicago apartment, were forced to deal with scatterbrained neighbor Howard Borden (Bill Daily). The fact that Borden remained in a perpetually confused state was made funnier (and a bit frightening) by the fact that he toiled as an airline pilot. Daily's sense of timing was far better than that of Borden, who made a habit of barging in on the Hartleys at the most inopportune times.

Bob arrived at work each day to a lack of respect. Receptionist Carol Kester Bondurant (Marcia Wallace) and orthodontist Jerry Robinson (Peter Bonerz) seemed more interested in goofing off than working and often made Bob the butt of their jokes. They hung around the receptionist desk and watercooler discussing the vagaries of their work or personal lives. Such scenes and dialogue fit perfectly on a show that embraced low-key verbal humor over physical comedy.

The same held true when Bob conversed with patients. The irony that their psychologist failed to cure them of their phobias and neuroses was secondary to the humor emanating from the banter between them and Hartley. The funniest of the bunch was the paranoid, self-deprecating Elliot Carlin (Jack Riley), who shot down every piece of advice tossed his way, and who managed to chip away at the emotional rock that was Bob Hartley.

Group therapy also proved a disaster as Elliot sought to massage his own ego by insulting the others, including meek, unconfident Emil Peterson (John Fiedler) and sweet senior Mrs. Bakerman (Florida Friebus), who whiled away her time knitting and didn't seem to have any psychological problems. The dysfunctional therapy group bares itself for all of Chicago to see on one episode, as its members convince Bob, whom they fear is ashamed of them, to conduct a session on live television. Hilarity ensues when they all clam up. The only one to express his feelings is Emil, who warned Bob before the show that his high-pitched voice tends to rise even higher when he gets nervous. With the cameras rolling, his voice gets so high as he speaks about having finally worked up enough courage to stand up to his wife that he is stricken with laryngitis. Fortunately for one and all, few in Chicago are watching, as the show is going head-to-head against the Bears on *Monday Night Football*.

Millions of Americans were, however, watching *The Bob Newhart Show*, which launched its lead character into television stardom. Newhart has remained one of the most embraced actors on television.

The Funniest Moment in TV History?

Millions of viewers were in for a shock and one long laugh as the final scene of *Newhart* played out. The show, which cast Bob Newhart as Vermont innkeeper Dick Loudon, ran on CBS from 1982 to 1990. In the last episode, viewers see only darkness as the scene begins. The Newhart character then turns on the light, rolls over in his bed, and exclaims, "Honey, you won't believe the dream I just had." The opposite light is illuminated to reveal Suzanne Pleshette as the live studio audience erupts in laughter and applause. The Newhart character explains that he had dreamed he was an innkeeper in "this crazy little town in Vermont."

Did You Know?

Series cocreator Lorenzo Music and wife Henrietta composed the theme song to *The Bob Newhart Show*, entitled "Home to My Emily."

They Said It

> **Emily:** [after Bob returned home to rearranged furniture] You hate it, right?
> **Bob:** I won't say I hate it; it's just alien to anything I've ever liked before.

Major Awards

EMMY AWARD NOMINATIONS (4)

1977 (2): Outstanding Comedy Series; Outstanding Lead Actress in Comedy Series (Suzanne Pleshette)
1978 (2): Outstanding Lead Actress in a Comedy Series (Suzanne Pleshette); Outstanding Film Editing in a Comedy Series (M. Pam Blumenthal for "A Jackie Story")

GOLDEN GLOBE NOMINATIONS (2)

1975 (1): Best TV Actor, Musical/Comedy (Bob Newhart)
1976 (1): Best TV Actor, Musical/Comedy (Bob Newhart)

Further Reading

Newhart, Bob. *I Shouldn't Even Be Doing This: And Other Things That Strike Me as Funny.* New York: Hyperion, 2007.
Sorenson, Jeff. *Bob Newhart.* New York: St. Martin's, 1988.

✳ 44 ✳

South Park

(1997–)

> **Voices:** Trey Parker (Eric Cartman, Stan Marsh, Mr. Garrison, Mr. Hankey), Matt Stone (Kyle Broflovski, Kenny McCormick, Leopold "Butters" Stotch, Tweek Tweak), Mona Marshall (Sheila Broflovski), Isaac Hayes (Chef), April Stewart (Sharon Marsh)
>
> **Created by:** Writers and producers Trey Parker and Matt Stone
>
> **Network:** Comedy Central
>
> **First Air Date:** August 13, 1997
>
> **Broadcast History:**
>   August 13, 1997—November 2012: Wednesday at 10:00–10:30 PM
>
> **Seasons:** 16
>
> **Episodes:** 237 (through November 2012)
>
> **Ratings History:** Never in Top 30

Overview

A third grader who seeks to avenge a humiliating experience at the hands of a high school student by having his parents killed, ground up into chili, and eaten by their son. Gnomes who sneak into the room of a little boy, steal the underpants out of his drawers, and take them to a cave, where they explain a three-step business model. The first step: Steal boys underwear. The third step: Make a profit. The gnomes are blank on that second step. Satan decides that Halloween belongs to him, so he throws a costume party in Los Angeles, and then laments that he has become as bad as the spoiled teens celebrating birthdays on the MTV reality show *My Super Sweet 16*. He

Front row: Kenny McCormick, Butters, Kyle Broflovski, Stan Marsh, and Eric Cartman.
Comedy Central/Photofest ©Comedy Central

is assured that he's not *that* rotten. Welcome to *South Park*, a sick, twisted, and down-right hilarious animated sitcom that is far too demented for network television. The result has been a run approaching two decades on Comedy Central and the love of millions of dedicated fans.

The show focuses on three vulgar kids who, in distant generations, would have had their mouths washed out with soap. The running gag revolves around their friend Kenny (Matt Stone), who is killed in an outrageous fashion in each show, thereby prompting the line that has proved to be one of the most embraced catchphrases in television history: "Oh my god, they killed Kenny!" No sweat, however. Kenny inevitably returns in the next episode.

The funniest, nastiest character in the fast-talking, manipulative, high-pitched trio is angry, racist, anti-Semitic, obese Eric Cartman (Trey Parker). He is easily the most foul-mouthed of the bunch, and he goes to great lengths to get what he wants—and damn any hapless victim who gets in his way. Cartman engages in frequent shouting matches with Kyle (also voiced by Stone), who tries in vain to end debates by calling him a "fat ass." Kyle is Jewish, but he bears little understanding of his heritage, despite the efforts of his parents to explain it. The most rational of the group is Stan (also Parker), who serves as a buffer between best friend Kyle and Cartman and often emerges with outrageous solutions to outrageous problems they often create themselves in their Colorado town of South Park.

Perhaps the strangest of all the strange side characters is delusional schoolteacher Mr. Garrison (Parker), who gives classroom lectures through a hand puppet he carries with him at all times. But every bit character boasts absurd idiosyncrasies. There is Chef, voiced by soul singer Isaac Hayes, a school lunch-counter worker who sings sexually inappropriate songs with students in easy earshot. There is Tweek Tweak (Stone), a hyperactive boy who drinks too much coffee and is the victim of the underpants-stealing gnomes. There is the Chinese dodge ball team striking fear into the South Park contingent after killing fellow children with ferocious firings (of course, the Chinese dodge ballers kill Kenny during a match). There are portrayals of Jesus as a talk show host and of Saddam Hussein embarking on a homosexual affair with Satan. There is even Mr. Hankey (Parker), a talking and singing pile of feces.

The show was the brainchild of former Fox television producers Trey Parker and Matt Stone, who have served as writers, producers, and character voices for *South Park*. Its characters were first seen in 1995, as part of a video Christmas card aired on that network. *South Park*, considered far too provocative for network TV or even mainstream cable, landed on Comedy Central and immediately thrived as marketing efforts maximized the show's popularity. Parker and Stone seem to embrace controversial topics they satirize in scripts and are unafraid to lampoon celebrities, for instance, scientologist Tom Cruise. In fact, the show even lampoons those they lampoon. The fourteenth season included an episode in which Cruise and other celebrities parodied by South Park residents plan to file a class action lawsuit against the town. Cruise promises to end the threat if the citizens can somehow present to him Muslim prophet Muhammad.

South Park proved to be a forerunner of other prime-time animated half-hour programs, for example, *Family Guy*, that stretched boundaries of good taste and tested censors. Its long run can be partially attributed to its home on one of the cable stations, which are sometimes far more forgiving for sagging ratings than their network counterparts. But it can also be explained by the huge legion of fans that have continued to watch the show since it debuted during the Bill Clinton administration.

How Kenny Is Killed

The strange ways in which Kenny is killed, generally at the end of episodes, seem endless and are often followed by his corpse being attacked by rats. The following are ten of the most gruesome ways in which this hapless *South Park* character has met his albeit temporary demise:
1. Impaled through the head by a flag pole
2. Wild turkey plucks out his eye
3. Head bitten off by Ozzy Osbourne
4. Vomits to death
5. Drowns in urine
6. Turned into duckbilled platypus and shot
7. Electrocuted by hospital emergency generator
8. Pulled under an escalator
9. Head pulled off at a football game
10. Crushed by a mining cart

Did You Know?

The Mr. Hankey, the Christmas Poo character in *South Park* was the brainchild of series cocreator Trey Parker, who recalled his childhood habit of not flushing the toilet. He was warned by his father that "Mr. Hankey" would climb out of the toilet and eat him if he continued failing to flush.

Major Awards

EMMY AWARD WINS (5)

2005 (1): Outstanding Animated Program, for Programming Less Than One Hour (for episode "Best Friends Forever")
2007 (1): Outstanding Animated Program, for Programming Less Than One Hour (for episode "Make Love not Warcraft")
2008 (1): Outstanding Animated Program, for Programming Less Than One Hour (for episode "Imaginationland")
2009 (1): Outstanding Animated Program, for Programming Less Than One Hour (for episode "Margaritaville")
2013 (1): Outstanding Animated Program (for episode "Raising the Bar")

EMMY AWARD NOMINATIONS, IN ADDITION TO WINS (8)

1998 (1): Outstanding Animated Program, for Programming Less Than One Hour (for episode "Big Gay Al's Big Gay Boat Ride")
2000 (1): Outstanding Animated Program, for Programming Less Than One Hour (for episode "Chinpoko Mon")
2002 (1): Outstanding Animated Program, for Programming Less Than One Hour (for episode "Osama Bin Laden Has Farty Pants")
2004 (1): Outstanding Animated Program, for Programming Less Than One Hour (for episode "Christmas in Canada)
2006 (1): Outstanding Animated Program, for Programming Less Than One Hour (for episode "Trapped in the Closet")
2010 (1): Outstanding Animated Program (for episode "200/201")
2011 (1): Outstanding Animated Program (for episode "Crack Baby Athletic Association")

Further Reading

Arp, Robert, ed. *South Park and Philosophy: You Know, I Learned Something Today*. Oxford, England: Blackwell, 2006.

McFarland, Melanie. "Oh My God, 'South Park' Killed a Decade!" *Seattle Post-Intelligencer*, September 29, 2006. Available online at www.seattlepi.com/ae/tv/article/Oh-my-God -South-Park-killed-a-decade-1216016.php.

Stall, Sam. *The South Park Episode Guide, Seasons 1-5*. Philadelphia, PA: Running Press, 2009.

Stone, Matt, and Trey Parker. *South Park Guide to Life*. Philadelphia, PA: Running Press, 2009.

✴ **45** ✴

Two and a Half Men

(2003–)

Cast: Jon Cryer (Alan Harper), Charlie Sheen (Charlie Harper), Angus T. Jones (Jake Harper), Holland Taylor (Evelyn Harper), Conchata Ferrell (Berta), Melanie Lynskey (Rose), Marin Hinkle (Judith Harper), Ashton Kutcher (Walden Schmidt), Jennifer Bini Taylor (Chelsea), Courtney Thorne-Smith (Lyndsey Mackelroy), Ryan Stiles (Dr. Herb Melnick), Graham Patrick Martin (Eldridge Mackelroy)

Created by: Executive producers Chuck Lorre and Lee Aronsohn

Network: CBS

First Air Date: September 22, 2003

Broadcast History:
September 22, 2003–May 2004: Monday at 9:30–10:00 PM
September 2005–May 2012: Monday at 9:00–9:30 PM
September 2012: Thursday at 8:30–9:00 PM

Seasons: 9

Episodes: 218

Ratings History: 2003–2004 (15), 2004–2005 (14), 2005–2006 (17), 2006–2007 (21), 2007–2008 (17), 2008–2009 (10), 2009–2010 (11), 2010–2011 (17), 2011–2012 (11)

Charlie Sheen, Jon Cryer, and Angus T. Jones. *CBS/Photofest ©CBS*

Overview

The once-taboo subject of sex had been used to elicit laughter and explore personal relationships between characters for three decades before *Two and a Half Men* premiered on the last night of summer in 2003, but it wasn't until that controversial sitcom debuted that more intricate sexual experiences were used as fodder for humor on network television. The spotlight on the foray into uncharted sexual conversation and activity was placed directly on narcissistic, boozing, middle-aged jingle writer Charlie Harper (Charlie Sheen), who paraded one young bimbo after another into the bedroom of his Malibu beach house for hours, even days, of erotic escapades, which he proudly discussed in lurid detail. The most frustrated of listeners was jealous and pitiful brother Alan, played in award-winning form by Jon Cryer, whose huge alimony and child support payments to vengeful wife Judith (Marin Hinkle) forced him to take up residence with Charlie (although how a seemingly successful chiropractor like Alan couldn't afford a home of his own remains a mystery).

The cast is peppered with colorful and funny characters. Among them is egotistical mother Evelyn (Holland Taylor), who feels rejected by her two sons—and for good reason. They can barely tolerate her presence and are bitter over their upbringing. The relationship between Evelyn and her sons spotlights a comedic strategy put forth by show creators Chuck Lorre and Lee Aronsohn and the writers that promotes a departure from typical characterizations and familial bonds. Evelyn merely feigns love and caring for her family. Alan's son Jake (Angus T. Jones), who was ten years old when the show was launched, is downright stupid. Manipulative, witty housekeeper Berta (Conchata Ferrell) is negligent in her duties, sarcastic to her employer (Charlie), and condescending toward Alan.

The side characters bring depth to the humor. Judith adds to the theme of dysfunctionality within the family unit by making it clear that she cannot wait to dump off her bratty, thoughtless son to Alan every week. New husband Dr. Herb Melnick (Ryan Stiles) has become friends with Alan and Charlie and has already become annoyed by his sniveling wife. And a pretty, but psychotic, young woman named Rose (Melanie Lynskey) pops in uninvited and unwanted at any time to stalk her prey—Charlie Harper. She once handcuffed herself to his refrigerator to remain close to him. Rose left for London as Lynskey was written off the show in 2007, but she has since made frequent appearances.

Rose played a role in a story line twist that began when Charlie temporarily shed his hedonistic ways and became engaged to girlfriend Chelsea (Jennifer Bini Taylor). The relationship faltered, whereupon Charlie flew to Paris to find Rose, whom he realized was his one true love. But it is revealed in a highly publicized ninth season premiere that he has been killed by a subway train in that French city. It is further suggested that Rose pushed him after learning that he cheated on her.

The adventures of Alan have featured trysts with several women, including mindless, sexy Kandi (April Bowlby), who quickly dumped him after they had won a half-million bucks in Vegas and wed, leaving the hapless younger Harper brother two sets of alimony payments to tie him down financially and increase his bitterness. He later embarked on a relationship with much more stable Lyndsey Mackelroy, played by former *Melrose Place* star Courtney Thorne-Smith. That patient soul managed to forgive Alan after he cheated on her and accidentally torched her house.

Sagging ratings were temporarily revived by the publicity surrounding the writing off of Charlie and the introduction of billionaire Walden Schmidt (Ashton Kutcher), who bought the house from Alan and allowed him to stay there. Walden has spent much of his time pining for his ex-wife and growing further depressed after new girlfriend Zoey (Sophie Winkleman) rejected his marriage proposal.

The sitcom has lost much of its comedic edge since losing Charlie. The sibling conflict is gone, and many fans are simply not as attracted to the Walden character. The credibility of the writing was questioned after the previously rebellious, long-haired, pot-smoking Jake enlisted in the army. Yet, the show has remained a ratings hit despite what some perceive as negative changes in story line and characters beyond the always entertaining Alan.

Two and a Half Men has been one of the most controversial sitcoms on television throughout its run. Its blatant sexual content has drawn criticism from social conservatives. But in the spirit of provocative comedies that have been launched since the early 1970s, it has been credited for taking chances and breaking new ground. Whether that ground was worthy of breaking will be debated long after the show is cancelled. That it is still going strong after nine seasons speaks for itself.

Sorry, Charlie

The end of Charlie Sheen's run on *Two and a Half Men* was certainly contentious. The highest-paid actor on American television, at $2 million per episode, claimed in early 2011 that he was underpaid and asked for Warner Bros. to raise his salary to $3 million per show. He gave a series of rambling interviews that coincided with his admission into drug and alcohol rehab. The son of noted actor Martin Sheen caused production of the show to be halted in February after he reportedly insulted cocreator and executive producer Chuck Lorre, who soon fired him. Sheen began starring as Dr. Charlie Goodson, an anger management therapist, on *Anger Management* on the cable network FX. The show was an immediate ratings hit.

Angus' Beef with His Show

The entertainment world was stunned in November 2012, when Angus T. Jones, who plays Jake on *Two and a Half Men*, slams the show as "filth" and begs people to stop watching it in a video that went viral. "I'm on *Two and a Half Men* and I don't want to be on it," he says in the video. "Please stop watching it. Please stop filling your head with filth." He adds that "you cannot be a God-fearing person and be on a television show like [*Two and a Half Men*]. I know I can't. I'm not OK with what I'm learning, what the Bible says, and being on that television show." Jones quickly apologized, but former star of the show Charlie Sheen called the program "cursed" and added that it was impossible for anyone to spend a decade in what he referred to as producer Chuck Lorre's "hive of oppression."

They Said It

> **Jake:** If drinking makes you feel bad, why do you drink?
> **Charlie:** Nobody likes a smart-ass, kid.
> **Jake:** You have to put a dollar in the swear jar. You said 'ass.'
> **Charlie:** Tell you what. Here's a twenty. That ought to cover me until lunch.

> **Charlie:** What do men have that women don't?
> **Jake:** Beards?
> **Charlie:** Lower.
> **Jake:** [in a lower voice] Beards?

> **Charlie:** What are you doing?
> **Alan:** Giving you a wedgie . . . where's your underwear?
> **Charlie:** I'm not wearing any, but thanks for scratching my ass.

> **Charlie:** I just thought you two might hit it off. I'm even making a little welcome basket for you to give to her.

Alan: So, she's beautiful, rich, and single. Why would she want me? I'm broke, middle-aged, twice-divorced, sleeping on your hide-a-bed, and sharing custody of a flatulent, underachieving son.
Charlie: We're gonna need a bigger basket.
Berta: We're gonna need chloroform and a rope.

Major Awards

EMMY AWARD WINS (9)

2005 (1): Outstanding Multi-Camera Sound Mixing for a Series or Special (Bruce Peters, Kathy Oldham, Bob La Masney, and Charlie McDaniel for "Can You Eat Human Flesh with Wooden Teeth?")
2006 (1): Outstanding Multi-Camera Picture Editing for a Series (Joe Bella for "That Special Tug")
2007 (2): Outstanding Cinematography for a Multi-Camera Series (Steven V. Silver for "Release the Dogs"); Outstanding Multi-Camera Picture Editing for a Series (Joe Bella for "Release the Dogs")
2009 (1): Outstanding Supporting Actor in a Comedy Series (Jon Cryer)
2011 (1): Outstanding Cinematography for a Multi-Camera Series (Steven V. Silver for "Hookers, Hookers, Hookers")
2012 (3): Outstanding Lead Actor in a Comedy Series (Jon Cryer); Outstanding Guest Actress in a Comedy Series (Kathy Bates for "Why We Gave Up Women"); Outstanding Cinematography for a Multi-Camera Series (Steven V. Silver for "Sips, Sonnets, and Sodomy")

EMMY AWARD NOMINATIONS, IN ADDITION TO WINS (38)

2004 (3): Outstanding Art Direction for a Multi-Camera Series (John Shaffner and Ann Margaret Shea for "Alan Harper, Frontier Chiropractor"); Outstanding Cinematography for a Multi-Camera Series (Steven V. Silver for "Camel Filters and Pheromones"); Outstanding Main Title Theme Music (Chuck Lorre, Lee Aronsohn, and Grant Geissman)
2005 (5): Outstanding Supporting Actress in a Comedy Series (Conchata Ferrell); Outstanding Supporting Actress in a Comedy Series (Holland Taylor); Outstanding Art Direction for a Multi-Camera Series (John Shaffner and Ann Margaret Shea for "It Was Mame, Mom" and "A Low, Guttural, Tongue-Flapping Noise"); Outstanding Cinematography for a Multi-Camera Series (Steven V. Silver for "Back Off, Mary Poppins"); Outstanding Multi-Camera Picture Editing for a Series (Joe Bella for "It Was Mame, Mom")
2006 (6): Outstanding Comedy Series; Outstanding Lead Actor in a Comedy Series (Charlie Sheen); Outstanding Supporting Actor in a Comedy Series (Jon Cryer); Outstanding Guest Actor in a Comedy Series (Martin Sheen for "Sleep Tight, Puddin' Pop"); Outstanding Cinematography for a Multi-Camera Series (Steven V. Silver for "Carpet Burns and a Bite Mark"); Outstanding Multi-Camera Sound Mixing for a Series or Special (Joe Bella for "That Special Tug")

2007 (5): Outstanding Comedy Series; Outstanding Lead Actor in a Comedy Series (Charlie Sheen); Outstanding Supporting Actor in a Comedy Series (Jon Cryer); Outstanding Supporting Actress in a Comedy Series (Conchata Ferrell); Outstanding Supporting Actress in a Comedy Series (Holland Taylor)

2008 (7): Outstanding Comedy Series; Outstanding Lead Actor in a Comedy Series (Charlie Sheen); Outstanding Supporting Actor in a Comedy Series (Jon Cryer); Outstanding Supporting Actress in a Comedy Series (Holland Taylor); Outstanding Hairstyling for a Multi-Camera Series or a Special (Pixie Schwartz, Krista Borrelli, Ralph M. Abalos, and Janice Zoladz for "City of Great Racks"); Outstanding Makeup for a Multi-Camera Series or a Special (Non-Prosthetic) (Janice Berridge, Peggy Nichols, Shelley Woodhouse, and Gabriel Solana for "City of Great Racks"); Outstanding Sound Mixing for a Comedy or Drama Series (Half-Hour) and Animation (Bruce Peters, Kathy Oldham, Bob La Masney, and Charlie McDaniel for "Is There a Mrs. Waffles?")

2009 (2): Outstanding Lead Actor in a Comedy Series (Charlie Sheen); Outstanding Hairstyling for a Multi-Camera Series or a Special (Pixie Schwartz, Krista Borrelli, Ralph M. Abalos, and Janice Zoladz for "I Think You Offended Don")

2010 (6): Outstanding Supporting Actor in a Comedy Series (Jon Cryer); Outstanding Supporting Actress in a Comedy Series (Holland Taylor); Outstanding Guest Actress in a Comedy Series (Jane Lynch for "818-JKLPUZO"); Outstanding Cinematography for a Half-Hour Series (Steven V. Silver for "Crude and Uncalled For"); Outstanding Hairstyling for a Multi-Camera Series or a Special (Pixie Schwartz, Krista Borrelli, Ralph M. Abalos, and Janice Zoladz for "That's Why They Call It Ballroom"); Outstanding Sound Mixing for a Comedy or Drama Series (Half-Hour) and Animation (Bruce Peters, Kathy Oldham, and Bob La Masney for "Fat Jokes, Pie, and Celeste")

2011 (1): Outstanding Supporting Actor in a Comedy Series (Jon Cryer)

2012 (1): Outstanding Multi-Camera Picture Editing for a Comedy Series (Joe Bella for "Why We Gave Up Women")

2013 (2): Outstanding Art Direction for a Multi-Camera Series; Outstanding Cinematography for a Multi-Camera Series

GOLDEN GLOBE NOMINATIONS (2)

2005 (1): Best Performance by an Actor in a TV Series, Musical/Comedy (Charlie Sheen)

2006 (1): Best Performance by an Actor in a TV Series, Musical/Comedy (Charlie Sheen)

Further Reading

Hurst, Brandon. *Apocalypse, Charlie: The Charlie Sheen Biography*. Montreal: Cogito Media Group, 2012.

Roush, Matt. "Roush Review: *Two and a Half Men*—The Sheen Is Gone." *TV Guide*, September 20, 2011. Available online at www.tvguide.com/News/Roush-Review-Men-1037765.aspx.

✬ **46** ✬
Make Room for Daddy
(1953–1964)

Cast: Danny Thomas (Danny Williams), Jean Hagen (Margaret Williams), Marjorie Lord (Kathy O'Hara "Clancey" Williams), Rusty Hamer (Rusty Williams), Sherry Jackson (Terry Williams #1), Penny Parker (Terry Williams #2), Angela Cartwright (Linda Williams), Sid Melton ("Uncle Charley" Halper), Louise Beavers (Maid #1), Amanda Randolph (Maid #2)

Created by: Producer Lou Edelman and writer Mel Shavelson

Network: ABC (1953–1957), CBS (1957–1964)

First Air Date: September 29, 1953

Last Air Date: September 14, 1964

Broadcast History:
September 29, 1953–April 1956: Tuesday at 9:00–9:30 PM
October 1956–February 1957: Monday at 8:00–8:30 PM
February 1957–April 1957: Thursday at 9:00–9:30 PM
October 1957–September 14, 1964: Monday at 9:00–9:30 PM

Seasons: 11

Episodes: 351

Ratings History: 1953–1957 (not in Top 30), 1957–1958 (2), 1958–1959 (5), 1959–1960 (4), 1960–1961 (12), 1961–1962 (8), 1962–1963 (7), 1963–1964 (9)

Sherry Jackson, Danny Thomas, Louise Beavers, Jean Hagen, and Rusty Hamer.
ABC/Photofest ©ABC

Overview

A new network home and a new woman transformed *The Danny Thomas Show* from just another sitcom into a smash hit. The changes allowed the program, known for its first three years as *Make Room for Daddy*, to remain on the airwaves for eleven seasons. That star Danny Thomas boasted a hit TV series at all seemed improbable after he bombed doing his nightclub routine as host of the *All-Star Revue* on NBC in 1952. He vowed never to return to the new medium, which he criticized as "only for idiots." His line has never been tied to television being referred to as "the idiot box"—that expression didn't come into vogue until several years later—but Thomas was back on the box in 1953 as star of his own sitcom.

What was then known as *Make Room for Daddy* spotlighted Danny Williams (Thomas) in his familiar role as a nightclub entertainer, husband to wife Margaret (Jean Hagen) and father to son Rusty (Rusty Hamer) and daughter Terry (Sherry Jackson, later played by Penny Parker). Among the story lines was Williams trying to maintain a strong relationship with his family despite long stretches on the road. On the show, Thomas displayed his all-around talents as a stand-up comedian, singer, and actor. Its original title was based on his experiences as an entertainer and father. It was borrowed from a phrase used in his real-life home; when he returned from touring, his children were forced to switch bedrooms to "make room for daddy."

The sitcom failed to attract significant viewership in its first four seasons on ABC. Sweeping changes, the likes of which have often doomed other shows, dramatically improved the fortunes of what was now *The Danny Thomas Show*. Margaret was killed off in 1956, after Hagen quit, leading to a season in which Williams was an eligible bachelor scouring the field with the aid of his kids to find a new woman. The show returned in the fall of 1957 on CBS, with new wife Kathy (Marjorie Lord) and her daughter Linda (Angela Cartwright) as mainstays of a revamped cast.

The new blood worked wonders. The show leaped out of comparative obscurity to number two in the Nielsen ratings during the 1957–1958 season, and it remained in the top twelve through 1964, when the network began airing only repeats. The Terry character was soon written off as a married woman after spending one season courting a nightclub performer played by Pat Harrington Jr., who gained greater fame in the 1970s and 1980s portraying handyman Dwayne Schneider in sitcom *One Day at a Time*.

The side characters, portrayed by several of the premier character actors in the history of the American sitcom, indeed played a role, literally and figuratively, in the success of *The Danny Thomas Show*. Among them were agents Phil Brokaw (Sheldon Leonard) and Jesse Leeds (Jesse White); salty "Uncle Charley" Halper (Sid Melton), owner of the nightclub in which Williams often performed, and bizarre Uncle Tonoose (Hans Conreid). All four enjoyed careers in television that spanned more than a half-century.

The show left the air near the top, ranking number twelve in the Nielsens in its final season. Thomas, Lord, and other cast members, including Cartwright and Hamer, who played a now-married Rusty, were brought back by ABC in 1970 and 1971 for *Danny Thomas in Make Room for Granddaddy*. The sentimental spin-off featured guest appearances from the likes of Bob Hope, Frank Sinatra, Milton Berle, and Lucille Ball, but they were all considered old guard in American entertainment by that time. Changing tastes on the sitcom scene limited it to just one season.

Cartwright's Early Career a Bonanza

Angela Cartwright was barely five years old when she debuted on *The Danny Thomas Show* in October 1957, but her performance was impressive enough to land her a part as one of the von Trapp children in the iconic 1965 film *The Sound of Music*. The British-born Cartwright was just getting started. She later played the role of Penny Robinson in the silly science fiction show *Lost in Space*, before embarking on a career in photography.

The Versatile Rosie Grier

One very large man who landed a role in *Danny Thomas in Make Room for Granddaddy* in 1970 was Roosevelt Grier, who played the star's piano-playing accompaniment at the nightclub. Grier already knew the pressure of performing. He did so every

Sunday as an All-Pro defensive lineman for the New York Giants and Los Angeles Rams in a football career that ran from 1955 to 1966. His varied talents included singing and needlepoint. The 285-pound Grier also worked as a bodyguard for presidential candidate Robert Kennedy in 1968. He was guarding Kennedy's wife Ethel when Sirhan Sirhan perpetrated the second Kennedy assassination in five years following the California primary. Grier wrestled the gun away from the shooter and subdued him.

They Said It

Margaret: Rusty, you don't take advantage of people just because they've got money.
Linda: I wouldn't take advantage of them, but I'd at least let them buy me a banana split.

Major Awards

EMMY AWARD WINS (5)

1954 (1): Best New Program
1955 (2): Best Situation Comedy Series; Best Actor Starring in a Regular Series (Danny Thomas)
1957 (1): Best Direction, Half Hour or Less (Sheldon Leonard for "Danny's Comeback")
1961 (1): Outstanding Directorial Achievement in Comedy (Sheldon Leonard)

EMMY AWARD NOMINATIONS, IN ADDITION TO WINS (17)

1955 (2): Best Supporting Actress in a Regular Series (Jean Hagen); Best Written Comedy Material (Danny Thomas)
1956 (6): Best Comedy Series; Best Single Program of the Year (for "Peter Pan Meets Rusty Williams"); Best Actor, Continuing Performance (Danny Thomas); Best Actress, Continuing Performance (Jean Hagen); Best Actress in a Supporting Role (Jean Hagen); Best Director, Film Series (Sheldon Leonard)
1958 (3): Best Continuing Performance by an Actor in a Leading Role in a Dramatic or Comedy Series (Danny Thomas); Best Direction, Half Hour or Less (Sheldon Leonard for "Danny Thomas Show"); Best Cinematography for Television (Robert De Grasse)
1959 (3): Best Comedy Series; Best Actor in a Leading Role (Continuing Character) in a Comedy Series (Danny Thomas); Best Direction of a Single Program of a Comedy Series (Sheldon Leonard for "Pardon My Accent")

1960 (2): Outstanding Directorial Achievement in Comedy (Sheldon Leonard); Outstanding Program Achievement in the Field of Humor
1961 (1): Outstanding Writing Achievement in Comedy (Charles Stewart and Jack Elinson)

Further Reading

Leonard, Sheldon. *And the Show Goes On: Broadway and Hollywood Adventures.* New York: Limelight Editions, 2004.
Thomas, Danny, and Bill Davidson. *Make Room for Danny.* New York: G. P. Putnam's Sons, 1991.

The Courtship of Eddie's Father

(1969–1972)

Cast: Bill Bixby (Tom Corbett), Brandon Cruz (Eddie Corbett), Miyoshi Umeki (Mrs. Livingston), James Komack (Norman Tinker), Kristina Holland (Tina Rickles)

Created by: Executive producer James Komack

Network: ABC

First Air Date: September 17, 1969

Last Air Date: June 14, 1972

Broadcast History:
September 17, 1969–September 1970: Wednesday at 8:00–8:30 PM
September 1970–September 1971: Wednesday at 7:30–8:00 PM
September 1971–June 1972: Wednesday at 8:30–9:00 PM
June 1972–June 14, 1972: Wednesday at 8:00–8:30 PM

Seasons: 3

Episodes: 73

Ratings History: Never in Top 30

Overview

From listening to the first note of the theme song "Best Friend," written by 1970s songwriter extraordinaire Harry Nilsson, viewers assumed they were about to watch an uplifting show in *The Courtship of Eddie's Father*. And they assumed right. This show was as positive in its message as the theme song was cheery.

The adaptation of a 1963 namesake film starring Glenn Ford and Ronnie Howard put a modern spin on a widower father raising a young son nine years after *The Andy*

Bill Bixby and Brandon Cruz. *ABC/Photofest ©ABC*

Griffith Show embraced the same premise with tremendous success. It revolved around magazine publisher Tom Corbett (Bill Bixby) and his inquisitive seven-year-old son Eddie (Brandon Cruz), who worked feverishly to get his dad hitched. Much of the humor revolved around the efforts of the young matchmaker, whose efforts were appreciated by his father despite the fact that they were in vain. The mutual love between father and son came across as genuine and sometimes a bit syrupy, but that was welcome in an era of divisiveness in the United States. Their heart-to-heart conversations highlighted the cuteness of Eddie and wisdom of his dad whether they were, as the theme song states, "talking man to man or talking son to son."

The charming side characters not only added depth and personality to the show, but racial and philosophical diversity that was still badly needed in the American sitcom at that time. Kind housekeeper Mrs. Livingston (Miyoshi Umeki) proved to be a guiding force for both Tom and Eddie, while magazine photographer Norman Tinker (James Komack) brought a grown hippie and free spirit flavor to his character and was always quite willing to give parenting advice to his friend and colleague. Ditzy blonde secretary Tina Rickles (Kristina Holland) provided some of the more manic moments. The excellence in the individual performances was duly noted. Bixby and Komack were nominated for Emmys and Umeki a Golden Globe. The show itself was nominated for an Emmy and a Golden Globe as the premier sitcom.

The Courtship of Eddie's Father attracted a limited viewership and never broke into the mainstream, especially among conservative audiences that rejected what was perceived as liberal fare. Strong competition on Wednesday nights from such popular variety shows as *The Glen Campbell Goodtime Hour* and *The Carol Burnett Show*, as well as the established western *The Virginian*, also played a role in it never cracking the Top 30 in the Nielsen ratings, but the program was significant in bridging the gap with quality programming between the purposely mindless sitcoms launched earlier in the decade and the socially and politically relevant sitcoms beginning in 1971 with *All in the Family*.

Did You Know?

Future movie star Jodie Foster appeared in five episodes as Eddie's friend Joey Kelly. She was six years old when *The Courtship of Eddie's Father* was launched in September 1969.

They Said It

> **Eddie:** Dad, who do I look like?
> **Tom:** You look just like your mother.
> **Eddie:** You mean she was a small boy?

Major Awards

EMMY AWARD NOMINATIONS (2)

1970 (1): Outstanding Comedy Series
1971 (1): Outstanding Continued Performance by an Actor in a Leading Role in a Comedy Series (Bill Bixby)

GOLDEN GLOBE NOMINATIONS (2)

1971 (2): Best TV Show; Best Supporting Actress, Television (Miyoshi Umeki)

Further Reading

Toby, Mark. *The Courtship of Eddie's Father.* New York: Paperback Library, 1963.

✶ **48** ✶

Sanford and Son

(1972–1977)

Cast: Redd Foxx (Fred Sanford); Demond Wilson (Lamont Sanford); Whitman Mayo (Grady Wilson); Don Bexley (Bubba Bexley); Nathaniel Taylor (Rollo Larson); LaWanda Page (Aunt Esther Anderson)

Created by: Producers Norman Lear and Bud Yorkin and writers Alan K. Simpson and Ray Galton

Network: NBC

First Air Date: January 14, 1972

Last Air Date: September 2, 1977

Broadcast History:
January 14, 1972–September 1977: Friday at 8:00–8:30 PM
April 1976–August 1976: Wednesday at 9:00–9:30 PM

Seasons: 6

Episodes: 136

Ratings History: 1972 (6), 1972–1973 (2), 1973–1974 (3), 1974–1975 (2), 1975–1976 (7), 1976–1977 (27)

Overview

Critics complained that Redd Foxx lowered rather than elevated the perceptions of African Americans presented by the media through his portrayal of Fred Sanford, a junk dealer in the Watts section of Los Angeles. They further criticized other characters on *Sanford and Son* for the same reason. Others countered that the show was an accurate depiction of contemporary urban black life in the United States and

Demond Wilson and Redd Foxx. *NBC/Photofest ©NBC*

very funny to boot. The former view was based on the belief that traits possessed by Sanford—laziness and deceitfulness, for example—were stereotypical of those given to black characters throughout the years. Those who disagreed cited moral son Lamont (Demond Wilson), who sought to keep his aging dad on a righteous path and cared for him, most often to his own detriment. They also alluded to equally low-quality white characters on modern television shows, namely the racist Archie Bunker.

Lamont was, in fact, Gilligan (the title character in silly 1960s sitcom *Gilligan's Island*) in reverse in relation to viewer frustration. They wanted to strangle the bumbling castaway for wrecking every rescue. They also wanted to strangle the smart and savvy Lamont for blowing every chance to maximize his personal and professional potential in life so he could stay with his dishonest dad and remain poor.

The show was created, in part, by Norman Lear, although it was an Americanized version of the British comedy *Steptoe and Son*. Everything Lear touched in the 1970s turned to gold, including breakthrough sitcom *All in the Family* and spin-offs *Maude* and *The Jeffersons*.

The choice of Foxx as the lead in *Sanford and Son* raised a few eyebrows. He was considered one of the most profane stand-up comedians of his day, but the show gave him a mainstream audience and thrust him in front of white viewers for the first time. His trademark sideways gait and such catchphrases as calling out to his deceased wife, "I'm coming to join you, Elizabeth" as he reeled backward with his hand over his heart when he was shocked by bad news, appealed to fans of all demographics. *Sanford and Son* could never have skyrocketed to number two in the Nielsen ratings twice and remained in the top seven in its first five seasons without tremendous white support.

A strong cast supplemented the talents of Foxx and Wilson. The two most prominent characters were friend Grady Wlson, played by Whitman Mayo, who garnered a Golden Globe nomination as a supporting actor for his performance, and holy roller Aunt Esther (LaWanda Page), who maintained a rooming house and a bitter feud with Fred. Esther often warned Fred that he would not be accepted into heaven, but rather be sent in the opposite direction, if he did not change his dishonest ways. Fred simply countered with one of many insults for Esther, for which he seemed to have an endless stock.

Fred did have one female supporter in patient girlfriend Donna Harris (Lynn Hamilton), a nurse who waited in vain for him to pop the question, which never came. The same plight awaited divorcee and mother Janet Lawson (Marlene Clark), who at least got a bit farther with Lamont. He did ask her to marry him, but the show ended in 1977 with the pair still engaged.

Those who defended *Sanford and Son* against critics who claimed it promoted negative black stereotypes cited the caricature portrayal of one of the only white characters on the show, a brainless cop known as Happy (Howard Platt), who butchered every attempt to relate to Fred and Lamont in inner city street lingo. The debate rages today among those who discuss race as it related to classic television programming, but what can't be debated is that *Sanford and Son* was the most embraced sitcom featuring black characters until a megahit known as *The Cosby Show* rolled around in the following decade and at least temporarily put to rest complaints about negative characterizations.

Hold the Mayo

Redd Foxx quit the sitcom in 1977, and in its place was a spin-off entitled *The Sanford Arms*, which was intended to star Wilson and Mayo. Wilson, however, scoffed at his salary offer. Mayo had already landed a starring role on a show on the same network called *Grady*, which lasted just one season. *The Sanford Arms*, which revolved around lead character Phil Wheeler (Theodore Wilson) buying the Sanfords out lock, stock, and barrel and converting their place into a hotel, lasted just a few episodes.

Did You Know?

Black actor Cleavon Little, who starred in the Mel Brooks comedy *Blazing Saddles*, turned down the part of Fred Sanford. Little, who recommended Foxx instead, had worked with Demond Wilson before, when the two teamed up to play burglars in an episode of *All in the Family*. Little would have needed some makeup to play Sanford. He was seventeen years younger than Foxx and only seven years older than Wilson.

They Said It

Fred: Listen, Esther, in the first place, you can't enter that contest because you're not eligible. See, one of the things you have to be is part of a certain race.
Woody: What race?
Fred: Human!

Lamont: They're predicting a massive earthquake on November 6.
Fred: November 6? That's only five days away!
Lamont: Don't worry about a thing, Pop. It's not possible.
Grady: Oh, I beg to differ with you, Lamont. Today is November 1 and it's extremely possible that November 6 is only five days away.

Major Awards

EMMY AWARD NOMINATIONS (7)

1972 (3): Outstanding New Series; Outstanding Series, Comedy; Outstanding Continued Performance by an Actor in a Leading Role in a Comedy Series (Redd Foxx)
1973 (2): Outstanding Comedy Series; Outstanding Continued Performance by an Actor in a Leading Role in a Comedy Series (Redd Foxx)
1974 (1): Best Lead Actor in a Comedy Series (Redd Foxx)
1976 (1): Outstanding Achievement in Video Tape Editing for a Series (Ken Denisoff and Robert Veatch for "Earthquake II")

GOLDEN GLOBE WIN (1)

1973 (1): Best TV Actor, Musical/Comedy (Redd Foxx)

GOLDEN GLOBE NOMINATIONS, IN ADDITION TO WIN (5)

1974 (2): Best TV Show, Musical/Comedy; Best TV Actor, Musical/Comedy (Redd Foxx)
1975 (2): Best TV Actor, Musical/Comedy (Redd Foxx); Best Supporting Actor, Television (Whitman Mayo)
1976 (1): Best TV Actor, Musical/Comedy (Redd Foxx)

Further Reading

Heitner, Devorah. "'This Ain't No Junk': Recuperating Black Television in the 'Post–Civil Rights' Era." *Jump Cut: A Review of Contemporary Media* 48 (Winter 2006). Available online at www.ejumpcut.org/archive/jc48.2006/TVblacks/text.html.
Starr, Michael Seth. *Black and Blue: The Redd Foxx Story*. New York: Applause Books, 2011.

✦ **49** ✦

The Beverly Hillbillies

(1962–1971)

Cast: Buddy Ebsen (Jed Clampett), Irene Ryan (Daisy "Granny" Moses), Donna Douglas (Elly May Clampett), Max Baer Jr. (Jethro Bodine), Raymond Bailey (Milburn Drysdale), Nancy Kulp (Jane Hathaway), Bea Benaderet (Cousin Pearl Bodine), Harriet MacGibbon (Margaret Drysdale)

Created by: Paul Henning

Network: CBS

First Air Date: September 26, 1962

Last Air Date: September 7, 1971

Broadcast History:
September 26, 1962–September 1964: Wednesday at 9:00–9:30 PM
September 1964–September 1968: Wednesday at 8:30–9:00 PM
September 1968–September 1969: Wednesday at 9:00–9:30 PM
September 1969–September 1970: Wednesday at 8:30–9:00 PM
September 1970–September 7, 1971: Tuesday at 7:30–8:00 PM

Seasons: 9

Episodes: 216

Ratings History: 1962–1963 (1), 1963–1964 (1), 1964–1965 (12), 1965–1966 (7), 1966–1967 (7), 1967–1968 (12), 1968–1969 (10), 1969–1970 (18), 1970–1971 (not in Top 30)

Buddy Ebsen, Irene Ryan, Max Baer Jr., and Donna Douglas. *CBS/Photofest ©CBS*

Overview

A new trend in the American sitcom began when old Jed Clampett (Buddy Ebsen) became a millionaire. *The Beverly Hillbillies* launched an era of escapism, and there was plenty to escape from in the 1960s—assassinations, riots, war, pollution, factions in American society tearing one another apart, literally and figuratively. The television powers that be decided that viewers yearned to take their minds as far away from reality as possible. They sought to create sitcoms with far-out premises.

No program was more successful than *The Beverly Hillbillies*, which featured a backwoods family that struck it rich. The story was told via one of the most memorable theme songs in television history, as family patriarch Jed Clampett, out hunting for food, nailed an oil gusher that transformed him into a multimillionaire. He and his family soon traded in their ramshackle cabin in the woods for a Beverly Hills mansion.

The comedy payoff was that Clampett, daughter Elly May (Donna Douglas), nephew Jethro Bodine (Max Baer Jr.), and Granny (Irene Ryan) remained incapable of transforming themselves into aristocrats. In fact, they continued to embrace the hillbilly lifestyle and remained woefully ignorant; Jethro beamed with pride at his sixth-grade education. The differences in breeding and education between the hillbillies and such characters as greedy, scheming Beverly Hills banker Milburn Drysdale

(Raymond Bailey) and assistant Jane Hathaway (Nancy Kulp) resulted in hilarious misconceptions.

Among the funniest involved real-life Los Angeles Dodgers pitcher Don Drysdale and general manager Leo Durocher, who invited Jed and Jethro to shoot a game of golf. Jed theorized that "golfs" are game birds that live in holes. He figured that golfs make for wonderful hunting after hearing that Mr. Drysdale shot nine holes and got fifty-seven.

The Beverly Hillbillies was the first of three highly rated rural shows in the 1960s created and produced by Paul Henning, who gained initial success in those roles with *The Bob Cummings Show* in the previous decade. The sensational ratings achieved by *The Beverly Hillbillies* gave Henning carte blanche at CBS and allowed him to launch two more highly popular rural series with *Petticoat Junction* and *Green Acres*.

The eight episodes that followed the assassination of President John F. Kennedy in November 1963 were among the highest rated in the history of the American sitcom. Included was one that aired on January 8, 1964, in which a kangaroo escapes into the neighborhood and Granny is stunned at the size of what she believes to be a giant jackrabbit. The success of the shows that followed the tragedy gave validity to the theory of escapism, but it should be pointed out that the show soared to number one in the Nielsen ratings in its first two seasons, most of which played out before the assassination that forever changed the nation.

It must also be noted that *The Beverly Hillbillies* mocked not only Jed and his extended family, but also the greed, prejudices, conceit, and ignorance of such educated and well-bred characters as Mr. Drysdale and his haughty wife Margaret (Harriet MacGibbon). But some critics saw it in a different light, panning it as a sitcom that poked fun at rural America. Among them was Paul Gould of the *New York Times*, who called it "rural no-think," and "perhaps the worst of the new season's entries" containing "every cliché in the book." Two years later, however, after the show soared to the top of the ratings, the same publication praised it for its mocking of pretentious people, which it conceded was a quality Americans embraced.

Each main character created visuals and passions that remain ingrained in the consciousness of viewers today—Jed whittling on the front steps, Jethro eating gigantic bowls of cereal (he even hawked Corn Flakes in commercials), Elly May caring for her animals, a stooped-over Granny slaving over a potful of possum stew. Even their vocabulary was memorable—animals were "critters," the pool was the "cement pond," and food was "vittles."

Many fans of the show believe it jumped the shark late in its run when it sought to expand beyond Beverly Hills and place the characters in Europe and New York, where it was filmed on location, but *The Beverly Hillbillies* had long before established a new wave of American television comedy. It succeeded in attracting audiences through its characterizations and story lines. The era of escapism might never have taken hold without this sitcom setting the standard.

Did You Know?

Buddy Ebsen turned down the role of the Tin Man in the iconic 1939 film *The Wizard of Oz*. He had originally been cast as the Scarecrow, but that was later given to Ray

Bolger. Ebsen originally accepted the part of the Tin Man but became allergic to the aluminum dust in the makeup he had to wear.

From Sexy Caterer to Grizzly Death

Sharon Tate, who was famously murdered in 1969 in the Charles Manson killings, appeared in fifteen episodes of *The Beverly Hillbillies* from 1963 to 1965. The beautiful actress and model assumed the role of an employee at a catering service.

"Flatt" Notes . . . and Scruggs

Fiddler Lester Flatt and banjo player Earl Scruggs teamed up as perhaps the most famous and accomplished bluegrass duo ever. They also gained fame through their connection to *The Beverly Hillbillies*. They not only provided the instrumentals to the theme song (which was composed by show creator Paul Henning and entitled "The Ballad of Jed Clampett"), they appeared and played on several episodes as friends of the family from back in the hills. The most famous hit for Flatt and Scruggs was the fast-paced instrumental "Foggy Mountain Breakdown," which was played in the 1967 movie *Bonnie and Clyde*.

They Said It

> **Granny:** Elly May done popped the buttons off her shirt again.
> **Jed:** Elly May carries herself proud with her shoulders throwed back.
> **Granny:** It ain't her shoulders that have been poppin' these buttons.

> **Mr. Drysdale:** [dictating a letter to Jane Hathaway] And furthermore, if you are late on your mortgage payment one more time you will be thrown into the street.
> **Jane:** Chief, she's eighty-five years old and in a wheelchair.
> **Mr. Drysdale:** Oh, I'm sorry. I didn't know . . . change that to read, you will be wheeled out into the street.

Major Awards

EMMY AWARD NOMINATIONS (7)

1963 (4): Outstanding Program Achievement in the Field of Humor; Outstanding Continued Performance by a (Lead) Actress in a Series (Irene Ryan); Outstanding Directorial Achievement in Comedy (Richard Whorf); Outstanding Writing Achievement in Comedy (Paul Henning)

1964 (2): Outstanding Continued Performance by a (Lead) Actress in a Series (Irene Ryan); Outstanding Directorial Achievement in Comedy (Richard Whorf)

1967 (1): Outstanding Performance by an Actress in a Supporting Role in a Comedy (Nancy Kulp)

GOLDEN GLOBE NOMINATION (1)

1964 (1): Best TV Show

Further Reading

Cox, Stephen. *The Beverly Hillbillies: A Fortieth Anniversary Wing-Ding.* Nashville, TN: Cumberland House, 2002.
Ebsen, Buddy. *The Other Side of Oz.* Hingham, MA: Donovan Publishing, 1994.

✴ **50** ✴

Night Court

(1984–1992)

Cast: Harry Anderson (Judge Harry T. Stone), John Larroquette (Dan Fielding), Richard Moll (Nastradamus "Moll" Shannon), Charles Robinson (Mac Robinson), Markie Post (Christine Sullivan), Marsha Warfield (Rosalind "Roz" Russell), Selma Diamond (Bailiff Selma Hacker), Paula Kelly (Public Defender Liz Williams)

Created by: Executive producer, director (two episodes), and writer Reinhold Weege

Network: NBC

First Air Date: January 4, 1984

Last Air Date: July 1, 1992

Broadcast History:
> January 4, 1984–March 1984: Wednesday at 9:30–10:00 PM
> May 1984–March 1987: Thursday at 9:30–10:00 PM
> March 1987–June 1987: Wednesday at 9:00–9:30 PM
> June 1987–July 1987: Wednesday at 9:30–10:00 PM
> July 1987–August 1987: Wednesday at 9:00–9:30 PM
> August 1987–March 1988: Thursday at 9:30–10:00 PM
> March 1988–April 1988: Friday at 9:00–9:30 PM
> May 1988–September 1988: Thursday at 9:30–10:00 PM
> October 1988–August 1990: Wednesday at 9:00–9:30 PM
> September 1990–January 1991: Friday at 9:00–9:30 PM
> January 1991–November 1991: Wednesday at 9:00–9:30 PM
> December 1991–May 1992: Wednesday at 9:30–10:00 PM
> May 1992–June 1992: Sunday at 9:30–10:00 PM
> June 1992–July 1, 1992: Wednesday at 9:30–10:00 PM

Seasons: 8

Episodes: 145

Ratings History: 1984–1985 (20), 1985–1986 (11), 1986–1987 (7), 1987–1988 (7), 1988–1989 (21), 1989–1990 (29), 1990–1991 (not in Top 30), 1991–1992 (not in Top 30)

Top from left: Richard Moll, Harry Anderson, and Charles Robinson; front from left: John Larroquette, Markie Post, and Marsha Warfield. *NBC/Photofest ©NBC*

Overview

It was a circus in a courtroom. There were no elephants, of course, but there were plenty of clowns. Welcome to *Night Court*, a funny slap in the face to all court shows that preceded it and one that must have had Perry Mason rolling over in his fictional grave. *L.A. Law* this was not. Of course, it's much harder to joke about crimes like murder than those committed by the parade of crackpots and losers that stood before judge Harry Stone (Harry Anderson), who tried in vain to maintain control when law, and especially order, had disintegrated within the first two minutes of each episode.

Anderson was no picture of authority himself. His youthful looks and dressed-way-down appearance had nobody, least of all the other characters working his courtroom, quaking in their shoes, but he handed down justice all the same with a glib, dismissive flair that kept his workplace loose and made his point with the accused. Some who had worked in the nocturnal arraignment courtrooms believed the show brought an air of realism despite its craziness. It has been pointed out that the cases Anderson tried were often inspired by actual cases from the Manhattan night court.

The humorous plot lines revolving around bizarre cases and oddball defendants combined with the quirky, unique personalities of the main characters to create one of the best comedies of its time. Despite frequent cast changes, the show maintained high quality. There was court clerk Lana Wagner (Karen Austin), who in her one season on the show worked to hide her sexual attraction to Anderson. There was replacement Mac Robinson (Charles Robinson), who brought a sarcastic but steadying influence to the courtroom. There was Selma Hacker (Selma Diamond), whose biting put-downs came from a throaty voice that sounded like it had been affected by the invasion of five packs of cigarettes a day. There was hulking bailiff "Bull" Shannon (Richard Moll), whose bald skull and six-foot, seven-inch height gave him the look of a monster in a suit and tie that belied his tender nature and childlike innocence.

But best of all there was Assistant District Attorney Dan Fielding, played by John Larroquette, who wore out a path to the dais at the Emmy Awards. His performance in that role earned him four consecutive Outstanding Supporting Actor in a Comedy Series honors. His character had the scruples of a grave robber. The loutish Fielding had a one-track mind, and that track was quite distant from the courtroom. His desire for sex dominated all other motivations.

Fielding grew most lustful for public defender Christine Sullivan (Markie Post), who arrived in the third season. Sullivan toned down her sexiness by wearing button-down suits, yet still caught the attention of Fielding and Anderson. Her character boasted perhaps the most intriguing personal story line in the show. She married undercover cop Tony Guillano (Ray Abruzzo) in 1990, but was soon divorced. Christine embarked on a love affair with Anderson that eventually cooled as well.

A year later, Dan's assistant, Phil Saunders (William Utay), was crushed by a piano, after which it was learned that he had earned millions on Wall Street and had left dishonest Dan in charge of his charitable foundation worth $10 million. When the dust settled, it was revealed that Phil's scheming twin brother Will had stolen all the money, and Dan nearly landed behind bars.

The Nielsen ratings for *Night Court* slipped considerably in the early 1990s, after remaining in the Top 30 throughout its first six seasons and peaking at number seven from 1986 to 1988, but there was one big blowout in the plot line in the final episode. A repentant Dan resigned to chase after Christine, who had been elected to Congress, and, in an appropriate twist for both character and crazy show, Bull left Earth altogether. He was abducted by midget aliens and flown off to planet Jupiter.

This sitcom could have been buried in the annals of 1980s television history under the avalanche of such brilliant and iconic sitcoms as *Cheers*, *The Cosby Show*, *Roseanne*, *Family Ties*, and *The Golden Girls*, but its loopy humor and memorable personalities have allowed it to maintain its place as one of the best shows of its era.

Quite a Quartet

The NBC lineup in which *Night Court* was included was among the best ever assembled. The courtroom sitcom followed *The Cosby Show*, *Family Ties*, and *Cheers*. Cosby show spin-off *A Different World* replaced *Family Ties* in 1988. The original four all placed in the top seven shows in the Nielsen ratings in the 1986–1987 season. *The Cosby Show*, *Family Ties*, and *Cheers* placed 1–2–3. *A Different World* opened at number two in 1987. One can argue that it rivaled the heavyweight CBS Saturday night lineup that peaked in the fall of 1973, with *All in the Family*, *M*A*S*H*, *The Mary Tyler Moore Show*, *The Bob Newhart Show*, and *The Carol Burnett Show*, although that quintet is widely considered the best of all time.

Did You Know?

Harry Anderson slipped out of his *Night Court* robes six times to portray one of the most intriguing recurring characters on *Cheers*. He played con man Harry "The Hat" Gittes, who hoodwinked anyone and everyone as a sly moneymaker. Harry helped the Cheers gang on occasion in their practical joke war against rival bar Gary's Old Towne Tavern.

They Said It

Mac: Bull has got himself a girlfriend.
Dan: Really? Animal, mineral, or vegetable?

Bull: [wearing nothing but underwear while approaching the others sitting at a cafeteria table] Hi, guys.
Harry: Bull?
Bull: Oh, don't worry, Your Honor. I'm just having one of those dreams where you show up to work in your underwear.
Harry: Bull, this isn't a dream.
Bull: It's not? Yikes.

Dan: You know, one of my college roommates actually contracted rabies. He died soon after. Got run over while chasing a car. [chuckles] Just kidding. He died of rabies.

Major Awards

EMMY AWARDS WINS (7)

1985 (1): Outstanding Supporting Actor in a Comedy Series (John Larroquette)
1986 (1): Outstanding Supporting Actor in a Comedy Series (John Larroquette)
1987 (2): Outstanding Supporting Actor in a Comedy Series (John Larroquette); Outstanding Editing for a Series, Multi-Camera Production (Jerry Davis for "Her Honor: Part I")
1988 (1): Outstanding Supporting Actor in a Comedy Series (John Larroquette)
1989 (2): Outstanding Sound Mixing for a Comedy Series or a Special (Klaus Landsberg, Craig Porter, and Allen Patapoff for "The Last Temptation of Mac"); Outstanding Technical Direction/Camera/Video for a Series (Robert G. Holmes, Leigh Nicholson, John Repczynski, Jeffrey Wheat, Rocky Danielson, and Tom Tcimpidis for "Yet Another Day in the Life")

EMMY AWARD NOMINATIONS, IN ADDITION TO WINS (23)

1984 (3): Outstanding Supporting Actress in a Comedy Series (Paula Kelly); Outstanding Individual Achievement, Costumers (Barbara Murphy for "Welcome Back, Mama"); Outstanding Lighting Direction (Electronic) for a Series (John Appelroth for "Bull's Baby")
1985 (5): Outstanding Comedy Series; Outstanding Lead Actor in a Comedy Series (Harry Anderson); Outstanding Supporting Actress in a Comedy Series (Selma Diamond); Outstanding Lighting Direction (Electronic) for a Series (John Appelroth for "Billie's Valentine"); Outstanding Videotape Editing for a Series (Jerry Davis for "The Blizzard")
1986 (4): Outstanding Lead Actor in a Comedy Series (Harry Anderson); Outstanding Achievement in Costuming for a Series (Dan Frank and Molly Harris Campbell for "Halloween, Too"); Outstanding Editing for a Series, Multi-Camera Production (Jerry Davis for "Hurricane: Part I and Part II"); Outstanding Lighting Direction (Electronic) for a Series (George Spiro Dibie for "Leon We Hardly Knew Ye")
1987 (4): Outstanding Comedy Series; Outstanding Lead Actor in a Comedy Series (Harry Anderson); Outstanding Achievement in Costuming for a Series (Dan Frank and Molly Harris Campbell for "A Day in the Life"); Outstanding Technical Direction/Electronic Camerawork/Video Control for a Series (Jerry Weiss, Rocky Danielson, Leigh Nicholson, John Repczynski, Jeffrey Wheat, and Tom Tcimpidis for "Murder")

1988 (2): Outstanding Comedy Series; Outstanding Lighting Direction (Electronic) for a Comedy Series (George Spiro Dibie for "Constitution: Part II")

1989 (1): Outstanding Lighting Direction (Electronic) for a Comedy Series (Robert Berry for "Danny Got His Gun: Part III")

1990 (1): Outstanding Technical Direction/Camera/Video for a Series (Robert G. Holmes, Rick Caswell, Rocky Danielson, Leigh Nicholson, Jeffrey Wheat, and Tom Tcimpidis for "Come Back to the Five and Dime Stephen King, Stephen King")

1991 (1): Outstanding Lighting Direction (Electronic) for a Comedy Series (Charles L. Barbee for "Hey Harry," "F'Cryin' Out Loud," and "It Is a Wonderful Life, Sorta")

1992 (2): Outstanding Individual Achievement in Lighting Direction (Electronic) for a Comedy Series (Charles L. Barbee for "A Guy Named Phantom: Part I"); Outstanding Technical Direction/Camera/Video for a Series (Robert G. Holmes, Rick Caswell, Rocky Danielson, Jeffrey Wheat, and Tom Tcimpidis for "A Guy Named Phantom: Part II")

GOLDEN GLOBE NOMINATIONS (2)

1985 (1): Best Performance by an Actress in a Supporting Role in a Series, Mini-Series, or Motion Picture Made for TV (Selma Diamond)

1988 (1): Best Performance by an Actor in a Supporting Role in a Series, Mini-Series, or Motion Picture Made for TV (John Larroquette)

Further Reading

Archive of American Television. "*Night Court.*" Available online at www.emmytvlegends.org/interviews/shows/night-court.

Tvtropes.org. "Series: *Night Court.*" Available online at http://tvtropes.org/pmwiki/pmwiki.php/Series/NightCourt?from=Main.NightCourt.

✹ 51 ✹

The Many Loves of Dobie Gillis

(1959–1963)

Cast: Dwayne Hickman (Dobie Gillis), Bob Denver (Maynard G. Krebs), Frank Faylen (Herbert T. Gillis), Florida Friebus (Winifred "Winnie" Gillis), Sheila James (Zelda Gilroy), Tuesday Weld (Thalia Menninger), Steve Franken (Chatsworth Osborne Jr.), Warren Beatty (Milton Armitage), Darryl Hickman (Dewey Gillis), William Schallert (Mr. Leander Pomfritt)

Created by: Max Shulman

Network: CBS

First Air Date: September 29, 1959

Last Air Date: September 18, 1963

Broadcast History:
    September 29, 1959–June 1962: Tuesday at 8:30–9:00 PM
    September 1962–June 1963: Wednesday at 8:30–9:00 PM

Seasons: 4

Episodes: 147

Ratings History: 1959–1960 (not in Top 30), 1960–1961 (23), 1961–1962 (21), 1962–1963 (not in Top 30)

Overview

The sitcom landscape was beginning to shift in the late 1950s. Such teenage characters as Ricky Nelson (*The Adventures of Ozzie and Harriet*) and Wally Cleaver (*Leave It to Beaver*) began to steal the spotlight from their parents. The focus on teens was greatly a result of the Baby Boomer youth culture emerging at that time. But the first sitcom

Bob Denver, Dwayne Hickman, Sheila James, and Steve Franken. *CBS/Photofest ©CBS*

that delved deeply into teenage angst was the iconic and creative *The Many Loves of Dobie Gillis*. Although not a syndication staple, viewers still recall the sight of Dobie (Dwayne Hickman) sitting on a bench in Central Park in New York, elbow on his knee and fist under his chin, striking the same thoughtful pose at *The Thinker*, the bronze statue resting majestically behind him. The inventiveness of this sitcom became apparent in the first scene of the first episode, in which Gillis gives a soliloquy to the camera, which became his trademark, about his favorite subject: girls.

> My name is Dobie Gillis and I like girls. What am I saying? I love girls! Love 'em! Beautiful, gorgeous, soft, round, creamy girls. Now, I'm not a wolf, mind you. No, you see a wolf wants lots of girls, but me? Well, I just want one. One beautiful, gorgeous, soft, round, creamy girl for my very own. That's all I want! One lousy girl! But I'll tell you a sad, hard fact. I'm never gonna get a girl. Never. Why? Because to get a girl you need money.

His speech set the tone for the series, which proved underappreciated in the television industry, leaving the air after four years having never even been nominated for an Emmy or Golden Globe, perhaps because it targeted youth. *The Many Loves of Dobie Gillis* was created by Max Shulman and based on his namesake book, published in 1951 and transformed into a movie entitled *The Affairs of Dobie Gillis* (1953). Shulman wrote all 147 episodes of the TV show.

His theme was the unrelenting drive of the star character to find love. The problem was that the only girl who yearned for him was classmate Zelda Gilroy (Sheila James), a plain Jane whom he liked only as a friend until a TV special in 1977 entitled *Whatever Happened to Dobie Gillis* had the two married with a son and running the grocery store owned by Dobie's father. Dobie was forever beaten by the better-looking and wealthier competition, including Chatsworth Osborne Jr. (Steve Franken, cousin of comedian and future U.S. senator Al Franken), who flaunted his status in front of the opposite sex, much to Dobie's dismay.

Franken was not one of the many young actors who used the sitcom as a springboard to fame and fortune in the entertainment industry. The most prominent was Bob Denver, who played Gillis's best friend, allergic-to-work beatnik Maynard G. Krebs. Denver was soon playing the bumbling Gilligan, who ruined one potential rescue after another on *Gilligan's Island*. Portraying fellow students on *The Many Loves of Dobie Gillis* for one season before moving on to movie stardom were Tuesday Weld, who played stunning Thalia Menninger, the target of Dobie's affection who was driven by finding a man with oodles of money, and future Oscar-winning director Warren Beatty, who assumed the role of handsome lady killer Milton Armitage. Weld earned a Golden Globe as Most Promising Newcomer following her year on the show and was nominated for an Academy Award for Best Supporting Actress in 1978 for her performance in the film *Looking for Mr. Goodbar*. Beatty blossomed into one of the most respected and prolific actors and directors of his time.

Hickman, on the other hand, will forever be remembered for playing thoughtful, but tortured, teenager Dobie Gillis despite a long career as a television actor. Gillis and the show itself had something in common in that they tried to find themselves. The story line took a dramatic turn in March 1961, when both Gillis and Krebs enlisted in the army, but by the start of the following season, they had left the service and enrolled at St. Peter Prior Junior College, where Gillis resumed his search for the woman of his dreams.

Onward and Upward

The young generation of actors was not the only one who had a monopoly on future success after toiling on *The Many Loves of Dobie Gillis*. Those who played adults also landed other prominent roles, particularly in television. The most prolific of the bunch was William Schallert, whose career has spanned more than six decades. He landed the part of the title character's father in the *Patty Duke Show* (1963–1966) and repeating roles on such hit shows as *Wild Wild West*, *Get Smart*, *Gunsmoke*, and *The Waltons*. Schallert also gained spots in the cast of such memorable television miniseries as *North and South* (in which he portrayed Confederate general Robert E. Lee) and *War and Remembrance*. Schallert played opposite Jean Byron, another cast member from *The Many Loves of Dobie Gillis*, as her husband in *The Patty Duke Show*.

Two actors who played mothers on the sitcom also enjoyed successful careers. Florida Friebus, who assumed the role of Winnie Gillis, later landed the part of a frequent patient of Dr. Robert Hartley on *The Bob Newhart Show*. Doris Packer, who played Mrs. Chatsworth, specialized in portraying wealthy, haughty snobs, which she did in such sitcoms as *Green Acres*, *The Andy Griffith Show*, and *The Beverly Hillbillies*.

They Said It

Maynard: Man, Dobie, you sure are getting forgetful. You left your lunch right on the table. Your mom sent me over with it.
Dobie: Oh, thanks a lot, Maynard. I'm awful hungry.
Maynard: I'm not.
Dobie: You're not hungry? How come?
Maynard: I just ate your lunch.

Major Awards

None

Further Reading

Denver, Bob. *Gilligan, Maynard, and Me*. New York: Citadel, 1993.
Hickman, Dwayne, and Joan Roberts Hickman. *Forever Dobie: The Many Lives of Dwayne Hickman*. New York: Birch Lane, 1994.

✷ **52** ✷

Maude

(1972–1978)

Cast: Bea Arthur (Maude Findlay), Bill Macy (Walter Findlay), Conrad Bain (Dr. Arthur Harmon), Rue McClanahan (Vivian Cavender Harmon), Adrienne Barbeau (Carol Traynor), Hermione Baddeley (Nell Naugatuck), Brian Morrison (Phillip Traynor, 1972–1976), Kraig Metzinger (Phillip Traynor, 1977–1978)

Created by: Producer and writer Norman Lear

Network: CBS

First Air Date: September 12, 1972

Last Air Date: April 29, 1978

Broadcast History:
September 12, 1972–September 1974: Tuesday at 8:00–8:30 PM
September 1974–September 1975: Monday at 9:00–9:30 PM
September 1975–September 1976: Monday at 9:30–10:00 PM
September 1976–September 1977: Monday at 9:00–9:30 PM
September 1977–November 1977: Monday at 9:30–10:00 PM
December 1977–January 1978: Monday at 9:00–9:30 PM
January 1978–April 29, 1978: Saturday at 9:30–10:00 PM

Seasons: 6

Episodes: 142

Ratings History: 1972–1973 (4), 1973–1974 (6), 1974–1975 (9), 1975–1976 (4), 1976–1977 (not in Top 30), 1977–1978 (not in Top 30)

Bea Arthur and Adrienne Barbeau. *CBS/Photofest ©CBS*

Overview

The notion that television actresses must portray women with at least a modicum of softness and femininity in appearance and communication was blown to bits on December 11, 1971. That was the date on which a blustery character named Maude Findlay, played by Bea Arthur, invaded the Bunker home on *All in the Family*.

Maude was a cousin of Edith and the polar opposite in political thought to Archie, with whom she argued bitterly. Maude expressed her hatred of Archie with a deep, booming voice, as well as an aggressiveness and lack of sensitivity (at least in regard to *his* feelings) rarely seen previously on a TV sitcom. Her appearance proved impressive enough to motivate CBS to provide her with a spin-off series that premiered the following September.

Arthur was cast as an upper-middle class liberal living with fourth husband and appliance store owner Walter (Bill Macy) in the town of Tuckahoe, New York. (Archie joked about Maude having killed off her other husbands with her personality and having seen one lying in his casket with a big smile on his face.) They lived with 27-year-old divorced daughter Carol (Adrienne Barbeau) and her young son Phillip (Brian Morrison 1972–1976, Kraig Metzinger 1977–1978), whom Walter considered stupid.

Maude spent much of her time imposing her will and forcing her opinions on others. She was proud of her independent spirit and determination. She was also proud of the burgeoning women's movement, which she backed with all the fervor she could muster. Show creator Norman Lear used *Maude* as a vehicle to advance his belief in taking a head-on approach to controversial issues that he himself had removed from the closet in the television industry.

The subject matter was placed squarely on the trail blazed by *All in the Family*. Serious social, personal, and economic issues were not merely discussed, but proved very real to members of the Findlay home. Walter battled alcoholism and struck Maude in the process of trying to become sober. He also lamented the failure of his business as it slid into bankruptcy and suffered a nervous breakdown. Maude went through menopause in a far more serious way than did cousin Edith in a manic episode of *All in the Family*. Maude also underwent an abortion several months before *Roe v. Wade* legalized it, which drew the ire of some viewers.

Rue McClanahan and Conrad Bain, who played the Harmon couple living next door, led a strong supporting cast. It comes as no surprise that wife Vivian had been divorced and husband Arthur widowed. Maude's deep-voiced maid Florida (Esther Rolle) displayed the wit, wisdom, and attractive personality that earned the successful spin-off series *Good Times*.

Maude remained a Top 10 hit in the Nielsen ratings until it plummeted out of the Top 30 during the 1976–1977 season. That prompted story line changes, including Walter announcing that he was retiring from the appliance business and the Harmons planning on leaving town. Maude was to continue a new career as a congresswoman, which began in the final three episodes of what became the final season because Arthur decided to abandon the series in 1987. The decision to cancel the show rather than replace her was a wise one. Her character, after all, was one of a kind.

Bea and Rue

The on-screen chemistry between Bea Arthur and Rue McClanahan led to their pairing in the 1980s and early 1990s series *The Golden Girls*. Such might not have been the case if the original casting of future *Everybody Loves Raymond* star Doris Roberts as Vivian in *Maude* had become a reality. The producers concluded that Roberts and Arthur were too similar, so they opted for McClanahan.

They Said It

Dr. Harmon: [looking at Maude's black eye and recalling Petey the Dog from the *Our Gang* comedies] If the *Our Gang* comedies ever come back, you could be the dog.
Maude: And if Mister Ed ever comes back, there'd be a part for you. I'm not talking about the part that talks.

Walter: [after Maude gave him an uncooked chicken following an argument] That chicken is frozen.
Maude: You think that's frozen, wait and see what you get in bed tonight.

Major Awards

EMMY AWARD WIN (1)

1977 (1): Outstanding Lead Actress in a Comedy (Bea Arthur)

EMMY AWARD NOMINATIONS, IN ADDITION TO WIN (11)

1973 (3): Outstanding Comedy Series; Outstanding New Series; Outstanding Continued Performance by an Actress in a Leading Role in a Comedy Series (Bea Arthur)
1974 (1): Best Lead Actress in a Comedy Series (Bea Arthur)
1976 (3): Outstanding Lead Actress in a Comedy Series (Bea Arthur); Outstanding Writing in a Comedy Series (Jay Folb for "The Analyst"); Outstanding Directing in a Comedy Series (Hal Cooper for "The Analyst")
1977 (1): Outstanding Art Direction or Scenic Design for a Comedy Series (Chuck Murawski for "Walter's Crisis")
1978 (3): Best Lead Actress in a Comedy Series (Bea Arthur); Outstanding Directing in a Comedy Series (Hal Cooper for "Vivian's Decision"); Outstanding Art Direction for a Comedy Series (Chuck Murawski for "The Wake")

GOLDEN GLOBE WIN (1)

1976 (1): Best Supporting Actress, Television (Hermione Baddeley)

GOLDEN GLOBE NOMINATIONS, IN ADDITION TO WIN (7)

1973 (2): Best TV Show, Musical/Comedy; Best TV Actress, Musical/Comedy (Bea Arthur)
1974 (1): Best TV Actress, Musical/Comedy (Bea Arthur)
1975 (1): Best TV Show, Musical/Comedy
1976 (1): Best TV Actress, Musical/Comedy (Bea Arthur)
1977 (1): Best Supporting Actress, Television (Adrienne Barbeau)
1978 (1): Best TV Actress, Musical/Comedy (Bea Arthur)

Further Reading

Hamamoto, Darrell Y. *Nervous Laughter: Television Situation Comedy and Liberal Democratic Ideology.* New York: Praeger, 1989.

✳ **53** ✳

Home Improvement

(1991–1999)

Cast: Tim Allen (Tim Taylor), Patricia Richardson (Jill Taylor), Earl Hindman (Wilson Wilson Jr.), Taran Noah Smith (Mark Taylor), Zachery Ty Bryan (Brad Taylor), Richard Karn (Al Borland), Jonathan Taylor Thomas (Randy Taylor), Debbe Dunning (Heidi Keppert)

Created by: Executive producers and writers Carmen Finestra, David McFadzean, and Matt Williams

Network: ABC

First Air Date: September 17, 1991

Last Air Date: September 17, 1999

Broadcast History:
September 17, 1991–August 1992: Tuesday at 8:30–9:00 PM
August 1992–September 1994: Wednesday at 9:00–9:30 PM
March 1994–May 1994: Wednesday at 8:00–8:30 PM
September 1994–July 1998: Tuesday at 9:00–9:30 PM
April 1997–May 1999: Tuesday at 8:00–8:30 PM
April 1999–September 17, 1999: Friday at 8:00–8:30 PM

Seasons: 8

Episodes: 204

Ratings History: 1991–1992 (5), 1992–1993 (3), 1993–1994 (1), 1994–1995 (2), 1995–1996 (7), 1996–1997 (9), 1997–1998 (10), 1998–1999 (10)

Tim Allen, Patricia Richardson, and Richard Karn. *ABC/Photofest ©ABC*

Overview

One would think that the host of an instructional television show about the most effective use of tools would be a whiz around the house, but when Tim Taylor pulled out a piece of equipment, souped up for maximum power, his wife and kids scurried to safety. That was the humorous paradox on *Home Improvement*, but it was certainly not the only aspect of the show that viewers found funny. How many sitcoms, after all, debut in the Top 10 of the Nielsen ratings and remain there for its duration? This one actually hit number one in its third season.

The lead character, played by stand-up comedian Tim Allen, perceived himself as a man's man. He loved tools, cars, and sports, especially his hometown Detroit teams. He also hosted a show called *Tool Time* alongside Al Borland, played by Richard Karn, who later starred as the host of television game show *Family Feud*. Although his instructions didn't always go as planned on the show, the credibility of Tim and his advice to viewers was never questioned. They believed he was merely attempting to prove what could go wrong if tools were not used properly. It was when he pulled out a drill or electric saw at home that all hell broke loose. And whenever anything would go wrong, he would emphasize the two words he believed could resolve any problem: "More power!"

The show revolved around Tim and his relationships with his wife, kids, Borland, and a mysterious neighbor known only as Wilson (Earl Hindman), who remained unseen until he took his final bows along with the rest of the cast as the curtain was lowered for the final time in 1999. Wilson sought to give Tim sage personal advice through the fence that divided their backyards, but it was Tim's interaction with Al that proved most contentious. His helper on *Tool Time* repeatedly proved to have greater skill in his craft, as well as audience appreciation, but Al was too shy and insecure to fight for more camera time. Tim kept him that way with frequent on-air put-downs about Al's bland personality and weight problems. Tim claimed his needling was not done maliciously, but rather as a form of male bonding.

Tim was not the most respected father on the block, either, although his wife and kids loved him. Elder sons Brad (Zachery Ty Bryan) and Randy (Jonathan Taylor Thomas) were typical (read: cruel) older brothers to youngest son Mark (Taran Noah Smith), particularly until the first two reached their teenage years. Brad was more popular and athletic than his brothers. Randy was the jokester of the group, but he grew more thoughtful in time. He and girlfriend Lauren (Courtney Peldon) later embraced environmental issues and even boycotted his father's employer, Binford Tools. They later ran off to save the rain forest in Costa Rica, but Thomas was really written off the show so he could pursue his college studies. Mark overcame a sudden, surprising, and brief Goth period. Jill (Patricia Richardson) grew as well as she pursued her master's degree in psychology.

Each character underwent personal upheavals in the series finale. Tim quit *Tool Time* after a falling out with his company, Al married his longtime love Trudy in a ceremony in the Taylor family backyard, and Jill took a job in Bloomington. Tim finally got something right when he successfully raised their house and wheeled it to that city to accommodate his wife.

Home Improvement didn't boast the flair, social impact, or element of surprise (at least until the final episode) of other sitcoms throughout the years, but its popularity was a testament to the consistent humor and intriguing characterizations it provided on a weekly basis to its millions of loyal viewers.

The *Tool Time* Girls

A sexy woman or two often helps ratings, and two sexy women helped the ratings of two shows—*Home Improvement* and *Tool Time*. The latter featured young beauties providing tools for the hosts. The first was Lisa, played by former *Baywatch* star Pamela Anderson, who left the show after two seasons. The second was Heidi (Debbe Dunning), whose real-life pregnancy gave the writers an opportunity to make her very realistically pregnant on the show. In one of the more manic episodes of *Home Improvement*, Tim was forced to deliver her baby.

They Said It

Randy: It's not junk. It's heavy metal.
Tim: It sounds like they're banging their heads on their guitars while they're getting their teeth drilled.
Randy: Hey, cool—you saw the video.

Wilson: Tim, it is not easy to change one's perception of things, but it can be very healthy. Some people might even say it's a growth experience.
Tim: Wilson, how far does this go? How do I really know you are who I think you are?
Wilson: Well how do I know you are who I think you are?
Tim: How do I know you're the one who said that?
Wilson: How do I know you heard what I said?
Tim: How do I know you're really here?
Wilson: Who else would have the time to come out and listen to this silly conversation?

Major Awards

EMMY AWARD WINS (7)

1992 (1): Outstanding Individual Achievement in Lighting Direction (Electronic) for a Comedy Series (Donald A. Morgan for "Luck Be a Taylor Tonight")
1993 (1): Outstanding Individual Achievement in Lighting Direction (Electronic) for a Comedy Series (Donald A. Morgan for "Bye Bye Birdie")
1994 (1): Outstanding Individual Achievement in Lighting Direction (Electronic) for a Comedy Series (Donald A. Morgan for "Twas the Blight")
1995 (1): Outstanding Individual Achievement in Lighting Direction (Electronic) for a Comedy Series (Donald A. Morgan for "My Dinner with Wilson")
1996 (1): Outstanding Individual Achievement in Lighting Direction (Electronic) for a Comedy Series (Donald A. Morgan for "Room without a View")
1998 (1): Outstanding Lighting Direction (Electronic) for a Comedy Series (Donald A. Morgan for "A Night to Dismember")
1999 (1): Outstanding Lighting Direction (Electronic) for a Comedy Series (Donald A. Morgan for "Mark's Big Break")

EMMY AWARD NOMINATIONS, IN ADDITION TO WINS (27)

1992 (2): Outstanding Comedy Series; Outstanding Individual Achievement in Editing for a Series, Multi-Camera Production (Alex Gimenez and Marco Zappia for "Stereo Typical")

1993 (4): Outstanding Comedy Series; Outstanding Lead Actor in a Comedy Series (Tim Allen); Outstanding Individual Achievement in Editing for a Series, Multi-Camera Production (Alex Gimenez and Marco Zappia for "To Build or Not to Build"); Outstanding Technical Direction/Camera/Video for a Series (Chris Donovan, Gary Allen, Greg Harms, Marvin Shearer, Randy Baer, Larry Gaudette, and Bob Kaufman for "Rites and Wrongs of Passage")

1994 (5): Outstanding Comedy Series; Outstanding Lead Actress in a Comedy Series (Patricia Richardson); Outstanding Individual Achievement in Editing for a Series, Multi-Camera Production (Roger Ames Berger and Marco Zappia for "It Was the Best of Tim's, It Was the Worst of Tim's"); Outstanding Individual Achievement in Sound Mixing for a Comedy Series or a Special (Klaus Landsberg, Charlie McDaniel, and John Bickelhaupt for "5th Anniversary Show"); Outstanding Technical Direction/Camera/Video for a Series (Chris Donovan, Gary Allen, Randy Baer, Victor Gonzalez, Larry Gaudette, and Bob Kaufman for "5th Anniversary Show")

1995 (3): Outstanding Individual Achievement in Editing for a Series, Multi-Camera Production (Roger Ames Berger and Marco Zappia for "Don't Tell Momma"); Outstanding Sound Mixing for a Comedy Series or a Special (Klaus Landsberg, Charlie McDaniel, and John Bickelhaupt for "Don't Tell Momma"); Outstanding Technical Direction/Camera/Video for a Series (Chris Donovan, Chris Shideler, Kenneth R, Shapiro, Richard Edwards, Gary Allen, Victor Gonzalez, Randy Baer, Marvin Shearer, Larry Gaudette, and Bob Kaufman for "Tool Time After Dark")

1996 (4): Outstanding Lead Actress in a Comedy Series (Patricia Richardson); Outstanding Individual Achievement in Editing for a Series, Multi-Camera Production (Roger Ames Berger and Marco Zappia for "The Longest Day"); Outstanding Individual Achievement in Sound Mixing for a Comedy Series or a Special (Klaus Landsberg, Charlie McDaniel, John Bickelhaupt, and Kathy Oldham for "A Taylor Runs Through It"); Outstanding Technical Direction/Camera/Video for a Series (Chris Shideler, Marvin Shearer, Victor Gonzalez, Gary Allen, Larry Gaudette, and Bob Kaufman for "The Longest Day")

1997 (3): Outstanding Lead Actress in a Comedy Series (Patricia Richardson); Outstanding Lighting Direction (Electronic) for a Comedy Series (Donald A. Morgan for "I Was a Teenage Taylor"); Outstanding Sound Mixing for a Comedy Series or a Special (Klaus Landsberg, Charlie McDaniel, John Bickelhaupt, and Kathy Oldham for "Wilson's World")

1998 (3): Outstanding Lead Actress in a Comedy Series (Patricia Richardson); Outstanding Sound Mixing for a Comedy Series or a Special (Klaus Landsberg, Charlie McDaniel, and John Bickelhaupt for "A Night to Dismember"); Outstanding Technical Direction/Camera/Video for a Series (Chris Shideler, Gary Allen, Jeff Barnes, Bettina Levesque, Larry Gaudette, Marvin Shearer, and Bob Kaufman for "A Night to Dismember")

1999 (3): Outstanding Music and Lyrics (Dan Foliart for the song "We've Got It All" for "The Long and Winding Road"); Outstanding Sound Mixing for a Comedy Series or a Special (Klaus Landsberg, Charlie McDaniel, John Bickelhaupt, and Kathy Oldham for "Love's Labor Lost: Part I"); Outstanding Technical Direction/Camera/Video for a Series (Chris Shideler, Gary Allen, Jeff Barnes, Bettina Levesque, Larry Gaudette, Marvin Shearer, and Bob Kaufman for "The Long and Winding Road")

GOLDEN GLOBE WIN (1)

1995 (1): Best Performance by an Actor in a TV Series, Musical/Comedy (Tim Allen)

GOLDEN GLOBE NOMINATIONS, IN ADDITION TO WIN (8)

1993 (1): Best Performance by an Actor in a TV Series, Musical/Comedy (Tim Allen)
1994 (3): Best TV Series, Musical/Comedy; Best Performance by an Actor in a TV Series, Musical/Comedy (Tim Allen); Best Performance by an Actress in a TV Series, Musical/Comedy (Patricia Richardson)
1995 (2): Best TV Series, Musical/Comedy; Best Performance by an Actress in a TV Series, Musical/Comedy (Patricia Richardson)
1996 (1): Best Performance by an Actor in a TV Series, Musical/Comedy (Tim Allen)
1997 (1): Best Performance by an Actor in a TV Series, Musical/Comedy (Tim Allen)

HUMANITAS PRIZE NOMINATION

1996: 30-Minute Category (Eliot Shoenman and Marley Sims)

Further Reading

Allen, Tim. *I'm Not Really Here.* New York: Hyperion Books, 1996.

The Jeffersons

(1975–1985)

Cast: Isabel Sanford (Louise Jefferson), Sherman Hemsley (George Jefferson), Roxie Roker (Helen Willis), Franklin Cover (Tom Willis), Paul Benedict (Harry Bentley), Marla Gibbs (Florence Johnston), Mike Evans (Lionel Jefferson), Zara Cully (Mother Jefferson)

Created by: Writer and producer Norman Lear

Network: CBS

First Air Date: January 18, 1975

Last Air Date: July 23, 1985

Broadcast History:
January 18, 1975–August 1975: Saturday at 8:30–9:00 PM
September 1975–August 1976: Saturday at 8:00–8:30 PM
November 1976–January 1977: Wednesday at 8:00–8:30 PM
January 1977–August 1977: Monday at 8:00–8:30 PM
September 1977–March 1978: Saturday at 9:00–9:30 PM
April 1978–May 1978: Saturday at 8:00–8:30 PM
June 1978–September 1978: Monday at 8:00–8:30 PM
September 1978–June 1979: Wednesday at 8:00–8:30 PM
January 1979–March 1979: Wednesday at 9:30–10:00 PM
March 1979–June 1979: Wednesday at 8:00–8:30 PM
June 1979–September 1982: Sunday at 9:30–10:00 PM
September 1982–December 1984: Sunday at 9:00–9:30 PM
January 1985–March 1985: Tuesday at 8:00–8:30 PM
April 1985: Tuesday at 8:30–9:00 PM
June 1985: Tuesday at 8:30–9:00 PM
June 1985–July 23, 1985: Tuesday at 8:00–8:30 PM

Seasons: 11

Episodes: 253

Ratings History: 1974–1975 (4), 1975–1976 (21), 1976–1977 (24), 1977–1978 (not in Top 30), 1978–1979 (not in Top 30), 1979–1980 (8), 1980–1981 (6), 1981–1982 (3), 1982–1983 (12), 1983–1984 (19), 1984–1985 (not in Top 30)

Marla Gibbs, Isabel Sanford, and Sherman Hemsley. *CBS/Photofest ©CBS*

Overview

In the hearts and minds of American viewers, the Jeffersons had been "movin' on up" long before they hightailed it out of Archie Bunker's neighborhood for a "deluxe apartment in the sky." George, Louise, and Lionel had established themselves as integral characters in the breakthrough and brilliant sitcom *All in the Family*. Not bad exposure—that show had been entrenched at number one in the Nielsen ratings for years before *The Jeffersons* was launched as one of the most successful spin-offs in television history.

George Jefferson (Sherman Hemsley) remained unseen in the first two seasons of *All in the Family*, as it was explained that he preferred not to step foot in that "honky house" occupied by the Bunkers, but Louise (Isabel Sanford) and son Lionel (Mike Evans) were immediately established as friends of the Bunker family—even the bigoted Archie. The man in the family presented in the first two seasons of *All in the Family* was George's younger brother Henry (Mel Stewart), who was equally combative in his verbal sparring with the intellectually unarmed Archie but lacked the sharp wit and stimulating personality that made George one of the funniest and purposefully abrasive and belligerent characters of his era. It came as a bit of a shock when he was introduced on *All in the Family* as Archie's equal in regard to bigotry, although on the opposite ends of the racial divide.

The generous and outgoing Louise was confrontational against George's unwillingness to compromise and open his mind, but she was otherwise quite contrasting to her irascible husband. The thoughtful, intelligent, and likeable Lionel arrived in the first *All in the Family* episode as a friend of Mike and Gloria. The Jefferson story line continued to be woven from there as they moved next door to the Bunkers and fell into insurance money from an accident that allowed George to quit his job as an apartment janitor and buy a dry cleaning store. His ambition and business savvy took over from there, as he built his business into a success that allowed him to whisk his family away to an apartment on New York's Upper East Side.

The move proved to be quite a culture shock, especially for George, who was not one to easily embrace new neighbors (particularly white folks). The most prominent were eccentric, hulking, and just plain weird Harry Bentley (Paul Benedict), who spent much of his time begging George to walk on his aching back, and Tom Willis (Franklin Cover), the target of George's put-downs for his naivetés and temerity for having wed a black woman, Helen (Roxie Roker), and his "zebra" daughter Jenny (Berlinda Tolbert). The heated conflict, however, revolved around Lionel falling in love with Jenny and eventually marrying her.

But it was two black actors that were recognized as critically acclaimed stars for their roles on *The Jeffersons*. The first was Sanford, who earned twelve Emmy or Golden Globe nominations for best lead actress in a comedy series, winning the former in 1981. The surprise was Marla Gibbs, who played sarcastic, witty housekeeper Florence Johnston. Gibbs earned a major role on the show after nailing her portrayal of a maid George hired to impress a client. By the time *The Jeffersons* was cancelled after an eleven-year run in 1985, Gibbs had snagged five Emmy nominations and one nomination for a Golden Globe.

Frequent and sometimes confusing cast changes might have played a role in the show dropping out of the Top 30 in the Nielsen ratings in the late 1970s, but it recovered to soar higher than ever early in the next decade. Evans departed after the first season to concentrate on helping launch a new sitcom entitled *Good Times*. He was replaced by stiff and unconvincing Damon Evans (no relation) but returned for two years before his character was written out of the show. Benedict also bolted for two years, as his character moved to Russia to further his career as a United Nations interpreter, but he also came back for the last two seasons.

The relationships between the characters shifted as the sitcom approached the end of the line in the early 1980s. George pulled an Archie Bunker, softening and growing more tolerant, particularly of Tom, with whom he finally established a sincere friendship. By the end of the show they had gone partners on a neighborhood bar they had often frequented, just as Archie had done in eventually transforming *All in the Family* into *Archie Bunker's Place*.

Late Bloomer

Zara Cully, who played the suspicious, but proud, mother of George Jefferson, took advantage of greater opportunities for black actors on television to amazingly begin her television career at the age of seventy-four with an appearance on the drama *Run for Your Life* in 1966, but Cully was no stranger to the theater. She worked locally in Jacksonville, Florida, as a producer, director, and performer, and also taught drama at Edward Waters College. She moved to Los Angeles to escape rampant racism in the

South. Cully landed roles on such serious shows as *Rod Serling's Night Gallery*, *Days of Our Lives*, and *Mod Squad* before being given the opportunity to display her comedic talents in two episodes of *All in the Family* and as a regular on *The Jeffersons* before succumbing to lung cancer in 1978.

Stunning Moment

The Jeffersons took a shocking and violent turn in a two-part episode in 1982, when George was stabbed by female gang members who had robbed him of his wallet and the ring he was planning on giving Louise for their wedding anniversary. He not only recovered in the second installment, but also tracked down the thief, put her on a better path in life, and motivated her to give him back the ring.

They Said It

> **Louise:** Lionel, you'd better go to your room. I don't want you to get hit by your father.
> **Lionel:** Why would dad hit me?
> **Louise:** Because I'm not sure just yet when I'm going to throw him!

> **Harry:** [looking through a telescope] I want to view the dog star.
> **George:** Lassie?
> **Harry:** No, Sirius.
> **George:** I am serious!

Major Awards

EMMY AWARD WINS (2)

1981 (1): Outstanding Lead Actress in a Comedy Series (Isabel Sanford)
1983 (1): Outstanding Video Tape Editing for a Series (Larry Harris for "Change of a Dollar")

EMMY AWARD NOMINATIONS, IN ADDITION TO WINS (12)

1979 (1): Outstanding Lead Actress in a Comedy Series (Isabel Sanford)
1980 (1): Outstanding Lead Actress in a Comedy Series (Isabel Sanford)
1981 (1): Outstanding Supporting Actress in a Comedy or Variety or Music Series (Marla Gibbs)
1982 (2): Outstanding Lead Actress in a Comedy Series (Isabel Sanford); Outstanding Supporting Actress in a Comedy or Variety or Music Series (Marla Gibbs)

1983 (2): Outstanding Lead Actress in a Comedy Series (Isabel Sanford); Outstanding Supporting Actress in a Comedy or Variety or Music Series (Marla Gibbs)

1984 (3): Outstanding Lead Actor in a Comedy Series (Sherman Hemsley); Outstanding Lead Actress in a Comedy Series (Isabel Sanford); Outstanding Supporting Actress in a Comedy Series (Marla Gibbs)

1985 (2): Outstanding Lead Actress in a Comedy Series (Isabel Sanford); Outstanding Supporting Actress in a Comedy Series (Marla Gibbs)

GOLDEN GLOBE NOMINATIONS (8)

1977 (1): Best TV Actress, Musical/Comedy (Isabel Sanford)

1978 (1): Best TV Actress, Musical/Comedy (Isabel Sanford)

1983 (1): Best Performance by an Actress in a TV Series, Musical/Comedy (Isabel Sanford)

1984 (1): Best Performance by an Actress in a TV Series, Musical/Comedy (Isabel Sanford)

1985 (4): Best TV Series, Musical/Comedy; Best Performance by an Actor in a TV Series, Musical/Comedy (Sherman Hemsley); Best Performance by an Actress in a TV Series, Musical/Comedy (Isabel Sanford); Best Performance by an Actress in a Supporting Role in a Series, Mini-Series, or Motion Picture Made for TV (Marla Gibbs)

HUMANITAS PRIZE NOMINATION

1978: 30-Minute Network or Syndicated Television (Roger Shulman and John Baskin)

Further Reading

McCrohan, Donna. *Archie & Edith, Mike & Gloria: The Tumultuous History of* All in the Family. New York: Workman, 1988.

"The Jeffersons." *Television Heaven.* Available online at www.televisionheaven.co.uk/jeffersons.htm.

✦ 55 ✦

Hogan's Heroes

(1965–1971)

Cast: Bob Crane (Colonel Robert Hogan), Werner Klemperer (Colonel Wilhelm Klink), John Banner (Sergeant Hans Schultz), Robert Clary (Corporal Louis LeBeau), Richard Dawson (Corporal Peter Newkirk), Ivan Dixon (Sergeant James Kinchloe), Larry Hovis (Sergeant Andrew Carter), Marya (Nita Talbot)

Created by: Producer and writer Bernard Fein and writer Albert Ruddy

Network: CBS

First Air Date: September 17, 1965

Last Air Date: July 4, 1971

Broadcast History:
    September 17, 1965–September 1967: Friday at 8:30–9:00 PM
    September 1967–September 1969: Saturday at 9:00–9:30 PM
    September 1969–September 1970: Saturday at 8:30–9:00 PM
    September 1970–July 4, 1971: Sunday at 7:30–8:00 PM

Seasons: 6

Episodes: 168

Ratings History: 1965–1966 (9), 1966–1967 (17), 1967–1968 (not in Top 30), 1968–1969 (not in Top 30), 1969–1970 (not in Top 30), 1970–1971 (not in Top 30)

Ivan Dixon, Bob Crane, Robert Clary, Larry Hovis, and Richard Dawson. *CBS/ Photofest ©CBS*

Overview

The horrors of World War II remained fresh in the hearts and minds of nearly all adult Americans when *Hogan's Heroes* was launched in the fall of 1965. The mere notion of creating a sitcom about a German prisoner of war camp when millions of potential viewers still had memories of a war that took 50 million lives and a Holocaust that killed 6 million Jews seemed to some incomprehensible. It had to be done tastefully, and that meant portraying the Germans as boobs consistently outsmarted by the crafty Americans. Never mind that the real Nazis in World War II were anything but the clownish figures represented in this show. That was the only way to make it work. And, boy, did it work.

Hogan's Heroes was among the most successful sitcom launches in television history, catapulting to number nine in the Nielsen ratings in its first year before dropping out of the Top 30 for good during the 1967–1968 season. The kookiest characters were indeed the Germans that ran Stalag 13, specifically Colonel Wilhelm Klink (Werner Klemperer) and Sergeant Hans Schultz (John Banner), whose fear of getting in trouble motivated him to utter his trademark lines: "I see nothing! I know nothing!"

One reason for the high ratings achieved by *Hogan's Heroes* in its first season was that some viewers were familiar with a 1953 movie directed by the legendary Billy Wilder entitled *Stalag 17*. The writers of that film—Donald Beban and Edmund

Trzcinski—believed the similarities between the two projects were striking enough to sue for copyright infringement. The judge, however, dismissed the case, citing the fact that the film was deadly serious, while the TV show was a comedy.

The fact that many of the actors were Jewish survivors of Nazi terror provided legitimacy and justification for the decision of CBS to place the show on the air. Klemperer had fled the Nazis, along with his father, noted composer Otto Klemperer. Banner had been imprisoned in a concentration camp, as had Robert Clary, who played French prisoner of war Louis LeBeau. The actors who portrayed German superior officers Albert Burkhalter (Leon Askin) and Wolfgang Hochstetter (Howard Caine) were also Jewish.

The American resistance in the show was headed by star character Colonel Robert Hogan (Bob Crane), whose analytic mind and craftiness resulted in schemes that repeatedly thwarted the plans of Klink and his commanders. Hogan became one of the few characters in the history of the American sitcom to kill, as he did a number of Germans during the course of the show. Fellow prisoners like LeBeau, Corporal Peter Newkirk (played by future *Family Feud* host Richard Dawson), Sergeant James Kinchloe (played by Ivan Dixon, one of the first regular black cast members on American television), and Sergeant Andrew Carter (Larry Hovis) aided Hogan in foiling the Germans.

The prisoners understood their importance to the Allied war effort, which is one reason why they showed no desire to escape. Another is that Stalag 13 bore no resemblance to the prisoner of war camps run by the Nazis in World War II. It boasted such amenities as a barber shop, a steam room, and a French chef who prepared delightful meals. But then, it was the era of escapism on American television and the farther from reality *Hogan's Heroes* became, the less it reminded viewers of the most destructive war in the history of mankind.

The Rise and Fall of Bob Crane

The 1978 murder of Bob Crane remains one of the great mysteries in American entertainment history. Crane was found with a cord wrapped around his neck and the unmistakable signs of having taken brutal blows to the head. The killer has yet to be determined, but Crane's death ended what had been an accomplished career with a promising future.

In 1949, Crane married high school sweetheart Anne Terzian, with whom he had three children. He emerged as the premier morning drive radio host in Los Angeles, interviewing such celebrities as Marilyn Monroe, Frank Sinatra, and Bob Hope before landing acting roles in such shows as *The Twilight Zone* and *The Dick Van Dyke Show* in the early 1960s. All seemed well when he was cast as the lead in *Hogan's Heroes*.

But there was a seedier side to Crane that would eventually cost him his life. He was a notorious womanizer and, as the investigation into his murder revealed, quite kinky in his sexual exploits. He had a penchant for videotaping his sexual activities and playing drums at topless bars in Los Angeles. It has been speculated that his reputation (he was on his second marriage at the time of his death) cost him movie and television gigs.

They Said It

Klink: [after Newkirk and Carter are found near the camp fence] Schultz, into the cooler they go. Throw away the key.
Carter: Don't we get a trial or anything?
Klink: This is Germany. Although I do appreciate your sense of humor.

Schultz: Colonel Hogan, if you ever escape . . .
Hogan: Yeah?
Schultz: Be a good fellow and take me with you.

Major Awards

EMMY AWARD WINS (2)

1968 (1): Outstanding Performance by an Actor in a Supporting Role in a Comedy (Werner Klemperer)
1969 (1): Outstanding Performance by an Actor in a Supporting Role in a Comedy (Werner Klemperer)

EMMY AWARD NOMINATIONS, IN ADDITION TO WINS (10)

1966 (3): Outstanding Comedy Series; Outstanding Continued Performance by an Actor in a Leading Role in a Comedy Series (Bob Crane); Outstanding Performance by an Actor in a Supporting Role in a Comedy (Werner Klemperer)
1967 (3): Outstanding Comedy Series; Outstanding Continued Performance by an Actor in a Leading Role in a Comedy Series (Bob Crane); Outstanding Performance by an Actor in a Supporting Role in a Comedy (Werner Klemperer)
1968 (3): Outstanding Comedy Series; Outstanding Performance by an Actress in a Supporting Role in a Comedy (Nita Talbot); Outstanding Achievement in Cinematography
1970 (1): Outstanding Performance by an Actor in a Supporting Role in a Comedy (Werner Klemperer)

Further Reading

Graysmith, Robert. *The Murder of Bob Crane: Who Killed the Star of Hogan's Heroes?* New York: Crown Publishing, 1993.
Shandley, Robert R. *Hogan's Heroes.* Detroit, MI: Wayne State University Press, 2011.

✶ **56** ✶

The Monkees

(1966–1968)

Cast: Davy Jones (Davy Jones), Mike Nesmith (Mike Nesmith), Peter
Tork (Peter Tork), Micky Dolenz (Micky Dolenz)

Created by: Executive producers Bob Rafelson and Bert Schneider

Network: NBC

First Air Date: September 12, 1966

Last Air Date: August 19, 1968

Broadcast History:
September 12, 1966–August 19, 1968: Monday at 7:30–8:00 PM

Seasons: 2

Episodes: 58

Ratings History: Never in Top 30

Overview

Perhaps the influence of the Beatles was felt less in the world of television than
in other aspects of American culture. The most important rock band in history
changed music, fashion, and philosophy more than they did the fare on the small
screen. There was, however, one notable exception. Their impact was all-pervasive
in the creation of the Monkees—whose level of popularity as a pop band could not
have been possible without the success of their albeit short-lived namesake sitcom.
The show was inspired by the free-form style of the first Beatles movie, *A Hard
Day's Night* (1964), which features rapid pacing, distorted focus, quick cutaways,

Davy Jones, Micky Dolenz, Peter Tork, and Mike Nesmith. *NBC/Photofest ©NBC*

fast and slow motion, and Fab Four hits interspersed within the action in appealing to the rock and roll generation. The Monkees followed suit just as the Beatles were shedding the last remnants of their wholesome, mop-top image to begin the musical foray into psychedelia.

Monkeemania was born not in the garage, where other 1960s bands made up of teenage buddies honed their skills, but of a test-tube approach. Each member was chosen as a result of auditions. The survivors were cute, diminutive Davy Jones; beanie-hatted, thoughtful Mike Nesmith; floppy-haired, babylike blond Peter Tork; and the manic Micky Dolenz. They were put together for the show, not for their musical talents. In fact, they neither wrote their own songs nor played their own instruments. Such might not have been the case had future *Buffalo Springfield* and *Crosby, Stills, Nash, and Young* singer/songwriter Stephen Stills, who was far more talented musically, agreed to be one of the quartet. He sought to keep publishing rights to his songs, which was denied, so he recommended his roommate Tork.

Their personalities and looks proved attractive, particularly to teenybopper girls, and the tunes written by such accomplished songwriters as Neil Diamond and the team of Tommy Boyce and Bobby Hart emerged as smash hits. Catchy numbers the likes of "Last Train to Clarksville," "I'm a Believer," "Daydream Believer," "A Little Bit Me, a Little Bit You," and "Pleasant Valley Sunday" soared to the top of the charts. Meanwhile, the humor and frenzied pace of the sitcom itself resonated with kids and critics alike. Occasional interviews with the band members used as filler provided thoughtful moments.

The show snagged an Emmy for Outstanding Comedy Series after its first season, and director James Frawley garnered another in each of its two years on the air. The show ran for only those two seasons before The Monkees grew discontented with their roles and sought, mostly in vain, to prove themselves as songwriters and musicians. That decision led to cancellation. Nesmith managed to make his mark musically, having in 1965 written "Different Drum," which Linda Ronstadt and the Stone Poneys turned into a hit two years later.

Although the original program has long been forgotten, subsequent generations have embraced the Monkees and their music. Their continued popularity motivated the creation of a new Monkees band and show in 1987, but the whole operation closed down after thirteen quite forgettable episodes.

A Purple Haze on a Pleasant Valley Sunday

The worst mismatch in the history of rock and roll concerts? It had to be brilliant psychedelic guitar wizard Jimi Hendrix opening for The Monkees for seven shows in the summer of 1967. While Hendrix played, the unappreciative teenybopper kids called out for their far less talented idols to replace him on stage. "Jimi would amble onto the stage, fire up the amps, and break out into 'Purple Haze,' and the audience would instantly drown him out with 'We want Daaavy!'" Micky Dolenz once recalled. "God, it was embarrassing."

Did You Know?

Bette Nesmith Graham, mother of Mike Nesmith, invented Wite-Out. She called it "Mistake Out" when she first marketed it in 1956. It quickly became a widely used office product.

They Said It

> **Mike:** Welcome to Swineville, Peter, a happy, sleepy, little hillbilly town where seemingly innocent, naïve people turn just like that . . . to a vengeful, hateful mob!
> **Peter:** How do you know that?
> **Mike:** Because these are my people.

Major Awards

EMMY AWARD WINS (2)

1967 (2): Outstanding Comedy Series; Outstanding Directorial Achievement in Comedy (James Frawley for "Royal Flush")

EMMY AWARD NOMINATION, IN ADDITION TO WINS (1)

1968 (1): Outstanding Directorial Achievement in Comedy (James Frawley for "The Devil and Peter Tork")

Further Reading

Dolenz, Micky. *I'm a Believer: My Life of Monkees, Music, and Madness.* New York: Cooper Square Press, 2004.

Lefcowitz, Eric. *Monkee Business: The Revolutionary Made-for-TV Band.* Port Washington, NY: Retrofuture Products, 2010.

Sandoval, Andrew. *The Monkees: The Day-to-Day Story of the 60s TV Pop Sensation.* San Diego, CA: Thunder Bay Press, 2005.

✳ **57** ✳

Rhoda

(1974–1978)

Cast: Valerie Harper (Rhoda Morgenstern Gerard), Julie Kavner (Brenda Morgenstern), Lorenzo Music (Carlton the Doorman), David Groh (Joe Gerard), Nancy Walker (Ida Morgenstern), Harold Gould (Martin Morgenstern)

Created by: Executive producers and writers James L. Brooks and Allan Burns

Network: CBS

First Air Date: September 9, 1974

Last Air Date: December 9, 1978

Broadcast History:
September 9, 1974–September 1975: Monday at 9:30–10:00 PM
September 1975–January 1977: Monday at 8:00–8:30 PM
January 1977–September 1978: Sunday at 8:00–8:30 PM
September 1978–December 9, 1978: Saturday at 8:00–8:30 PM

Seasons: 5

Episodes: 106

Ratings History: 1974–1975 (6), 1975–1976 (7), 1976–1977 (not in Top 30), 1977–1978 (25), 1978–1979 (not in Top 30)

Valerie Harper, Nancy Walker, and Julie Kavner. *CBS/Photofest ©CBS*

Overview

It takes a special show to turn an unseen character into a household name, but Carlton the Doorman became a mini celebrity for his role on *Rhoda*. Granted, the man who answered the buzzer in the apartment building on this sitcom sounding either drunk or stoned didn't become a star for his voice. Lorenzo Music was already one of the top producers in television, and he assumed that role in twenty-five episodes of *Rhoda*; no one else gained stardom in this *Mary Tyler Moore Show* spin-off. Title character Rhoda (Valerie Harper) had already established herself on that sitcom, and sister Julie Kavner didn't earn fame until she became the voice of Marge Simpson on *The Simpsons* eleven years after *Rhoda* bit the dust. Despite strong competition in the mid- to late 1970s from the likes of *All in the Family*, *Sanford and Son*, *The Mary Tyler Moore Show*, and *M*A*S*H*, *Rhoda* blossomed into a ratings hit in its first two seasons before several severe detours in the story line, it can be argued, took a toll on viewership.

Rhoda left Minneapolis to return to New York and fell in love with Joe Gerard (David Groh), the divorced father of 10-year-old son Donny (Todd Turquand) and owner of a wrecking company. She had blossomed from an insecure, slightly overweight woman into a self-assured beauty by the time she arrived in the Big Apple, where she had been born and raised. Rhoda, who had been desperately seeking romance on *The Mary Tyler Moore Show*, first moved in with Brenda before marrying Joe in a one-hour special episode broadcast in the second month of the first season.

It was one happy occasion for mother Ida (Nancy Walker) and father Martin (Harold Gould), perhaps the two most engaging and intriguing characters on the program. Walker had carved her niche as Rhoda's neurotic, overprotective mother in several episodes of *The Mary Tyler Moore Show* before earning three Emmy nominations and two nominations for Golden Globes for playing the same part in the spin-off.

Rhoda and Joe moved into the apartment building (complete with Carlton the Doorman) in which Brenda and Rhoda had previously resided, but the life of a housewife suited neither Rhoda nor the comedic success of the show, so she reverted to her Minneapolis days and opened a window dressing business. That still didn't satisfy the powers that be, who began focusing more on the single, unconfident, and overweight Brenda and her pursuit of love and happiness. The show, however, was not called *Brenda*. Despite high ratings, the producers decided the life of a single woman would create more opportunities for humor than the life of a married one. Writer/producer Charlotte Brown complained in an issue of *TV Guide* that life was too idyllic for Rhoda and that the character had lost her vulnerability and role as an underdog.

So, despite the outward appearance of a happy marriage, Rhoda and Joe were separated and later divorced. The latter was soon phased out and, lo and behold, the ratings plummeted. The show struggled to find its way. Many of the episodes spotlighted Rhoda and Brenda seeking men together. A strange and seemingly unrealistic pairing had Rhoda developing a relationship with vain, arrogant Vegas entertainer Johnny Venture (Michael Delano), while Brenda dated a musician from the same town who was seen in only seven episodes during the course of three seasons.

More shifts in the story line were in the offing as the new season rolled around in 1977. Rhoda accepted work at a struggling costume company, Brenda landed a new boyfriend, and Martin left Ida. Fans of the show complained that changes were made for the sake of change and that realism was tossed out the window. The show was finally cancelled in 1978, leaving some to wonder why the producers didn't leave well enough alone and maintain an original premise that landed *Rhoda* in the heady position of number six in the Nielsen ratings.

No Chance to Groh in Prime Time

After being written out of *Rhoda* in 1977, David Groh never landed further work as a prime-time TV regular. He did play D. L. Brock, one of Bobbie Spencer's husbands, in *General Hospital* in the mid-1980s before his character was killed off. Groh, who worked on Broadway as well, appeared on such shows as *Police Story*, *Fantasy Island*, *Kate & Allie*, *Murder She Wrote*, *Melrose Place*, *Baywatch*, and *Law and Order*.

Did You Know?

Rhoda debuted on September 9, 1974, to the highest Nielsen rating for the week. The seventh episode, in which Rhoda marries Joe, attracted an estimated 50 million viewers.

They Said It

Rhoda: [in the opening credits] I decided to move out of the house when I was twenty-four. My mother still refers to this as the time I ran away from home.

Major Awards

EMMY AWARD WINS (2)

1975 (1): Outstanding Lead Actress in a Comedy Series (Valerie Harper)
1978 (1): Outstanding Continuing Performance by a Supporting Actress in a Comedy Series (Julie Kavner)

EMMY AWARD NOMINATIONS, IN ADDITION TO WINS (15)

1975 (4): Outstanding Comedy Series; Outstanding Continuing Performance by a Supporting Actress in a Comedy Series (Julie Kavner); Outstanding Continuing Performance by a Supporting Actress in a Comedy Series (Nancy Walker); Outstanding Writing in a Comedy Series (Norman Barasch, Carroll Moore, David Lloyd, Lorenzo Music, Allan Burns, James L. Brooks, and David Davis for "Rhoda's Wedding")

1976 (4): Outstanding Lead Actress in a Comedy Series (Valerie Harper); Outstanding Continuing Performance by a Supporting Actress in a Comedy Series (Julie Kavner); Outstanding Continuing Performance by a Supporting Actress in a Comedy Series (Nancy Walker); Outstanding Single Performance by a Supporting Actress in a Comedy or Drama Series (Ruth Gordon for "Kiss Your Epaulets Good-bye")

1977 (3): Outstanding Lead Actress in a Comedy Series (Valerie Harper); Outstanding Continuing Performance by a Supporting Actress in a Comedy Series (Julie Kavner); Outstanding Single Performance by a Supporting Actress in a Comedy or Drama Series (Nancy Walker for "The Separation")

1978 (4): Outstanding Lead Actress in a Comedy Series (Valerie Harper); Outstanding Continuing Performance by a Supporting Actress in a Comedy Series (Nancy Walker); Outstanding Lead Actor for a Single Appearance in a Drama or Comedy Series (Judd Hirsch for "Rhoda Likes Mike"); Outstanding Single Performance by a Supporting Actor in a Comedy or Drama Series (Harold Gould for "Happy Anniversary")

GOLDEN GLOBE WIN (1)

1975 (1): Best TV Actress, Musical/Comedy (Valerie Harper)

GOLDEN GLOBE NOMINATIONS, IN ADDITION TO WIN (8)

1975 (1): Best Supporting Actress, Television (Julie Kavner)
1976 (3): Best TV Actress, Musical/Comedy (Valerie Harper); Best Supporting Actress, Television (Julie Kavner); Best Supporting Actress, Television (Nancy Walker)
1977 (2): Best Supporting Actress, Television (Julie Kavner); Best Supporting Actress, Television (Anne Meara)
1979 (2): Best TV Actress in a Supporting Role (Julie Kavner); Best TV Actress in a Supporting Role (Nancy Walker)

Further Reading

Armstrong, Jennifer Keishin. *Mary and Lou and Rhoda and Ted: And All the Brilliant Minds Who Made* The Mary Tyler Moore Show *a Classic*. New York: Simon & Schuster, 2013.
Harper, Valerie. *I, Rhoda*. New York: Gallery Books, 2013.

✳ **58** ✳

The Addams Family

(1964–1966)

Cast: Carolyn Jones (Morticia Addams), John Astin (Gomez Addams), Jackie Coogan (Uncle Fester), Ted Cassidy (Lurch), Blossom Rock (Grandmama), Ken Weatherwax (Pugsley Addams), Lisa Loring (Wednesday Addams), Felix Silla (Cousin Itt)

Created by: Writer Charles Addams

Network: ABC

First Air Date: September 18, 1964

Last Air Date: September 2, 1966

Broadcast History:
September 18, 1964–September 2, 1966: Friday at 8:30–9:00 PM

Seasons: 2

Episodes: 64

Ratings History: 1964–1965 (23), 1965–1966 (not in Top 30)

Overview

How many times can you laugh at Thing emerging from a box with the daily mail? How many times can you laugh at Morticia snipping off the roses and arranging the stems? How many times can you laugh watching Uncle Fester sleeping on a bed of nails? Now you know why *The Addams Family* lasted just two seasons, but they were two very funny seasons because they were a very funny, albeit creepy, family. *The Addams Family* was the brainchild of Charles Addams, who had originally created the macabre group as a comic strip in *New Yorker* magazine, which began publishing it in 1938. It was an ideal television adaptation for the escapist programming of the 1960s.

Front row, from left: John Astin, Lisa Loring, Carolyn Jones, and Ken Weatherwax; back row: Ted Cassidy. *ABC/Photofest ©ABC*

Unlike the happy-but-ghoulish Munsters (which, ironically, ran the same two years on CBS), who were offshoots of such monsters as Frankenstein and Dracula, the Addams family consisted of kooky people. Even pile-of-hair Cousin Itt (Felix Silla) was a human with a sped-up voice (it was once slowed down to reveal he was a fine Shakespearean actor). Okay, Thing was only a hand, but he did have human feelings.

The head of the family was Gomez (John Astin), who exuded passion about everything in his life, including his stock (Consolidated Fuzz), his yoga (he spent much of his time smoking a cigar while standing on his head or swinging from the chandelier), and his shapely wife Morticia (Carolyn Jones), who drove him crazy when she spoke French. He was aflame with desire for his spouse, which she tempered to bring him back into focus with the matters at hand and in consideration that this was 1960s television. Morticia was far more calm and sensible, at least in an Addams line of thinking, as she spent much of her time feeding the lion and knitting three-armed sweaters for kin.

Then there was the suspicious, kooky, bald-as-a-cue ball Fester, played to the hilt by Jackie Coogan. His solution to any problem with a guest was to "shoot him in the back," and there were plenty of problems with guests from the moment the front gates clanged shut behind them and towering harpsichord-playing butler Lurch (Ted Cassidy), whose face cracked when he tried to manage a rare smile, removed their hats within seconds of their arrival. One can only imagine their shock when Gomez began puffing on a cigar that he pulled out of his shirt pocket without lighting it. Or when he showed them his model trains, only to place them on a collision course and, with great anticipation, blow them up upon impact. Or when Thing popped out of his box to greet them. Or when a roaring lion came traipsing down the stairs. Or when Morticia began to smoke—literally. And if they were unfortunate to stay for dinner, they were in for a real treat with the dishes prepared by Grandmama (Blossom Rock), for instance, eye of newt or puree of aardvark.

Son Pugsley (Ken Weatherwax) and daughter Wednesday (Lisa Loring), who explained to guests what happened to her beloved headless Marie Antoinette doll by running her finger past her throat, were happy until they were forced to attend school, where they were read fairy tales that painted witches and goblins in a negative light. Thus inspired, Morticia embarked on authoring children's books based on experience that promoted love for such beings, but in an attempt to turn his wife away from writing, Gomez turned the tables by changing her words and entitling the book *A Treasury of Mean Witches, Evil Giants, Wicked Goblins, and Other Bedtime Stories*.

The show inspired two *Addams Family* movies in the early 1990s. The first is easily the finer effort. It features a Thing that actually flits about the home and a cast, including Angelica Huston as Morticia and Raul Julia as Gomez, that lives up to the standards set by the wonderful Jones and Astin.

Kid Coogan

Jackie Coogan was one of the most accomplished child actors in the early years of film. He was a mere seven years old when he played his most famous role as the lead character in *The Kid*. He also starred in film adaptations of such literary classics as *Oliver Twist*, *Huckleberry Finn*, and *Tom Sawyer*.

Did You Know?

John Astin, whose second of three wives was Academy Award winner Patty Duke, landed parts in three episodes of *Rod Serling's Night Gallery*. His character was killed in all of them, and he wound up in hell in two of them.

They Said It

Gomez: [during a flashback in which he just met Morticia] Has anyone ever told you, you have the softest brown eyes?
Morticia: No. Besides, my eyes are blue.
Gomez: No wonder nobody's ever told you.

Gomez: [to a magazine photographer] *Strike Magazine* has been one of our favorites.
Morticia: We simply devour it from cover to cover.
Uncle Fester: Aw, it's delicious.

Gomez: The L stands for Lucifer.
Morticia: Very appropriate for a politician.

Major Awards

None

Further Reading

Cox, Stephen. *The Addams Chronicles*. Nashville, TN: Cumberland House, 1998.
Miserocchi, Kevin. *Charles Addams: The Addams Family: An Evolution*. Petaluma, CA: Pomegranate Communications, 2010.

✴ **59** ✴

Designing Women

(1986–1993)

Cast: Dixie Carter (Julia Sugarbaker), Delta Burke (Suzanne Sugarbaker), Annie Potts (Mary Jo Shively), Jean Smart (Charlene Frazier Stillfield), Meshach Taylor (Anthony Bouvier), Jan Hooks (Carlene Frazier Dobber), Julia Duffy (Allison Sugarbaker), Alice Ghostley (Bernice Clifton), Judith Ivey (B. J. Poteet)

Created by: Writer Linda Bloodworth-Thomason and director Harry Thomason

Network: CBS

First Air Date: September 29, 1986

Last Air Date: May 24, 1993

Broadcast History:
    September 29, 1986–November 1986: Monday at 9:30–10:00 PM
    December 1986–January 1987: Thursday at 9:30–10:00 PM
    February 1987: Sunday at 9:00–9:30 PM
    March 1987–February 1988: Monday at 9:30–10:00 PM
    February 1988–June 1988: Monday at 8:30–9:00 PM
    June 1988–September 1989: Monday at 9:30–10:00 PM
    September 1989–October 1989: Monday at 10:00–10:30 PM
    November 1989–September 1992: Monday at 9:30–10:00 PM
    September 1992–May 1993: Friday at 9:00–9:30 PM
    May 1993: Monday at 9:00–10:00 PM

Seasons: 7

Episodes: 164

Ratings History: 1986–1987 (not in Top 30), 1987–1988 (not in Top 30), 1988–1989 (not in Top 30), 1989–1990 (22), 1990–1991 (11), 1991–1992 (6), 1992–1993 (not in Top 30)

Annie Potts, Jean Smart, Delta Burke, and Dixie Carter. *CBS/Photofest ©CBS*

Overview

Sometimes the comic timing between two actors in a new sitcom is so precise and their interaction so natural that it seems as if they had worked together before. Such was the case with Delta Burke and Dixie Carter on *Designing Women*. The only difference is that they had indeed worked with one another before. The pair had teamed up four years earlier in the albeit unsuccessful 1982 sitcom *Filthy Rich*. That show was created by Linda Bloodworth-Thomason, who had not forgotten their chemistry when she wrote *Designing Women*. She cast Burke as fading glamour girl Suzanne Sugarbaker and Carter as passionately liberal widowed sister Julia Sugarbaker, who was as outspoken a feminist as any character in television history.

The two helped run a decorating business called Sugarbakers in Atlanta, Georgia, along with Charlene Frazier Stillfield, played by Jean Smart, and Mary Jo Shively, portrayed by the always likeable Annie Potts. The dialogue, however, rarely touched upon work, but rather personal relationships both inside and outside the group, which proved to be the driving force of this character-driven comedy. The most intriguing of the four was three-time divorcee Suzanne, who sought desperately to maintain the sexiness that had made her a beauty pageant contestant, and who flirted with men in an attempt to convince herself that she had lost nothing. The most prominent supporting character was former con Anthony Bouvier (Meshach Taylor), who played the role of the delivery man for the business who was rarely seen in action and later became a partner.

Designing Women did not set the world on fire when it debuted in late September 1986, but it attracted a loyal audience that grew when CBS found it a permanent home on Monday nights in the winter of 1987. By 1989, it had jumped to number twenty-two in the Nielsen ratings, and it peaked at number six before dropping out of the Top 30 in its final season.

The story lines expanded in time as Charlene's marriage to U.S. Air Force captain Bill Stillfield, coincidentally or not, matched the time frame of the ratings boost in 1989. The couple added a baby girl named Olivia. But Smart was not long for the show. Her character was replaced by sister Carlene (Jan Hooks), who arrived in Atlanta to help take care of Olivia and remained on the program after Charlene was written off with the explanation that she had moved to England to be with Bill, who was stationed in that country.

Meanwhile, tragedy struck, as Julia's boyfriend Reese (Hal Holbrook) died of a heart attack. By that time the show was on its last legs despite still-strong ratings. It has been speculated that its demise was the inability of Burke to keep her weight down, thereby making it difficult for the writers to continue portraying her as a sexy character. Her photos were splashed across the tabloids until she was written off the show in 1991, with the explanation that she had moved to Japan and sold her share of the business to cousin Allison, played by Julia Duffy, who had proven to be far more humorous as the wonderfully childish, spoiled Stephanie Vanderkellen in *Newhart*.

Designing Women targeted female viewership with great success. Its premise has been compared to that of *The Golden Girls*, only with a younger cast, but it lacked the warmth and charm, which perhaps was never intended. Critics have called it a bit preachy in its feminism, but it achieved success in creating strong female characters with distinct personalities and motivations.

Bringing in the Vets

Two veterans of American entertainment strengthened the cast of *Designing Women*. One was Alice Ghostley, who played an elderly and peculiar friend of the Sugarbakers named Bernice Clifton. The Tony Award-winning actress, who generally played rather meek and scatterbrained characters, performed in such notable 1960s films as *To Kill a Mockingbird*, *Please Don't Eat the Daisies*, and *The Graduate* before landing recurring roles in television sitcoms *Bewitched*, *Designing Women*, and *Evening Shade*.

Hal Holbrook starred in *Evening Shade*, but he had gained his greatest acclaim well before that as an actor in miniseries and TV specials. He won an Emmy for his role in *Pueblo* (1973) and his portrayal of Abraham Lincoln in *Lincoln* (1974). Holbrook had also earned one for Outstanding Continued Performance by an Actor in a Leading Role in a Dramatic Series in 1970 for his work in *The Bold Ones: The Senator*. The roles in *Designing Women* and *Evening Shade* proved to be a departure for him, as he had previously performed mostly in dramas, historical and otherwise.

Did You Know?

Both Jean Smart and Delta Burke married men they met on the set of *Designing Women*. Smart wed Richard Gilliland, who played Mary Jo's boyfriend. Burke married guest star Gerald McRaney, who was portraying one of Suzanne's three ex-husbands.

They Said It

Julia: Suzanne, if sex were fast food, there'd be an arch over your bed.

Mary Jo: Anthony, where have you been all morning?
Anthony: The question should be, 'Where have I been all night?' I'll tell you where I've been. I was locked in the basement of Suzanne's house!
Allison: Oh, were you locked in there? I thought I heard something.
Anthony: Did it sound anything like someone shouting, 'Let me out of here, bitch!?'

Major Awards

EMMY AWARD WIN (1)

1988 (1): Outstanding Achievement in Hairstyling for a Series (Judy Crown and Monique De Sart for "I'll Be Seeing You")

EMMY AWARD NOMINATIONS, IN ADDITION TO WIN (17)

1987 (2): Outstanding Directing in a Comedy Series (Jack Shea for "The Beauty Contest"); Outstanding Costume Design for a Series (Cliff Chally for "Oh Suzannah")
1988 (2): Outstanding Writing in a Comedy Series (Linda Bloodworth-Thomason for "Killing All the Right People"); Outstanding Editing for a Series, Multi-Camera Production (Roger Bondelli for "Killing All the Right People")
1989 (3): Outstanding Comedy Series; Outstanding Supporting Actor in a Comedy Series (Meshach Taylor); Outstanding Costume Design for a Series (Cliff Chally for "Come on and Marry Me, Bill")
1990 (6): Outstanding Comedy Series; Outstanding Lead Actress in a Comedy Series (Delta Burke); Outstanding Directing in a Comedy Series (Harry Thomason for "They Shoot Fat Women, Don't They?"); Outstanding Costume Design for a Series (Cliff Chally for "The Rowdy Girls"); Outstanding Editing for a Series, Multi-Camera Production (Judy Burke for "The First Day of the Last Decade of the Entire 20th Century"); Outstanding Sound Mixing for a Comedy Series or

a Special (Larry Lasota, Anthony Constantini, Doug Gray, and Rick Himot for "Tornado Watch")

1991 (3): Outstanding Comedy Series; Outstanding Lead Actress in a Comedy Series (Delta Burke); Outstanding Costume Design for a Series (Cliff Chally for "Keep the Home Fires Burning")

1992 (1): Outstanding Supporting Actress in a Comedy Series (Alice Ghostley)

GOLDEN GLOBE NOMINATIONS (2)

1990 (1): Best TV Series, Musical/Comedy
1991 (1): Best TV Series, Musical/Comedy

Further Reading

Bernstein, Fred. "Pulling Itself out of the Ratings Waste Heap, *Designing Women* Becomes TV's Trashy New Smash." *People Weekly*, April 20, 1987. Available online at www.people .com/people/archive/article/0,,20096104,00.html.

✳ **60** ✳

NewsRadio

(1995–1999)

Cast: Dave Foley (Dave Nelson), Stephen Root (Jimmy James), Andy Dick (Matthew Brock), Maura Tierney (Lisa Miller), Vicki Lewis (Beth), Joe Rogan (Joe Garrelli), Phil Hartman (Bill McNeal), Khandi Alexander (Catherine Duke), Jon Lovitz (Max Lewis)

Created by: Executive producer and writer Paul Simms

Network: NBC

First Air Date: March 21, 1995

Last Air Date: July 13, 1999

Broadcast History:
March 21, 1995–January 1996: Tuesday at 8:30–9:00 PM
January 1996–July 1996: Sunday at 8:30–9:00 PM
June 1996–August 1996: Tuesday at 8:30–9:00 PM
September 1996–February 1997: Wednesday at 9:00–9:30 PM
March 1997–July 1997: Wednesday at 8:00–8:30 PM
June 1997–August 1997: Sunday at 8:30–9:00 PM
July 1997–March 1998: Tuesday at 8:30–9:00 PM
March 1998–May 1998: Wednesday at 8:00–8:30 PM
May 1998–August 1998: Tuesday at 8:30–9:00 PM
September 1998–December 1998: Wednesday at 9:30–10:00 PM
November 1998–July 1999: Tuesday at 8:30–9:00 PM

Seasons: 4

Episodes: 97

Ratings History: Never in Top 30

Vicki Lewis, Andy Dick, Dave Foley, Maura Tierney, Stephen Root, Phil Hartman, and Khandi Alexander; seated front: Joe Rogan. *NBC/Photofest ©NBC*

Overview

If not for the availability of one former *Saturday Night Live* comedian to replace another, the run of *NewsRadio* might have ended prematurely. It didn't last long enough as it was for its loyal fans. The stunning and tragic murder of *SNL* alum Phil Hartman in 1998 nearly killed the show, but Jon Lovitz came to the rescue and *NewsRadio* remained on the air for another season. All good things come to an end, but at least this one survived one more year.

Following the lead of such acclaimed sitcoms as *Taxi*, *Barney Miller*, and *Cheers*, the scenes in *NewsRadio* rarely strayed from the newsroom. The story line revolved around the all-news radio station WNYX in New York and its news director Dave Nelson (Dave Foley), who just came from Wisconsin and was overwhelmed by his responsibilities and domineering station owner Jimmy James (Stephen Root), but resolute in his desire to make the most of his opportunity. His efforts were in vain, however, as he slowly lost his sanity in the wake of the wackiness and ineptitude that he was forced to deal with in one episode after another.

The fast pace of the show gave it a slapstick quality that the television comedy world had abandoned for a generation. It also brought out the talents of Hartman, who played self-absorbed anchor Bill McNeal; partner Catherine Duke (Khandi Alexander); and oversensitive, incompetent reporter Matthew Brock (Andy Dick).

Although the cameras never intruded on the home lives of the characters, their personal relationships were explored in depth. Included was a hot-and-cold romance between Dave and sharp news writer Lisa Miller (Maura Tierney), whose interest in her boss was tempered by her feelings that she should have been given his job. That story line ended abruptly in the last season when Lisa married Johnny Johnson (Patrick Warburton).

The writers sometimes even strayed into fantasy plot lines, giving the sitcom a surreal flavor. They also refused to ignore Hartman's demise and simply place a new face into the McNeal role. The setting for the first episode of the last season was his funeral. Each of his coworkers shed tears, except for the always-oblivious Matthew, who was under the impression that Bill had been sent to Afghanistan. The writers further recognized their fallen comrade by replacing him with Max, who earned the position because he had been Bill's close friend and colleague, just as Lovitz was to Hartman when they worked together on *Saturday Night Live*.

Not that Max worked out particularly well. He was not only unprofessional, but as was eventually revealed, his name wasn't really Max. The ultimate phony (a perfect role for Lovitz) used aliases and different personas in the thirty-seven jobs he had held in the past twenty years.

The loss of Hartman did not doom *NewsRadio* immediately, but the show had arguably lost its most popular character and never fully recovered. Its short, four-year run made it a bit of a flash-in-the-pan when examined in the lens of television history, and its viewership was small in comparison to some of the most recognized sitcoms of its era, but many of its fans still consider it one of the most creative shows ever produced.

The Emerging Star

Patrick Warburton had yet to emerge as a TV star when he played Johnny Johnson, the love interest and eventual husband of Lisa on *NewsRadio*, but he had made a mark a few years earlier playing the understated, dimwitted David Puddy, on-again, off-again boyfriend of Elaine Benes on *Seinfeld*. Warburton had also acted in such notable sitcoms as *Murphy Brown*, *Designing Women*, and *Ellen*, but he didn't land a major part in a successful comedy until 2007, when he assumed the role of Jeff Bingham in *Rules of Engagement*.

Did You Know?

The name of each album produced by legendary rock band *Led Zeppelin* was used as an episode title in *NewsRadio*.

They Said It

Dave: [reading cards from the complaint box] 'You suck.' 'You suck.' 'Howard Stern rules.' 'If you can read this you are a dork.' 'Coupon for one free kiss from Joe if you are a girl.' 'We need more complaint cards.' 'Coupon for one free kiss from Joe if you are a guy.'

Joe: Hey.

Dave: [pulling out a fortune cookie slip] 'You will go on a journey, happy long time.' 'Matthew is a moron.' 'No I'm not.' 'Yes you are.' 'No I'm not infinity.' 'Yes you are infinity plus one.' And this one, 'I have doobie in my funk,' which I assume is some sort of reference to the Parliament Funkadelic song, 'Chocolate City.' Uh, 'You got peanut butter in my chocolate. You got chocolate in my peanut butter. Together they taste like crap.' 'Matthew has been staring at me all day . . . and I like it.' I don't think I get this one, it says, 'I try to be good hard-worker-man, but refrigemater so messy, so so messy.'

Lisa: I think that one's probably from Milos, the janitor.

Dave: Oh. Refrigem . . . oh, then that one's legitimate. [continuing reading the complaint cards] 'Who's the black private dick who's the sex machine with all the chicks.' Bill, Beth, Lisa, Matthew, Joe: 'SHAFT.'

Bill: I thought we'd all enjoy that.

Dave: [reading one last card] And, 'Help, I'm being held prisoner in a complaint box,' which is actually kinda funny.

Major Awards

EMMY AWARD WIN (1)

1998 (1): Outstanding Costuming for a Series (Luellyn Harper and Carol Lupo for "Sinking Ship")

EMMY AWARD NOMINATIONS, IN ADDITION TO WIN (2)

1997 (1): Outstanding Costuming for a Series (Luellyn Harper for "Awards Show")
1998 (1): Outstanding Supporting Actor in a Comedy Series (Phil Hartman)

Further Reading

Ashby, Emily. "NewsRadio." *Common Sense Media*. Available online at www.commonsense media.org/tv-reviews/newsradio.

✴ **61** ✴

Mary Hartman, Mary Hartman

(1976–1978)

Cast: Louise Lasser (Mary Hartman), Greg Mullavey (Tom Hartman), Mary Kay Place (Loretta Haggers), Graham Jarvis (Charlie Haggers), Dody Goodman (Martha Shumway), Philip Bruns (George Shumway), Debralee Scott (Cathy Shumway), Claudia Lamb (Heather Hartman), Bruce Solomon (Sergeant Dennis Foley), Victor Kilian (Raymond Larkin)

Created by: Executive producer Norman Lear

Network: Syndicated

First Air Date: January 6, 1976

Last Air Date: 1978

Seasons: 2

Episodes: 325

Ratings History: Never in Top 30

Overview

Was nothing sacred in America by the mid-1970s? Richard Nixon had besmirched the presidency. The sanctity of marriage had been destroyed by a skyrocketing divorce rate. Even Babe Ruth was turning over in his grave as Hank Aaron had wiped out his home run record, which had stood for a half-century. But satirizing the soap opera—the most serious of American television programming? *That* was going too far. And it sure was funny.

TV viewers could hardly believe their eyes and ears in 1976, when they tuned into a syndicated sitcom called *Mary Hartman, Mary Hartman*. Why was it syndicated? Because show creator Norman Lear pitched it to all the networks and was sent packing,

Standing from left: Mary Kay Place, Graham Jarvis, Greg Mullavey, Claudia Lamb, Louise Lasser, and Victor Kilian; sitting from left: Dody Goodman, Philip Bruns, and Debralee Scott. *Columbia Pictures/Photofest ©Columbia Pictures*

the words *too controversial* ringing in his ears. One might wonder how executives could turn back the man who created *All in the Family* and how that show wasn't deemed too controversial five years earlier, but that question was forever left to ponder. The networks certainly had second thoughts when Louise Lasser, who played the pigtailed title character, wound up on the covers of *Rolling Stone* and *People* magazines.

Mary Hartman, Mary Hartman never approached the level of ratings or critical acclaim as that breakthrough Lear comedy, but it did get people talking. Lear sought to create a social satire that would draw in audiences through captivating plot lines and characters. It proved to be a departure from all other sitcoms, not merely because it ran five nights a week and featured strong dramatic elements. It also exaggerated typical soap opera story lines and poked fun at American commercialism.

The gullible, dimwitted title character took all advertising claims for gospel, but her concerns about the relative merits of freeze-dried coffee and fresh perked turned out to be the least of her problems. She was burdened with factory-worker husband Tom (Greg Mullavey), who was stuck in perpetual adolescence; brooding preteen daughter Heather (Claudia Lamb), who detested her; ignorant parents George (Philip Bruns) and Martha (Dody Goodman); and crackpot grandfather Raymond Larkin (Victor Kilian).

The catastrophes came one after another. By the end of the first season, Raymond had been revealed as the "Fernwood Flasher" and had reacted to his arrest with stupefying nonchalance, Heather had been kidnapped and held hostage by a mass murderer, best friend and aspiring country singer Loretta Haggers (Mary Kay Place) had been paralyzed, George had disappeared behind the blind spot of his car's rearview mirror, Tom's high school basketball coach had drowned in a bowl of chicken soup, and child evangelist Jimmie Joe Jeeter, whose father was mayor of Fernwood, had been electrocuted by a stray television wire that landed in his bathtub. Welcome to *Green Acres* with death.

At the end of the first season, the story line took another detour when Mary was invited to New York (where she promptly got mugged) to appear on the nationally televised *David Susskind Show* for being, hilariously, "America's Typical Consumer Housewife." She suffered a nervous breakdown on the air after revealing to the world that Tom was impotent, and she then landed in a psychiatric ward. Sure, why not?

Lasser left the show, but not before she had been seduced into having an affair by local cop Dennis Foley (Bruce Solomon), who had been involved in prosecuting Raymond for revealing his private parts to the good citizens of Fernwood. Following her departure, the title of the show became *Forever Fernwood*. The George Shumway character, now played by Tab Hunter, returned with the explanation that he had fallen into a chemical vat and his body had been restored through plastic surgery.

The sitcom lost some steam before cancellation, but CBS (the first network to have rejected *Mary Hartman, Mary Hartman*) added reruns of episodes to its late-night lineup in 1980. The show had come and gone quickly, like a tornado, leaving mundane and predictable television programming in its wake.

Focus on Fernwood

The popularity of *Mary Hartman, Mary Hartman* led show creator Norman Lear to launch another satire fictionally based in Fernwood, Ohio, as a summer replacement in 1977, entitled *Fernwood 2-Night*. It was hosted with biting sarcasm and great insincerity by idiotic, insensitive Jerry Hubbard (Fred Willard) and arrogant Barth Gimble (Martin Mull). Mull had appeared in *Mary Hartman, Mary Hartman* as a wife beater who was killed off when he impaled himself on an aluminum Christmas tree. The pair invited the strangest of guests, including a housewife who was campaigning to have her aunt posthumously gain sainthood because she made wonderful raisin bread. Gimble and Hubbard also booked a Jewish person named Morton Rose, who was caught speeding through all-Protestant Fernwood. They opened up the phone lines for a "Talk to a Jew" call-in segment.

Did You Know?

Louise Lasser was married to legendary filmmaker Woody Allen for three years. She acted in several of his early films, including *Take the Money and Run* (1969), *Bananas* (1971), and *Everything You Always Wanted to Know About Sex * But Were Afraid to Ask* (1972).

They Said It

Cathy: You know, isn't it ironic that if one of us had to get it, it's a miracle it was you.

Mary: I know, I must have been born under an unlucky star. You know I have filled out entry blanks for every single drawing in the supermarket for the last twelve years, and the only thing I ever won was a coupon for a small little jar of tomato paste. But they were out of tomato paste, and by the time they got more in, my coupon had expired. And now I have venereal disease.

Major Awards

EMMY AWARD WINS (2)

1976 (1): Special Classification of Outstanding Program and Individual Achievement (writers Ann Marcus, Jerry Adelman, and Daniel Gregory Browne)

1977 (1): Outstanding Continuing Performance by a Supporting Actress in a Comedy Series (Mary Kay Place)

Emmy Award Nominations, in Addition to Wins (2)

1976 (2): Special Classification of Outstanding Program and Individual Achievement (producers Norman Lear and Viva Knight); Special Classification of Outstanding Program and Individual Achievement (Louise Lasser)

Further Reading

Lockwood, Daniel. *The Mary Hartman Story*. New York: Bolder Books, 1976.

McCormack, Ed. "Mary Hartman's Secret Recipe for Mock Cornball Surprise." *Rolling Stone Magazine*, March 25, 1976. Available online at http://maryhartmanmaryhartmanphoto graphs.yolasite.com/197603rollingstone.php.

⟡ **62** ⟡

That Girl

(1966–1971)

Cast: Marlo Thomas (Ann Marie), Ted Bessell (Donald Hollinger), Lew Parker (Lew Marie), Bernie Kopell (Jerry Bauman)

Created by: Executive producers and writers Sam Denoff and Bill Persky

Network: ABC

First Air Date: September 8, 1966

Last Air Date: September 10, 1971

Broadcast History:
   September 8, 1966–April 1967: Thursday at 9:30–10:00 PM
   April 1967–January 1969: Thursday at 9:00–9:30 PM
   February 1969–September 1970: Thursday at 8:00–8:30 PM
   September 1970–September 10, 1971: Friday at 9:00–9:30 PM

Seasons: 5

Episodes: 136

Ratings History: Never in Top 30

Overview

Mary Tyler Moore is often given credit for her contribution to the burgeoning women's movement of the late 1960s and early 1970s for playing the first television role of a woman neither tied to or dependent in any way on a man in her personal life. That acclaim is well deserved. But it must be recognized that *That Girl* star Marlo Thomas blazed a trail for Moore by portraying a single woman in Ann Marie who was motivated equally by her career as she was in maintaining a relationship with a man, in this case

Marlo Thomas and Ted Bessell. *ABC/Photofest ©ABC*

boyfriend and then fiancé Donald Hollinger (Ted Bessell). Although her pursuits as an actress were greatly failures, adding to the comic development of her character, that the story line centered on her professional yearnings forever changed the role of women on television. The daughter of entertainment icon Danny Thomas also emerged as one of the most outspoken advocates of women's rights in the television industry.

Ann arrived in New York City from rural Brewster, New York. She landed bit parts in plays and commercials but spent the entire run of the sitcom seeking her big break in vain with passion and enthusiasm that never waned. She continued her quest with zeal despite losing out on big role after big role in ways that might have led viewers to believe she was destined for failure, for example, the episode in which getting her finger caught in the kitchen sink causes her to miss her Broadway debut. Her inability to strike it rich as an actress forced her to accept far less exciting and satisfying work, but her spirits were always buoyed by Donald, whose encouragement came across as genuine.

The contrasting personalities between the grounded Donald and the flighty Ann, who got herself into predicaments worthy of Lucy Ricardo (for instance, getting swallowed by a rollaway bed, which displayed Thomas's flair for physical comedy), proved to be one reason for the show's critical success, which belied its lukewarm ratings. Thomas gained Emmy nominations for her role as a leading actress in four of five years on the show. Yet, like the Ann Marie character who couldn't land the breakout role, she failed to take home the prize, although she did earn a Golden Globe for Best Female TV Star in 1967.

The only other significant character was Lew Marie (Lew Parker), Ann's father, whose mistrust of Donald was never explained outside of an overprotective nature. Parker played the part with greater aplomb than did some of the other bit characters, none of whom could match the attractiveness of personality established by Thomas and Bessell.

The banter between Ann and Donald was downright charming, thanks greatly to show creators and writers Sam Denoff and Bill Persky, whose talents and previous success writing episodes for *The Dick Van Dyke Show* all but ensured success. The show earned a measure of distinctiveness and pulled in viewers by starting before the theme song, which was rare for that era. The story line for each episode was established when someone pointed to Ann and said, with emphasis, "That Girl!" A close-up of Ann Marie then cued the opening credits and theme music. That, too, proved memorable as a wide-eyed and beaming Ann was shown soaking in the excitement of New York, from flying a kite in Central Park to staring at the marquees on the theaters of Broadway.

The importance of *That Girl* in the social fabric of American entertainment has been underappreciated since it hit the airwaves, overwhelmed by the greatness and significance of *The Mary Tyler Moore Show*, which has also been far more successful in syndication. But the work of Thomas and her show should not be placed in the dustbin of history. It must be remembered that she refused to accept the recommendation of NBC to marry Donald because of the implication that it would be the ultimate goal for a female character. That decision cemented Thomas's place as a television trailblazer.

Beyond Ann Marie

Marlo Thomas remained active in the women's liberation movement and acting after *That Girl* was cancelled in 1971, but it was her work with children that proved most influential. She spearheaded the creation of the record entitled *Free to Be . . . You and Me* in 1972, which sought to lure kids away from gender and racial stereotyping. Little could Thomas have imagined that the record would immediately go platinum. That inspired Thomas and her friends to follow up with a companion book and television special, both of which were well received. Thomas won an Emmy as producer and star of a TV special in 1974, and ABC, which aired it, earned a Peabody Award the following year.

Did You Know?

Aside from Thomas and Bessell, no actor performed in more than half of the 136 episodes of *That Girl*. Lew Parker was next with sixty-five, followed by Bernie Kopell as friend Jerry Bauman, with just thirty-one.

They Said It

> **Ann:** [to the head of an acting workshop] Mr. Benedict, I'm a little confused about how my character should be played.
> **Jules Benedict:** [slowly] Much . . . much . . . better.

> **Ann:** That's what I love about the theater! You know what I mean, Donald? One day you're nobody, and the next, Ethel Merman is stuffing your cabbage!

Major Awards

EMMY AWARD NOMINATIONS (7)

1967 (1): Outstanding Continued Performance by an Actress in a Leading Role in a Comedy Series (Marlo Thomas)
1968 (3): Outstanding Continued Performance by an Actress in a Leading Role in a Comedy Series (Marlo Thomas); Outstanding Writing Achievement in Comedy (Danny Arnold and Ruth Brooks Flippen for "The Mailman Cometh"); Outstanding Directorial Achievement in Comedy (Danny Arnold for "That Girl")
1970 (1): Outstanding Continued Performance by an Actress in a Leading Role in a Comedy Series (Marlo Thomas)
1971 (2): Outstanding Continued Performance by an Actress in a Leading Role in a Comedy Series (Marlo Thomas); Outstanding Continued Performance by an Actor in a Leading Role in a Comedy Series (Ted Bessell)

GOLDEN GLOBE WIN (1)

1967 (1): Best TV Star, Female (Marlo Thomas)

GOLDEN GLOBE NOMINATION, IN ADDITION TO WIN (1)

1967 (1): Best TV Show

Further Reading

Douglas, Susan J. *Where the Girls Are: Growing Up Female with the Mass Media.* New York: Times Books, 1994.
Thomas, Marlo. *Growing Up Laughing: My Story.* New York: Hyperion, 2011.
———. *The Right Words at the Right Time.* New York: Atria Books, 2004.

✳ **63** ✳

Kate & Allie

(1984–1989)

Cast: Susan Saint James (Kate McArdle), Jane Curtin (Allie Lowell),
Frederick Koehler (Charles "Chip" Lowell), Allison Smith (Jennie
Lowell), Ari Meyers (Emma McArdle)

Created by: Writer Sherry Coben

Network: CBS

First Air Date: March 19, 1984

Last Air Date: September 11, 1989

Broadcast History:
  March 19, 1984–September 1986: Monday at 9:30–10:00 PM
  September 1986–September 1987: Monday at 8:00–8:30 PM
  September 1987–November 1987: Monday at 8:30–9:00 PM
  December 1987–June 1988: Monday at 8:00–8:30 PM
  July 1988–August 1988: Saturday at 8:00–8:30 PM
  August 1988–September 1988: Monday at 9:00–9:30 PM
  December 1988–March 1989: Monday at 8:30–9:00 PM
  March 1989–June 1989: Monday at 10:30–11:00 PM
  June 1989–September 11, 1989: Monday at 8:00–8:30 PM

Seasons: 6

Episodes: 122

Ratings History: 1983–1984 (8), 1984–1985 (17), 1985–1986 (14),
  1986–1987 (19), 1987–1988 (not in Top 30), 1988–1989 (not in
  Top 30)

Clockwise from left: Jane Curtin, Susan Saint James, Ari Meyers, Allison Smith, and Frederick Koehler. *CBS/Photofest ©CBS*

Overview

Many sitcoms have featured unmarried folks living in New York City. Included among them were such highly popular shows as *Seinfeld*, *Friends*, and *The Odd Couple*. But two divorced women with three kids between them sharing an apartment in the Big Apple? Now, *that* was a new twist. That was *Kate & Allie*.

   The Odd Couple billed itself as a comedy about two divorced men trying not to drive one another crazy. *Kate & Allie* boasted the same theme with teenage children tossed into the mix. Jane Curtin played Allie Lowell in her first significant role since the breakup of the original *Saturday Night Live* cast in 1980. Her character was a bit like a female Felix Unger. Allie was straitlaced, hardworking, and far too old-fashioned and unprepared for the wild New York dating scene. Kate McArdle (Susan Saint James) was an Oscar Madison only in her desire to help her roommate find a life partner. Unlike Allie, she embraced new trends in fashion and lifestyle.

Show creator Sherry Coben was new to the world of sitcoms. She had written 120 episodes of the short-lived soap opera *Ryan's Hope* early in the decade and then faded from the scene after crafting *Kate & Allie*. But this show was an artistic, critical, and ratings success. It earned Emmy nominations for Outstanding Comedy Series three straight years, while Curtin snagged two Outstanding Lead Actress wins.

The story line strayed little from the immediate family and their rather communal existence. Both Kate and Allie grew dissatisfied with their lots in life professionally, leading in the spring of 1987—the middle of the show's five-year run—to them teaming up to launch a catering business. Soon, Kate's daughter Emma (Ari Meyers) and Allie's daughter Jennie (Allison Smith) enrolled at Columbia University. Both remained at home until the former opted for a room in a dorm and the more freewheeling lifestyle embraced by her mother. Jennie grew jealous of Emma, forcing Allie to give her daughter more freedom.

Expanding personal relationships took the show in new directions and lower Nielsen ratings in the last two seasons, after it had remained in the Top 20 in its first four years. Allie married sportscaster Bob Barsky (Sam Freed) in the 1988 season premiere and moved out. The problem of separating the two main characters was solved when Bob landed a job in Washington, D.C., that forced him to commute to New York, and Kate moved in with Allie and son Chip (Frederick Koehler). Meyers was written off the show as Emma transferred to UCLA in her desire to be closer to her father. Kate remained unattached despite the unwanted advances from building superintendent Lou Carello (Peter Onorati). *Kate & Allie* was far from a breakthrough sitcom, but it strengthened the role of independent women on television.

Susan Was Showing

Susan Saint James played a single woman in *Kate & Allie*, which didn't preclude her from becoming pregnant on the show, but the writers opted against that story line, so when Saint James did get pregnant during the second season, they had some hiding to do. They placed props in front of her and had Kate recovering from a broken leg, which allowed her to lift her leg up to shield the evidence. A flashback episode in which Kate was pregnant allowed her to show her pregnancy.

They Said It

> **Jennie:** [talking with her mother about her virginity] What you're saying is that I should wait.
> **Allie:** Definitely, yes.
> **Jennie:** But that the choice is mine.
> **Allie:** Unfortunately, yes.

Major Awards

EMMY AWARD WINS (3)

1984 (2): Outstanding Lead Actress in a Comedy Series (Jane Curtin); Outstanding Directing in a Comedy Series (Bill Persky for "A Very Loud Family")
1985 (1): Outstanding Lead Actress in a Comedy Series (Jane Curtin)

EMMY AWARD NOMINATIONS, IN ADDITION TO WINS (9)

1984 (3): Outstanding Comedy Series; Outstanding Lead Actress in a Comedy Series (Susan Saint James); Outstanding Video Tape Editing for a Series (Marco Zappia for "Dear Diary")
1985 (3): Outstanding Comedy Series; Outstanding Lead Actress in a Comedy Series (Susan Saint James); Outstanding Directing in a Comedy Series (Bill Persky for "Landlady")
1986 (2): Outstanding Comedy Series; Outstanding Directing in a Comedy Series (Bill Persky for "Chip's Friend")
1987 (1): Outstanding Lead Actress in a Comedy Series (Jane Curtin)

GOLDEN GLOBE NOMINATIONS (3)

1985 (2): Best TV Series, Musical/Comedy; Best Performance by an Actress in a TV Series, Musical/Comedy (Jane Curtin)
1986 (1): Best TV Series, Musical/Comedy

HUMANITAS PRIZE

1987: 30-Minute Category (Bob Randall)

HUMANITAS PRIZE NOMINATION

1988: 30-Minute Category (Bob Randall and Bill Persky)

Further Reading

O'Connor, John J. "'Kate & Allie,' about 2 Divorced Women, on CBS." *New York Times*, March 19, 1984.

✳ **64** ✳

Gomer Pyle, U.S.M.C.

(1964–1970)

Cast: Jim Nabors (Private Gomer Pyle), Frank Sutton (Sergeant Vincent "Vince" Carter), Ronnie Schell (Private Duke Slater), Roy Stuart (Corporal Chuck Boyle), Ted Bessell (Private Frankie Lombardi), Barbara Stuart (Bunny), Allan Melvin (Sergeant Charlie Hacker), Elizabeth MacRae (Lou Ann Poovie)

Created by: Producer and writer Aaron Ruben

Network: CBS

First Air Date: September 25, 1964

Last Air Date: September 9, 1970

Broadcast History:
 September 25, 1964–June 1965: Friday at 9:30–10:00 PM
 September 1965–September 1966: Friday at 9:00–9:30 PM
 September 1966–August 1967: Wednesday at 9:30–10:00 PM
 September 1967–September 1969: Friday at 8:30–9:00 PM
 July 1970–September 9, 1970: Wednesday at 8:00–8:30 PM

Seasons: 5

Episodes: 150

Ratings History: 1964–1965 (3), 1965–1966 (2), 1966–1967 (10), 1967–1968 (3), 1968–1969 (2)

Frank Sutton and Jim Nabors. *CBS/Photofest ©CBS*

Overview

Sometimes the chemistry between two characters can carry a show. That of bumbling, naïve U.S. Marine private Gomer Pyle (Jim Nabors) and his exasperated sergeant, Vince Carter (Frank Sutton), was undoubtedly the key to ratings success. The sitcom was a spin-off of *The Andy Griffith Show*, in which Pyle played a happy-go-lucky, clueless hillbilly gas station attendant. The trend toward absurd premises that permeated the 1960s television comedy scene made his joining the toughest military branch in the United States a natural fit. Just as Andy Griffith had been launched on an episode of *The Danny Thomas Show*, *Gomer Pyle, U.S.M.C.* began on an episode of *The Andy Griffith Show*, when Gomer met his sergeant for the first time. By the middle of the show, Carter had grown so angry and frustrated with his new recruit that he forced him to wear a bucket on his head.

In early episodes (only in the first season, when Gomer was in boot camp, was the show in black-and-white), Carter believed that the private was attempting to get the best of him, reasoning that nobody could be so backward and inept, but he soon realized that Gomer was indeed that clumsy and incompetent, and he worked with very limited success to turn his "prized knucklehead" into a marine. Carter, who was no Einstein himself, eventually gained an understanding that he was a father figure to Gomer, who adored him and always looked after what he perceived as his best interests in his personal life, with albeit mostly disastrous results.

The contrasts between the two personalities strengthened the comedy. Gomer was laid-back, Carter intense. Gomer was forgiving, Carter vengeful. Gomer was a meddler, Carter yearned to be left alone. The result was that the latter often blew his cork at Gomer, who remained understanding no matter how explosive the dressing down. Perhaps the funniest episode revolved around a $50 bet made by Carter and rival sergeant Charlie Hacker (Allan Melvin), in which the former had to go twenty-four hours without yelling. Hacker used Gomer as his weapon, sending him into Carter's barracks to annoy and anger him. Carter's anger became so bottled up that, seething and silent as his facial expressions matched the torture he felt inside, he sped his jeep into the mountains, stumbled up a hill, stomped his feet up and down, and screamed at the top of his lungs.

Fellow marines the likes of Hacker, Private Duke Slater (Ronnie Schell), and Corporal Chuck Boyle (Roy Stuart) only served to raise and lower tensions between Gomer and Sergeant Carter, but the story line and plot lines did expand a bit when they played off their girlfriends. Gomer's girl was southern belle Lou Ann Poovie (Elizabeth MacRae), who arrived in 1967 to seek her fame and fortune as a singer. There was only one problem—she had no talent. After fending off the advances of Carter and Slater, she fell for the more sincere Gomer, and the two gullible, sweet characters remained a couple for the remainder of the series. The more hardened Bunny (Barbara Stuart) was every bit the match for her boyfriend, Carter. She was cynical of his intentions and quite capable of standing up to him despite his prodigious temper.

One might think that a military show would struggle to survive in the midst of the increasingly unpopular Vietnam War, but such was not the case with *Gomer Pyle*, which remained in the Top 10 in the Nielsen ratings and twice peaked at number two. Although Carter's crew sometimes participated in maneuvers, there was nothing in the show to remind viewers of the thousands of U.S. soldiers getting killed halfway around the world. In fact, the show hit number two during the 1968–1969 season, when U.S. troop levels peaked at more than 500,000.

The writers sought to keep the show fresh, so they used a variety of settings and multiepisode series. They placed Carter's unit on a U.S. Navy ship (Gomer frustrated and infuriated his sergeant by puncturing holes in their raft three times). They had the boys participating in a Hollywood movie entitled *Leathernecks of the Air*, in which Carter continually blew his one line ("OK, let's hear it for Henshaw!"). They sent the two main characters to the nation's capital, where the masterfully voiced Gomer displayed his surprising talents before fellow marines.

By the end of the series, Gomer had become a better soldier and a far more confident person than when he arrived in Carter's platoon, but he still screwed up enough to drive his sergeant crazy. And that's what the show was all about.

Reversal of Roles through Rarebit

One of the most popular episodes of *Gomer Pyle* revolves around a passion for Welsh rarebit, which makes Gomer sleepwalk. He bursts into Carter's barracks in the wee hours of the morning and, in a show of temper never before displayed, wakes him up and screams at him for alleged mistreatment. Carter is ready to get him tossed in the brig when Boyle wises him up to the fact that Gomer is fast asleep. Carter follows Gomer to the restaurant in which he had been eating the sleepwalking stimulus and chows down on a plate of it himself. Hilarity ensues that night as the two meet in the middle of the camp and a meek Carter apologizes profusely for every furious charge Gomer yells at him. It takes Boyle to wake them up and return them to their normal personalities.

Did You Know?

One of the privates in Carter's platoon was intellectual Lester Hummel, played by William Christopher, who gained greater fame as Captain Father John Francis Patrick Mulcahy in *M*A*S*H*.

They Said It

> **Andy Taylor:** [in the pilot episode as he sees Gomer with a bucket on his head] Psst. Hey, Gomer.
> **Gomer:** [removes bucket] Hey, Andy. How'd you know it was me under this thing?
> **Andy:** I just took a guess. What's wrong?
> **Gomer:** Nothin'. Why do you ask?
> **Andy:** Well, Gomer, whenever I see a man sittin' by hisself in a Quonset hut with a bucket on his head, I've just gotta ask, 'What's wrong?'

> **Carter:** [to Gomer] All I can say is, if the idea of desertion ever crossed your mind, you'll never find a better time to look into it.

Major Awards

None

Further Reading

Beranek, Susan N. *A Book of Tribute Jim Nabors: A Man of Comfort and Joy.* Bloomington, IN: Xlibris Corporation, 2011.

✵ **65** ✵

Our Miss Brooks

(1952–1956)

Cast: Eve Arden (Connie Brooks), Gale Gordon (Osgood Conklin), Jane Morgan (Margaret Davis), Robert Rockwell (Philip Boynton), Richard Crenna (Walter Denton), Gloria McMillan (Harriet Conklin)

Created by: Writer and director Al Lewis

Network: CBS

First Air Date: October 3, 1952

Last Air Date: May 11, 1956

Broadcast History:
October 3, 1952–June 1955: Friday at 9:30–10:00 PM
October 1955–September 1956: Friday at 8:30–9:00 PM

Seasons: 4

Episodes: 154

Ratings History: 1952–1953 (22), 1953–1954 (14), 1954–1955 (not in Top 30), 1955–1956 (not in Top 30)

Overview

The transition from radio to television proved seamless for some shows and a disaster for others. *Our Miss Brooks* can be placed squarely in the former category. One of the most popular radio staples of the late 1940s emerged as a hit in the early days of the new medium, although it earned greater critical acclaim than viewership. It snagged Best Situation Comedy Emmy nominations in 1953, 1954, and 1955. Yet, the radio

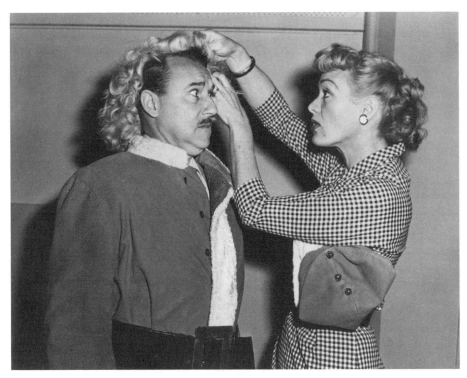

Gale Gordon and Eve Arden. *Photofest*

program continued one year beyond the run of its television namesake. The fact that both shows thrived simultaneously confirmed their popularity and that of star Eve Arden, who received much of the praise for their success. She gained fame as a movie actress before her radio show hit the airwaves, landing a role in the classic *Stage Door* alongside emerging comedienne Lucille Ball (with whom she forged a lifetime friendship) and earning a Best Supporting Actress Oscar for her performance in *Mildred Pierce* (1945).

In *Our Miss Brooks*, she portrayed a wisecracking high school English teacher named Connie Brooks, with an eye for biology instructor and handsome, but painfully shy, bachelor Philip Boynton (Robert Rockwell). Her foil and constant tormentor was hotheaded principal Osgood Conklin (Gale Gordon), who lost his temper over the mildest of provocations. But like most sitcoms of that era and well beyond, the focus on the main characters extended to their domestic lives. Plots sometimes revolved around her relationship with her compassionate landlord, Margaret Davis (Jane Morgan), and simpleton student Walter Denton (Richard Crenna).

The depth and likeability of the cast and thoughtfulness of the writing set *Our Miss Brooks* apart from less memorable sitcoms. Brooks was not a one-dimensional character. She shielded her uncertainties and lack of self-confidence by making jokes.

She felt pain in her inability to attract Boynton and anxiety about a tirade by Conklin that always seemed to be right around the corner. But her quick wit most often gave her the upper hand in social situations. One of these instances takes place in a 1952 episode in which Daisy Enright (Mary Jane Croft), a rival for Boynton's affections, seeks to paint herself as a younger woman in front of the handsome biology teacher as the subject turns to the early days of television.

> **Enright:** [to Boynton] I remember . . . when I was in my teens . . . there weren't very many stars on television.
>
> **Brooks:** When you were in your teens, there weren't many stars on the flag.

Sagging ratings in the mid-1950s forced changes in the story line. Brooks was transferred to an elementary school, but her conflicts continued with Conklin, who magically took over as principal of that building. Denton was written out of the script, as was Boynton. Connie was no longer a pursuer of a man, but rather the love interest of gym teacher Gene Talbot (Gene Barry). That character failed to attract audiences, prompting a return of Boynton as *Our Miss Brooks* neared its demise. Connie never did get her man for television audiences, but there was a happy ending on the big screen. A namesake film brought back the original cast and featured Brooks and Boynton tying the knot. *Our Miss Brooks* has been largely forgotten by future generations, but it remains one of the finest and perhaps most thoughtful sitcoms of its era.

Planting the Seeds of Success

Actor Richard Crenna, who played the love interest of Connie Brooks in the sitcom, was just twenty-six years old when the show hit the airwaves. He remained one of the busiest actors in Hollywood for the next half-century. Crenna starred in numerous programs and earned Emmy nominations for his work in both *The Real McCoys* (1957–1963) and *Slattery's People* (1964–1965). He played significant roles in such shows as *All's Fair* (1976–1977), *It Takes Two* (1982–1983), and *Judging Amy* (2002–2003). He also directed eight episodes of the immensely popular *Andy Griffith Show* in 1963 and 1964.

Not *That* Al Lewis

One would assume that the Al Lewis who served as writer and director of most *Our Miss Brooks* episodes was the same one that starred as Grandpa Munster in the 1960s sitcom *The Munsters*.

One would assume wrong. The Al Lewis in question was far older and not an actor. He remained close to *Our Miss Brooks* star Eve Arden throughout her career. He toiled as a producer on *The Eve Arden Show* (1957–1958) and six episodes of *The Mothers-in-Law* (featuring Arden) in 1967.

They Said It

> **Connie:** [after having locked Osgood in a refrigerator] You look much better than when I saw you last, sir.
> **Osgood:** Well, I've defrosted since then.

Major Awards

EMMY AWARD WINS (1)

1954 (1): Best Female Star of Regular Series (Eve Arden)

EMMY AWARD NOMINATIONS, IN ADDITION TO WIN (6)

1953 (1): Best Situation Comedy
1954 (1): Best Situation Comedy
1955 (3): Best Situation Comedy Series; Best Actress Starring in a Regular Series (Eve Arden); Best Supporting Actor in a Regular Series (Gale Gordon)
1956 (1): Best Actress, Continuing Performance (Eve Arden)

Further Reading

Arden, Eve. *The Three Phases of Eve*. New York: St. Martin's, 1985.

✴ **66** ✴

The Adventures of Ozzie & Harriet

(1952–1966)

Cast: Ozzie Nelson (Ozzie Nelson), Harriet Hilliard (Harriet Nelson), Ricky Nelson (Ricky Nelson), David Nelson (David Nelson), Don DeFore (Syd "Thorny" Thornberry)

Created by: Ozzie Nelson

Network: ABC

First Air Date: October 3, 1952

Last Air Date: September 3, 1966

Broadcast History:
October 3, 1952–June 1956: Friday at 8:00–8:30 PM
October 1956–September 1958: Wednesday at 9:00–9:30 PM
September 1958–September 1961: Wednesday at 8:30–9:00 PM
September 1961–September 1963: Thursday at 7:30–8:00 PM
September 1963–January 1966: Wednesday at 7:30–8:00 PM
January 1966–September 3, 1966: Saturday at 7:30–8:00 PM

Seasons: 14

Episodes: 435

Ratings History: 1952–1953 (not in Top 30), 1953–1954 (not in Top 30), 1954–1955 (not in Top 30), 1955–1956 (not in Top 30), 1956–1957 (not in Top 30), 1957–1958 (not in Top 30), 1958–1959 (not in Top 30), 1959–1960 (not in Top 30), 1960–1961 (not in Top 30), 1961–1962 (not in Top 30), 1962–1963 (not in Top 30), 1963–1964 (29), 1964–1965 (not in Top 30), 1965–1966 (not in Top 30)

The Nelsons: David, Harriet, Ozzie, and Ricky. *ABC/Photofest ©ABC*

Overview

It was the late 1950s. David Cassidy was just a kid hanging around his home in West Orange, New Jersey. John Travolta was a toddler in the same state, barely out of diapers. Their foray into the realm of teen idolatry would have to wait. That of Ricky Nelson had already come and gone. The oh-so-cute, real-life son of Ozzie and Harriet Nelson emerged as the first TV heartthrob. His popularity as an actor and early rock-and-roll icon motivated the decision to allow him to perform his latest songs on the show before the final credits rolled. Teenage girls swooned when he lip-synched Fats Domino's "I'm Walkin'" in 1957. A music star was born.

Several television stars were born as soon as ABC aired the first of a whopping 435 episodes of *The Adventures of Ozzie & Harriet* in the fall of 1952, but the show had already permeated the American consciousness as a popular radio program launched in 1944. The roles of Ricky and brother David were played by other actors until 1948, before being assumed by the actual kids. That created what emerged as the first family television show, one that mirrored reality, at least for the Nelsons, if not for most American families of the 1950s and early 1960s, with problems and conflicts that were not considered proper subject matter in that era. The spotlight throughout remained on Ozzie and Harriet, as well as Ricky, who grew up before our eyes, going from little boy when he joined the cast, to teen singing sensation, to twenty-five-year-old husband when the program finally bit the dust in 1965, after an amazing fifteen seasons.

The Adventures of Ozzie & Harriet set the tone for a genre of television shows in the 1950s that focused on what was perceived as sterile and pleasant family life. The postwar Baby Boom brought about an era of large, mostly white families migrating to exploding suburban areas. The sitcom was a forerunner of others soon to follow that would embrace the same theme, for example, *The Danny Thomas Show* (*Make Room for Daddy*), *Father Knows Best*, and *Leave It to Beaver*. The plot rarely extended beyond the four family members. No other character appeared in more than ninety-six episodes, as the show experienced frequent cast changes among the bit characters throughout its run.

Most puzzling was the role of Ozzie beyond fatherhood. Unlike other TV dads, he spent an inordinate amount of time at home, although in a 1957 episode he does claim to have been an orchestra leader and his wife a singer. Such a boast maintained a sense of realism—they indeed performed in those real-life roles in the 1930s. Further realism was achieved through exterior shots of the Nelson's actual Los Angeles home. In the late 1950s, Ozzie, who wrote many of the episodes and directed all but four (he turned the duties over to son David occasionally in 1963 and 1964), even convinced the network to cave on his demand to show Harriet and himself occupying the same bed. The image of a married couple in such a sleeping arrangement remained unseen until a decade later.

The story lines reflected the experiences of the Nelson family as David and Ricky aged. Unlike other fictional and real-life fathers that railed against rock-and-roll music, Ozzie supported Ricky in his pursuit of a music career, which exploded. The teen sensation struck it rich during the run of the show with such hits as "Hello Mary Lou" and number-one smashes "Poor Little Fool" and "Travelin' Man." His pleasant voice and nonthreatening stage presence made him a favorite of both kids and adults.

Neither parent pretended to serve as a moral compass that their kids were forced to follow blindly. Although viewers understood that the problems that cropped up weekly in the Nelson household were far less critical than those in their own lives, which could not be solved in a half-hour, the experience provided a soothing effect. The Nelsons as seen on television were not a fictional family. They were a real one in the hearts and minds of Americans. They were friends that allowed millions of viewers into their homes once a week. While their kids grew up, so did David and Ricky.

But the country was changing by the early 1960s. Its innocence began to dissipate on a November day in Dallas, when President John F. Kennedy was gunned down. Even though it would take another eight years before television sitcoms began to embrace the social and political issues of the times, cancellation was near. The wives of David (June Blair) and Ricky (Kristin Harmon) joined the cast in the 1960s. David graduated from law school to join a firm in which Ricky later toiled as a clerk. The story lines dabbled in their professional lives, but ABC showed many reruns from the early 1950s as the run of the sitcom neared its end. The last original episode featured Ozzie seeking to purchase a pool table to place in the empty bedroom once occupied by his sons.

The Adventures of Ozzie & Harriet was a reflection of a simpler time. It mirrored the bond felt by growing families throughout the nation and the realization of how important family members were to one another following a war that killed so many of them.

The Next Generation of Nelsons

Talent and notoriety in the Nelson family didn't end with Ricky. His daughter Tracy, who was born during the run of the show in 1963, embarked on an acting career that took hold as a cast member of the critically acclaimed *Square Pegs* in 1982. She starred in *Father Dowling Mysteries* several years later and has since landed parts in such notable shows as *Family Ties*, *Melrose Place*, *Murphy Brown*, *Will & Grace*, and *Seinfeld*. Particularly memorable was her role in the latter. She played the girlfriend of George Costanza, who was accused of dating her only because she bore a striking resemblance to best buddy Jerry Seinfeld.

Ricky Nelson's sons Gunnar and Matthew took a different route to brief stardom. They launched a pop rock band named simply *Nelson*, which hit the scene in the early 1990s with the album *After the Rain*, which features the number-one hit "(Can't Live without Your) Love and Affection." Their fame was fleeting, however, as their popularity gave way under the weight of the emerging grunge phenomenon and their inability to make *After the Rain* anything more than a one-hit wonder.

From Thorny to George

Veteran actor Don DeFore spent five seasons as Nelson neighbor Syd "Thorny" Thornberry on *The Adventures of Ozzie & Harriet*. DeFore gained greater notoriety, however, in the early 1960s as George Baxter in the hit series *Hazel*. DeFore also served as president of the National Academy of Television Arts and Sciences in 1954 and 1955, and he was greatly responsible for the Emmy Awards being broadcast on national TV for the first time on March 7, 1955.

They Said It

> **Ricky:** Tell me this—does June make a big scene every time you take your wedding ring off?
> **David:** No—but that's probably because I never take it off.

Ricky: I don't see how you can help it. I guess it's just that I haven't gotten used to wearing it yet. How'd you get used to it?

David: Well, June took care of that right from the start. She bought me a ring a little too small, slipped it on my finger, and then started fattening me up.

Major Awards

EMMY AWARD NOMINATIONS (3)

1953 (1): Best Situation Comedy
1955 (2): Best Supporting Actor in a Regular Series (Don DeFore); Best Art Direction of a Filmed Show (Frank Durlauf)

Further Reading

Barringer, Felicity. "Dialogue That Lingers: 'Hi Mom,' 'Hi, Pop,' 'Hi, David,' 'Hi, Rick.'" *New York Times*, October 9, 1994. Available online at www.nytimes.com/1994/10/09/weekin review/word-for-word-adventures-ozzie-harriet-dialogue-that-lingers-hi-mom-hi-pop-hi .html.
Selvin, Joel. *Ricky Nelson: Idol for a Generation.* Chicago: Contemporary Books, 1991.

✳ **67** ✳

My World and Welcome to It

(1969–1970)

Cast: William Windom (John Monroe), Joan Hotchkis (Ellen Monroe), Lisa Gerritsen (Lydia Monroe), Harold J. Stone (Hamilton Greeley), Henry Morgan (Philip Jensen)

Created by: Writer and director Melville Shavelson (based on the namesake book written by James Thurber)

Network: NBC

First Air Date: September 15, 1969

Last Air Date: March 9, 1970

Broadcast History:
September 15, 1969–March 9, 1970: Monday at 7:30–8:00 PM

Seasons: 1

Episodes: 26

Ratings History: Not in Top 30

Overview

The silly premises and equally silly story lines that permeated the world of American sitcoms in the 1960s had not yet been put to rest by September 15, 1969, when a thoughtful show entitled *My World and Welcome to It* debuted on NBC. After all, U.S. involvement in the Vietnam War was at its peak, and the television powers that be still deemed escapism as necessary fare. Their beliefs were far from unwarranted, as such sitcoms as *The Beverly Hillbillies*, *Bewitched*, *Gomer Pyle, U.S.M.C.*, and *Green Acres* remained hugely popular.

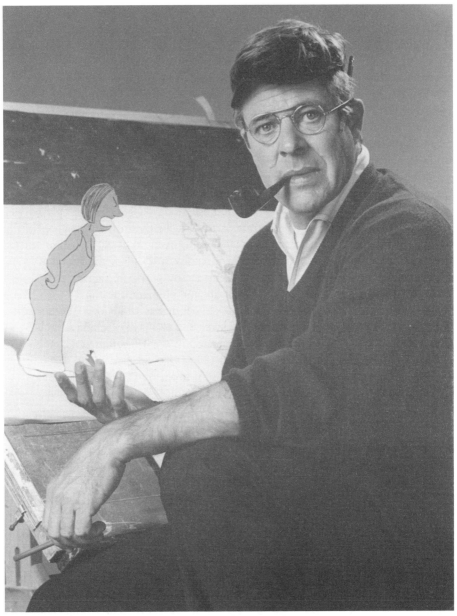

William Windom. *NBC/Photofest ©NBC*

But, as Bob Dylan had so famously expressed several years earlier, the times they were a-changin'. More sophisticated, imaginative sitcoms were beginning to find their way onto the small screen. Among them was *My World and Welcome to It*, which was based on the works of creative writer James Thurber, who critiqued American society through humor and observation and expressed dissatisfaction with his lot in life. There was just one problem with the show: It failed to attract viewers. The ratings could not match the critical acclaim, and the show was cancelled after just one season. But then, when you place a program head-to-head against the wildly popular *Gunsmoke* on Monday nights, what could NBC have expected? The sitcom did, however, gain enough respect to win an Emmy for Outstanding Comedy Series in 1970, and earn Windom another for Outstanding Continuing Performance by an Actor in a Leading Role.

The show revolved around highly imaginative writer and cartoonist John Monroe (William Windom) and featured both animation and the playing out of his daydreams, interspersed with live action to express his feelings. In one scene, he pictures a sexy neighbor, played by Lee Meriwether, who is merely grabbing her mail out of her mailbox, dancing erotically for him in a skintight sparkly red dress.

John dreamed of being king of his castle but feared domination by wife Ellen (Joan Hotchkis), who did at least subtly and kindly boss him around. He used humor to express his resentment of women, including young daughter Lydia, played well enough by Lisa Gerritsen to land her the part of Phyllis Lindstrom's daughter in *The Mary Tyler Moore Show*. John was a defeated man, strong enough to dream, but too weak to take charge of his life and, deep down, in love with Ellen and loving of Lydia.

Perhaps American viewers were not ready for the rather restrained, subtle, conversational humor and combination of real life and animation featured in *My World and Welcome to It*. The disdain of a laugh track, which was standard in 1960s sitcoms, indicated that Thurber and show creator Melville Shavelson, who combined to write all twenty-six episodes, did not intend to garner huge guffaws. They didn't even get enough chuckles. That—along with the popularity of *Gunsmoke*—resulted in this sitcom biting the dust after just one year, as if it had been shot down by Dodge City marshal Matt Dillon himself, although CBS did pick it up for summer evening reruns in 1972.

Profound Part for Windom

William Windom was among the most versatile actors in American entertainment. He thrived in theater, film, and television, in both dramatic and comedic roles, for more than sixty years. One standout performance was in the breakthrough sitcom *All in the Family* in 1971. Windom played a rich car dealership owner named Eddie Frazier, who was revered by Archie Bunker for his wealth. Archie invited him and the old army gang over for a get-together, where it was revealed that Frazier was miserable because his son wanted nothing to do with a father he perceived as unscrupulous and immoral. Windom excelled at portraying a broken man who was painfully sad on the inside, despite his wealth, and happy on the outside in an attempt to maintain his standing as a huge success to his old comrades-in-arms.

They Said It

> **Ellen:** You never took the time to get comfy with your own daughter. She'd look lovely to you.
> **John:** We just don't have anything in common. Take the international situation. I don't want to discuss it, but she does.

Major Awards

EMMY AWARD WINS (2)

1970 (2): Outstanding Comedy Series; Outstanding Continued Performance by an Actor in a Leading Role in a Comedy Series (William Windom)

EMMY AWARD NOMINATION, IN ADDITION TO WINS (1)

1970 (1): Outstanding Achievement in Any Area of Creative Technical Crafts (Wilfred M. Cline, Howard A. Anderson, and Bill Hansard)

Further Reading

Thurber, James. *My World, and Welcome to It*. Orlando, FL: Harcourt, 1942.

✳ **68** ✳

The Bob Cummings Show

(1955–1959)

Cast: Robert Cummings (Bob Collins), Rosemary DeCamp (Margaret MacDonald), Ann B. Davis (Charmaine "Shultzy" Schultz), Dwayne Hickman (Chuck MacDonald), Isabel Randolph (Isabel), Nancy Kulp (Pamela)

Created by: Paul Henning

Network: NBC (1955, 1957–1959), CBS (1955–1957)

First Air Date: January 2, 1955

Last Air Date: September 15, 1959

Broadcast History:
January 2, 1955–September 1955: Sunday at 10:30–11:00 PM
July 1955–September 1957: Thursday at 8:00–8:30 PM
September 1957–September 15, 1959: Tuesday at 9:30–10:00 PM

Seasons: 5

Episodes: 173

Ratings History: Never in Top 30

Overview

The disconnect between television viewers and critics has been pronounced, particularly in the 1950s, 1960s, and 1970s. Such sitcoms as *Gomer Pyle, U.S.M.C.*, *Green Acres*, and *Gilligan's Island* were panned by critics and combined to win zero Emmys, but all were ratings smashes. Other shows, including *Square Pegs*, *Buffalo Bill*, and *My World and Welcome to It*, earned critical acclaim but bombed in the ratings and were quickly dispatched into the dustbin of television history.

Ann B. Davis, Rosemary DeCamp, Robert Cummings, and Isabel Randolph. *NBC/ Photofest ©NBC*

The Bob Cummings Show falls squarely into the latter category, although it did last five seasons. It failed to crack the Top 30 in the Nielsen ratings, yet it earned two Emmy Awards and a slew of nominations, including three for Best Comedy Series. One might have assumed that a show about a bachelor photographer who worked with beautiful models would have at least cornered the market on young and middle-aged male viewers, but the ratings suggested otherwise.

The show indeed revolved around Bob Collins (Cummings), who juggled his career and the dating scene with limited success. His escapades with the women who would come and go in his life resulted in confusion for the star character, who shared an apartment with widowed sister Margaret (Rosemary DeCamp) and her son Chuck (Dwayne Hickman). Jealousy reared its ugly head as neighbor Pamela (Nancy Kulp) and secretary Charmaine (Ann B. Davis) competed in vain for Bob's affection against the bevy of models that drew his interest.

The subject of sex never arose in that program, or any other, until the floodgates opened in the early 1970s, but it was certainly implied. Pamela and Charmaine aggressively pursued the handsome photographer while he played the role of wolf in chasing after such seductive models as those played by busty Joi Lansing and 1955 Miss Sweden Ingrid Goude. Even grandfather Josh, who was portrayed by Cummings, stared at the models surrounding his grandson as sexy eye candy.

The sitcom continued to raise the stock in the entertainment world of creator Paul Henning, who had previously written twenty-six episodes of *The George Burns and Gracie Allen Show.* He served as writer and producer of *The Bob Cummings Show* before creating, writing, and producing such 1960s ratings smashes as *The Beverly Hillbillies, Petticoat Junction,* and *Green Acres.* It's no wonder that Kulp landed a major role as secretary Jane Hathaway on the first of those hits.

Kulp wasn't the only cast member to ride the sitcom to further success. Hickman, a mere college student when he landed his part, gained greater fame playing the title character in the highly acclaimed *The Many Loves of Dobie Gillis.* Davis, who snagged the only two Emmy Awards won by *The Bob Cummings Show,* waited more than a decade to find her next big role as housekeeper Alice on *The Brady Bunch.*

The show bounced from NBC to CBS and back to NBC without striking it rich in the ratings. It was even picked up by ABC in October 1959, where it ran under the title *Love That Bob* as a daytime comedy for fourteen months.

Same Title, Not the Same Success

Bob Cummings didn't take long to find another sitcom after *The Bob Cummings Show* left the air. Another show with the same title and a different story line hit the small screen on CBS in October 1961. It featured Cummings as an aviator and amateur sleuth named Bob Carson. It lasted a mere five months and twenty-two episodes, during which time its title was changed to *The New Bob Cummings Show,* before it was cancelled.

In 1964, Cummings starred in a sitcom entitled *My Living Doll,* alongside Julie Newmar, who would soon take on the role of Catwoman on the *Batman* TV series. *My Living Doll* left the air after one year, after which Cummings never acted as a regular in any series. He did land guest-starring appearances in such 1960s and 1970s staples as *Green Acres, Bewitched, Here's Lucy, Love, American Style,* and *Love Boat.*

They Said It

> **Margaret:** How is Crazy Lips?
> **Bob:** Oh, brother.
> **Margaret:** Well, you can't have everything, and she has a very nice figure.
> **Bob:** Yeah, that she has, that she has . . . 36–23–36–23.
> **Margaret:** What's that last 23?
> **Bob:** Her IQ.

Major Awards

EMMY AWARD WINS (2)

1958 (1): Best Continuing Supporting Performance by an Actress in a Dramatic or Comedy Series (Ann B. Davis)

1959 (1): Best Supporting Actress (Continuing Character) in a Comedy Series (Ann B. Davis)

EMMY AWARD NOMINATIONS, IN ADDITION TO WINS (15)

1956 (6): Best Comedy Series; Best Actor, Continuing Performance (Robert Cummings); Best Actress in a Supporting Role (Ann B. Davis); Best Producer, Film Series (Paul Henning); Best Director, Film Series (Rod Amateau for "Return of the Wolf"); Best Editing of a Television Film (Stanley Frazen and Guy Scarpitta for "Miss Coffee Break")

1957 (2): Best Continuing Performance by a Comedian in a Series (Robert Cummings); Best Supporting Performance by an Actress (Ann B. Davis)

1958 (2): Best Comedy Series; Best Continuing Performance by an Actor in a Leading Role in a Dramatic or Comedy Series (Robert Cummings)

1959 (5): Best Comedy Series; Best Actor in a Leading Role (Continuing Character) in a Comedy Series (Robert Cummings); Best Supporting Actress (Continuing Character) in a Comedy Series (Rosemary DeCamp); Best Writing of a Single Program of a Comedy Series (Paul Henning and Dick Wesson for "Grandpa Clobbers the Air Force"); Best Editing of a Film for Television (Robert Crawford for "Grandpa Clobbers the Air Force")

✵ **69** ✵

Coach

(1989–1997)

Cast: Craig T. Nelson (Hayden Fox), Jerry Van Dyke (Luther Van Dam), Shelley Fabares (Christine Armstrong Fox), Bill Fagerbakke (Dauber Dybinski), Clare Carey (Kelly Fox)

Created by: Writer, director, and producer Barry Kemp

Network: ABC

First Air Date: February 28, 1989

Last Air Date: August 6, 1997

Broadcast History:
February 28, 1989: Tuesday at 9:30–10:00 PM
March 1989–June 1989: Wednesday at 9:00–9:30 PM
June 1989–August 1989: Tuesday at 9:30–10:00 PM
August 1989–September 1989: Wednesday at 9:30–10:00 PM
November 1989–November 1992: Tuesday at 9:30–10:00 PM
November 1992–July 1993: Wednesday at 9:30–10:00 PM
July 1993–July 1994: Tuesday at 9:30–10:00 PM
August 1994–March 1995: Monday at 8:00–8:30 PM
March 1995–May 1995: Wednesday at 9:30–10:00 PM
June 1995–January 1996: Tuesday at 9:30–10:00 PM
February 1996–May 1996: Tuesday at 8:30–9:00 PM
May 1996–September 1996: Tuesday at 9:30–10:00 PM
September 1996–October 1996: Saturday at 9:00–9:30 PM
December 1996–August 6, 1997: Wednesday at 8:30–9:00 PM

Seasons: 8

Episodes: 200

Ratings History: 1989-1990 (18), 1990-1991 (18), 1991-1992 (10), 1992-1993 (6), 1993-1994 (6), 1994-1995 (not in Top 30), 1995-1996 (14), 1996-1997 (not in Top 30)

Jerry Van Dyke, Craig T. Nelson, and Bill Fagerbakke. *ABC/Photofest ©ABC*

Overview

What is amazing is that fans of *Coach* actually knew what day and time it was scheduled to air often enough to maintain its standing as one of the top-rated shows of its era. The network bounced it around like a Ping-Pong ball for eight seasons, placing it on every day of the week but Friday and Sunday, and all four time slots between 8 p.m. and 9:30 p.m. The fact that it achieved Nielsen ratings in the Top 18 in every season but two and peaked twice at number six is a testament to all involved in the production.

The show revolved around Hayden Fox (Craig T. Nelson), who coached the usually woebegone Screaming Eagles football team at fictional Minnesota State University. Hayden showed a passion for the sport and a yearning to win and maintain discipline, all of which were tempered by his desire to mold his players into young men with a kind, caring approach. He was assisted by bumbling, mindless assistant

Luther Van Dam (Jerry Van Dyke) and stereotypical dumb jock Dauber Dybinski (Bill Fagerbakke), a former Screaming Eagles player who joked about his status as a perennial student before graduating with three bachelor's degrees.

Hayden's personal life remained in the spotlight as well. He married steady girlfriend Christine Armstrong (Shelley Fabares), who was far more organized and intelligent than her husband-to-be. Christine was only one of the women in his life. Hayden's love for eighteen-year-old daughter Kelly (Clare Carey) from a previous marriage caused him to be overprotective and suspicious of suitors, including her eventual spouse and mime (of course, everyone hates mimes) Stuart Rosebrock (Kris Kamm). *Coach* often pitted men versus women in battle of the sexes competitions, with the latter emerging victorious. Along with their strong characterizations of women (Christine and Kelly), that was one reason the show appealed to both men and women.

The sitcom also evolved. Hayden's hard work finally paid off in 1990, when he guided the Screaming Eagles to a winning season and a berth in the mythical Pioneer Bowl. Soon thereafter, Christine was tempted by a lucrative job offer and nearly left town, leading Hayden to realize just how much he loved and needed her and motivating him to propose to her on the air early in the 1992–1993 season. One can understand why he was far more successful in his love life than Luther, whose inadequacies caused him to bounce from one romance to the next without satisfaction.

Meanwhile, the show bounced from one location to another in its seventh season. Hayden landed a job as a professional football coach with the fictional Orlando Breakers and bolted to Florida, along with his two assistants. A new cast of characters, including bizarre team owner Doris Sherman (Katherine Helmond), failed to revive the foundering program. The comedic tempo was lost, and the show relied heavily on real football stars, including Walter Payton, Dick Butkus, and Mike Ditka, and such broadcasting heavyweights as Larry King and Al Michaels, to survive. The Breakers fared poorly on the field, and Hayden did no better when asked to write a book about dealing with defeat.

Even the birth of Fox baby Timothy couldn't save the sitcom from extinction. It had become apparent that it had jumped the shark when the Foxes jumped to Orlando. The final episode featured Hayden turning down a $17 million contract to stay with the Breakers and the couple moving back to Minnesota to aid Christine in her career. Dauber hung around to coach the team to two Super Bowls and embark on a new career as a sports commentator.

Coach fell victim to the same malady that weakened the legacy of other sitcoms: the desperation to resuscitate a dying show. But it was fun and funny before its setting went from snowy to sunny.

Dick's Little Brother

Dick Van Dyke was striking it rich, literally and figuratively, as the title character in one of the most successful sitcoms in television history; however, his brother wasn't so fortunate. Jerry, who played a somnambulist banjo player in episodes of *The Dick*

Van Dyke Show, struggled most of his career to find a television role in which he could maximize his vast talents, which included impeccable timing and delivery. The closest the younger Van Dyke came to finding such a part was as Dave Crabtree in the bizarre mid-1960s sitcom *My Mother the Car*. He had turned down the title role in *Gilligan's Island* and nearly became Don Knotts's replacement in *The Andy Griffith Show*. It wasn't until almost a quarter-century later that Van Dyke found professional fulfillment as Luther Van Dam in *Coach*.

Did You Know?

Coach creator Barry Kemp, who also launched the popular 1980s sitcom *Newhart*, based the main character of his new show on University of Iowa football coach Hayden Fry, thus the identical first name of the lead character. Kemp was an alma mater of that school.

They Said It

Hayden: You graduated from college and now you won't wash my car?
Dauber: Uh-huh.
Hayden: You see, this is why I hate education.

Major Awards

EMMY AWARD WINS (2)

1992 (1): Outstanding Lead Actor in a Comedy Series (Craig T. Nelson)
1996 (1): Outstanding Guest Actor in a Comedy Series (Tim Conway for "The Gardener")

EMMY AWARD NOMINATIONS, IN ADDITION TO WINS (14)

1990 (2): Outstanding Lead Actor in a Comedy Series (Craig T. Nelson); Outstanding Supporting Actor in a Comedy Series (Jerry Van Dyke)
1991 (4): Outstanding Lead Actor in a Comedy Series (Craig T. Nelson); Outstanding Supporting Actor in a Comedy Series (Jerry Van Dyke); Outstanding Guest Actor in a Comedy Series (Tom Poston for "Diamonds Are a Dentist's Best Friend"); Outstanding Editing for a Series, Multi-Camera Production (Andrew Chulack for "The Break-Up")
1992 (2): Outstanding Supporting Actor in a Comedy Series (Jerry Van Dyke); Outstanding Individual Achievement in Editing for a Series, Multi-Camera Production (Andrew Chulack for "A Real Guy's Guy")

1993 (2): Outstanding Supporting Actress in a Comedy Series (Shelley Fabares); Outstanding Individual Achievement in Editing for a Series, Multi-Camera Production (Andrew Chulack for "Vows")

1994 (4): Outstanding Supporting Actor in a Comedy Series (Jerry Van Dyke); Outstanding Supporting Actress in a Comedy Series (Shelley Fabares); Outstanding Individual Achievement in Editing for a Series, Multi-Camera Production (Andrew Chulack for "The Luck Stops Here"); Outstanding Individual Achievement in Sound Mixing for a Comedy Series or a Special (Dana Mark McClure, Charlie McDaniel, and Craig Porter for "Pioneer Bowl")

GOLDEN GLOBE NOMINATIONS (5)

1992 (1): Best Performance by an Actor in a TV Series, Musical/Comedy (Craig T. Nelson)

1993 (1): Best Performance by an Actor in a TV Series, Musical/Comedy (Craig T. Nelson)

1994 (2): Best TV Series, Musical/Comedy; Best Performance by an Actor in a TV Series, Musical/Comedy (Craig T. Nelson)

1995 (1): Best Performance by an Actor in a TV Series, Musical/Comedy (Craig T. Nelson)

Further Reading

"Coach." *Common Sense Media*. Available online at www.commonsensemedia.org/tv-reviews/coach.

✴ 70 ✴

The Flintstones

(1960–1966)

Voices: Alan Reed (Fred Flintstone), Jean Vander Pyl (Wilma Flintstone, Pebbles Flintstone), Mel Blanc (Barney Rubble, Dino the Dinosaur), Bea Benaderet (Betty Rubble #1), Gerry Johnson (Betty Rubble #2), Don Messick (Bamm-Bamm Rubble), Harvey Korman (The Great Gazoo)

Created by: Animators William Hanna and Joseph Barbera

Network: ABC

First Air Date: September 30, 1960

Last Air Date: September 2, 1966

Broadcast History:
September 30, 1960–September 1963: Friday at 8:30–9:00 PM
September 1963–December 1964: Thursday at 7:30–8:00 PM
December 1964–September 2, 1966: Friday at 7:30–8:00 PM

Seasons: 6

Episodes: 166

Ratings History: 1960–1961 (18), 1961–1962 (21), 1962–1963 (30), 1963–1964 (not in Top 30), 1964–1965 (not in Top 30), 1965–1966 (not in Top 30)

Wilma Flintstone, Bamm-Bamm Rubble, Barney Rubble, Betty Rubble, Pebbles Flintstone, and Fred Flintstone. *ABC/Photofest ©ABC*

Overview

Even those who don't like *The Flintstones* must give credit for creativity. Birds that use their long beaks as record needles and require nudging when they fall asleep to prevent skipping? Elephants that twirl around and squirt water out of their trunks to water lawns? Pterodactyl airplanes? Welcome to the Stone Age, complete with televisions, telephones (OK, those are never explained), and pet dinosaurs.

The main characters in the first prime-time cartoon were lifted right out of *The Honeymooners*. Fred Flintstone (voiced by Alan Reed) was more than a reasonable facsimile of Ralph Kramden, and best buddy Barney Rubble (voiced by the incomparable Mel Blanc) was a short Ed Norton in caveman clothing. They followed the same pursuits as those they imitated—bowling, shooting pool, and embracing their membership at the Loyal Order of Water Buffaloes lodge, where Fred once earned the honor of being named Grand Poobah. The only difference (aside from living a million years earlier) was that Barney could hold a grudge. Fred had a temper that did Ralph proud, but his friend could be equally stubborn, leading to such feuds as the doozy over a backyard pool.

Fred and Barney might never have remained friends if not for peacemaker wives Wilma Flintstone (Jean Vander Pyl) and Betty Rubble (voiced by accomplished sitcom actress Bea Benaderet until 1964). They, too, had their disagreements, but their friendship overcame all obstacles and all would be well in their families by the end of each episode.

All was also well with *The Flintstones* for three seasons. The announcement that Wilma was about to be pregnant (okay, they didn't *use* that word) was trumpeted by Fred at the end of one episode, and the birth of Pebbles (who said nothing but "ga-ga" and "goo-goo" for three years) did not significantly alter the story line, but, in 1964, the show jumped the shark and decided to mix Stone Age with a futuristic invasion in the form of an alien/genie named "The Great Gazoo" (Harvey Korman), who worked his magic in trying to keep the boys out of trouble. He created Fred and Barney clones so they could go bowling and still take their wives out to dinner. The only absurdity was that their doubles only uttered two things to Wilma and Betty: "Yes, yes, yes" and "No, no, no." Gazoo also accompanied the Flintstones and Rubbles into the future as the show went beyond jumping the shark to jumping into outer space.

The writers worked to tie *The Flintstones* in with modern pop culture, particularly the exploding rock-and-roll scene. In one episode, noted San Francisco band *The Beau Brummels* are transformed into the animated *Beau Brummelstones* to sing their real-life hit "Laugh, Laugh." In another, a rock band that is promoted to be from another planet called the *Way Outs* hits Bedrock, causing panic. Even Fred gets involved in one episode, substituting for youth idol Rock Roll and performing a dance called The Twitch in front of an audience of screaming teenagers. The show also delved heavily into the world of Hollywood, as it sought to attract adult viewers, as well as kids. Names of famous actors were changed to fit the prehistoric setting, thereby turning Ann-Margret into Ann Margrock, Ed Sullivan into Ed Sullystone, and Tony Curtis into Stony Curtis.

But it would seem to be no coincidence that *The Flintstones* fell out of the Top 30 in the Nielsen ratings, where it was housed in its first three seasons, when Gazoo appeared and the plot lines expanded well beyond the town of Bedrock. Gone was the comedy based on the interrelationships of the Flintstones and Rubbles, as well as the humor surrounding Fred and his demanding boss, Mr. Slate (John Stephenson), at the Slate Rock and Gravel Company.

Although *The Simpsons* has wrested away the distinction as the most memorable animated sitcom in American television history, *The Flintstones* remains an iconic and beloved show, one that has inspired a hit movie and several animated spin-offs.

Flintstones Flick

The Flintstones movie of 1994 did not raise the critical success to the level of its cast, which included Academy Award winners Elizabeth Taylor and Halle Berry, John Goodman, Rick Moranis, Rosie O'Donnell, and Elizabeth Perkins. Unlike the TV show, Fred (Goodman) and Barney (Moranis) are colleagues at the quarry in the film, in which Fred lends the Rubbles money to adopt Bamm-Bamm. Barney seeks to repay Fred by switching intelligence tests with him that were used to determine promotions. Barney scores so high and Fred so low that the former is elevated to an executive position and the latter fired. The movie was mostly panned by critics, although the *New York Times* praised Taylor for her performance as Wilma's mother and Berry as Fred's sexy secretary.

Did You Know?

Mr. Slate voice John Stephenson also served as the narrator in thirty-three episodes of *Dragnet* in 1967. Stephenson acted in such prominent programs as *The George Burns and Gracie Allen Show*, *The Beverly Hillbillies*, *Gomer Pyle, U.S.M.C.*, *Hogan's Heroes*, and *Perry Mason*, and he lent his voice to the cartoons *Top Cat*, *Wacky Races*, *Jonny Quest*, and *Scooby-Doo, Where Are You?*

They Said It

> **Fred:** How can you be so stupid?
> **Barney:** Hey, that's not very nice. Say you're sorry.
> **Fred:** I'm sorry you're stupid.

> **Fred:** Yabba-dabba-doo!

> **Fred:** Hey, why don't you hold out your hand when you're making a left turn?
> **Rock Quarry:** Left turn? I was going straight.
> **Fred:** Look, buster, you're at fault and I can prove it. I got a disinterested witness here, my neighbor and best friend, Barney Rubble. Go ahead, Barney, tell him just how it happened.
> **Barney:** You drove through a boulevard stop, Fred, and hit that man's car.

Major Awards

EMMY AWARD NOMINATION (1)

1961 (1): Outstanding Program Achievement in the Field of Humor

Further Reading

Beck, Jerry. *The Flintstones: The Official Guide to the Cartoon Classic*. Philadelphia, PA: Running Press, 2011.

Emmy Awards and Nominations

At the end of each chapter, I have included the nominees and winners of Emmy Awards through 2012. For the top fifteen shows, I have cited the individuals who received awards in the crafts categories (editing, sound mixing, cinematography). Emmy details for the remaining shows only cite the categories.

Emmy Award Winners for Best Comedy Series

Note: Although the Emmys were first awarded in 1949, an award for comedy was not bestowed until 1952. The title of the award has changed numerous times since "Best Comedy Show" was awarded to *The Red Skelton Hour*. Each change is indicated in parentheses.

1952	*The Red Skelton Hour* (Best Comedy Show)
1953	*I Love Lucy* (Best Situation Comedy)
1954	*I Love Lucy*
1955	*Make Room for Daddy* (Best Situation Comedy Series)
1956	*The Phil Silvers Show* (Best Comedy Series)
1957	*The Phil Silvers Show* (Best Series, Half Hour or Less; this was not limited to comedy)
1958	*The Phil Silvers Show* (Best Comedy Series)
1959	*The Jack Benny Program*
1960	none (an episode of the *Art Carney Special* received the award for Outstanding Program Achievement in the Field of Humor)
1961	*The Jack Benny Program* (Outstanding Program Achievement in the Field of Humor)
1963	*The Dick Van Dyke Show*
1964	*The Dick Van Dyke Show* (Outstanding Program Achievement in the Field of Comedy)
1965	*The Dick Van Dyke Show* (Outstanding Program Achievements in Entertainment)

1966	*The Dick Van Dyke Show* (Outstanding Comedy Series)
1967	*The Monkees*
1968	*Get Smart*
1969	*Get Smart*
1970	*My World and Welcome to It*
1971	*All in the Family*
1972	*All in the Family*
1973	*All in the Family*
1974	*M*A*S*H*
1975	*The Mary Tyler Moore Show*
1976	*The Mary Tyler Moore Show*
1977	*The Mary Tyler Moore Show*
1978	*All in the Family*
1979	*Taxi*
1980	*Taxi*
1981	*Taxi*
1982	*Barney Miller*
1983	*Cheers*
1984	*Cheers*
1985	*The Cosby Show*
1986	*The Golden Girls*
1987	*The Golden Girls*
1988	*The Wonder Years*
1989	*Cheers*
1990	*Murphy Brown*
1991	*Cheers*
1992	*Murphy Brown*
1993	*Seinfeld*
1994	*Frasier*
1995	*Frasier*
1996	*Frasier*
1997	*Frasier*
1998	*Frasier*
1999	*Ally McBeal*
2000	*Will & Grace*
2001	*Sex and the City*
2002	*Friends*
2003	*Everybody Loves Raymond*
2004	*Arrested Development*
2005	*Everybody Loves Raymond*
2006	*The Office*
2007	*30 Rock*
2008	*30 Rock*
2009	*30 Rock*
2010	*Modern Family*
2011	*Modern Family*
2012	*Modern Family*
2013	*Modern Family*

Shows That Won Best Comedy Series More Than Once

FIVE TIMES

Frasier   (1994, 1995, 1996, 1997, 1998)

FOUR TIMES

The Dick Van Dyke Show	(1963, 1964, 1965, 1966)
All in the Family	(1971, 1972, 1973, 1978)
Cheers	(1983, 1984, 1989, 1991)
Modern Family	(2010, 2011, 2012, 2013)

THREE TIMES

The Phil Silvers Show	(1956, 1957, 1958)
The Mary Tyler Moore Show	(1975, 1976, 1977)
Taxi	(1979, 1980, 1981)
30 Rock	(2007, 2008, 2009)

TWICE

I Love Lucy	(1953, 1954)
The Jack Benny Program	(1959, 1961)
Get Smart	(1968, 1969)
The Golden Girls	(1986, 1987)
Murphy Brown	(1990, 1992)
Everybody Loves Raymond	(2003, 2005)

Emmy Award Wins

Note: This list includes all winners as of 2012, in descending order.

Frasier	37
The Mary Tyler Moore Show	29
Cheers	28
The Simpsons	28
All in the Family	22
Taxi	18
Murphy Brown	18
Modern Family	18

Will & Grace	16
30 Rock	16
The Dick Van Dyke Show	15
Everybody Loves Raymond	15
M*A*S*H	14
The Golden Girls	11
Seinfeld	10
Two and a Half Men	9
The Phil Silvers Show	8
The Jack Benny Program	7
Get Smart	7
Night Court	7
Home Improvement	7
Malcolm in the Middle	7
Father Knows Best	6
The Andy Griffith Show	6
The Cosby Show	6
Friends	6
Arrested Development	6
Make Room for Daddy	5
Family Ties	5
Family Guy	5
The Big Bang Theory	5
South Park	5
The Office	5
I Love Lucy	4
Soap	4
Wonder Years	4
Roseanne	4
Bewitched	3
The Odd Couple	3
Barney Miller	3
Kate & Allie	3
The Larry Sanders Show	3
The Bob Cummings Show	2
Hogan's Heroes	2
The Monkees	2
My World and Welcome to It	2
Rhoda	2
Mary Hartman, Mary Hartman	2
The Jeffersons	2
Coach	2
Curb Your Enthusiasm	2
The Honeymooners	1
Our Miss Brooks	1
Happy Days	1
Maude	1
Designing Women	1
NewsRadio	1

Emmy Award Nominations

Note: This list includes all nominees as of 2013, in descending order.

Cheers	119
M*A*S*H	109
30 Rock	109
Frasier	107
Will & Grace	83
The Simpsons	76
Everybody Loves Raymond	69
The Golden Girls	68
Seinfeld	68
The Mary Tyler Moore Show	67
Murphy Brown	62
Friends	62
Modern Family	57
All in the Family	56
The Larry Sanders Show	56
Two and a Half Men	47
The Office	44
Curb Your Enthusiasm	37
Taxi	34
Home Improvement	34
Malcolm in the Middle	33
Barney Miller	32
Night Court	30
The Cosby Show	29
Wonder Years	28
The Big Bang Theory	26
The Dick Van Dyke Show	25
Roseanne	25
Arrested Development	23
Bewitched	22
Make Room for Daddy	22
I Love Lucy	20
The Jack Benny Program	20
Father Knows Best	19
Family Ties	19
Family Guy	19
The Phil Silvers Show	18
Designing Women	18
The Bob Cummings Show	17
Soap	17
Rhoda	17
Coach	16
The Odd Couple	15
Get Smart	14

The Jeffersons	14
Hogan's Heroes	12
Maude	12
Kate & Allie	12
South Park	12
The George Burns and Gracie Allen Show	11
The Andy Griffith Show	9
Happy Days	8
Our Miss Brooks	7
The Beverly Hillbillies	7
That Girl	7
Sanford and Son	7
The Bob Newhart Show	4
Mary Hartman, Mary Hartman	4
The Adventures of Ozzie and Harriet	3
The Honeymooners	3
The Monkees	3
My World and Welcome to It	3
NewsRadio	3
Leave It to Beaver	2
The Courtship of Eddie's Father	2
The Flintstones	1

Most Emmy Awards in a Single Year

All in the Family (1972)	7
30 Rock (2008)	7
All in the Family (1978)	6
Taxi (1981)	6
Frasier (2004)	6
Modern Family (2010)	6

Most Emmy Nominations in a Single Year

30 Rock (2009)	24
30 Rock (2008)	18
Modern Family (2011)	16
30 Rock (2010)	15
30 Rock (2013)	15

The Just-Missed List:
Top 10 Sitcoms from
Each Decade

Note: Sitcoms are listed by year of launch.

1950s

The Goldbergs (1949–1951)
The Life of Riley (1949–1958)
I Married Joan (1952–1955)
Mr. Peepers (1952–1955)
My Little Margie (1952–1955)
Private Secretary/The Ann Sothern Show (1953–1961)
December Bride (1954–1961)
The Real McCoys (1957–1963)
The Donna Reed Show (1958–1963)
Dennis the Menace (1959–1963)

1960s

My Three Sons (1960–1972)
Hazel (1961–1966)
The Lucy Show (1962–1968)
My Favorite Martian (1963–1966)
The Patty Duke Show (1963–1966)
Gilligan's Island (1964–1967)
The Munsters (1964–1966)
I Dream of Jeannie (1965–1970)
Family Affair (1966–1969)
The Brady Bunch (1969–1974)

1970s

Chico and the Man (1974–1978)
Good Times (1974–1979)
One Day at a Time (1975–1984)
Welcome Back, Kotter (1975–1979)
Alice (1976–1985)
Laverne and Shirley (1976–1983)
Three's Company (1977–1984)
Mork & Mindy (1978–1982)
WKRP in Cincinnati (1978–1982)
Benson (1979–1986)

1980s

Newhart (1982–1990)
Square Pegs (1982–1983)
Alf (1986–1990)
It's Garry Shandling's Show (1986–1990)
Perfect Strangers (1986–1993)
A Different World (1987–1993)
Married . . . with Children (1987–1997)
The Days and Nights of Molly Dodd (1987–1991)
The Tracey Ullman Show (1987–1990)
Dear John (1988–1992)

1990s

Dream On (1990–1996)
Evening Shade (1990–1994)
The Fresh Prince of Bel-Air (1990–1996)
Mad about You (1992–1999)
Ally McBeal (1997–2002)
Dharma and Greg (1997–2002)
Just Shoot Me (1997–2003)
That '70s Show (1998–2006)
Sex and the City (1998–2004)
Futurama (1999–2013)

2000s

Scrubs (2001–2010)
Entourage (2004–2011)
It's Always Sunny in Philadelphia (2005–)
How I Met Your Mother (2005–)
My Name Is Earl (2005–2009)
Weeds (2005–2012)
The New Adventures of Old Christine (2006–2010)
Ugly Betty (2006–2010)
Nurse Jackie (2009–)
Parks and Recreation (2009–)

APPENDIX C

Ten Best Spin-Offs

Note: Only starring recurring characters from previous shows.

1. *Frasier* (from *Cheers*)
2. *Maude* (from *All in the Family*)
3. *The Jeffersons* (from *All in the Family*)
4. *Rhoda* (from *The Mary Tyler Moore Show*)
5. *Gomer Pyle* (from *The Andy Griffith Show*)
6. *Laverne and Shirley* (from *Happy Days*)
7. *A Different World* (from *The Cosby Show*)
8. *Good Times* (from *Maude*)
9. *Benson* (from *Soap*)
10. *Fish* (from *Barney Miller*)

APPENDIX D

Fifty Funniest Male Characters

1. George Costanza (Jason Alexander: *Seinfeld*)
2. Archie Bunker (Carroll O'Connor: *All in the Family*)
3. Louie DePalma (Danny DeVito: *Taxi*)
4. Barney Fife (Don Knotts: *The Andy Griffith Show*)
5. Ted Baxter (Ted Knight: *The Mary Tyler Moore Show*)
6. Ralph Kramden (Jackie Gleason: *The Honeymooners*)
7. Robert Barone (Brad Garrett: *Everybody Loves Raymond*)
8. Fred Sanford (Redd Foxx: *Sanford and Son*)
9. Homer Simpson (Dan Castellaneta: *The Simpsons*)
10. Sheldon Cooper (Jim Parsons: *The Big Bang Theory*)
11. Larry David (Larry David: *Curb Your Enthusiasm*)
12. Frasier Crane (Kelsey Grammer: *Frasier*)
13. Alan Harper (Jon Cryer: *Two and a Half Men*)
14. Peter Griffin (Seth MacFarlane: *Family Guy*)
15. Cliff Huxtable (Bill Cosby: *The Cosby Show*)
16. Norm Peterson (George Wendt: *Cheers*)
17. Fred Mertz (William Frawley: *I Love Lucy*)
18. Ed Norton (Art Carney: *The Honeymooners*)
19. Jack McFarland (Sean Hayes: *Will & Grace*)
20. Hank Kimball (Alvy Moore: *Green Acres*)
21. Alf (Paul Fusco: *Alf*)
22. Hank Kingsley (Jeffrey Tambor: *The Larry Sanders Show*)
23. Bart Simpson (Nancy Cartwright: *The Simpsons*)
24. Hawkeye Pierce (Alan Alda: *M*A*S*H*)
25. Dan Fielding (John Larroquette: *Night Court*)
26. Niles Crane (David Hyde Pierce: *Frasier*)
27. Alex P. Keaton (Michael J. Fox: *Family Ties*)
28. George Jefferson (Sherman Hemsley: *All in the Family, The Jeffersons*)
29. Maxwell Smart (Don Adams: *Get Smart*)
30. Frank Costanza (Jerry Stiller: *Seinfeld*)
31. Michael Scott (Steve Carell: *The Office*)

32. Will Smith (Will Smith: *The Fresh Prince of Bel-Air*)
33. Ernie Bilko (Phil Silvers: *The Phil Silvers Show*)
34. Cosmo Kramer (Michael Richards: *Seinfeld*)
35. Gomez Addams (John Astin: *The Addams Family*)
36. Stewie Griffin (Seth MacFarlane: *Family Guy*)
37. Cameron Tucker (Eric Stonestreet: *Modern Family*)
38. Phil Dunphy (Ty Burrell: *Modern Family*)
39. Sergeant Vince Carter (Frank Sutton: *Gomer Pyle, U.S.M.C.*)
40. Barney Stinson (Neil Patrick Harris: *How I Met Your Mother*)
41. Arthur "Fonzie" Fonzarelli (Henry Winkler: *Happy Days*)
42. Eddie Haskell (Ken Osmond: *Leave It to Beaver*)
43. Al Bundy (Ed O'Neill: *Married . . . with Children*)
44. Felix Unger (Tony Randall: *The Odd Couple*)
45. Dwight Schrute (Rainn Wilson: *The Office*)
46. Kirk Morris (Jere Burns: *Dear John*)
47. Eric Cartman (Trey Parker: *South Park*)
48. Buddy Sorrell (Morey Amsterdam: *The Dick Van Dyke Show*)
49. Herman Munster (Fred Gwynne: *The Munsters*)
50. Colonel Wilhelm Klink (Werner Klemperer: *Hogan's Heroes*)

APPENDIX E

Fifty Funniest Female Characters

1. Lucy Ricardo (Lucille Ball: *I Love Lucy*)
2. Gracie Allen (Gracie Allen: *The George Burns and Gracie Allen Show*)
3. Elaine Benes (Julia Louis-Dreyfus: *Seinfeld*)
4. Roseanne Conner (Roseanne Barr: *Roseanne*)
5. Carla Tortelli (Rhea Perlman: *Cheers*)
6. Marie Barone (Doris Roberts: *Everybody Loves Raymond*)
7. Maude Findley (Bea Arthur: *Maude*)
8. Murphy Brown (Candice Bergen: *Murphy Brown*)
9. Edith Bunker (Jean Stapleton: *All in the Family*)
10. Sue Ann Nivens (Betty White: *The Mary Tyler Moore Show*)
11. Florence Johnston (Marla Gibbs: *The Jeffersons*)
12. Karen Walker (Megan Mullally: *Will & Grace*)
13. Liz Lemon (Tina Fey: *30 Rock*)
14. Rebecca Howe (Kirstie Alley: *Cheers*)
15. Rhoda Morgenstern (Valerie Harper: *The Mary Tyler Moore Show, Rhoda*)
16. Granny (Irene Ryan: *The Beverly Hillbillies*)
17. Lois Wilkerson (Jane Kaczmarek: *Malcolm in the Middle*)
18. Blanche Dubois (Rue McClanahan: *The Golden Girls*)
19. Molly Flynn (Melissa McCarthy: *Mike and Molly*)
20. Margaret Houlihan (Loretta Swit: *M*A*S*H*)
21. Christine Campbell (Julia Louis-Dreyfus: *The New Adventures of Old Christine*)
22. Ethel Mertz (Vivian Vance: *I Love Lucy*)
23. Jessica Tate (Katherine Helmond: *Soap*)
24. Phyllis Lindstrom (Cloris Leachman: *The Mary Tyler Moore Show*)
25. Rose Nylund (Betty White: *The Golden Girls*)
26. Jill Taylor (Patricia Richardson: *Home Improvement*)
27. Diane Chambers (Shelley Long: *Cheers*)
28. Estelle Costanza (Estelle Harris: *Seinfeld*)
29. Suzanne Sugarbaker (Delta Burke: *Designing Women*)
30. Connie Brooks (Eve Arden: *Our Miss Brooks*)
31. Sally Solomon (Kristen Johnston: *3rd Rock from the Sun*)

32. Mary Richards (Mary Tyler Moore: *The Mary Tyler Moore Show*)
33. Phoebe Buffay (Lisa Kudrow: *Friends*)
34. Endora (Agnes Moorehead: *Bewitched*)
35. Leslie Knope (Amy Poehler: *Parks and Recreation*)
36. Gloria Delgado Pritchett (Sofia Vergara: *Modern Family*)
37. Louise Jefferson (Isabel Sanford: *The Jeffersons*)
38. Patty/Cathy Lane (Patty Duke: *The Patty Duke Show*)
39. Laverne DiFazio (Penny Marshall: *Laverne and Shirley*)
40. Bernadette Rostenkowski (Melissa Rauch: *The Big Bang Theory*)
41. Lisa Douglas (Eva Gabor: *Green Acres*)
42. Stephanie Vanderkellen (Julia Duffy: *Newhart*)
43. Morticia Addams (Carolyn Jones: *The Addams Family*)
44. Dalia Royce (Carly Chaikin: *Suburgatory*)
45. Susie Greene (Susie Essman: *Curb Your Enthusiasm*)
46. Meg Griffin (Mila Kunis: *Family Guy*)
47. Berta (Conchata Ferrell: *Two and a Half Men*)
48. Jess Day (Zooey Deschanel: *New Girl*)
49. Ann Marie (Marlo Thomas: *That Girl*)
50. Aunt Esther Anderson (LaWanda Page: *Sanford and Son*)

Index

About the Author

Martin Gitlin is a freelance writer based in Cleveland. As a newspaper journalist in the 1990s, he has won more than forty-five awards. Since 2006, he has had more than seventy books published, including *The Baby Boomer Encyclopedia* and *The Great American Cereal Book*, which was featured in the *New York Times* and *Time Magazine*.